PENROSE MEMORIAL LIBRARY
WHITMAN COLLEGE
WALLA WALLA WASHINGTON 99362

Presidential Elections and American Politics
Voters, Candidates, and Campaigns since 1952

Withdrawn by
Whitman College Librar

D0089732

PENROSE MEMORIAL LIBRARY
WHITMAN COLLEGE
WALLA WALLA, WASHINGTON 99362

The Dorsey Series in Political Science
Consulting Editor Samuel C. Patterson *The University of Iowa*

PENROSE MEMORIAL LIBRARY
WHITMAN COLLEGE
WALLA WALLA WASHINGTON 99362

Presidential Elections
and
American Politics

Voters, Candidates, and Campaigns
since 1952

HERBERT B. ASHER

Professor of Political Science
The Ohio State University

1980   Revised Edition

THE DORSEY PRESS
Homewood, Illinois   60430

Irwin-Dorsey Limited   Georgetown, Ontario   L7G 4B3

JK
1965
1A83
1980

© THE DORSEY PRESS, 1976 and 1980

All rights reserved. No part of this publication may be
reproduced, stored in a retrieval system, or transmitted,
in any form or by any means, electronic, mechanical,
photocopying, recording, or otherwise, without the prior
written permission of the publisher.

ISBN 0-87094-210-7 (hardbound)
ISBN 0-256-02322-0 (paperbound)
Library of Congress Catalog Card No. 79–54419

Printed in the United States of America

1 2 3 4 5 6 7 8 9 0 ML 7 6 5 4 3 2 1 0

Whitman College
Library

SEP 2 3 '03
G
Acquisitions Dept.
DEC 1 1 2003

For my Mother and the memory of my Father

Preface

The same organizing framework is used as in the first edition, namely analyzing presidential elections from the perspective of citizens and candidates. All of the chapters have been updated and a new chapter added on the 1976 election. In addition, the section on the media has been expanded into a separate chapter, reflecting my view that media influences on presidential politics have grown tremendously. The section on turnout in Chapter 2 has also been expanded.

Acknowledgments

Many people assisted in various ways in the preparation of this revision. My graduate assistant, Sandra Davis, did a superb job in helping with the data analysis and the preparation of background papers. Patti Kirst and Clyde Wilcox also assisted in the data analysis and David Harding, Marcia Myers, and Jeff Spellerberg also prepared useful background materials. Marcia also assisted with many other aspects of the project. The Department of Political Science and the College of Social and Behavioral Sciences of The Ohio State University provided many resources (some unbeknownst to them). Herb Weisberg read the revised manuscript and made numerous thoughtful suggestions. The reviewers of the first edition—Thomas Cronin, Hugh Bone, and Sam Patterson—made many recommendations about revisions from which I have profited. Finally, much of the data utilized in the book was made available by the Inter-University Consortium for Political and Social Research which of course bears no responsibility for any of the analyses and interpretations presented herein.

January 1980   Herbert B. Asher

Preface to the First Edition

This book analyzes presidential elections from the dual perspectives of the candidate seeking support in the electorate and the citizen choosing between competing candidates. Elections are viewed as the interplay between citizens and candidates with each imposing constraints upon the behavior of the other. Hence, the book is organized into two major sections, the first part focusing on factors influencing citizens' voting choices and the second on conditions affecting candidates' strategic choices.

Too often students believe that politics began with their own political maturity. Therefore, change is a major theme throughout the book, reflecting my concern that students become aware that political arrangements and behavior are not immutable. The first part of the book (Chapters 2 through 6) on citizen voting behavior in presidential elections since 1952 emphasizes trends and developments that have given shape to the electoral politics of the mid-1970s. Chapters 5 and 6 combine the more analytical work of political scientists with the more descriptive efforts of political journalists to give the student some sense of the issues and candidates that have dominated presidential elections since 1952.

Part II of the book (Chapters 7 through 11) also incorporates change as a central theme. Wherever possible, the most recent developments in campaign financing reforms and primary election arrangements have been included. An extensive section on the media, especially television, is included in Chapter 8 because of my belief that insufficient attention has been given to the effects of the mass media on the conduct of American politics.

Throughout the book, I was guided by the belief that academic political scientists had a lot to say to students about the practical world of presidential politics. The presentation of the results of empirical political science research has been kept fairly straightforward with figures and percentage tables being the most common modes of data presentation. In examining the finished product, I am quite confident that students will find the more quantitative sections readily understandable. Sections of Chapter 3 on party identification and Chapter 4 on the issue voting controversy may be overly detailed for some classroom purposes; thus, the instructor might selectively assign sections of these chapters.

Acknowledgments

I owe a large debt to many people for assistance in the preparation of this book. My graduate assistant, Susan Howell, provided invaluable aid in the data analysis. I am pleased that my book was finished before her dissertation; I hope there was no causal connection between the two outcomes. John Russell proved to be a master of the library and prepared a number of useful background papers. Other students who provided assistance at various stages of the project were Dean Lorimor, Janis Salis, Richard Schottenstein, Ronald Taylor, Jay Zenitsky, and Cliff Zukin.

The reviewers of the manuscript—Donald B. Johnson, Michael R. King, Samuel C. Patterson, W. Phillips Shively, David A. Smeltzer, and Thomas Wolanin—made many significant contributions to the development of the book and I am pleased to acknowledge their assistance. Larry Baum, Richard Hofstetter, John Kessel, and Herb Weisberg, Ohio State colleagues, and Norman Ornstein of Catholic University served as patient and thoughtful sounding boards at a number of important points and made many helpful suggestions. Donald Van Meter, another Ohio State colleague, was a valuable source of advice about the technical aspects of writing a book. Michael Kagay and Greg Caldeira were extremely generous in providing me with their most recent results on the six partisan attitude components discussed in Chapters 5 and 6. Joseph Elton brought to my attention the material from the Republican Leadership Conference used in Chapter 11. I am indebted to Pete Allen and his friends for providing me the immediate motivation to undertake this book. The Department of Political Science and the Polimetrics Laboratory at Ohio State University provided numerous resources including research assistance, computer time, Xeroxing, and typing that greatly facilitated the completion of the book. I appreciate the work of Karen Carty, Connie DeVeau, and Becky Howe in typing various parts of the manuscript. The SRC/CPS data utilized in this book were made available by the Inter-University Consortium for Political and Social Research. Neither the Center for Political Studies nor the Consortium bear any responsibility for the analyses or interpretations presented herein.

As this book was being written, my father was enduring a lengthy illness culminating in his death in May 1975. The strain of his illness was borne almost entirely by my mother who sacrificed three years of her life to make his life more bearable. Jean Glucksman, May Powers, and Mildred and Nat Segal were extremely kind and helpful during my father's illness and made my mother's burden less wearisome. I will always be grateful for their kindness.

Herbert B. Asher

Contents

PART II

1

American Presidential Elections

INTRODUCTION

Even before the inauguration of Jimmy Carter as the 39th President of the United States on January 20, 1977, the 1980 presidential campaign had begun. On the Republican side, political commentators began to speculate shortly after Gerald Ford's defeat in 1976 about the identity of the Republican challenger to Carter in 1980. Would Ford seek the nomination again? Would Ronald Reagan easily capture the Republican nomination now that Ford did not have the advantage of presidential incumbency? Would some relatively unknown Republican emerge from obscurity to win the nomination as Carter had done in 1976 on the Democratic side? Would the Republicans have a large field of candidates as did the Democrats in 1976? The 1980 Republican presidential contest formally began with the announcement of

1

candidacy by Representative Philip Crane of Illinois in August of 1978, more than two years before the election itself.

On the Democratic side, the actions, accomplishments, and failures of the Carter administration were continually interpreted in terms of their implications for the 1980 presidential contest. When Carter's popularity ratings continued to plunge and his problems with Congress continued to grow in the first 18 months of his presidency, speculation became rampant about Carter being a one-term President who would either be defeated for reelection, defeated for renomination, or would choose not to run at all. The short-term boost given to presidential popularity and prestige by the Camp David summit meeting between Carter, Prime Minister Begin of Israel, and President Sadat of Egypt temporarily quieted talk of a one-term Presidency. But soon, thereafter, the 1980 presidential contest became a central consideration in the media's interpretation of political events. Thus, when Senator Edward Kennedy gave an impassioned speech in favor of early adoption of a national health insurance program at the Democratic mid-term conference in Memphis in December, 1978, observers were quick to wonder whether this signified the beginning of a Kennedy challenge to Carter's renomination. Likewise, the 1978 mid-term election results were widely analyzed in terms of what they said about 1980 and Carter's prospects. In particular, Jerry Brown's reelection as Governor of California by an overwhelming margin was seen by many political analysts as providing Brown a major impetus should he challenge Carter's renomination.

As the inflation rate soared and as the energy crisis worsened in the first half of 1979, speculation about the future of the Carter Presidency became rampant, with much of the talk devoted to the possibility of a draft-Kennedy movement despite Kennedy's proclaimed support for Carter. Public opinion polls reflected the decline in Carter's popularity, as evidenced in a "CBS News"/*New York Times* survey conducted in early June 1979, which showed that only 30 percent of Americans approved of Carter's job performance, 52 percent disapproved, and the rest had no opinion. Even among Democrats, disapproval outweighed approval by a margin of 41 to 39. When Democrats were asked who they preferred for their 1980 presidential nomination, 52 percent said Kennedy, 23 percent Carter, and 8 percent Brown. On the issues of the economy, foreign policy, and energy, Carter received the approval of only 20, 36, and 19 percent of Americans. Thus as the 1980 presidential season drew near, the incumbent President seemed to be in deep political trouble. Certainly 1980 would be a test of the power of incumbency.

In November 1979, Edward Kennedy and Jerry Brown both formally announced their candidacies for the Democratic presidential nomination. A few days earlier, Iranian students seized the U.S. embassy in Teheran, an event that soon escalated into a major international confrontation. The plight of the American hostages and President Carter's efforts to resolve the situation provided an excellent example of how a foreign policy crisis can (at least temporarily) bolster the standing of the incumbent President as the nation rallies behind his actions. A poll conducted by the Louis Harris organization in late November 1979, during the midst of the Iranian crisis showed that the wide Kennedy lead over Carter in mid-1979 had largely vanished. Of course, poll results could change dramatically once again; the point is that major events provide unusual opportunities (and risks) for an incumbent President.

What this brief recounting of events indicates is that for some Americans—prospective candidates and their staff, public opinion pollsters, and political commentators and journalists—presidential politics is always in season. But for the average citizen the presidential contest may only be salient during the general election campaign every four years, and then perhaps only in the latter weeks of the campaign. Citizen involvement in the presidential race is largely confined to the later, highly visible stages of the campaign; but for the candidate and the campaign team, the serious effort now extends into years. This difference in political attention and activity suggests that presidential elections can be viewed from two differing perspectives —that of the citizen who selects the nation's leader and that of the candidate who seeks support from the citizenry. Elections involve the interaction between citizens and candidates, and it is this interplay that provides the organizing themes of this book. Part I of the book deals with elections from the perspective of citizens, focusing on such topics as the determinants of the citizen's vote and examining such factors as party identification and the candidates and issues unique to an election. Part II concentrates on campaign strategy and the conduct of presidential campaigns, mainly from the vantage point of political elites such as candidates and party strategists.

Unfortunately, there are disparities in the information available for the analysis of citizen versus elite behavior. On the citizen side, numerous surveys and public opinion polls provide detailed information about the attitudes and preferences of voters. Of particular importance is the series of national sample surveys conducted since 1948 by the Survey Research Center and the Center for Political Studies of the University of Michigan. These surveys (hereafter referred to as SRC/CPS) are designed to explain and not simply predict electoral outcomes, and are an invaluable source of data for studying citizen behavior over time since many of the same or similar questions were asked at each election. Other important sources of information about citizen behavior are the public opinion polls conducted regularly by, among others, the Gallup and Harris organizations and the National Opinion Research Center, and the election statistics and census information published periodically by the U.S. government.

Unlike voters, political elites such as candidates and party strategists are far less accessible and much of their behavior is less public. While published statements and documents may be available, one must recognize that public utterances may have strategic purposes, such as winning support or covering up problems, and therefore may not accurately reflect elite preferences and motivations. Similarly, the various interpretations of elite behavior published by respected observers of American politics should not necessarily be viewed as factual or correct since each author (including myself) has certain values and preferences which influence his or her analysis of political events. This results in sharply different interpretations being given to the same event or set of events. An example of this situation is provided by two books written on the 1972 election—*Fear and Loathing: On the Campaign Trail '72* by Hunter Thompson, who was covering the election for *Rolling Stone,* and *The Making of the President 1972* by Theodore White, who has written a series of best-selling books on presidential elections since 1960. In discussing Richard Nixon, Thompson (1973: 416) wrote, "it is Nixon himself who represents that dark, venal and incurably violent side of the American character almost every other country in the world has learned to fear and despise." White (1973: 484), on the other hand, would have rated Richard Nixon (as of March 17, 1973) "as one of the major Presidents of the twentieth century, in a rank just after Franklin Roosevelt, on a level with Truman, Wilson, Eisenhower, Kennedy." Clearly, Thompson and White must be basing their evaluations on different criteria of performance.

Hence, we often find ourselves speculating about the reasons and motivations underlying elite behavior, campaign tactics, and the like.

Speculation is not necessarily bad, but it may force us to leave many interesting questions without definitive answers. For example, did Senator Goldwater really believe in 1964 that there were millions of conservative citizens just waiting for the opportunity to vote for a genuine conservative candidate? Did Lyndon Johnson know in 1964 that his promises to keep American soldiers out of a land war in Southeast Asia would soon be broken? Did Richard Nixon in 1968 really have a plan for peace in Vietnam in his coat pocket that he could not or would not reveal for fear of upsetting the Paris peace negotiations? All of these questions are at the heart of politics, yet we are less able to answer them conclusively than we are to investigate the bases of vote choice by the average citizen. We might note that the above questions have been addressed by a number of journalists and political commentators. For example, David Halberstam (1972) writes that even as Lyndon Johnson was campaigning on a platform of peace in 1964, plans were being drawn up for a much larger American involvement in Vietnam. This does not prove that Johnson deliberately deceived the American electorate since governments by necessity must plan for contingencies that they hope will never arise. However, Johnson was less than forthright about the existence of these plans. In summary, the evidence available about elite behavior and motivations is often less satisfactory than the extant information about citizens.

THE 1952–1976 ERA

Our aim in this book is to understand the dynamics of presidential elections. As such, we are not content simply to describe a specific election in unique terms; rather we want to develop a more general approach that will enable us to comprehend the similarities and dissimilarities in elections over time and perhaps even to project to future elections. Thus, we will analyze the seven presidential elections from 1952 through 1976 with an eye toward offering some informed commentary about future elections.

These seven elections are instructive to study for a variety of reasons, including the basic fact that they span an unusually diverse period of American history, ranging from the relatively tranquil and issueless 1950s to the more turbulent and issue-oriented 1960s and 1970s. The elections of this era are characterized by the decline in the importance of traditional New Deal-economic prosperity issues and the rise of new issues centering on race, war, and lifestyles, although the raging inflation and threats of recession in the mid and late 1970s have served to focus national attention once again on traditional economic issues, albeit in somewhat modified form.

The 1952–76 era includes elections in which candidate personality was of paramount importance (1952 and 1956), an election in which religion played a major role (1960), contests in which race and civil rights were both above and beneath the surface (1964 and 1968), a race in which a third-party candidate almost forced the election into the House of Representatives (1968), an election in which one party scored a smashing victory (1972) only to have the significance of that victory called into question by subsequent revelations of serious misdeeds, and a contest (1976) in which a veritable unknown won the presidential nomination of his party and defeated the incumbent President in November. The circumstances under which Presidents left office in this period suggest the volatility and diversity of the era. One President (Eisenhower) left office to widespread acclaim and affection, another (Kennedy) was assassinated, another (Johnson) was practically prevented from seeking reelection, another (Nixon) was forced to resign from office in the face of inevitable impeachment in the House of Representatives and conviction in the Senate, and another (Ford) suffered one of the rare electoral defeats of an incumbent President despite his personal popularity with the electorate. In short, these were exciting, hopeful, and tragic times, and as such are fascinating to study.

Beyond the fact of their intrinsic interest, the presidential elections between 1952 and 1976 are important to analyze since they span a period in which significant trends in American politics occurred. In this era, the conduct of presidential campaigns underwent substantial change, as did the composition of the electorate itself. Furthermore, citizen evaluations of the political system, including political parties and elections, became markedly less positive. And at the elite level, there was a fundamental shift in the meanings of the ideological labels that often occupy prominent positions in presidential election contests. Moreover, the tragedies of the 1960s and 1970s led to revisions in prescriptions for the ideal President as well as suggestions for new criteria to be considered in assessing presidential performance. Finally, the years 1952–76 can be viewed as a transitional period during which the partisan alignments emerging from the 1930s depression gradually weakened to be replaced by a structure of partisan allegiances as yet unclear. All of the above-mentioned trends and topics and their implications for American presidential politics are discussed briefly in the following sections.

Changes in the Conduct of Campaigns

The advent of television in the 1950s drastically altered the conduct of presidential campaigns and the strategies used in winning the presidential nomination; television made it possible for candidates to go directly to the public on a massive scale, thereby reducing reliance on the party organization. Observers have bemoaned the impact of television on politics, citing the tremendous increase in the cost of campaigns, which may be a contributing factor to shady fund-raising practices. Furthermore, the effective use of television requires skilled media personnel; hence, campaigns are increasingly being managed by market research and advertising companies, to the detriment of the political party organizations. The prominence of media experts in campaigns has led to overblown descriptions of the influence of television, a topic addressed in Chapter 9.

The late 1960s and 1970s also witnessed substantial reforms in the presidential selection process. Public funding was provided to the presidential candidates for the first time, in 1976. More importantly, in the decade since 1968 the political parties, especially the Democrats, adopted a series of reforms designed to make the presidential nomination process more open and democratic. These reforms in conjunction with media coverage of the presidential selection process have dramatically changed the way in which a presidential nomination is obtained and the role of the political party in that process, themes developed in Chapters 9 and 10.

Changes in the Characteristics of the Electorate

The eligible electorate expanded dramatically between 1952 and 1976. In particular, the role of black citizens, especially in the South, changed markedly. From systematic disenfranchisement and low levels of participation, black citizens today are in certain cases more politically active than their white compatriots. The extension of the vote to 18-years-olds has also increased the eligible electorate; 11 million citizens were added to the list of potential voters in 1972.

Certain characteristics of the electorate have changed noticeably in the two decades since 1952. For example, in 1952 more than two fifths of the electorate had only an eighth-grade education or less, while by 1976 this proportion was under 15 percent. At the other end of the education continuum, less than 15 percent of the people had had some college education in 1952, while by 1976 the percentage had more than doubled. Given the emphasis in classical democratic theory on the competence of the individual citizen to make informed, rational decisions (a topic developed in Chapter 4), the trend toward higher educational levels cannot be ignored in assessing the performance of the American electoral system.

Another changing characteristic, the effect of which is difficult to identify precisely, is the age distribution of the American electorate. In the 1960s the electorate was becoming younger as the World War II baby boom reached voting age. As younger people generally have weaker attachments to political parties (a theme expanded upon in Chapter 3), the presence of a large segment of potentially mobilizable young voters could have a substantial impact on American politics under the proper conditions. However, with the influx of the postwar baby boom now over and with the gradual reduction in U.S. birth rates, the long-range trend appears to be one of an increasingly older electorate.

Changes in Citizen Evaluations of the Political System

In addition to changes in the characteristics of the electorate, there have been potentially significant trends in the public's attitudes toward the political system. Of particular interest is the loss of confidence in government, indicated by responses to a set of five questions asked periodically by SRC/CPS; these responses are presented in Table 1.1. The table indicates a dramatic increase in cynicism toward government, a trend that predates the Watergate affair. Substantial rises in cynicism occurred between 1964 and 1968; for example, in this period the percentage of citizens believing that government was run for the benefit of a few big interests rose by 13 percent, while the percentage saying that the government could be trusted to do what is right only some of the time jumped by 16 percent. Between 1972 and 1973, the period of Watergate revelations, there were additional, sharp increases in levels of cynicism. For example, the percentage of citizens who believed that quite a few government officials were a little crooked rose by 17 points, while the percentage of citizens who thought government was run for the benefit of big interests jumped

TABLE 1.1
Trends in Trust in Government, 1958–76
(in percentages)

Attitudes of Trust or Distrust	Response Categories	Year							
		1958	1964	1968	1970	1972	1973	1974	1976
1. How much of the time do you think you can trust the government in Washington to do what is right?	Always	16	15	8	7	7	4	3	4
	Most of the time	59	63	55	48	47	30	35	31
	Some of the time	24	22	37	45	46	66	63	65
	Total	99	100	100	100	100	100	101	100
	Number of cases	1,711	1,423	1,310	1,539	1,286	1,383	2,413	2,727
2. Would you say the government is pretty much run by a few big interests looking out for themselves or that it is run for the benefit of all of the people?	For benefit of all	—	69	56	45	47	28	27	27
	Few big interests	—	31	44	55	53	72	73	73
	Total		100	100	100	100	100	100	100
	Number of cases		1,335	1,212	1,423	1,223	1,317	2,270	2,565
3. Do you think that people in the government waste a lot of money we pay in taxes, waste some of it, or don't waste very much of it?	Not much	11	7	4	4	3	3	1	3
	Some	44	45	35	27	28	22	23	21
	A lot	45	48	61	69	69	75	76	76
	Total	100	100	100	100	100	100	100	100
	Number of cases	1,704	1,413	1,309	1,555	1,303	1,394	2,458	2,772
4. Do you feel that almost all of the people running the government are smart people who usually know what they are doing, or do you think that quite a few of them don't seem to know what they are doing?	Know what they are doing	61	72	61	54	56	53	52	47
	Don't know what they are doing	39	28	39	46	44	47	48	53
	Total	100	100	100	100	100	100	100	100
	Number of cases	1,681	1,386	1,280	1,508	1,262	1,348	2,378	2,660
5. Do you think that quite a few of the people running the government are a little crooked, not very many are, or do you think hardly any of them are crooked at all?	Hardly any	28	19	20	17	17	12	10	14
	Not very many	46	51	54	50	48	35	43	42
	Quite a few	26	30	26	33	36	53	47	44
	Total	100	100	100	100	100	100	100	100
	Number of cases	1,670	1,383	1,283	1,517	1,284	1,373	2,412	2,684

Source: SRC/CPS election studies of 1958, 1964, 1968, 1970, 1972, 1973, 1974, and 1976.

by 19 points. These percentage increases are equal to about 20 million Americans; hence the growth of distrust cannot be ignored by leaders and potential leaders.

Note that even with the resignation of Richard Nixon in 1974 and the passing of the Watergate affair into history, citizen confidence in government had not by 1976 resumed the high levels characteristic of the early 1960s. This suggests that the sources of cynicism and dissatisfaction go beyond mere displeasure with incumbent officeholders. Arthur Miller (1974) found that one reason for the decline in political trust between 1964 and 1970 was citizen dissatisfaction with federal government actions on various issues, particularly Vietnam and civil rights. Miller identified two groups of cynics—cynics of the left and cynics of the right—who disagreed with federal government policies. The cynics of the left were generally favorable to political and social change and thought that many social and political ills could be cured by changing the existing political system. For example, cynics of the left thought that urban riots could best be prevented by solving the problems of poverty and unemployment. Cynics of the right were more supportive of the existing political arrangements and favored authorities who would act to control disruptive elements by whatever means necessary. Thus, cynics of the right tended to believe that urban unrest should be handled by the use of police force. The point is that both groups of cynics were dissatisfied with governmental policies since they perceived these policies as being middle-of-the-road, that is, some distance from their own preferred positions.

These findings have direct relevance for our discussion in Chapter 12 of possible political realignment in the United States. Miller's research suggests that dissatisfaction is more policy related than personality oriented; therefore, simply changing the incumbent leadership, for example, the President, may not necessarily reduce the level of distrust. Miller's research also suggests that the common political maxim that political parties and candidates should seek to occupy the center ground on issues may not be the wisest strategy, both in terms of winning elections and inspiring confidence in the electorate that the government is capable of solving problems. Of course, another source of distrust in government is dissatisfaction with the incumbent leadership, which eventually may be generalized to the political system at large; hence, replacement of that leadership may produce some increase in popular confidence in government. But if dissatisfaction is largely rooted in policy concerns, then leaders must at some point confront these issues. And if the issues and problems are themselves intractable, this bodes poorly for governmental performance that would be likely to generate public confidence.

There are also important trends in public support for the institutions of elections and the political party system. Jack Dennis (1970) found that the institution of elections received widespread support in the electorate, particularly with respect to beliefs that it is the duty of citizens to vote. Dennis also found more negative evaluations of the political party system in comparison to the electoral system. For example, in response to a question as to which part of the government had done the best job in recent years, only about 4 percent of a 1973 sample of citizens said the political parties compared to 45 percent for Congress, 26 percent for the Supreme Court, and 25 percent for the President, this at a time when the President was under widespread attack (Dennis, 1974: 11a). These varying perceptions of elections versus parties are laid out clearly in Figure 1.1, which shows the percentage of citizens believing that political parties and elections help make the government responsive to the people. Note that while

FIGURE 1.1
Trends in Evaluations of Political Parties and Elections

Percentage of respondents saying that the institution helps a good deal in making government pay attention to the people

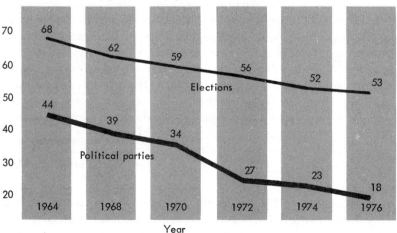

Year

Sources: SRC/CPS surveys of 1964, 1968, 1970, 1972, 1974, and 1976. The actual questions were: "How much do you feel that political parties help to make the government pay attention to what the people think: a good deal, some, or not much?" and "How much do you feel that having elections makes the government pay attention to what the people think: a good deal, some, or not much?"

elections are evaluated more positively, both trend lines slope down-ward, indicating decreased support for both elections and parties. For most Americans, political parties are largely seen as irrelevant in pro-moting governmental responsiveness.

It is clear that political parties are held in relatively low esteem by citizens. Popular attitudes toward the parties are reflected in the pridefully uttered statement, "I vote for the man, not the party," in the common description of party workers as hacks, and in the wide-spread disdain expressed about party patronage positions. Political parties were never specifically mentioned in the Constitution and were often referred to pejoratively as factions by the founding fathers.

The negative evaluation of parties is paradoxical, given the central role that they play in the organization and processes of electoral poli-tics. The decline in popular support for the political parties has been a source of major concern for numerous observers of American politics. A political scientist, Walter Dean Burnham, has written (1970: 132–33):

> . . . the New Deal might come to be regarded one day as a temporary if massive deviation from a secular trend toward the gradual disap-pearance of the political party in the United States. It is clear that the significance of the party as an intermediary link between voters and rulers has again come into serious question. . . .
>
> It seems fairly evident that if this secular trend toward politics without parties continues to unfold, the policy consequences will be profound. To state the matter with utmost simplicity: Political par-ties, with all their well-known human and structural shortcomings, are the only devices thus far invented by the wit of Western man which with some effectiveness can generate countervailing collective power on behalf of the many individually powerless against the rela-tively few who are individually—or organizationally—powerful. Their disappearance could only entail the unchallenged ascendancy of the latter unless new structures of collective power were developed to replace them. . . . This contingency, despite recent publicity for the term "participatory democracy," seems precisely what is not likely to occur. . . .

In a similar vein, David Broder, a respected political journalist, wrote a book entitled *The Party's Over* in which he expressed fear for the disintegration of the political parties. He cited as evidence for his concern the increase in the number of citizens who do not identify with either political party and the tremendous jump in the number of split-ticket votes cast in recent years, topics addressed more fully in

Chapter 3. Broder also discussed the weakening of the party organization, citing such causes as the reduction in the number of patronage positions brought about by civil service reforms; the advent of technology, particularly television, that makes the party organization less necessary to conduct campaigns; and the increase in political work done by volunteers who have loyalties to candidates and not to parties. To Broder's list might be added the newly adopted campaign financing and delegate selection reforms, which to a substantial degree have taken the traditional political party organization out of the business of nominating and electing its own presidential candidates.

The implications of these trends will be considered further in our discussion of potential partisan realignment in the United States in Chapter 12. For now, we might note that the weakening of partisan attachments and the party organization is likely to lead to vote decisions based upon factors other than party, and campaigns conducted by persons other than party elites. Furthermore, the decline in the two traditional parties may facilitate the emergence of new organizations built around different issues or principles, or both. While it is fashionable to criticize the Republican and Democratic Parties as archaic and unresponsive, despite the far-reaching party reforms instituted in recent years, it should be noted that parties perform several critical functions (Sorauf, 1972: 54–55):

> ... the American parties ... serve democracy by reaffirming and promoting its basic values. The very activities of the two gigantic and diversified American parties promote a commitment to the values of compromise, moderation, and the pursuit of limited goals. They also encourage the political activity and participation that a democracy depends on. ...
>
> In addition, the parties offer an operating mechanism for the processes of democracy. By organizing aggregates of voters, the major American parties express the demands and wishes of countless Americans with meaningful political power. They are mobilizers of both democratic consent and dissent. By channeling choices into a few realistic alternatives, they organize the majorities by which the country is governed. ... The party is, moreover, the instrument of compromise among competing claims on public policy. ... To put the matter briefly, the political parties have helped fashion a workable system of representation for the mass democracies of the twentieth century.

The possible demise of the traditional political parties without any clear indication as to what is likely to emerge as their replacement is a situation that should be viewed with mixed feelings. This is not to say that the two-party system should be preserved as is, no matter its shortcomings, but rather that replacement of the present party system offers no necessary assurances of improvement.

Changes in Political Discourse and Images of the Ideal President

In addition to trends in popular evaluations of government, the years 1952–76 witnessed startling changes in the meanings given to political labels, such as liberal and conservative—changes with important consequences for our understanding of American politics and our assessment of the Presidency as an institution of government. Despite the tendency of labels to distort and oversimplify, their use in political discourse often serves as a useful shorthand to describe where an individual stands on a broad range of issues. Throughout the 1950s and up through the mid-1960s, the meanings of such terms as liberal and conservative were fairly clear, particularly when applied to political elites rather than to the average citizen. For example, a conservative was commonly portrayed as a person opposed to federal government intervention in the economy and society. Knowing this general position, one could predict fairly accu a ely how a conservative would feel about a variety of domestic social welfare programs, such as federal aid to education and public housing. A liberal, on the other hand, was most often described as an advocate of federal intervention.

Because of their different policy preferences, conservatives and liberals had different opinions about the optimal relative strength of the Congress versus the President. The liberals favored a strong, activist President and viewed the Congress with its seniority system, conservative southern committee chairmen, and Rules Committee (particularly during the Kennedy administration) as a major roadblock to progressive legislation. Conservatives, on the other hand, looked to Congress to block the advances of an activist President. The liberal idealization of presidential power reached its peak in 1964 and 1965 during the Johnson administration when presidential initiatives led to congressional passage of two major civil rights bills and a host of domestic welfare programs, many of which had been bottled up in Congress for years.

Until the late 1960s and 1970s, it appeared that power was flowing to the President at the expense of the Congress, the process reaching its culmination during the Johnson and Nixon administrations when an unpopular, costly, and undeclared war continued to be prosecuted in the face of ever-rising congressional opposition. Also in this period the presidential staff grew tremendously, with many key presidential aides not subject to Senate confirmation. This trend peaked in the Nixon administration, with such powerful Nixon assistants as H. R. Haldeman and John Ehrlichman frequently contemptuous of Congress, and such important officials as the Director of the Office of Management and Budget, responsible for the impoundment of congressionally approved funds, not subject to congressional approval. (The Director of OMB is now subject to congressional confirmation.) The very basic issue of the accountability of the President and his aides to the public and to the Congress was raised in the controversy over executive privilege; the Attorney General of the United States taunted the members of a congressional committee that if the Congress was not satisfied with the President's behavior, it had the option to impeach him. The growth of the White House staff, coupled with the tendency of presidential aides not to want to be the bearers of bad news, led to the increased isolation of the President from diverse sources of information. This was especially true of President Nixon whose personal style tended to be that of a loner; this isolation is often cited as an important contributor to his extensive political difficulties.

Given the apparently unlimited ends to which a President could employ his power, the attitudes of liberals and conservatives toward the relative power of the Congress and the President and the role of the federal government began to change in the late 1960s. Johnson's conduct of the Vietnam War was a major catalyst in this change, as were the abuses of presidential power (enemies lists, illegal wiretaps, burglaries) revealed during the Nixon administration. Beyond presidential misconduct, there was a growing concern about centralized government acting as Big Brother; these fears were exacerbated by the development of computer-related technology that made it possible for the government to maintain massive data banks on its citizens. Liberals no longer sanctified presidential and national power, recognizing that such power could be put to good and bad ends. Liberals praised the Congress for its attempts to resist presidential incursions in such areas as impoundment of funds, control over the national budget, war powers, and executive privilege. Conservatives, however, tended to rally behind the President (especially Nixon), particularly in the areas of foreign policy and fiscal affairs. Conservatives warned of tying the hands of the President and at times berated the Congress for its efforts to regain power. Liberals, who had once been firm supporters of foreign aid and international involvement, were now dubbed the New Isolationists because of their reaction to the Vietnam War and to American military aid policies that resulted in American allies fighting each other with American-supplied arms. Conservatives did not switch en masse to an endorsement of presidential initiatives in the realm of foreign affairs, although they did provide the bulk of the President's support in Congress on the war powers issue. Actions of the Nixon administration contributed further to the confusion in the meaning of liberal and conservative. A "conservative" administration instituted peacetime wage and price controls, formulated budgets with sizable deficits, etstablished diplomatic contact with the People's Republic of China and detente with the Soviet Union, and used agencies of the federal government to invade the privacy and rights of citizens, all actions that one would not normally associate with a conservative administration.

The meanings of the terms liberal and conservative were further muddied by the rise of new issues in the 1970s that did not coincide with the New Deal issues that had traditionally divided liberals and conservatives (and Democrats and Republicans). Whereas liberals had traditionally supported and conservatives opposed governmental intervention in the economy, the advent of such issues as drug regulation, abortion, and sexual behavior often witnessed liberals opposing governmental involvement and conservatives favoring governmental regulation to protect traditional values. The rise of the feminist, the environmental, and the consumer movements placed issues on the political agenda that did not neatly fit into existing ideological and partisan labels. The issues confronting the United States in the late 1970s are represented pictorially in Figure 1.2.

The graph in Figure 1.2 is of course an oversimplification of reality, as are the labels that anchor each dimension. Nevertheless, the graph suggests that when the issue domain is characterized by at least two dimensions, it becomes very difficult to classify a person under the overarching label of liberal or conservative. For example, how does one label the citizen who favors federal sponsorship of social welfare programs, but who strenuously objects to recent liberal trends in lifestyles? Given two dimensions, one can envisage four ideal ideological types—the economic and lifestyle liberal, the economic and lifestyle conservative, the economic liberal and lifestyle conservative, and the economic conservative and lifestyle liberal. Despite the possi-

FIGURE 1.2

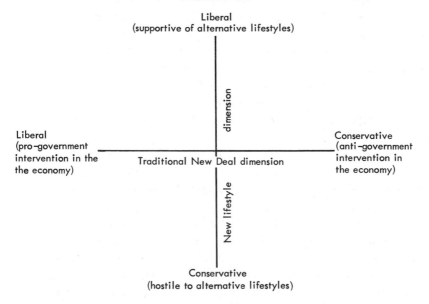

bility of at least four clusters of issue positions, there are usually only two major candidates in presidential contests, which may result in many voters believing that their own policy preferences are not adequately represented by the available choices. There is currently a minor party (the Libertarian Party) that explicitly takes the conservative position on the economic dimension and the liberal position on the lifestyle dimension, thereby providing the electorate with another choice, but one with poor prospects of victory.

The complexity of the issue space depicted in Figure 1.2 may help explain a number of seeming paradoxes of contemporary American politics. One such paradox is a citizenry that increasingly calls itself conservative even as it registers strong majorities in favor of traditional liberal social welfare programs. There may be no inconsistency here if the sources of conservative identifications are stances on new issues and not positions on New Deal issues. A related paradox is the decline in the proportion of Americans expressing identification with the Republican Party even as the proportion labeling themselves conservative has risen. Perhaps the conservative GOP is not winning new adherents or keeping old ones because it is associated with conservative stances on the wrong kinds of issues, a point elaborated in the final chapter.

The late 1970s witnessed the onset of the tax revolt heralded by the passage of Proposition 13 (the Jarvis-Gann Amendment) in California, which sparked similar measures in other states and heightened congressional awareness of taxpayer discontent. Related to the tax revolt was the growing perception that government, particularly the government in Washington, was the source of problems rather than the solver of problems. The attack on a powerful national government would seem to be a natural conservative and Republican issue, given the lengthy record of conservative opposition to federal initiatives and the fact that the government (particularly the Congress and the bureaucracy) has been dominated by Democrats supportive of an activist federal government. Yet even here ideological labels and partisan associations become confusing. Even as Americans are upset with the federal government, they still strongly support federally sponsored programs in the areas of housing, health care, education, environment, and aging. Moreover, it was Carter the Democrat who ran as an outsider attacking the Washington establishment in 1976 even though that establishment was largely Democratic. It was Jerry Brown the Democrat who became a leading proponent of the thesis that government was limited in its problem-solving capabilities. As the tax revolt became stronger, the Democrats in Congress, ostensibly a very liberal contingent with a lengthy record of supporting federal initiatives, were quite successful in co-opting traditional Republican and conservative rhetoric about fiscal responsibility and limiting governmental growth. Despite his initial opposition to Proposition 13, Jerry Brown was so successful in implementing it that many observers of California politics began to refer to the issue as the Jarvis-Brown Amendment. No wonder citizens have difficulty sorting out what ideological and party labels really signify. Some commentators have semifacetiously suggested that the most advantageous political stance for a prospective candidate to take today is to be a Democrat who sounds like a Republican.

Additional complications in the interpretation of political labels are introduced when one recognizes the need to distinguish between political discourse at the elite versus the citizen level. The average citizen generally does not think about politics in such broad, overarching terms as liberal and conservative; rather, citizens tend to view politics more from a self-interest perspective. Thus, we must be careful not to impose interpretations on citizen attitudes and behavior that may be inappropriate. Philip Converse (1974: 310–311) argues that the interpretation of the 1952 election outcome as a move to the right was correct only at the elite level where more conservative Republicans replaced Democrats in office. But survey data showed little evidence suggesting that the individual citizen had moved toward a more conservative position. The question of how average citizens conceptualize politics will be discussed extensively in Chapter 4.

Unlike citizens, elites such as candidates for office are likely to have more coherent views of current political affairs and rely more upon general criteria for evaluating political events. That is, the assertion that a candidate is a conservative gives one a lot of information about that candidate's stands on a wide variety of issues, while the same would not likely hold for the average citizen. An example of this situation occurred in the 1950s where positions on international and domestic issues were related at the elite level, but not so for citizens. Knowing whether a citizen preferred liberal or conservative policies in the realm of domestic affairs gave one no clue as to where the person stood on issues of internationalism versus isolationism. In contrast, domestic and international issue positions were related at the elite level: domestic liberals tended to be internationalists and domestic conservatives isolationists (Converse, 1974: 324–329). The impact of foreign policy events since the 1950s, particularly the Vietnam War, has upset this neat pattern.

Thus, we presently find in contemporary America substantial confusion as to what it means to be a conservative or a liberal. Many political commentators find themselves in the position of Haynes Johnson of the *Washington Post,* who wrote (1974):

> Like so many of my generation, I grew up convinced of certain political facts. Franklin Roosevelt was my hero, the Democrats were my party, and ideologically I was a Liberal. A strong central government was essential and we, the people, could rely on that government to exercise its powers to insure that the greatest number derived the greatest benefits. . . .
>
> Now I find myself in a peculiar position. In private conversation with such [conservatives] as George Will and James Buckley, I discover far more areas of intellectual agreement than disagreement. I want to limit the powers of the state to preserve the delicate checks and balances . . . and to protect the individual against the tyranny of the mob.
>
> I am a new Conservative with no place to go politically. . . .

*   *   *   *   *

Who, then, are today's Liberals and today's Conservatives? Is the Liberal the one who unquestionably permits the President to retain his vast powers? Is the Conservative the one who would sharply limit them? . . . Is the Liberal the person who wants to expand federal authority? Is the Conservative the one who believes the greatest failure has been the erosion of state and local authority? And what, realistically, does he propose to do about it?

Quite clearly, we must exercise great care in applying political labels; to label supporters of George Wallace as conservative fails to recognize that on many social welfare issues they were more liberal (more supportive of federal government intervention) than supporters of Richard Nixon in 1968.

The events of the 1960s and 1970s that have led observers to question the meaning of political labels have also led to analyses of the personality of the President as a variable that influences presidential performance. Whereas earlier writers on the Presidency stressed the situational factors that impinged upon the President and scarcely mentioned presidential personality, today numerous scholars, including James Barber (1972) and Ernest Hargrove (1974), have proclaimed the importance of presidential personality in comprehending presidential performance. Hargrove (1974: 8–9) argues that "at key moments of crisis the personality of the President is the decision system," and that the "presidential personal style of authority is the crucial variable in what the top leaders of the executive branch know, consider, and debate. . . ." Hargrove therefore suggests that the ideal President is one who combines a democratic character with political skills, and he offers five criteria for assessing potential Presidents (1974: 31–32):

1. . . . Any signs of self-pity, the personalization of conflict and issues, fundamental self-doubt, and rigidity and defensiveness under attack are danger signs.
2. . . . We must also ask about old-fashioned moral character and integrity. Is a man good to his word? Does he tell the truth? . . .
3. There must be evidence of a democratic style of authority drawn from actual leadership positions and experience. . . .
4. The ability to persuade others that a moral question is at stake . . . is vital. . . .
5. The leader must be able to think and act politically and devise strategies and tactics of persuasion that can draw upon diverse sources of support.

Hargrove emphasizes the importance of the first three criteria, in part because recent Presidents, especially Johnson and Nixon, have not measured up well against them and have suffered accordingly. The problem arises as to how the average voter is to identify potential candidates whose personality attributes do not measure up. The voter is not a trained psychologist, nor is personality analysis as precise a science as some might claim. Perhaps the grueling process of obtaining the presidential nomination helps weed out candidates who cannot bear up under extreme pressures, although one might argue that running for President and serving as President are two different matters. In certain cases there is clear-cut evidence of personality flaws in the candidate prior to the election. For example, Richard Nixon's 1962 press conference, after losing the California governorship, in which he declared to the press that they "wouldn't have Nixon to kick around any more," might be considered a prime example of the self-pity about which Hargrove warns. Likewise, Nixon's book *Six Crises* provides numerous examples of the personalization of conflict. But the availability of these indicators of personality weakness did not prevent Richard Nixon from being elected President; nor is it clear that they should have since if the initial Watergate breakin had not occurred, the Nixon administration today might be highly acclaimed, regardless of the personality of the President. The point is that it is difficult to know, except after the fact, how various personality types will behave under differing stressful situations. Thus, the voter is most often in the position of choosing between candidates on the basis of party or issues or more surface aspects of candidate personality, such as whether a person appears trustworthy or resolute or whatever. But how the essential personality of the candidates is to become a basis for candidate choice by the voters is unclear, and such a criterion will likely remain a remote concern to the electorate at large.

1952–1976 as a Transitional Era

When placed in a historical perspective, the 1952–76 period raises some basic questions about the future shape of partisan alignments in the United States. The 1952–76 presidential election outcomes varied markedly despite the fact that the Democratic Party was commonly viewed as the majority party throughout the era. The 1952 victory of Dwight Eisenhower marked the first Republican presidential success since the election of Herbert Hoover in 1928. The narrow 1968 and massive 1972 victories of Richard Nixon, the candidate of the minority party, led many political commentators to speculate whether the Republican Party was about to supplant the Democrats as the national majority party—that is, whether a substantial shift or realignment in the basic party loyalties of the nation was about to occur.

The politics of the 1952–76 years was in part a legacy of the realignment of the 1930s in which the nation moved from majority Republican to majority Democratic, due mainly to the impact of the Great Depression and the efforts of the Roosevelt administration to alleviate the economic miseries. Prior to 1932, the first Roosevelt election, the GOP was the dominant party nationwide, although the South was heavily Democratic. The 1928 candidacy of Catholic New Yorker Al Smith attracted to the Democratic Party many urban northern, Catholic immigrant voters and repelled many traditional Protestant Democrats, especially in the South, because of the religious factor. This is graphically illustrated in the first column of Table 1.2, which shows that five normally Democratic southern states went Republican in 1928. Since the 1930s, it has been common to refer to the majority Democratic support for FDR as the New Deal coalition, composed primarily of the South, labor, urban Catholics, and blacks.

The New Deal coalition reached its peak strength in the 1936 presidential and congressional elections and thereafter suffered erosion so that the 1936 Roosevelt sweep of 46 of 48 states and 60.8 percent of the total vote had by 1944 fallen to 53.4 percent of the vote, although Roosevelt carried 37 states. Prior to the election of Eisenhower in 1952, the most serious threat to the dominance of the New Deal coalition occurred in 1948 when Harry Truman was challenged not only by the Republican candidate Thomas Dewey but also by third- and fourth-party candidates from the right and left wings of the Democratic Party. Of these latter two challenges, the more notable was that raised by Strom Thurmond, then Governor of South Carolina, whose States' Rights candidacy carried the four deep southern states of South Carolina, Alabama, Mississippi, and Louisiana. The immediate cause of the Dixiecrat revolt was the adoption of a liberal civil rights platform at the Democratic National Convention, a major controversy that previewed North-South splits in the Democratic Party based on race-related matters in the 1960s.

The apparent decline of the New Deal coalition has raised the question of the likely futures of the Democratic and Republican Parties. After the 1968 and 1972 Republican presidential victories, some observers thought the country was in the midst of a realignment from Democratic to Republican dominance. After the debacle suffered by the Republicans in the mid-term elections in 1974, the Democratic presidential victory in 1976, and the minimal gains regis-

TABLE 1.2

Presidential Voting in the South since 1928

	1928	1932	1936	1940	1944	1948	1952	1956	1960	1964	1968	1972	1976	No. of Times Parties Won Dem.	Rep.	Other
Alabama	D	D	D	D	D	SR	D	D	D	R	W	R	D	9	2	2
Arkansas	D	D	D	D	D	D	D	D	D	D	W	R	D	11	1	1
Florida	R	D	D	D	D	D	R	R	R	D	R	R	D	7	6	0
Georgia	D	D	D	D	D	D	D	D	D	R	W	R	D	10	2	1
Louisiana	D	D	D	D	D	SR	D	R	D	R	W	R	D	8	3	2
Mississippi	D	D	D	D	D	SR	D	D	D	R	W	R	D	9	2	2
North Carolina	R	D	D	D	D	D	D	D	D	D	R	R	D	10	3	0
South Carolina	D	D	D	D	D	SR	D	D	D	R	R	R	D	9	3	1
Tennessee	R	D	D	D	D	D	R	R	D	D	R	R	D	7	6	0
Texas	R	D	D	D	D	D	R	R	D	D	D	R	D	9	4	0
Virginia	R	D	D	D	D	D	R	R	R	D	R	R	R	6	7	0
No. of states won by Democrats	6	11	11	11	11	7	7	6	8	6	1	0	10			

Key to abbreviations: R—Republican, D—Democratic, SR—States' Rights, W—Walace.
Source: *Politics in America*, ed. IV (Washington, D.C.: Congressional Quarterly, Inc., 1974), p. 87; *Guide to 1976 Elections* (Washington, D.C.: Congressional Quarterly, Inc., 1977), p. 25.

tered by the GOP in 1978, speculation centered on whether the GOP was consigned to permanent minority party status, with prospects of occasionally winning the Presidency because of internal contradictions in the national Democratic coalition. Some analysts assert that instabilities inherent in the Democratic coalition will yet result in Republican dominance, while others envisage the Democratic Party constructing a new majority coalition. These and other possible outcomes will be analyzed in the final chapter. For now, we will define more systematically some of the terms used in the above discussion.

Angus Campbell (1966) of the Michigan Survey Research Center has developed a threefold typology of presidential elections. He labels the first kind of election "maintaining," the chief characteristic of which is that the majority party (the party commanding a majority of voters' professed allegiances) wins the election. The second type of election is termed "deviating"; this is an election in which the basic partisan loyalties of the electorate do not change much, but the influence of forces specific to the election leads to the defeat of the majority party. The Eisenhower victories of 1952 and 1956 are commonly viewed as deviating elections, resulting mainly from Eisenhower's immense popular appeal. Survey evidence about party loyalties as well as the congressional election results (the Republicans controlled Congress in only the first two of the eight Eisenhower years) are often cited to show that the Democrats were still the majority party in the Eisenhower years.

The third type of election discussed by Campbell is called "realigning" and refers to a situation in which the basic partisan attachments of the electorate change, resulting in a new partisan balance, one possible outcome being the previous majority party becoming the minority and vice versa. Other outcomes are possible; James Sundquist (1973) asserts that realignment can occur when one or both of the major parties is replaced or when third parties are absorbed into the existing party system. When supporters of George Wallace and the American Independent Party in 1968 voted heavily for Richard Nixon in 1972, many observers thought that the Wallace candidacy had served as a way station for Democrats en route to becoming Republicans. However, survey evidence showed that the Wallace adherents maintained their Democratic partisan loyalties and supported Carter strongly in 1976.

Realignment occurs infrequently, but when it does, it is usually associated with severe crises and upheavals, such as wars or depressions.

The best example of realignment thus far in this century is the transformation in party loyalties brought on by the depression of the 1930s. Other elections generally referred to as realigning occurred in 1860, when the relatively new Republican Party elected its presidential candidate (Abraham Lincoln) for the first time, and in 1896, when almost balanced partisan competition in the post-Civil War era gave way to a period of Republican dominance as the GOP made sizable gains in the Northeast. Rather than talk about a specific realigning election, some observers (MacRae and Meldrum, 1960) argue that we should speak in terms of a realigning era or period, thereby recognizing that realignment is an ongoing process, the end result of which depends upon a variety of factors, including elite behavior, societal conditions, and chance. The validity of this point is illustrated by the fact that the peak Democratic strength was reached in 1936 even though 1932 is commonly viewed as the critical or realigning election.

A more elaborate classification of presidential election has been presented by Gerald Pomper; a schematic representation of his classification is presented in Figure 1.3. The major contribution of

FIGURE 1.3
Pomper's Classification of Presidential Elections

Stability of Electoral Cleavage	Fate of Majority Party	
	Victory	Defeat
Continuity	Maintaining	Deviating
Change	Converting	Realigning

Source: Gerald M. Pomper, *Elections in America* (New York: Dodd, Mead & Co., Inc., 1968), fig. 2, p. 104. Reprinted by permission of Dodd, Mead, & Co., Inc., copyright 1968.

Pomper's typology is the category of a "converting election," an election in which the majority party wins, but the nature of its support coalition changes. Pomper's classification is useful since it explicitly incorporates two dimensions of electoral outcomes: the electoral fate of the majority party and the stability/instability in the existing electoral cleavages. The converting category suggests that one example of realignment in the United States would have the Democratic Party remain as the majority but have the sources of Democratic support shift substantially. Pomper labels the 1964 election "converting" since the Democrats were victorious and won increased support in the

Northeast and Midwest, while losing tremendous support in the South, particularly the five deep southern states of South Carolina, Georgia, Alabama, Louisiana, and Mississippi (where Johnson received only 13 percent of the vote). Campbell, however, would classify the 1964 election as "maintaining."

We cannot say with certainty whether we are currently in a realignment era of Republican ascendancy or in an era of a permanent majority status for the Democrats; the ultimate outcome depends upon a configuration of forces, some of which cannot yet be charted. We can note, however, that, until the 1976 presidential election, sectional realignment appeared to have taken place as the once Democratic Solid South seemed to have become the Republican Solid South, at least in presidential voting. Whereas Roosevelt carried all of the southern states in 1932 with vote tallies above 85 percent in all the deep southern states, in 1972 McGovern failed to carry a single southern state and in 1968 Humphrey carried only Texas, eking out a tiny plurality over Nixon mainly because of the presence of Wallace in the race. In 1976 the South appeared solidly Democratic once again as native son Carter swept the entire region, with the exception of Virginia. The statewide presidential voting patterns of the South are presented in Table 1.2.

Before one concludes too hastily that the South has returned to the Democratic fold, it should be noted that Carter did *not* win a majority of the white vote in the region, although his performance far surpassed that of Humphrey and McGovern. Carter's success to a large extent depended on overwhelming support from black voters. Hence the South still seems like fertile ground for the Republicans unless the Democrats continue to nominate southerners or candidates with issue and ideological stances particularly attuned to southern preferences. However, the latter move would undoubtedly hurt the party among other elements of its support coalition, such as labor and blacks. On the state and local levels, Republican dominance in the South is very far from established. In fact, in recent years moderate Democrats with good ties to the national Democratic Party have been successful in winning southern governorships and in replacing conservative patriarchs who have departed from Congress. We will return to the topic of realignment in Chapter 12, where we will focus on various aspects of realignment, including the groups most likely to realign and the issues likely to bring about various realignment outcomes. There we will explicitly consider an alternative scenario, namely that of de-alignment, in which the shape of the present party system is maintained even as it becomes progressively weaker.

A PERSONAL ASSESSMENT OF ELECTIONS

Before turning to Part I and citizen voting behavior, I should make clear my evaluation of elections and their role in a democratic political system. Obviously, elections occupy a central role in democratic theory, especially as they provide a linkage between the preferences of citizens and the actions of government. Elections serve a legitimizing function in that they presumably enable leaders to act in the name of the people. Numerous consequences of elections are often suggested. For example, it is argued that elections promote stability in the political system since they provide a regularized means for making potentially controversial decisions about political succession (even though two of our four most recent Presidents took office by means other than elections). Furthermore, it is argued that decisions made by popularly elected officials are more likely to receive the support of a citizenry responsible for choosing its leaders in the first place. At the individual level, the claim is often made that participation in elections (and other forms of political activity) contributes to the fullest growth of the individual.

While there is little dispute that elections serve as a mechanism whereby citizens choose their leaders, there is a major controversy over the significance of elections with respect to the policies subsequently adopted by the elected officials. What significance can elections have, some people ask, if the voter is forced to choose between two evils? What does it mean to talk of a choice when the competing candidates do not differ in important respects? How meaningful are elections if the victorious candidate subsequently reneges on campaign promises?

All of these questions have been raised about American presidential elections in recent years, and not only by people with a radical viewpoint. For example, the underlying thesis of the Goldwater campaign in 1964 was that there existed a vast number of conservative voters who refrained from voting because the Republican Party offered candidates too similar to the Democrats. If the GOP were to nominate a genuine conservative, the argument went, millions of "stay-at-home" voters would flock to the polls to elect Goldwater. Richard Nixon and John Kennedy were often referred to as Tweedle-dee and Tweedle-dum in 1960; Barry Goldwater promised "a choice, not an echo" in 1964. In 1968, at the height of the "New Politics," the two major parties nominated familiar representatives of the old politics— Richard Nixon and Hubert Humphrey. George Wallace claimed that there was "not a dime's worth of difference between them," and evidently many voters agreed with him. A study of the Vietnam positions of Humphrey and Nixon by two political scientists (Page and Brody, 1972) showed that there was scarcely any difference between the candidates as determined from campaign speeches, this in a year when Vietnam was a major issue with the Democrats attempting to defend their record and the Republicans promising to end the war in ways unspecified. In 1976, the subtleties, nuances, and shadings of meaning expressed by the candidates, especially Carter, left many voters wondering just how the candidates differed.

Do the above examples indicate that presidential elections offer no choice to the voter? Not necessarily. By counterexample, we can cite McGovern and Nixon as two candidates certainly representing sharply differing positions across a wide spectrum of issues in 1972. Likewise, there were substantial differences between Humphrey and Nixon on matters ranging from general philosophy of government to specific issues of social welfare and arms control. Who could deny that Adlai Stevenson was ahead of his time in raising the issue of disarmament in 1956? The point is that there are differences between the candidates, sometimes large, sometimes small. At times these differences are on issues of immediate concern to the voter; at other times the voter seems to be left without a choice. In most cases, there is no single candidate with whom one agrees on all issues; rather, one must decide which issues are most important to him or her and vote accordingly. Some observers call this selecting "the lesser of two evils." Perhaps so, but if presidential elections are to yield definitive results, the list of alternatives must be kept relatively narrow, although there is nothing sacred about the number two.

The charge is often raised that once elected the victorious candidate may break his campaign promises. An amusing article by political satirist Art Buchwald makes this point very effectively. Buchwald wrote about what would have happened had Barry Goldwater and not Lyndon Johnson been elected in 1964. He asserted that had Goldwater won the United States would have become entangled in a major land war in Southeast Asia that involved hundreds of thousands of American troops and cost billions of dollars. Fortunately, Buchwald concluded, Lyndon Johnson, the peace candidate, won the election and thus this war never occurred.

But in prosecuting the Vietnam War did Johnson really violate a mandate for peace? John Kessel (1968: 290) reports that about 63 percent of the people who favored pulling out of Vietnam voted for Johnson in 1964. He also reports, however, that Johnson received almost 52 percent of the vote from those citizens who favored taking a stronger stand in Vietnam even if it meant invading North Vietnam. Or consider the case of conservative Republicans who supported Richard Nixon in 1968, in part because of his long-time opposition to Communist expansion abroad and to federal intervention at home. Did Nixon violate a trust by seeking detente with China and the Soviet Union and by instituting wage and price controls? Were not his China and Soviet policies bold ventures that held promise for building "a structure of peace?" In short, when does breaking campaign promises or changing from past behavior constitute a serious violation of trust? Campaign promises are made within a political, social, and economic context that can change dramatically during the four years of a President's term. Insisting that a President adhere faithfully to outmoded promises may lead to irrelevent and even disastrous policies. But where is the line between duplicity and flexibility? The individual citizen will have to make that judgment on his or her own grounds and behave accordingly. As a final point here, a political scientist (Pomper, 1968: 187) has studied party platforms from 1944 to 1964 and generally found a high rate of fulfillment of party planks; fewer than 10 percent of party promises were totally ignored. Of course, if promises are kept on a large number of relatively minor issues and broken on one key issue, the voter may still feel seriously betrayed.

If elections at times do not offer meaningful choices and at other times campaign promises are broken, then where does this leave the average voter? Perhaps the central question of Part I of this book should be "Why does the citizen vote at all?" rather than "Why does the citizen vote as he or she does?" I think there are several good reasons to vote. One is to punish incumbents and parties who have performed less than admirably. In this situation, voting becomes a sanction to be employed after the fact. The vote signifies that one is unhappy with what has transpired, but may have little policy directive for future governmental actions. This view of voting constitutes a procedural view of democracy in which the defining characteristic of a democratic political system is free and open competition among competing sets of elites. The role of citizens in such a system is a minimal one—the selection of leaders who are then free to make policy decisions unconstrained by popular directives. If the people are not content with the incumbents' performance, they can vote them out of office at the *next* election.

I would argue that the procedural view is a fairly accurate description of contemporary American politics; this in no way implies an endorsement of a limited role of the voters. While my assessment may be disturbing to the reader, one should recognize that leaders often engage in anticipatory behaviors that result in indirect influence on policy decisions for the citizen. That is, the argument is made that since leaders want to remain in office they try to anticipate what the people want and act accordingly, thereby resulting in indirect citizen inputs into decisions. The notion of anticipatory behavior by elites, if accepted too uncritically, can very quickly lead to overly optimistic evaluations of citizen influence. Some observers agree that leaders engage in anticipatory behavior, but what they try to anticipate is what they can get away with and not what the people want. Other observers have a markedly different view of the American political system, arguing that it provides maximum citizen initiative in decision making. Again, the reader must make his or her own evaluations.

Before turning to Chapter 2, it is appropriate for me to explicitly lay out my own values and preferences here so the reader can evaluate subsequent arguments more knowledgeably. I think that elections are consequential, that it is worthwhile to vote, and that reasonable choices are often available. In particular, I think the types of public policies likely to be adopted differ, depending upon whether Democratic versus Republican versus some third set of elites control the national government, although after observing the actions of recent Congresses, I am less confident about this assertion. I am not content with a procedural or elitist view of democracy, which assigns citizens to a minor role in influencing governmental policies, yet I recognize this as a fact of political life because of inequalities in the distribution of resources necessary to exercise influence, widespread citizen disinterest on many issues, and the presence of uncontrollable external forces that impinge upon leaders. Besides voting, there are other kinds of participatory behaviors that may more directly affect elite behavior; protests, demonstrations, even riots may quickly obtain desired responses from leaders. Furthermore, there are elections other than presidential elections (e.g., referenda) in which one's vote is more likely to have a direct bearing on the outcome and to have a clearer policy import. Yet all of these provisos suggest to me, not that voting in presidential elections is futile, but rather that greater efforts must be made to organize, to mobilize, to vote, and to carefully scrutinize the behavior of officials if government is to remain at least minimally controllable. Perhaps elected officials such as Presidents cannot be controlled effectively. If so, it becomes even more important to place in office persons of good intentions and conscience who, in exercising relatively unlimited power, will not bring dishonor to the country and its people.

Part I

2

A Framework for Analyzing
Citizen Voting Behavior

Many different forces have influenced presidential election outcomes since 1952, and in order to analyze citizen voting behavior systematically we need terminology that will facilitate comparisons over time. Thus, we talk of two kinds of forces that affect election outcomes—long-term and short-term forces. Long-term forces are those that exhibit continuity across a series of elections and include the generalized images that many people have of the political parties. For some people, the Democratic Party is the party of prosperity and the Republican is the party of depression. For others, the Democrats are the party of war and the Republicans the party of peace. These generalized images reflect historical events: the Great Depression commenced during a Republican administration, while World Wars I and II and the Korean and Vietnam Wars all broke out in Democratic administrations. These images do vary, depending upon the specific election context. For example, Donald Stokes (1966) shows that the traditional Republican advantage in the area of foreign policy was eroded by the Goldwater candidacy in 1964; Goldwater was seen by many voters at that time as being too impulsive in the foreign policy arena.

The long-term force that has received the greatest attention from political scientists and political practitioners is the basic distribution of partisan loyalties in the electorate, commonly called "party identification." Party identification is a psychological commitment or attachment to a political party that normally predisposes one to evaluate that party and its candidates in a favorable light. The distribution of party attachments has remained fairly stable over the series of elections we are studying, as indicated in Table 2.1. In fact, the Democratic Party has had a sizable advantage over the Republicans in partisan loyalties since the 1930s.

We will talk much more about party identification in Chapter 3. The important point for now is that had the long-term force of party identification been the only influence on presidential elections since 1952, then the Democrats should have won every election in that period, assuming a fairly even split in the independent vote and reasonably comparable turnout rates among each party's supporters. Yet not only did the Democrats lose four of the seven elections, in three of the four they were solidly trounced by the Republicans, as shown in Table 2.2.

Obviously, then, we must look beyond party identification for explanations of election outcomes since 1952. We must search for unique features of each election that help account for departures from the prevailing patterns of party loyalties. These unique features are the short-term forces, examples of which include Carter's *Playboy* interview and Ford's misstatement about Soviet domination in Eastern Europe in 1976, the Eagleton affair, and the short-lived McGovern $1,000 per person welfare program in 1972, the violence-torn Democratic National Convention in Chicago in 1968, perceptions of Barry Goldwater as "trigger-happy" in 1964, Kennedy's Catholicism in 1960, and Eisenhower's personal appeal in 1952 and 1956. Two types of short-term forces will be examined in this book—the candidates and the issues specific to each election.

The analysis of issues and candidates occupies a prominent place in the social psychological approach to the study of elections. This approach focuses on a set of attitudes that is viewed as the immediate

TABLE 2.1
The Distribution of Party Identification in the United States, 1952–1978
(in percentages)

	Year													
	1952	1954	1956	1958	1960	1962	1964	1966	1968	1970	1972	1974	1976	1978
Strong Democrat	22	22	21	23	21	23	26	18	20	20	15	17	15	15
Weak Democrat	25	25	23	24	25	23	25	27	25	23	25	21	25	24
Independent leaning Democratic	10	9	7	7	8	8	9	9	10	10	11	13	12	14
Pure Independent	5	7	9	8	8	8	8	12	11	13	13	15	14	14
Independent leaning Republican	7	6	8	4	7	6	6	7	9	8	10	9	10	9
Weak Republican	14	14	14	16	13	16	13	15	14	15	13	14	14	13
Strong Republican	13	13	15	13	14	12	11	10	10	10	10	8	9	8
Apolitical, don't know ..	4	4	3	5	4	4	2	2	1	1	3	3	1	3
Total percent ..	100	100	100	100	100	100	100	100	100	100	100	100	100	100

Source: SRC/CPS election surveys, Center for Political Studies, University of Michigan.

TABLE 2.2
Election Returns and Turnout Rate, 1952–1976

Candidates	Popular Vote	Percent of Total Vote	Presidential Turnout Rate
1952			
Dwight D. Eisenhower (Rep.)	33,936,137	55.1	61.6
Adlai E. Stevenson (Dem.)	27,314,649	44.4	
1956			
Dwight D. Eisenhower (Rep.)	35,585,245	57.4	59.3
Adlai E. Stevenson (Dem.)	26,030,172	42.0	
1960			
John F. Kennedy (Dem.)	34,221,344	49.7	62.8
Richard M. Nixon (Rep.)	34,106,671	49.5	
1964			
Lyndon B. Johnson (Dem.)	43,126,584	61.1	61.9
Barry M. Goldwater (Rep.)	27,177,838	38.5	
1968			
Richard M. Nixon (Rep.)	31,785,148	43.4	
Hubert H. Humphrey (Dem.)	31,274,503	42.7	60.9
George C. Wallace (AIP)	9,901,151	13.5	
1972			
Richard M. Nixon (Rep.)	47,170,179	60.7	55.5
George S. McGovern (Dem.)	27,171,791	37.5	
1976			
Jimmy Carter (Dem.)	40,829,046	50.1	54.4
Gerald R. Ford (Rep.)	39,146,006	48.0	

Sources: *Guide to U.S. Elections* (Washington, D.C.: Congressional Quarterly Inc., 1975); *Guide to 1976 Elections* (Washington, D.C.: Congressional Quarterly Inc., 1977); *Statistical Abstract of the United States: 1971*, 92d ed. (Washington, D.C.: U.S. Bureau of the Census, 1971); and *Statistical Abstract of the United States: 1977*, 98th ed. (Washington, D.C.: U.S. Bureau of the Census, 1977).
The presidential turnout rate is based on the number of citizens of voting age who cast votes in the presidential contest.

determinant of the vote decision. An early work with a social psychological orientation was *The Voter Decides* by Angus Campbell and his associates, a study of the 1952 election. The authors were concerned with the psychology of the voting choice, arguing that the immediate determinants of human behavior are to be found in one's attitudes and perceptual organization of the environment rather than in one's social position or demographic characteristics, such as race and religion. Campbell and his colleagues were particularly interested in why voters chose one candidate over another. They identified three attitudinal variables that help answer this question: party identification, issue orientation, and candidate orientation. Party identification will be considered extensively in the next chapter, while issue and candidate orientations are recurrent themes in Chapters 4 through 7.

Probably the most influential work in the social psychological tradition is *The American Voter,* a study of the 1952 and 1956 Eisenhower-Stevenson elections by Angus Campbell and his associates. The authors examined six attitudes that were presumed to be strongly related to the partisan direction of one's vote. Each of the attitudes could easily be classified under the general headings of candidate-related and issue-related attitudes. The six partisan attitudes studied were:

1. Attitudes toward the personal attributes of Eisenhower.
2. Attitudes toward the personal attributes of Stevenson.
3. Attitudes toward the groups involved in politics and the questions of group interest affecting them.
4. Attitudes toward the issues of domestic policy.
5. Attitudes toward the issues of foreign policy.
6. Attitudes toward the comparative record of the two parties as managers of government.

Thus, in 1952 and 1956, samples of the mass electorate were asked a variety of questions about the parties, candidates, and issues. The flavor of this approach is captured by the following responses from an interview of an Ohio farm woman reported in *The American Voter* (p. 236).

> (Like about Democrats?) I think they have always helped the farmers. To tell you the truth, I don't see how any farmer could vote for Mr. Eisenhower. (Is there anything else you like about the Democratic Party?) We have always had good times under their Administration. They are more for the working class of people. Any farmer would be a fool to vote for Eisenhower.
>
> (Dislike about Democrats?) No, I can't say there is.
>
> (Like about Republicans?) No.
>
> (Dislike about Republicans?) About everything. (What are you thinking of?) They promise so much but they don't do anything. (Anything else?) I think the Republicans favor the richer folks. I never did think much of the Republicans for putting into office a military man.
>
> (Now I'd like to ask you about the good and bad points of the two candidates for President. Is there anything in particular about Stevenson that might make you want to vote for him?) I think he is a *very smart* man. (Is there anything else?) I think he will do what he says, will help the farmer. We will have higher prices. (Anything else?) No.
>
> (Is there anything in particular about Stevenson that might make you want to vote against him?) No. But I have this against Stevenson,

but I wouldn't vote against him. In the Illinois National Guards he had Negroes and whites together. They ate and slept together. I don't like that. I think Negroes should have their own place. I don't see why they would want to mix.

(Is there anything in particular about Eisenhower that might make you want to vote for him?) No.

(Is there anything in particular about Eisenhower that might make you want to vote against him?) Yes. He favors Wall Street. I don't think he is physically able, and he will step aside and that Richard Nixon will be President. (Anything else?) To tell the truth, I never thought he knew enough about politics to be a President. He is a military man. He takes too many vacations and I don't see how he can do the job.

In general, *The American Voter* demonstrated that the behavior of the electorate was better understood when all six attitudes were examined rather than focusing only on one. For example, one could predict correctly how three fourths of the electorate would vote by simply relying on their attitudes toward Eisenhower. When all six partisan attitudes were examined, the correct prediction rate rose to 86 percent (Campbell et al.: p. 74). More impressively, at the same time that information about the six partisan attitudes was collected, the respondents were asked to indicate how they intended to vote, which, in effect, were the voters' own predictions about their November vote. It turned out that one could predict slightly better how a person would actually vote by relying on partisan attitudes rather than his or her own statement of vote intention. This clearly suggests the importance of partisan attitudes to vote choice.

The six partisan attitudes are obviously not independent of the voter's party identification. That is, attitudes toward the candidates, issues, performance of the parties, and the like are very likely to be influenced by one's party identification. It is argued in *The American Voter* that party identification serves as a perceptual screen through which the elements of politics are evaluated. This implies that party identification may lead to selective processes in the collection, retention, and interpretation of political communications. For example, the long-time Democrat may be more receptive to information favorable to his own party and detrimental to the Republicans and may be more likely to retain or remember supportive information. Kurt and Gladys Lang (1968) documented a number of selective processes that viewers of the Kennedy-Nixon television debates in 1960 employed to achieve congruence between their party and candidate loyalties and their perceptions of the performances of Kennedy and Nixon in the first debate, often described as a "victory" for Kennedy. They analyzed the response of Nixon supporters to the first debate as follows (1968: 243–45):

> Nixon's performance in the first debate undermined the image of the superior debater most of his supporters had held. The keen disappointment many of them felt was translated into votes for Kennedy only among those few whose choice was founded on rather weak party identification. Most countered Nixon's shaky performance by one or more of three techniques: isolation, selective perception, and personalization.
>
> Isolation (in the sense of denying the relevance of information to behavioral commitment) has already been noted in the pre-debate responses of Kennedy backers who minimized debating skill as a test of political competence. Now it was the pro-Nixon group who, despite the fact that they had supported evaluations of their candidate by referring to his debating skills, no longer emphasized such skills when his performance proved disappointing.
>
> Selective perception is illustrated by claims that both candidates had been "primed beforehand," an observation often documented by "Kennedy's ability to rattle off figures." Nixon's claim to the presidency was most often justified after the debate by his long advocacy of "sound policies." The candidate's performance was ignored, while the policies he advocated came in for extra attention. . . .
>
> The technique of personalization is perhaps a special variant of selective perception. It involves molding essentially ambiguous attributes into an unfavorable personal image of the opposition, and vice versa. For example, one of his supporters remarked on Nixon's "not smiling at all, being ill at ease, and on the defensive," but then went on to interpret this as being "more careful, more subtle, and thinking over a problem. . . ."

The Lang's work clearly demonstrates that people selectively structure and even misperceive their environment in many instances to bring new information into harmony with their existing beliefs.

Thus, recognizing that party identification influences one's partisan attitudes, we can array the long- and short-term forces affecting the vote decision as illustrated in the accompanying diagram:

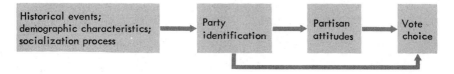

The terms in this diagram should be viewed in relation to their temporal proximity to the vote decision. Partisan attitudes which include attitudes about the short-term forces in an election are the most immediate determinants of the vote. Party identification is viewed as more remote from the vote decision, generally influencing vote through its impact on partisan attitudes. Note, however, that an arrow is drawn directly from party identification to vote; that is done to reflect those citizens who make their vote choice solely on the basis of party without reference to specific issue and candidate attitudes. This type of voter is typified by the following interview responses from a California woman in *The American Voter* (p. 247):

> (Like about Democrats?) I'm a Democrat. (Is there anything you like about the Democratic Party?) I don't know.
>
> (Dislike about Democrats?) I'm a Democrat, that's all I know. My husband's dead now—he was a Democrat. (Is there anything you don't like about the party?) I don't know.
>
> (Like about Republicans?) I don't know.
>
> (Dislike about Republicans?) I don't know.
>
> (Like about Stevenson?) Stevenson is a good Democrat. (Is there anything else about him that might want to make you vote for him?) No. Nothing.
>
> (Dislike about Stevenson?) I don't know. (Is there anything about him that might make you want to vote against him?) No.
>
> (Like about Eisenhower?) I don't know. (Is there anything about Eisenhower that might make you want to vote for him?) I don't know.
>
> (Dislike about Eisenhower?) I don't know. (Is there anything about him that might make you want to vote against him?) No.

Clearly this is a citizen for whom partisan loyalty is the paramount concern.

Finally, in our diagram, the basic distribution of party identification in the electorate is seen as produced by major historical events (e.g., the Great Depression) and processes (e.g., the receptivity of urban Democratic machines to immigrant populations) that differentially affected various groups in society. The distribution of party identification tends to be maintained by a family-dominated political socialization process (discussed in Chapter 3) even when memory of the crucial historical era has faded into the dim past. Hence we include demographic characteristics like race and religion in our diagram as furthest away from the vote decision, although these characteristics may become extremely important under appropriate circumstances.

For example, the impact of religion on the 1960 Kennedy-Nixon election was far more immediate than the diagram indicates. Because of the salience of Kennedy's Catholicism to many voters in 1960, religion was transformed to the status of an immediate attitudinal determinant with major consequences for voting behavior.

This diagram oversimplifies reality, particularly as it treats the relationship between party identification and partisan attitudes, especially those attitudes that are issue related. One can imagine a person changing loyalty to a party or forging a new loyalty on the basis of some issue or set of issues very crucial to him or her. The discussion of the possibility of major political realignment in the last section of this book reflects the potential power of "new" issues to upset the traditional alignments forged during the New Deal that focused on issues of economic prosperity. For now, we might simply speculate that one reason why the Democratic Party no longer routinely carries the South in presidential elections is because many white southern Democrats see their national party and its candidates as taking too liberal and interventionist a position on matters of civil rights and social welfare and too tolerant a position on a variety of "social" issues dealing with lifestyles, law and order, and the like. Whether this means that white southern Democrats are inexorably converting to Republicanism is a topic we leave to later. The point is that issues can and do influence partisan attachments.

We can now more systematically restate the framework to be employed in Part I by treating the presidential vote in any election as being composed of two components—the normal or baseline vote and deviations from the normal vote. The term *normal vote* usually refers to the partisan division of the vote that would occur if the long-term force of party identification were the only force influencing the election outcome, or if party identification was operating and the short-term forces canceled themselves out; that is, the pro-Republican forces balanced the pro-Democratic forces. The normal vote has actually been calculated by Philip Converse (1966); the expected vote outcome when there are no short-term forces, or when the short-term forces cancel, is about 54 percent to 46 percent in favor of the Democratic Party.[1]

The other component of the vote is the *deviations* from the normal

---

[1] Converse computed the normal vote on data from 1952–60. A recalculation of the normal vote with more recent data yields essentially the same result. See Miller (1979).

vote, and these deviations are a result of the short-term forces operating in a specific election. Two examples may help to clarify this notion. For example, Converse (1966: 31) decomposed the nonsouthern presidential vote in 1952 into its two components for both Protestants and Catholics, as shown in the accompanying table:

Non-South	Long-Term Expected Proportion Democratic, Normal Vote	Short-Term Deviation of 1952 Vote from Expected Vote
Protestants	44%	−13% *
Catholics	64	−13

* A negative deviation means a vote more Republican than normal.

These numbers mean that the normal Democratic vote for Protestants is 44 percent and for Catholics 64 percent. The actual Democratic vote in 1952 for Protestants and Catholics was 31 and 51 percent. These 13 percent deviations for each religious group are due to the short-term forces acting on the 1952 election. Since the short-term component produced identical deviations for Protestants and Catholics, this implies that it was not related to any religious issue. Undoubtedly, the major part of the 13 percent deviation in each group is to be explained by the attractiveness of Eisenhower's personality.

Richard Boyd (1972) performed a normal vote analysis of the 1968 election by determining the expected vote for persons who took different positions on a variety of issues and comparing the expected vote with the actual vote. Some results of his research are presented in Table 2.3, which shows how various issue positions affected the support for the candidates in 1968. For example, the expected Democratic vote for those people who thought the civil rights movement was moving too fast was 54 percent, yet the actual Democratic vote was only 33 percent, a deviation of 21 percent, which shows that Humphrey suffered a substantial erosion in expected vote support from persons in this category. Notice that the Democratic vote was actually 2 percentage points higher than expected among respondents who thought the civil rights movement had proceeded too slowly. Similarly, note that the Democrats got fewer votes than expected from all categories of Vietnam position, although the loss was smallest from the status quo category, a position commonly identified with the Johnson administration.

TABLE 2.3
A Normal Vote Analysis on Three Selected Issues for the 1968 Election
(in percentages)

Issue	Position	Expected Democratic Vote	Actual Democratic Vote	Deviation
One's position about whether the civil rights movement is moving too fast.	Too fast	54	33	—21
	About right	62	52	—10
	Too slow	68	70	+ 2
One's position about what the United States should do about the Vietnam War.	Withdraw	58	46	—12
	Same policy	58	50	— 8
	Escalate	55	31	—24
One's position about whether the government should help people get health care.	Should	65	55	—10
	Should not	45	21	—24

Source: Extracted from figures presented in Richard W. Boyd, "Popular Control of Public Policy: A Normal Vote Analysis of the 1968 Election," *American Political Science Review* 66 (June 1972), pp. 429–49. A negative deviation means a vote less Democratic than normal.

The main reason we have discussed the normal vote concept is that it helps us to disentangle the effects of short-term and long-term forces and its leads us to view any election outcome as the result of short-term forces acting upon a certain distribution of partisan loyalties in the electorate. It should be noted that the use of the normal vote concept as well as the classification of presidential elections discussed in Chapter 1 make sense only if there is some stability in partisan affiliations from which one can then calculate a baseline or normal vote. That is, if there is little continuity in party loyalties across a series of elections, then it is difficult to determine a normal vote as well as identify which is the majority party, thereby calling into question the applicability of our classification of elections. Fortunately, there was substantial continuity in partisan allegiances in the first half of the period we are investigating; this gives us a baseline from which to analyze current developments in electoral commitments.

Converse (1966: 15) distinguishes between two general kinds of short-term forces that can produce deviations from the normal vote: forces of stimulation, which act to increase turnout, and partisan forces that tend to favor one party over the other and thus influence the election outcome directly. These partisan forces receive substantial attention in the chapters on issues and candidates, so we will conclude this chapter by discussing patterns and determinants of turnout in presidential elections since 1952.

TURNOUT IN PRESIDENTIAL ELECTIONS SINCE 1952

As shown in the last column of Table 2.2, turnout in presidential elections has dropped steadily after reaching a peak in 1960. The reasons for this decline have sparked a major controversy, with some analysts citing institutional factors, such as registration requirements, and others emphasizing psychological determinants, such as citizen dissatisfaction with the political system. The various explanations will be discussed shortly; for now it is important to note that turnout has declined even as the act of voting has been made easier. For example, there has been a major relaxation of residency requirements and an easing of registration procedures. In 1960, about half the population lived in states where the state residency requirement for voting was one year; counties and municipalities also had their own residency requirements. Obviously in a highly mobile society many people were disenfranchised by such conditions. Today a series of court decisions has led to a shortening of residency requirements in state and local elections, while the Voting Rights Act Amendments of 1970 forbade residency requirements of more than 30 days for presidential elections. Since young people and upper-status individuals tend to be the most mobile, the relaxation of residency requirements should contribute to higher voting rates among those groups. Likewise, many states have eased their registration procedures by, for example, conducting registration at multiple sites throughout the community, by publicizing more widely the opportunities and procedures for registration, and by making it more difficult to strike a person from the election rolls. Hence, the decline in turnout since 1960 might have been larger had not residency and registration requirements been weakened.

Contemporary turnout rates are not as high as those in the last half of the 19th century when presidential turnout averaged more than 75 percent and approached 82 percent in 1876. Turnout fell sharply in the early years of the 20th century, to an average of just over 50 percent by the 1920s, then gradually increased reaching a contemporary peak in 1960, and has since declined once again. If turnout figures are based on the total adult population, then American turnout rates seem low in comparison to the 80 to 90 percent figures commonly observed in Western European parliamentary elections. These comparisons are misleading since European turnout rates are often constructed on the basis of registered voters and not the total adult population. More important, most Western European nations make registration a much easier task than it is in the United States, where registration procedures often deter people from voting. Also, many nations have compulsory voting or at least impose sanctions on citizens who do not vote. For example, in Italy citizens who do not vote have their official documents marked as "failed to vote," which can create problems in obtaining other governmental papers. This threat may be one reason for the very high Italian turnout, which regularly exceeds 90 percent. The point is that American turnout would undoubtedly be much higher if the United States adopted registration and voting procedures similar to those used in many Western European nations; we will return to this point later.

One institutional development that served to lower turnout was the extension of the suffrage to 18-year-olds. The Voting Rights Act extension of 1970 gave young people the franchise for federal elections, and the ratification of the 26th Amendment to the Constitution extended the franchise of 18-year-olds to all elections. These actions increased the potential universe of voters by more than 11 million in 1972. Because young citizens vote at a lower rate than their elders, their recent enfranchisement has served to lower the turnout rate.

Probably the most important development in increasing the opportunities for registration and voting has been the breakdown of the legal barriers, particularly in the South, that had prevented blacks and other minorities from voting. The 24th Amendment to the Constitution abolished the poll tax, while congressional passage in 1965 of the Voting Rights Act enabled federal examiners to register citizens in counties (mostly southern) where literacy tests were used and fewer than 50 percent of the people were registered. Low registration rates in conjunction with literacy tests were viewed as evidence of discriminatory administration of the tests and hence justified federal intervention. Moreover, a number of organizations sponsored massive mobilization and registration drives among blacks. That these activities of the federal government and private organizations were highly successful in registering blacks is evidenced by the figures in Table 2.4. For example, less than 7 percent of Mississippi blacks were registered prior to passage of the Voting Rights Act, while three years after passage the percentage had jumped to about 60 percent. Note that white registration levels also increased sharply. This may represent a countermobilization by whites in response to increased black participation.

TABLE 2.4
Voter Registration Rates in the South Before
and After the Voting Rights Act of 1965, by Race

State	Percent Registered			
	1960	1964	1968	1976
Alabama				
Nonwhite	13.7	19.3	51.6	58.4
White	63.6	69.2	89.6	79.3
Arkansas				
Nonwhite	38.0	40.4	62.8	94.0
White	60.9	65.5	72.4	62.6
Florida				
Nonwhite	39.4	51.2	63.4	61.1
White	69.3	74.8	81.4	61.3
Georgia				
Nonwhite	29.3	27.4	52.6	74.8
White	56.8	62.2	80.3	65.9
Louisiana				
Nonwhite	31.1	31.6	58.9	63.0
White	76.9	80.5	93.1	78.4
Mississippi				
Nonwhite	5.2	6.7	59.8	60.7
White	63.9	69.9	91.5	80.0
North Carolina				
Nonwhite	39.1	46.8	51.3	54.8
White	92.1	96.8	83.0	69.2
South Carolina				
Nonwhite	13.7	37.3	51.2	56.5
White	57.1	75.7	81.7	58.4
Tennessee				
Nonwhite	59.1	69.5	71.7	66.4
White	73.0	72.9	80.6	73.7
Texas				
Nonwhite	35.5	53.1*	61.6	65.0
White	42.5		53.3	69.1
Virginia				
Nonwhite	23.1	38.3	55.6	54.7
White	46.1	61.6	63.4	61.6

* A breakdown by race is not available.
Sources: *Political Participation: A Report of the United States Commission on Civil Rights* (Washington, D.C.: U.S. Government Printing Office, 1968), pp. 12–13; and *Statistical Abstract of the United States: 1977* (Washington, D.C.: U.S. Bureau of the Census, 1977), p. 507.

Although the 1976 figures in Table 2.4 indicate that registration levels in a number of southern states declined since 1968, nevertheless the overall gap between southern and nonsouthern registration rates narrowed because of even larger declines in registration outside the South. Likewise, the difference in turnout across the regions dropped dramatically by 1976 because of migration patterns to and from the

South, the sizable increase in southern voting brought on by actions of the federal government, and the presence (in 1976) of a native southerner at the head of the Democratic ticket. Thus, southern turnout in 1952 was about 40 percent compared to a nonsouthern rate of almost 70 percent. But by 1976 the difference had fallen to about 6 percent.

Table 2.5 illustrates the turnout trends in the 50 states and the District of Columbia since 1960—the recent high point in presidential

TABLE 2.5
Turnout in Presidential Elections by States, 1960–1976

State	Year				
	1960	1964	1968	1972	1976
Alabama	30.8	35.9	52.7	43.4	47.3
Alaska	43.7	44.0	50.0	48.3	53.5
Arizona	52.4	54.8	49.9	48.1	47.8
Arkansas	40.9	50.6	54.2	48.1	51.1
California	65.8	63.9	61.0	59.9	51.4
Colorado	69.2	68.0	64.8	60.1	61.0
Connecticut	76.1	70.7	68.8	66.3	62.5
Delaware	72.3	68.9	68.3	62.3	58.5
District of Columbia	(X)	38.7	34.5	43.2	32.8
Florida	48.6	51.2	53.1	49.3	49.8
Georgia	29.3	43.3	43.9	37.9	43.5
Hawaii	49.8	51.3	53.8	50.4	48.6
Idaho	79.7	77.2	73.4	63.2	60.7
Illinois	75.5	73.2	69.3	62.7	61.1
Indiana	76.3	73.5	70.7	60.8	61.0
Iowa	76.5	72.9	69.8	63.3	63.6
Kansas	69.6	65.1	64.8	59.0	59.5
Kentucky	57.7	53.3	51.2	48.4	49.2
Louisiana	44.6	47.3	54.8	44.3	50.5
Maine	71.7	65.1	66.4	61.1	65.2
Maryland	56.5	54.1	54.4	50.3	50.3
Massachusetts	75.0	70.0	67.4	62.0	61.0
Michigan	72.2	67.9	65.7	59.5	58.3
Minnesota	76.4	75.8	73.8	68.4	71.7
Mississippi	25.3	33.9	53.3	45.0	49.8
Missouri	71.5	67.1	64.3	57.5	58.4
Montana	70.2	69.3	68.1	67.7	63.5
Nebraska	70.6	66.5	60.9	56.0	56.2
Nevada	58.3	52.1	54.3	50.9	47.6
New Hampshire	78.7	72.4	69.6	64.2	59.2
New Jersey	70.8	68.8	66.0	60.0	58.5
New Mexico	61.7	62.0	60.7	57.6	54.3
New York	66.5	64.8	59.9	56.6	50.6
North Carolina	52.9	52.3	54.4	43.4	43.6
North Dakota	78.0	71.4	70.0	67.9	68.8

48

TABLE 2.5 *(continued)*

	Year				
State	*1960*	*1964*	*1968*	*1972*	*1976*
Ohio	70.7	66.6	63.3	57.5	55.1
Oklahoma	63.1	63.4	61.2	56.9	56.4
Oregon	72.0	68.9	66.6	61.7	62.3
Pennsylvania	70.3	67.9	65.3	56.1	54.7
Rhode Island	75.1	71.6	67.2	62.0	63.5
South Carolina	30.4	39.4	46.7	38.6	41.5
South Dakota	77.6	74.2	73.3	68.8	64.1
Tennessee	49.8	51.7	53.7	43.6	49.9
Texas	41.2	44.6	48.7	45.4	47.9
Utah	78.2	78.4	76.7	68.5	69.1
Vermont	72.4	70.3	64.1	61.1	56.2
Virginia	32.8	41.1	50.1	45.5	48.1
Washington	71.9	71.8	66.0	63.8	61.3
West Virginia	77.9	75.5	71.1	62.4	58.6
Wisconsin	72.9	69.5	66.5	62.0	65.5
Wyoming	73.3	74.3	67.0	63.6	58.8

Source: *Statistical Abstract of the United States: 1977*, 98th ed. (Washington, D.C.: U.S. Bureau of the Census, 1977), p. 511.

turnout nationally. A comparison of the 1960 and 1976 turnout rates shows that voting participation increased in only 11 states over this period and that 10 of the 11 states were in the South. Hence, if turnout trends were analyzed for nonsouthern states only, the decline would be even more pronounced, which would further heighten concerns about the viability of voting and elections as instruments of popular control.

The Determinants of Turnout

Turnout is sensitive to characteristics of the individual citizen as well as to properties of the political system in which elections are conducted. With respect to political system attributes, the 50 states have the major responsibility for election administration, which includes such matters as registration and absentee ballot procedures, the hours in which the polls are open, and many more. One might hypothesize that states that make registration and absentee voting easy and keep the polls open longer will, ceteris paribus, have higher turnout. The nature of a state's political party system can also affect turnout. One might expect turnout to be higher where the competition between the two parties is more evenly balanced and citizens therefore see their votes as being more consequential for the election outcome. The effects of election administration and party competition on turnout are demonstrated in a study done by three political scientists (Kim, Petrocik, and Enokson, 1975) on presidential voting in 1960. Their research shows that one reason for the low southern turnout in 1960 (and earlier) was the presence of election laws designed to hinder participation and the absence of meaningful party competition in the general election. By implication, as legal barriers have been struck down in the South and as the region has become more politically competitive, one would expect that southern turnout would increase and begin to approach levels outside the South. That, of course, is the pattern observed for the 1960–76 period. Moreover, Wolfinger and Rosenstone (1977: 57–58) argue that, as the older generations of southerners who were socialized in an era of nonparticipation depart the political scene, southern and nonsouthern turnout rates will further converge.

Individual characteristics can also affect turnout, and here we might distinguish between such demographic or background variables as race, education, and place of residence versus attitudinal variables, such as interest in politics, feelings about the obligation to vote, and concerns about the election outcome. It should be recognized that systemic factors do not affect all citizens uniformly; rather, their impact will depend on the individual characteristics of citizens. For example, election laws designed to deter participation are most likely to be effective among citizens with little interest in politics in the first place; citizens highly interested in politics will more readily overcome legal obstacles to participation.

Table 2.6 presents the turnout rate in 1976 by selected background characteristics of Americans. A fair summary statement is that the electorate is disproportionately white, middle-aged, and of higher socioeconomic status.[2] More specifically, the table indicates that turnout is positively related to education and age; that is, the more educated and older (but not the oldest) groups have higher turnout rates. The more highly educated vote with greater regularity because they tend to have more information about politics, be more aware of the

---

[2] Until very recently, there had been a small but statistically significant difference in the turnout rates of men and women, with men voting at a higher rate. This difference has almost vanished for a number of reasons: the dying out of the older female age cohort, socialized at a time when women's political role was more passive, the higher proportion of women going on to higher education today, and the greater number of women in the work force.

TABLE 2.6
Turnout in the 1976 Election by Population Characteristics

Characteristic	Percent Turnout	Characteristic	Percent Turnout
Sex		Employment status	
Male	59.6	Employed	62.0
Female	58.8	Unemployed	43.7
Race/ethnicity		Not in labor force	56.5
White	60.9		
Black	48.7	Length of residence in community	
Spanish origin	31.8	Less than 1 year	44.4
Residence		1–2 years	56.6
Metropolitan	59.2	3–5 years	64.2
Nonmetropolitan	59.1	6 years or more	72.4
North and West	61.2		
South	54.9	Age	
Education		18–20 years	38.0
8th grade or less	44.1	21–24	45.6
9–11	47.2	25–34	55.4
High school graduate	59.4	35–44	63.3
Post-high school		45–64	68.7
education	73.5	65 and over	62.2

Source: *Statistical Abstract of the United States: 1977*, 98th ed. (Washington, D.C.: U.S. Bureau of the Census, 1977), pp. 508–9.

impact of government on citizens, and feel that they are competent to influence government (Milbrath, 1965: 122–123). Younger citizens have lower turnout rates in part because they have other important matters, such as career and family decisions, vying for their attention along with political affairs, while the oldest age groups have lower voting rates because of the physical and financial burdens of age (Converse, 1963) and because of their lower average level of education (Wolfinger and Rosenstone, 1977). Moreover, as shown in Table 2.6, turnout is highly sensitive to length of residence in the community; and since young people tend to be the most mobile segment of the community, they are least able to establish the community roots that facilitate participation.

Turnout also tends to be higher among high income and occupation groups. Milbrath (1965: 116–21) cites three reasons for this situation: such groups tend to be better educated, they are more likely to perceive that they have a stake in politics, and they are more likely to interact with persons active in politics. Robert Lane (1959: 233–34) cites some additional factors that help explain why lower-status citizens do not participate as much, including the basic fact that such individuals do not have as much of the resources (e.g., time and money) which are conducive to participation and voting. He also argues that the social roles and norms of lower-status citizens tend to encourage more passive political behavior in comparison to the norms of middle- and upper-class citizens.

Among religious groups, Jews and Catholics tend to have higher turnout rates while white citizens generally still vote more regularly than black citizens. One reason why black citizens do not vote as much is that they are disproportionately in the lower levels of income, occupation, and education, characteristics associated with lower levels of political activity in general. The difference in black and white turnout rates has narrowed substantially since the 1950s throughout the nation, reaching a minimum outside the South in 1964 when the gap in black and white turnout rates was less then 3 percent (72.0 versus 74.4 percent respectively). This occurrence probably reflected the fact that in 1964 blacks had the strongest positive incentives to support Lyndon Johnson, who pushed the Civil Rights Act through Congress, and vote against Barry Goldwater, who opposed the act.[3] The gap between black and white turnout rates actually widened to more than 10 percent in 1968, 1972, and 1976, although this difference is much less than that observed in the 1950s. Note that the ethnic category with the lowest turnout in Table 2.6 is people of Spanish origin. Although this is a very broad classification—which does not distinguish between citizens of Puerto Rican origin who reside mainly in cities of the northeastern United States, nor between Mexican-Americans who live mainly in the Southwest and California —the very low turnout of Hispanics suggests they are a potentially rich target for political mobilization. In many areas, particularly in the Southwest where geographical concentration may be readily convertible into political power, there is a rising political consciousness and an increasingly effective political organization among Hispanics. Moreover, when Congress extended the Voting Rights Act for seven

---

[3] When one looks at types of political participation other than voting, such as campaign activity and contacting public officials, the differences in white and black participation rates varies markedly. In a nationwide study, Verba and Nie found that whites were about twice as likely to contact public officials about a problem, in part because most officials are white. For other types of political activity, however, blacks were just as likely, if not more so, to participate as whites. And when the effects of the lower social class characteristics of blacks were eliminated, blacks performed many political activities at rates substantially higher than whites. One reason for this was the presence among blacks of a group consciousness. Verba and Nie wrote: "Consciousness of race as a problem or a basis of conflict appears to bring those blacks who are conscious up to a level of participation equivalent to that of whites. Or, to put it another way, this awareness overcomes the socioeconomic disadvantages of blacks and makes them as active as whites." See Verba and Nie (1972: 149–73).

years in 1975, it also added guarantees to protect the voting rights of Spanish-speaking Americans, thereby providing the institutional and legal basis upon which a major mobilization effort might be built.

A number of attitudinal factors that affect turnout were identified in *The American Voter* (pp. 89–115). Party identification has an impact on turnout; people with stronger attachments to a party vote at higher rates than those with weaker or nonexistent attachments. *The American Voter* also found that the more involved in politics a person was, the more likely that person was to vote. Citizens with higher levels of interest in politics, greater concern about the election outcome, and greater feelings of effectiveness in influencing political affairs were more apt to vote. And, as suggested previously, it is citizens in the higher-status categories who tend to have higher levels of political interest, concern, and effectiveness. A respectable proportion of people with low interest, little concern about the election, and low efficacy with respect to politics actually voted, and *The American Voter* attributed this to a sense of citizen duty which was socialized in the person by civics courses, media appeals, and the like. The good citizen is commonly described as the one who performs his civic duty of voting.

The Turnout Controversy

The reasons for the decline in turnout, the effectiveness of possible remedies, and the consequences of low voter turnout for the political system have been controversial topics in recent political debate. With respect to the decline in turnout, one line of argument emphasizes the depressing effects on turnout of institutional barriers, particularly restrictive registration systems. It is observed that turnout among registered voters is very high (averaging about 84 percent in the five national elections between 1968 and 1976, according to Census Bureau reports) and that therefore the turnout problem can be reduced to registering more citizens by creating a more facilitative registration system. The obvious flaw in this argument is that institutional barriers have been weakened substantially since 1960, yet throughout this period turnout has fallen. Hence, although registration requirements may deter some people from voting, they cannot account for the decline in turnout in the past two decades.

In a very comprehensive study of the effects of registration laws on turnout, Rosenstone and Wolfinger (1978) argued that if the most permissive laws were on the books in all 50 states, national turnout would increase by about 9 percent. The most important reforms they identified were expanding the hours during which one could register and establishing a deadline for registration much closer to election day. The liberalized registration laws they analyzed would still leave a registration system in which the primary responsibility of registering fell upon the citizen, in contrast to most European democracies where the government takes the initiative in enrolling citizens by such means as door-to-door registrars and postcard registration. Hence, Rosenstone and Wolfinger argue that if relatively minor changes in registration laws could increase turnout by 9 percent, then a revamped system in which government plays a more active role could increase turnout substantially more.

Their analysis is very convincing, but it does not account for the drop in turnout. In fact, if liberalized registration laws increased voting by 9 percent, voting participation would be back only to its 1960 level. Moreover, demographic changes in the electorate, such as rising educational levels and the passing of the oldest generation (characterized by lower female participation), suggest that turnout should be increasing rather than the reverse. The one demographic change that does help account for lower turnout is the age distribution of Americans, which has become more skewed to the youngest and oldest adults since 1960. Because a greater proportion of Americans are in the youngest and oldest age cohorts and because these cohorts tend to have the lowest turnout rates (see Table 2.6), turnout has declined. Boyd (1979: 5) cites a Census Bureau estimate that 30 percent of the decline in turnout since 1964 can be traced to the changing age distribution of the electorate. Overall, institutional and demographic explanations of turnout trends are neither definitive nor complete, and thus we turn to individual attitudes and motivations as possible sources of the decline in turnout.[4]

---

[4] One speculative, institutional explanation of turnout decline concerns the American election calendar. Boyd (1979: 5–9) observes that Americans have many opportunities to vote beyond the presidential contest; in addition to the multitude of offices on the November ballot, there are primary elections, referenda, special tax levies, and so forth. It may be that citizens are voting but not always in the presidential contest. Boyd further notes (1974: 7) that between 1932 and 1976 the number of states holding their gubernatorial election simultaneous with the presidential contest has fallen from 34 to 14. If the gubernatorial contest and the concommitant political party activity helped stimulate overall turnout, then the current separation of the two races may help explain the decline in presidential turnout. Of course, the downward trend in turnout has been evident in most election contests.

In Chapter 1 we detailed the decline in trust in government (Table 1.1) and the loss of confidence in elections and political parties (Figure 1.1) as being institutions that promote governmental responsiveness. And Table 2.1 indicates a weakening of party loyalties in the past decade. It is certainly plausible to expect that as support for various political institutions goes down, the rate of nonvoting will increase. Many citizens believe that voting is not worth the effort, that government is distant and unresponsive, that the bureaucracy is an incomprehensible, uncontrollable maze, and that the link between one's vote and policy outcomes is minimal at best. Various polls have shown that attitudes toward presidential candidates have become more negative, with fewer voters able to see meaningful differences in the choices offered them. Reiter (1977) found that the decline in turnout has occurred mainly among white citizens of low education and low income. He speculates the reason this group is dropping out of the electorate at a faster rate is that the available party choices that do not include a workers' party or a socialist party are least relevant to lower-status citizens.

All of the above attitudinal explanations emphasize voter discontent and antipathy toward the political system. Yet voters may refrain from voting because of a basic sense of satisfaction with the course of politics. A recent study of nonvoting (Hadley, 1978) established six categories of nonvoters, the first of which was labeled the "positive apathetics"—satisfied citizens who thought voting was unnecessary and who comprised 35 percent of all nonvoters. In Hadley's scheme, only 18 percent of the nonvoters were classified as physically, or legally disenfranchised, which means that institutional reforms could at best have only a marginal effect in increasing turnout. In a polemical conclusion, Hadley asserts that politicians emphasize institutional reforms that would increase turnout to avoid the unpleasant fact that many Americans despise politicians or at least see them as irrelevant.

Hence, many factors are possible sources of the downward trend in turnout, but the various pieces of the puzzle have not yet been fit together. For those who interpret low turnout as a sign of voter satisfaction, the decline in voting rates poses no problems. In fact, some analysts (e.g., Berelson, Lazarsfeld, and McPhee, chapter 14) would argue that low turnout can provide political leadership flexibility in decision making and contribute to the maintenance and stability of the political system. But for other observers, nonvoting has more worrisome ramifications. Substantial nonvoting may indicate a low degree of legitimacy accorded by the citizenry to the political system. Moreover, the presence of numerous citizens not actively involved in politics suggests the existence of a large pool of potentially mobilizable voters who might succumb to the antidemocratic blandishments of a charismatic demagogue in a time of crisis. And if elections do have policy consequences, then the question arises whether the policy preferences of voters differ from those of nonparticipants; it may be that nonvoting results in certain policy alternatives being ignored.

This is all we will say directly about turnout, although we might note that turnout can be as influential in affecting the election outcome as the partisan forces to be discussed in the next chapters. If parties appeal differentially to a variety of societal groups, then the party with supporters characterized by higher turnout rates is obviously in a more advantageous position. It is commonly cited that the groups associated with the Democratic Party exhibit lower turnout levels. Thus turnout becomes an important strategic consideration for the candidate attempting to build a majority coalition. For example, the McGovern hope to win an overwhelming proportion of the youth vote in 1972, even if achieved (and it was not), was still a fragile strategy since young people have traditionally had very low turnout rates. As another example, it is argued that if black voters had turned out in 1968 for Hubert Humphrey at the same rate they did for Lyndon Johnson in 1964, then Humphrey might have carried a few additional states, which at the least might have thrown the election into the House of Representatives. Finally, we might simply observe that in all the presidential elections since 1952 the difference in vote totals between the two major party candidates was far less than the number of eligible citizens who did not vote. If large numbers of nonvoters could be mobilized to vote, this would directly influence the kinds of electoral strategies that major and minor party candidates would adopt.

3

Party Identification

INTRODUCTION

As was noted earlier, the long-term force of party identification has occupied a central place in the analysis of American presidential elections. In the United States, party identification is commonly viewed as a psychological attachment or feeling of loyalty to a political party that develops during childhood and becomes more intense the longer one is identified with that party. While party identification predisposes one to vote for the party to which one is attached, it is not synonymous with vote—as evidenced by the substantial defection of Republican loyalists from Goldwater in 1964 and of Democratic partisans from McGovern in 1972. In the European context, it has been argued that party identification may be somewhat indistinguishable from vote intention and perhaps not represent any long-standing commitment to a party, although the evidence is far from conclusive on this point.[1]

FUNCTIONS OF PARTY IDENTIFICATION

Party identification is often described as serving useful functions for the individual citizen and for the political system of which he or she is a part. At the individual level, it is argued that party identification provides a vantage point from which the citizen can more economically collect and evaluate information about political affairs and behave accordingly. The citizen requires some screening device to make the burdens of collecting and evaluating information manageable; party identification provides that device and thereby eases the difficulties involved in making decisions about a broad range of political matters. Of course, as described in Chapter 2, the reliance on party identification as an orienting framework toward politics may lead to a highly selective acquisition and interpretation of political information and to selective evaluations of candidates, upsetting results to those who (somewhat naively) believe that political decisions can and should be made divorced from a partisan context. Roberta Sigel (1964) found, for example, in a 1960 study that perceptions of the qualities of Kennedy and Nixon were strongly influenced by one's partisan loyalties. While Democrats and Republicans overwhelmingly agreed on the traits that the ideal President should possess, they strongly disagreed as to which of the two presidential candidates best measured up to the ideal, with Democrats favoring Kennedy and Republicans Nixon.

This argument does not imply that attachment to a party causes one to screen out all information unfavorable to one's party and its candidates; if such were the case, then there would be very few instances of partisans defecting from their party to support the candidate of the opposition. Yet in 1964 and 1972 there were substantial defections from the Republican and Democratic candidates. Furthermore, when citizens have changed their partisan affiliation (as might occur in a realigning era), certainly information unfavorable to the initial partisan loyalties must have filtered through the voters' perceptual screens. Finally, one would expect that the screening effect of party identifica-

---

[1] For a discussion of some of this literature, see Shively (1972).

tion would be weaker among younger voters, whose attachments to the parties tend to be less intense, a point elaborated upon shortly.

At the system level, it is argued that the presence of widespread partisan attachment helps maintain the stability of the political system. This function of party identification has been analyzed by Jack Dennis and Donald McCrone, who write (1970: 247):

> Party system stability, in the sense of a persisting configuration of organized partisan competition, is a function of how widely rooted in mass public consciousness is the sense of identification with the parties. Two aspects of mass identification are important: (a) the extent of partisan identification as measured by the proportion of the general public who identify themselves psychologically with one or another of the parties, however intensely; (b) the intensity of party affiliation, seen as the percent of identifiers who have a strong (and thus, more enduring) sense of commitment to one of the parties.

This argument states that political systems characterized by widespread and enduring partisan attachments are more likely to remain immune to profound upheavals brought on by severe societal stresses, such as depression and war. Thus, for some observers whose major concern is the maintenance of the stability of the political system, the existence of widespread partisan loyalties becomes highly desirable. Hence the fact that in recent years there has been a marked decrease in the proportion of Americans identifying with one of the two major parties (as was shown in Table 2.1) is a source of genuine worry to these observers who fear that an uncommitted electorate will be more susceptible to the appeals of a demagogue under the appropriate circumstances. While there is certainly a conservative or status quo bias in this argument, it is instructive to note that in the 1968 presidential election the nonsouthern vote of George Wallace came disproportionately from young voters and not from the older age cohorts, a finding that surprises many students. As Converse and his colleagues (1969: 1103) note, "Wallace captured less than 3% of the vote among people over 70 outside the South, but 13% of those under 30, with a regular gradient connecting these two extremes." The explanation for this finding is that young people generally have weaker attachments to the two major parties and therefore are more susceptible to the appeals of a third-party candidacy. Evidence supporting this explanation is presented in Table 3.1, which breaks down the various classes of partisan identifiers into age groups. There are two key points to be made about the table. First, the proportion of Independents is much

TABLE 3.1
Party Identification by Age Cohorts, 1976
(in percentages)

Party Identification	Age				
	18–20	21–30	31–54	55–70	71 and over
Democrat					
Strong	8	10	14	20	24
Weak	27	26	25	26	22
Independent					
Democrat	15	18	11	9	6
Independent	22	19	15	11	7
Republican	14	11	11	8	5
Republican					
Weak	11	12	15	15	19
Strong	2	5	9	11	17
Total	99	101	100	100	100
Number of cases ...	132	722	1,037	626	286

Source: 1976 CPS election study.

higher among younger age cohorts than older ones. For example, in the 18–20 age cohort, more than half were Independents of one type or another, while in the oldest age group less than one fifth were Independents. Second, the relative frequency of strong versus weak partisan identifiers differs sharply across age cohorts. For example, only 10 percent of the youngest age cohort are strong (more intense) Democrats or strong Republicans, compared to 41 percent of the oldest age group, with fairly regular gradients in the intermediate age categories. Thus, party identification serves as a conservatizing force; and the decline in partisan attachments has major implications for the future of American politics, a theme developed in the last chapter.

THE MEASUREMENT AND CONCEPTUALIZATION OF PARTY IDENTIFICATION

We have talked about citizens' attachments to the Democratic and Republican Parties and whether these attachments are strong or weak. Now we will discuss how the partisan affiliations of American citizens are determined. The most common way of measuring party identification is simply to ask people whether they consider themselves to be Democrats, Republicans, or Independents. This question is evidently a very meaningful one for a substantial proportion of the American adult population—as witnessed by the fact that, from 1952 to 1976, between 63 and 74 percent of the electorate could cite an allegiance to one of the two parties when questioned about their partisan loyalties (see Table 2.1). This widespread level of identification with a political party is not characteristic of all Western nations; for example, Converse and Dupeux (1966: 277) found that in France only 45 percent of the people could identify with one of the major parties or splinter groups.

The Survey Research Center of the University of Michigan has measured party identification by a two-part question that yields a more refined categorization of partisan affiliation beyond the three basic choices of Democrat, Republican, and Independent; the question reads as follows:

> "Generally speaking, do you think of yourself as a Republican, a Democrat, an Independent, or what?" Those who classified themselves as Republicans or Democrats were then asked, "Would you call yourself a strong (Republican, Democrat) or a not very strong (Repubican, Democrat)?" Those who termed themselves Independents were then asked, "Do you think of yourself as closer to the Republican or Democratic Party?"

This two-part question yields the sevenfold classification of party identification employed in Table 2.1—strong Republican, weak Republican, Independent Republican, Independent, Independent Democrat, weak Democrat, and strong Democrat.

Note that to be classified a "pure" Independent, a person would have had to have answered the first question "Independent"; and said that he or she was closer to neither the Democratic or Republican Parties in reply to the second question. Similarly, to be classified a weak Democrat requires a response of "Democrat" to the first question and a reply of "not very strong" to the second. For certain purposes we will rely on the simple threefold categorization of party identification, while for others we will employ the more elaborate classification.

This two-part question reflects a conceptualization of partisanship that assumes Independent represents the middle point of a single continuum ranging from strong Democrat to strong Republican and that Democratic and Republican identifications are opposite points along this continuum. Although this unidimensional conceptualization of party identification seems intuitively plausible and has had substantial payoff in understanding election outcomes, today numerous investigators (e.g., Van Wingen and Valentine, 1978; Weisberg, 1978) are proposing multidimensional perspectives on partisanship. Weisberg argues that independence may be a separate entity with which people can identify, regardless of whether they are neutral between the two parties. Moreover, Republican versus Democratic loyalty may not be polar opposites; certainly citizens can simultaneously like or dislike both parties. Hence, Weisberg advocates a three-dimensional approach, consisting of attitudes toward the Republican Party, the Democratic Party, and independence. One immediate payoff of this multidimensional perspective is the ability to distinguish between party loyalists openly hostile toward the opposition party versus those indifferent to it. Clearly, one would expect greater loyalty toward one's party in the former case; two researchers (Maggiotto and Piereson, 1977) found that evaluations of the other party exerted an independent effect on vote above and beyond the influence of one's own party loyalty.

A number of anomalous results are generated by the two-part question just described. For example, one would expect (assuming a single continuum) that strong identifiers would be more loyal than weak identifiers to their party and that the weak identifiers would in turn be more faithful than the independent leaners. Yet a quick glance at Figures 3.9 and 3.10 reveals that more often than not the independent leaners were more loyal than the weak identifiers in supporting their party's presidential nominee.[2]

In a related vein, research by John Petrocik (1974) has revealed that independent leaners are more likely than weak identifiers to be involved in politics, as evidenced by such indicators as one's general interest in politics, one's concern over the election outcome, and one's attentiveness to campaigns. This result is somewhat surprising if we

---

[2] Shively (1977) provides an intriguing argument why independent leaners exhibit high loyalty to their party's nominee. He suggests that leaners are true Independents who, in response to the second part of the party identification question, are simply reporting their intended vote in the upcoming election. Hence, almost by definition, leaners demonstrate strong loyalty to a party. Other analysts (Miller and Miller, 1977) view leaners more as covert partisans rather than as true Independents. The fact that in Table 3.2 leaners scarcely differ from weak partisans in their evaluations of a number of political stimuli suggests that a stronger case can be built for treating leaners as partisans rather than as pure Independents. Moreover, as shown in Table 3.6, independent leaners overwhelmingly identified in 1976 with the party that they leaned toward in 1972; this would suggest that their leaning preference is more than mere vote intention. Finally, if leaning is simply a matter of vote intention, then the frequency of independent leaners should increase as the election draws near and more Independents make their vote decision. Yet an analysis of the distribution of party identification, by time of interview, shows no increase in the proportion of independent leaners among citizens interviewed closer to Election Day. In general, there seems to be a consensus developing that independent leaners should be treated as partisans and not as Independents.

think of weak identifiers as having more intense partisan feelings than independent leaners, which would lead us to expect that more intense partisans would be more likely to be involved in politics. However, our expectation is incorrect, the main reason being that independent leaners, while less partisan, tend to have characteristics generally associated with higher levels of political involvement. More specifically, Petrocik found that leaners as compared to weak identifiers tended to have higher income and educational levels and were more likely to be white and reside outside the South, characteristics traditionally linked to higher involvement rates.

Petrocik concludes that with respect to partisan objects the sevenfold classification yields expected results, with weak partisans behaving in a more partisan fashion than independent leaners. But even these conclusions must be hedged a bit by the information presented in Table 3.2, which gives the mean evaluation of four partisan objects—the two political parties and the major presidential candidates in 1976—for each category of party identification. These evaluations are obtained by a thermometer scale, which asks respondents to indicate how warm or cold they feel toward an object along a 0 to 100 continuum, where 100 represents the warmest (most positive) evaluation and 0 the coldest. The analogy to a thermometer is helpful to the person making the evaluation. Thus, the first entry of 80 in Table 3.2 means that the average rating of Democrats by strong Democrats was 80, a very warm or positive rating as expected. Likewise, the mean evaluation of Democrats by strong Republicans was only 49.

Note that the differences in the mean ratings of the various objects for weak identifiers versus leaners of the same party are often very small and sometimes in the opposite direction than expected. For example, there is no difference in ratings of Democrats by independent and weak Republicans. Yet if weak Republicans are really more partisan than independent Republicans, we would expect their assessments of Democrats to be lower. Similarly, observe that there are scant differences in the evaluations made of Republicans and Carter by weak versus independent Democrats. In general, Table 3.2 indicates numerous instances where the discriminatory power of the sevenfold classification of party identification is at best minimal, which suggests that for certain purposes a smaller number of categories might be more appropriate and that alternative conceptualizations of partisanship need to be considered.

There is an additional conceptual problem with party identifica-

TABLE 3.2

Mean Evaluations of Four Partisan Objects in 1976, by Party Identification*

Object	Strong Democrats	Weak Democrats	Independent Democrats	Independents	Independent Republicans	Weak Republicans	Strong Republicans
Democrats.........	80	68	64	58	55	55	49
Republicans........	50	53	53	54	61	64	75
Carter............	82	71	69	60	48	53	38
Ford	43	56	52	63	70	72	81

* Table entries are mean thermometer ratings. The higher the rating, the more positive or favorable the evaluation of the object.
Source: CPS 1976 Election Study.

tion that merits attention. Some observers, such as Walter DeVries and V. Lance Tarrance, the authors of *The Ticket-Splitter*, have argued that political scientists rely too much on attitudinal measures of partisanship rather than measures based upon actual behavior. For example, DeVries and Tarrance classify people as Independents not by responses to a survey question but according to their actual voting behavior. Thus, an Independent for them is a person who cast a split-ticket vote, that is, supported candidates of both parties at the same election. Given their different definition of an Independent, it is not surprising that DeVries and Tarrance's description of Independents differs from other analyses.

In general, different measures of what is thought to be the same basic concept are likely to lead to disparities in research findings. This phenomenon is illustrated in the work of Everett Ladd and Charles Hadley (1973–74) who employed an attitudinal and a behavioral measure of party identification to measure the similarity in policy preferences of Democrats and Republicans. Their attitudinal measure of partisanship was a standard survey item, while they defined behavioral Republicans and behavioral Democrats as voters who supported the same party's presidential nominees in two consecutive elections. Thus, the self-identified (attitudinal) Democrat who voted for Eisenhower in 1952 and 1956 would be classified a behavioral Republican. Ladd and Hadley found that with the attitudinal measure, Republican and Democratic adherents took fairly similar positions on a wide variety of issues, while they were much further apart when measured behaviorally. In general, Ladd and Hadley found that behavioral Democrats were more liberal than their self-identified Democratic counterparts, while behavioral Republicans were more conservative.

Thus, the reader might ask which definition or measurement strategy is the correct one. The answer is that neither one is right or wrong; the choice between the two must be made on conceptual grounds and for the purposes of one's analysis. A self-identification measure of party identification is to me more useful, for when people do not vote according to their proclaimed identification, it leads us to ask the crucial question "why?" Hence, we again return to our use of party identification as a base line from which to assess the impact of other factors impinging on the vote decision. Ladd and Hadley (p. 32) note that in times of rapid social change and partisan realignment, self-identification may lag behind actual behavior. That is, people may continue to identify with a party even though they no longer support its presidential candidates. Perhaps this is the situation in the South today where Democratic identification hangs on in the face of increasingly Republican behavior. But even in this situation the self-identification measure seems superior. If one conceptualizes realignment as a process occurring over time, then the ultimate outcome of realignment is in doubt. The fact that identification may lag behind behavior helps contribute to the uncertainty of the realignment outcome. Should events change suddenly, the lagged identification may facilitate people moving back to their original party. For example, we might speculate that the Watergate scandals and economic problems of the 1970s, coupled with the lagged Democratic identification in the South, made it easier for Southerners who supported Republican candidates in recent presidential elections to return to the Democratic Party and Jimmy Carter in 1976. The main point is that for the kinds of questions that concern us in this book, the attitudinal measure of party identification is preferable.

One final methodological point about party identification concerns the concealed, or undercover, partisan.[3] Some observers argue that a substantial proportion of citizens who claim to be Independents have simply hidden their partisan attachments, perhaps because they believe it is more socially desirable to be an Independent rather than a partisan. These observers then assert that a person's actual voting record would be a better indicator of his or her true party identification than responses to the party affiliation questions commonly used in surveys. It should be noted that if party identification was measured by how a person voted, then it could not be used to explain voting behavior since it would be synonymous with voting behavior. Table 3.3 shows that the amount of concealed partisanship is likely very low. It is the 23 percent of the Independents who have always or mostly always voted for the same party that represent the potential undercover partisans. Potential should be emphasized, for people may be Independents and just by coincidence vote for the same party across a number of elections; this is more likely for younger voters who have had fewer opportunities to participate in elections. One way that true Independents might wind up voting for the same party across a series of elections is for the Independents to be ideologically committed

---

[3] Note that the problem of the concealed partisan refers to pure Independents who have given no indication of any party preference in response to the two-part party identification question. In contrast, the leaning Independents have indicated a preference between the parties.

TABLE 3.3
Relation of Strength of Party Identification to Partisan
Regularity in Voting for President, 1976
(in percentages)

Consistency of Presidential Vote	Strength of Partisanship			
	Strong Party Identifiers	Weak Party Identifiers	Independents Leaning to Party	Independents
Voted always or mostly for same party	69	48	28	23
Voted for different parties ..	31	52	72	77
Total	100	100	100	100
Number of cases ...	616	915	472	263

Source: 1976 CPS election study. The question used to establish party consistency of voting was this: "Have you always voted for the same party or have you voted for different parties for President?"

conservatives or liberals without any overt partisan commitments. While this situation is not very common, such an Independent might consistently vote for the same party since that party generally offered more ideologically compatible candidates.

Even if the 23 percent of the Independents who consistently voted for the same party were all concealed partisans, they still total only slightly more than 2 percent of the sample. And if we examine Independents over 35 who have had the opportunity to vote in numerous elections, the percentage generally voting for the same party drops to 15 percent. Thus, the problem of the undercover partisan is not a very worrisome one.

In summary, party identification is most often measured by a self-report technique where citizens give verbal responses to a survey question about their partisanship. While there may be some slight systematic distortion in the verbal responses as compared to the actual behavior, people can be readily assigned to the three broad categories of Democrat, Republican, and Independent. For certain purposes, a more elaborate classification of party identification may be warranted, although we should be careful not to get unnecessarily complicated. How we measure a concept has important consequences for the results we obtain; since party identification occupies such a prominent position in the discussion of presidential elections, we have discussed problems of conceptualization and measurement in unusual detail.

THE DEVELOPMENT AND TRANSMISSION OF PARTY IDENTIFICATION

As was stated earlier, citizens tend to acquire a party identification fairly early in their lives. In a study of school children in eight cities, Hess and Torney (1967: 90) found that only about 20 percent of a sample of fourth graders could not recognize what the terms Democrat and Republican meant, while almost half of the children could express a clear partisan preference. Similarly, in a study of New Haven youngsters, Fred Greenstein (1965: 71) found that by fourth grade more than 60 percent of the students could cite a partisan preference. Hence, it is meaningful to talk of the partisan attachments of young children; however, the policy content and informational support of this partisanship is weak to nonexistent. Greenstein discovered, for example, that only a third of the fourth graders could name one public official from either of the two parties and fewer than one in five students could name a leader from each party. He also found that perceptions of issue differences between the parties were uncommon. These early partisan loyalties, despite being devoid of policy and informational content, may be consequential for what the child subsequently learns about the parties. That is, these early attachments may so facilitate the selective acquisition of information about parties that one's initial loyalties tend to be reinforced.

It is widely agreed that the family plays the greatest role in the child's acquisition of partisanship. In a nationwide study of high school seniors conducted in 1965, Jennings and Niemi (1974: 41) found substantial agreement in parental and child partisan affiliations, as shown in Table 3.4. The Jennings and Niemi evidence is particularly interesting since it is based upon responses from both the child and his parents and does not rely on the child's report of his parent's partisanship, which can be subject to serious distortion.

One factor that affected the degree of correspondence between the parents' and the child's identification was the politicization of the family. Correspondence was higher in situations where the parents engaged in political conversations frequently and where the child had a high level of interest in public affairs. Jennings and Niemi argue that in such situations there are more cues about the parents' political leanings and a greater likelihood that the child will accurately pick up such cues. Thus, the greater correspondence in party loyalties in politicized families is due to greater perceptual accuracy on the part

TABLE 3.4
Student Party Identification by Parental Party Identification*
(in percentages)

Student Party Identification	Parental Party Identification		
	Democrat	Independent	Republican
Democrat	66	29	13
Independent	27	53	36
Republican	7	17	51
Total	100	100	100
Number of cases	914	442	495

* Party identification was measured by the standard SRC/CPS question. The categories of Democrat and Republican include strong and weak identifiers, while the Independent category includes leaners and pure Independents.

Source: *The Political Character of Adolescence: The Influence of Family and Schools,* by M. Kent Jennings and Richard G. Niemi (copyright © 1974 by Princeton University Press), table 2.2, p. 41.

of children in recognizing their parents' partisanship (Jennings and Niemi, 1974: 47–49).

The family plays the dominant role in the transmission of partisan attitudes, although it is less important with respect to other political attitudes.[4] Within the family, it has been traditional to describe the father's political role as dominant. This image of male political dominance arose in part because in some of the earlier studies of voting it was not uncommon for the wife to say that she was going to vote the way her husband voted. The work of Jennings and Langton (1969) calls into question the simplistic notion of male political dominance, particularly in the child's acquisition of partisan attachment. Jennings and Langton showed that in cases where the mother and father had different identifications, the child was more likely to take on the partisan affiliation of the mother; the appropriate evidence is shown in Table 3.5. While the advantage for the mother is not overwhelming, it does suggest that we reject any unqualified notion of male political dominance.

One explanation given for the mother's relatively advantageous position is simply that the child spends much more time with the mother in his or her formative years and therefore develops closer

---

[4] For evidence that the family's role is less with respect to the transmission of political attitudes that are not overtly partisan, see Jennings and Niemi (1968).

TABLE 3.5
**Student's Party Identification in Cases in Which the
Parents' Party Identification Differs**
(in percentages)

| Parents' Partisanship | | Students' Partisanship | | | | No. of |
Mother	Father	Democrat	Independent	Republican	Total	Cases
Democrat	Republican	44	21	35	100	37
Republican	Democrat	29	38	33	100	23

Source: M. Kent Jennings and Kenneth P. Langton, "Mothers versus Fathers: The Formation of Political Orientations among Young Americans," *The Journal of Politics* 31 (May 1969), table 3, p. 341.

affective ties with the mother. While Jennings and Langton examine additional factors that affect the relative influence of the father versus the mother on the child, the basic result of the mother having greater influence still holds. For example, where the mother is more politically active in campaigns than the father, the child's identification agrees with the mother's over the father's by a margin of 59 percent to 28 percent, or a 31 percent advantage for the mother. But where the father is more politically active, his advantage over the mother in the child's loyalties is only 6 percent (36 percent versus 30 percent).

The actual learning of partisanship by children occurs via a process of identification, described by Hess and Torney (p. 21) as consisting of "the child's imitation of the behavior of some significant other person—usually a parent, or a teacher—when the adult has not attempted to persuade the child of his viewpoint." Thus, the learning of party identification is not a conscious activity; rather it is an informal process centered mainly in the family. One reason why the family is so crucial in this area is that other potential agents of political learning, such as teachers and school curricula, studiously avoid getting enmeshed in partisan questions.[5]

---

[5] For a discussion of the effects of the school and school curriculum, see Hess and Torney (1967: 93–115) and Langton and Jennings (1968). Rather than saying that the school has no impact on partisanship, it might be more accurate to say that the school moves children away from partisanship toward independence. Jennings and Niemi observe that in comparison to the younger children studied by Hess and Torney and by Greenstein, the high school seniors they analyzed had a higher proportion of Independents. They attribute this to the impact of the school and teachers, arguing that "attempts to keep 'partisan bickering' out of the classroom as well as direct inculcation of the norm that one should vote for the man and not the party probably counteract the partisan cues which many children receive at home." See Jennings and Niemi, *The Political Character of Adolescence,* p. 263.

THE STABILITY OF PARTY IDENTIFICATION AT THE INDIVIDUAL LEVEL

Although the child usually acquires a partisan orientation at an early age, this does not mean that these early loyalties necessarily remain unchanged. As the child matures, he or she increasingly encounters new situations—for example, college and the work group—in which the partisan cues may be vastly different from those of the child's home environment, thereby creating pressures toward a change in identification. Likewise, as the child reaches adulthood, more information is acquired about the parties and their policies and candidates, which may lead to switches from the child's original identification. For example, white youngsters growing up in the South may initially affiliate with the Democratic Party until they learn that the national party is responsible for a series of civil rights programs anathema to them; a move to the Republican Party may then follow.

Overall, however, there is substantial stability in the party loyalties of Americans. The best evidence of stability is provided by panel data obtained by repeated interviews with the *same* people over time, which enable one to observe directly any changes in partisanship that are occurring. Two major panel studies of the American electorate are available, one spanning the 1956–1958–1960 period and the other encompassing 1972–1974–1976. Table 3.6 presents the relationship between the partisanship professed by a sample of Americans in 1972 and the partisanship of these same respondents in 1976.

Although the assessment of partisan stability in Table 3.6 would appear to be straightforward, the task is complicated by problems inherent in the conceptualization of stability and in the actual measurement of partisanship. Given that the two-part party identification question assigns respondents to one of seven possible categories, does stability then refer to both the direction and the strength of partisanship? That is, should a person who at one time point is a strong Democrat and at the next is a weak Democrat be considered stable or unstable in his or her partisanship? If one defines stability to mean constancy in both direction and intensity, then the more numerous the categories of partisanship, the less likely identical responses will be given over time. Hence, as shown in Table 3.6, the level of stability with the sevenfold classification is about 50 percent compared to over 74 percent (the sum of the percentages within the broken lines) when party identification is trichotomized as Democrat (strong and weak),

TABLE 3.6
The Stability of Partisanship between 1972 and 1976

1972 Partisanship	1976 Partisanship						
	Strong Dem.	Weak Dem.	Ind. Dem.	Ind.	Ind. Rep.	Weak Rep.	Strong Rep.
Strong Dem.	8.9	3.7	.8	.3	.1	.1	.1
Weak Dem.	5.0	13.0	3.2	1.7	.6	.9	.2
Ind. Dem.	1.5	3.5	4.3	.8	1.0	.2	.1
Ind.	.6	1.0	1.7	4.9	2.2	.9	.1
Ind. Rep.	.5	.4	1.0	2.6	4.8	1.8	.5
Weak Rep.	.1	.7	.2	.8	2.7	7.4	2.4
Strong Rep.	.3	.4	.2	.2	.9	4.1	6.5

Total percentage = 100
Source: CPS 1972–1976 election panel. Table entries are corner or total percentages based on a total of 1,276 panel respondents who expressed a partisanship in both 1972 and 1976. The proportion stable is simply the percentage of respondents who gave identical responses over time.

Independent (leaners and pure Independents), and Republican (strong and weak). A third estimate of stability of just under 80 percent (the sum of the percentages within the solid lines) is obtained if the independent leaners are included with the partisans rather than with the pure Independents. The decision as to which of the three estimates gives the most accurate assessment of stability depends upon what one requires of party identification to call it stable.

Analyses of the 1956–1958–1960 panel have yielded varying judgments of stability. Dreyer (1973) concluded that party identification was very stable, with only random changes occurring over time. Dobson and St. Angelo (1975), in contrast, argue (as do Brody (1977) and

Macaluso) that partisanship changes were not random but instead were responsive to real world events. More specifically, they found that Republicans of all levels of intensity were less stable than Democrats between 1956 and 1958, but that between 1958 and 1960 supporters of both parties behaved more similarly. They attribute this pattern to the Republican-associated recession of 1958. A very similar pattern holds in the 1972–1974–1976 panel. Between 1972 and 1974 (the Nixon resignation year), Republicans were much more likely than Democrats to shift away from their partisanship, a difference that practically vanished between 1974 and 1976.

Hence, party identification and particularly its strength component seem sensitive to political conditions. Yet this finding probably should not alter our judgment of stability since the preponderance of observed shifts are intraparty (e.g., from strong Republican to weak Republican) rather than interparty, although it does call into question assertions about the early learning of partisanship and its subsequent intensification over the life cycle. At the least, the direction and intensity of party identification probably should be viewed as conceptually distinct, the former being very stable and long-term and the latter being more responsive to the immediate political environment.

The stability of party identification is further demonstrated by comparing it to the constancy of other political attitudes and attachments. For example, citizens' party loyalties are far more stable than their attitudes on a wide range of prominent political issues. Likewise, few attachments, with the exception of such loyalties as religious affiliation, exceed the durability of party identification. Finally, responses to a survey question that queried citizens as to whether their partisanship had ever changed provide additional evidence of partisan stability. Figure 3.1 indicates great stability in loyalties, even allowing for some distortion in the recall of prior partisanship. Note that in all years at least 69 percent of the strong and weak partisans of each party recall having always been affiliated with that party. Further observe that throughout this period, particularly in 1972, higher proportions of Republicans recall a different past identification. Perhaps this is a fragment of evidence suggesting a pro-Republican realignment. Or perhaps the decline in the proportion of stable partisans in both parties simply reflects the weakening of party ties discussed in Chapter 1. In either event, the major conclusion to be drawn from the panel data and the recall question is that stability in partisanship is still very high.

FIGURE 3.1
Proportion of Strong and Weak Identifiers
Recalling Stable Partisanship by Party, 1952–1976

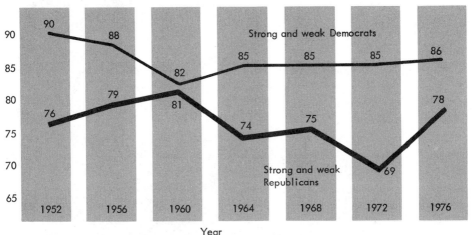

Percentage of strong and weak identifiers
recalling stable partisanship

Year

Sources: SRC/CPS studies of 1952, 1956, 1960, 1964, 1968, 1972, and 1976.

Although the panel data yielded valuable evidence about partisan stability over a four-year period, their limited time span makes them less helpful in studying two related questions, namely whether citizens become more conservative politically as they age and whether partisan loyalties become more intense over time.[6] With respect to the former question, it is commonplace in popular discussions of politics to assert that as adults get older, they get more conservative. Conservative in this context can mean a lot of different things, including an unwillingness to accept new ideas and a rigidity in thought. Or it might refer to more overtly political matters, as in the assertion that older people become more conservative politically and hence more Republican

---

[6] Because such questions entail studying people over much longer time periods than four years and because panel data are very difficult and costly to collect over a lengthy time span, social scientists often rely on cohort analysis to make longitudinal inferences. Cohort analysis requires multiple surveys with different respondents conducted at different points in time. Respondents are then assigned to age-defined cohorts and the behavior of these cohorts is traced over time. The CPS presidential election surveys, which have been conducted quadrennially since 1952, are a prime data source for cohort analysis. Imagine that the respondents in the 1952 CPS survey are divided into age groups, such as 21–24, 25–28, 29–32, 33–36, and the like. Then the 21–24 cohort in 1952 will be the 25–28 cohort in the 1956 survey, the 29–32 cohort in the 1960 survey, and so on, and hence the behavior of the cohort (and not the individual) can be examined over time.

since the Republican Party presumably takes the more conservative, status quo (opposition to federal intervention) position on a wide range of public policy issues. Table 3.1 might seem to provide some evidence that aging and Republicanism go together since the oldest age group is the most Republican and the youngest age group the least Republican. This is shown in Figure 3.2, which presents the propor-

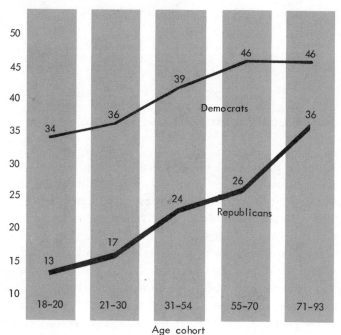

FIGURE 3.2
Percentage of Strong and Weak Identifiers
by Party in Various Age Cohorts, 1976

Source: 1976 CPS election study.

tion of strong and weak Democrats and Republicans in each age group in the 1972 electorate. Actually, Figure 3.2 shows increases for both parties in older age groups due to the decline in the number of Independents. But it is the case that the GOP is relatively stronger in the oldest age group.

While the trends portrayed in Figure 3.2 appear to show increasing Republicanism with age, there are two basic processes that could be producing the observed patterns. One process attributes the increase in Republicanism directly to the effects of aging; this is commonly referred to as a "life-cycle effect" in the sense that becoming more conservative is seen as an integral part of aging. But an alternative explanation argues that older citizens are more Republican because they learned their partisanship in a more Republican era. Hence, their greater Republicanism is not due to any consequence of aging but is simply a generational effect reflecting the fact that this age cohort of citizens grew up in a more Republican era and is therefore more Republican even today because of the relative stability of partisan orientations over time. For example, the citizens in the 71–93 age group in Figure 3.2 reached the age of 21 between 1904 and 1926 and in most cases acquired their initial partisanship prior to 1932, a period of Republican dominance in partisan allegiances. Thus, the relatively stronger position of the Republican Party in this age group simply reflects the maintenance of a Republican advantage that dates back to the 1920s.

The relative importance of life cycle versus generational effects has sparked a major controversy among academic investigators. *The American Voter* (pp. 149–67) found substantial generational effect associated with the Great Depression and the New Deal and also observed that older citizens were somewhat more likely to switch from the Democrats to the Republicans than the reverse. But overall, *The American Voter* found little evidence sustaining the notion that aging leads to Republicanism. John Crittenden (1962, 1969–70) found that the aging process does produce sizable conversions to Republicanism, although Neal Cutler (1969–70) has criticized this research as based upon faulty methodology. A more recent study by Glenn and Hefner (1972) concludes that there is no evidence for the proposition linking aging to Republicanism.

With respect to the intensification of partisanship, political analysts have long observed that older citizens exhibit stronger party loyalties than their younger counterparts; see Table 3.1 for an example of the positive relationship between age and strength of party identification. The question is what processes might account for the more intense loyalties of older citizens and, again, the life cycle versus generational controversy becomes relevant. Converse (1969, 1976, 1979) has espoused an intuitively appealing life-cycle explanation, which asserts that the longer a person supports a political party, the stronger the loyalties to that party will become; repeated and enduring commitment results in more intense commitment. The life-cycle explanation implies that as older citizens with firmer loyalties pass from the electorate they are replaced by younger cohorts with intensifying party loyalties, thereby leaving the overall level of party support relatively unchanged.

Employing a cohort analysis, Abramson (1976, 1979) did not observe an increase in partisan intensity among age cohorts over time as would be predicted by the life-cycle explanation. Hence, he argued that the stronger party attachments of older citizens represent generation and not life-cycle effects because the older generation was socialized into partisanship at a time when party labels and loyalties were more meaningful. Thus the older generation was imprinted with a stronger sense of partisanship at a young age and has carried this imprint over time. Abramson asserts that the young cohorts of today receive weak partisan cues and that the resulting weak attachments will be characteristic of them even as they identify with a political party over a lengthy period.[7]

Additional evidence challenging the life-cycle explanation is provided by a two-wave panel study (Jennings and Niemi, 1975) of a sample of high school seniors and their parents. Between 1965 and 1973, the proportion of Independents among the youth *rose* by 12 percent and the proportion of strong identifiers fell by a half—movements opposite those predicted by the life-cycle notion. For the parents there was greater partisan stability over the eight-year period, with only a slight decline in the proportion of intense partisans. It is possible that life-cycle effects were operative in this era only to be outweighed by even stronger period effects centered on such political crises as Viet Nam, race relations, and Watergate.

In terms of the potentiality for realignment, the generational explanation implies that the weaker partisan attachments of the contemporary youth generation will continue to remain weak, resulting in a citizenry more susceptible to mobilization. The life-cycle process predicts that younger cohorts will acquire more of a partisan colora-

---

[7] There are a number of substantive and methodological issues in the Converse-Abramson debate, dealing with such matters as appropriate cohort analysis techniques, the difficulty in sampling the youngest cohorts, and the possibility of period effects in addition to life-cycle and generational influences. See Converse (1976, 1979) and Abramson (1976, 1979). A period effect results from particular political circumstances and events that may differentially affect various segments of the population. The Viet Nam War, issues relevant to race relations, and Watergate have produced period effects in the post-1964 era.

tion as they mature and thereby be more resistant to realignment. We will return to these themes in the last chapter.

We mentioned earlier the possibility that party identification may lag behind actual changes in voting behavior. This notion is given some support by the trends presented in Figure 3.3, which shows the

FIGURE 3.3
Proportion of Strong and Weak Identifiers
Reporting Consistent Presidential Vote by Party, 1952–1976

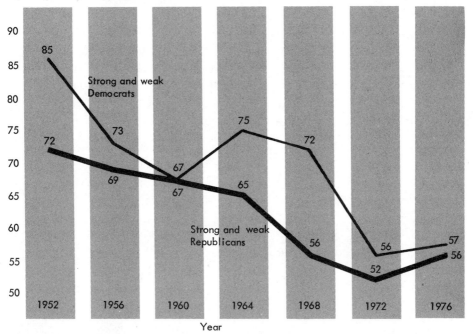

Percentage of strong and weak identifiers
reporting consistent presidential vote

Sources: SRC/CPS studies of 1952, 1956, 1960, 1964, 1968, 1972, and 1976.

proportion of Democrats and Republicans who claim to have voted for the same party for President all or most of the time. Observe that there is a sizable decline in the proportion of partisans citing consistent loyalty in presidential voting, a decline far greater than the trends toward increased instability in party identification shown in Figure 3.1. This suggests that actual voting behavior fluctuates more widely than partisan attachments.

Further evidence about changing behavior in the light of relatively stable partisan loyalties is provided by an examination of the extent of split-ticket voting over time. DeVries and Tarrance (1972: 30–33) show that there has been an upward trend in the number of congressional districts carried by a presidential candidate of one party and a House nominee of another party. For example, in 1920, only 3.2 percent of congressional districts exhibited split outcomes; by 1944 the comparable percentage was 11.2; and in 1968, the percentage of split outcomes had risen even more sharply to 31.6. Similar trends characterize the election results for Governor and U.S. Senator within a state; the greatest incidence of split outcomes in these two races occurs in the 1960s and 1970s. More direct evidence about the extent to which citizens cast split-ticket votes is provided by the SRC/CPS surveys. Figure 3.4 indicates the proportion of citizens who report having split their ticket for the offices of President and U.S. Representative. Note that split-ticket voting increases over time for all three partisan groups, with the highest levels generally occurring in 1972 and 1976. As expected, split-ticket voting among a party's adherents is highest when

FIGURE 3.4
Trends in Split-Ticket Voting by Party, 1952–1976

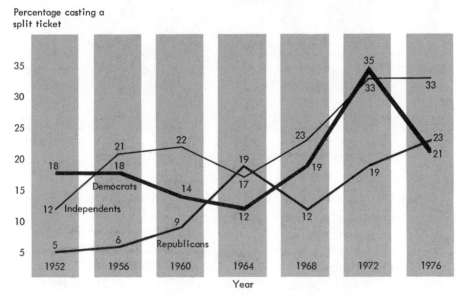

Sources: SRC/CPS studies of 1952, 1956, 1960, 1964, 1968, 1972, and 1976.

the presidential nominee is relatively unpopular—Goldwater in 1964 for Republicans and McGovern in 1972 for Democrats.[8]

In summary, there is still great stability in the partisanship professed by individual citizens. Most Americans who have a partisan affiliation say that they have always identified with that party. Despite the constancy in citizens' partisan allegiances, a number of trends— the increase in split-ticket voting and the rise in voters' support for presidential candidates from different parties—in the past two decades raises the possibility that partisan ties are weakening. Thus, while the stability of partisan attachments might lead one to assert that realignment is unlikely, these other indicators suggest caution in accepting such a conclusion, especially if one gives credence to the idea that psychological attachments to a party lag behind actual voting behavior.

THE STABILITY OF PARTY IDENTIFICATION IN THE AGGREGATE

Although the partisanship of individual citizens has remained fairly stable, there have been significant trends in the overall distribution of partisanship in the electorate, the most noteworthy being the huge rise in the number of citizens claiming to be Independents, so that today Independents outnumber Republican partisans. Of course, if one treats leaning Independents as partisans rather than as pure Independents, then the growth of independence is not nearly as impressive.

As depicted in Figure 3.5, the major increase in Independents occurred between 1964 and 1972, with little additional growth since 1972. Overall, the gain in Independents about equals the decline in Democratic identifiers, although this does not mean Democrats have been switching to a position of independence. In fact, the major source of the increase is to be found in the party affiliations of the young generation. In 1964, 33 percent of the 21- to-24-age cohort were Independents, compared to over 50 percent in 1972. Likewise, 28 percent of the 25- to 34-year-olds were Independents in 1964, a figure that

---

8 One reason why split-ticket voting has increased is the greater electoral support given congressional incumbents even by supporters of the opposite party. An analysis of any pair of federal races or of state and local contests would indicate trends in split-ticket voting similar to those in Figure 3.4.

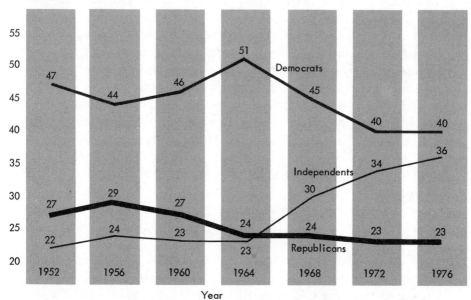

FIGURE 3.5
The Proportions of Partisans and Independents, 1952–1976*

Percentage of electorate

* The independent category includes pure independents and leaners, while the partisan categories include strong and weak identifiers.
Sources: SRC/CPS surveys of 1952, 1956, 1960, 1964, 1968, 1972, and 1976.

jumped to 47 percent by 1972. In contrast, the older generation has not witnessed as substantial an increase in independence. For example, between 1964 and 1972 the proportion of Independents among citizens over 65 years old increased only 10 percent (from 14 to 24 percent Independent).

Thus, the young generation without solid attachments to a political party becomes a prime source of any potential realignment. It is reasonable to expect that as these young citizens age, a sizable proportion will find a home in one of the two political parties even if they never become as partisan as the older generation. But on what basis will they make this choice? One possibility is that the preponderance of these young citizens will end up as adherents of the party preferred by their parents. It appears, however, that the influence of the family has declined somewhat, perhaps to be replaced by the impact of political events, issues, and candidates. If so, we are again saying that the future shape of the party system is unpredictable.

THE SOCIAL CHARACTERISTICS OF PARTISANS

It is a fact of American political life that support for the Democratic and Republican Parties varies among different racial, religious, nationality, and economic groups. American politics is often discussed in terms of the black vote or the union vote or the Catholic vote, indicating that blocs of citizens may have distinctive partisan allegiances. Yet despite the relative homogeneity of these various groups, it should be noted that, with the exception of blacks and Jews, it is uncommon for any group to give more than 60 percent of its vote to a party. Thus, we are correct in saying that the Democratic Party usually wins many more votes from union members and Catholics than does the Republican Party; it is also correct, however, to say that the Republican Party receives a substantial minority of the votes cast by Catholics and union members. Thus, the parties attract rather heterogeneous support even though they appeal to certain groups much more than others.

The clearest manifestation of the differential support that the parties receive from various social groups is reflected in the concern expressed by New York politicians, especially Democrats, that the voter be offered balanced tickets of candidates for office. By balanced is meant that there should be at least one candidate from each major voting bloc that supports a party. In the New York City Democratic context, this requirement for a balanced ticket means that Italian and Irish Catholics, Jews, blacks, and, more recently, Puerto Ricans should be well represented on the slate of candidates. At the national level, balance in a presidential ticket usually refers to regional, ideological, and, for Democrats, religious balance. Thus, in 1972, most of the candidates prominently mentioned as possible running mates for George McGovern, a Protestant, were Catholics, a recognition that the Democratic Party had a sizable Catholic constituency to please. In 1976, Walter Mondale added geographical and especially ideological balance to the Carter ticket; his close ties and identification with the liberal and labor wings of the Democratic Party helped shore up potentially weak areas for Carter.

Parties have a differential appeal to citizens with varying social characteristics because citizens do not act politically in a vacuum divorced from the influence of relevant others; rather, Americans belong to a large number of groups, many of which are relevant for partisan preferences. The most important group is the primary group of the family, where many citizens acquire their initial partisanship.

But many secondary groups to which an individual belongs, while entailing less group interaction than the family, still have notable consequences for political behavior. Such groups as religious and occupational organizations, while usually not overtly political, influence or appear to influence partisan choice either because members of the group have shared politically relevant experiences or because the group reflects consequential political events of a previous era or because the group has the resources to educate and mobilize its members toward political goals, as when labor unions rally their membership behind candidates endorsed by union governing bodies. For example, Catholics are on the whole more Democratic than non-Catholics, not because the Democratic Party currently espouses specifically pro-Catholic policies but because of historical circumstance and the economic location of Catholic citizens in an earlier generation. That is, the Democratic Party welcomed the massive waves of Catholic immigrants in the early part of this century and facilitated the movement of Catholics into the political system. Furthermore, Catholics were disproportionately of the lower and working class when the Great Depression struck; it was the Democratic Party that proposed policies that were viewed as more beneficial to disadvantaged groups. These Catholic Democratic loyalties, while less relevant to contemporary America, are maintained in part by a socialization process and by particular events, such as recessions and Democratic nomination of Catholic candidates; such events tend to resurrect the older images of the Democratic Party as the party more beneficial to Catholic citizens.

The most interesting aspect of group loyalties is that frequently the members of the group do not see the political relevance of the group nor do they perceive the group as having any significant impact on their behavior. Yet situations can arise in which the original basis of the group attachment assumes new life. For example, probably the most basic and most investigated social characteristic is social class, defined in a multitude of ways. While class cleavages are not as prominent in the United States as they are in other societies, the Democratic and Republican Parties are perceived somewhat differently in terms of which class they favor, with the Democrats seen as the working-class party and the GOP as the middle-class party. These class-related perceptions of the two parties have weakened in recent decades, although the presence of economic crises is likely to make class a more potent factor in partisan choice. The point is that the differential loyalties of various groups to the two parties most often have a "rational" basis in some past set of events. These loyalties may gradually decay as the original rationale for them fades into the past. But if the original basis for the loyalties become prominent once again, then these loyalties may be reinforced. This is why the Democratic Party tries to contest elections on New Deal-economic issues; if voters make their choices on the basis of such concerns, the Democratic Party is likely to fare very well at election time.

Research has indicated that blacks are more Democratic than whites, and Catholics and Jews more Democratic than Protestants (outside the South), and lower- and working-class citizens more Democratic than middle- and upper-class citizens. These general patterns have held throughout the 1952–76 period, although there have been some noteworthy deviations, which are discussed below.

Figure 3.6 presents trends in Democratic identification among religious groups. The proportion of Catholics who are strong and weak identifiers with the Democratic Party has declined by 11 percent from a peak in 1960, the year in which the Democrats nominated a Catholic candidate for President. Southern Protestant loyalties to the Democratic Party have eroded even more markedly, a decline that would be sharper if black citizens were excluded from the analysis. Yet the Democrats still claim greater allegiance from Catholics and southern Protestants than does the GOP. Nonsouthern Protestants have traditionally been less Democratic, and there has been no consistent trend in their loyalties; while among Jews, Democratic strength is still solid though not as high as in the 1950s.

Within racial categories, the greatest volatility has occurred among black citizens, especially in the South. This is not surprising since southern blacks have only recently become electorally active, and did not have the opportunity to develop as firm loyalties to a political party as did citizens who had been voting for a long time. Voting for a party regularly increases one's commitment to that party, an effect not very important among southern blacks given their recent achievement of the franchise. In 1960, only half of all blacks claimed to be Democrats, while in 1968, this proportion had jumped to 88 percent, an almost unheard of degree of partisan loyalty by a group. But between 1968 and 1972, black identification with the Democratic Party plummeted by almost 20 percentage points as the number of black Independents rose tremendously.

Miller and his associates (1973: 86) posit that the drop in black

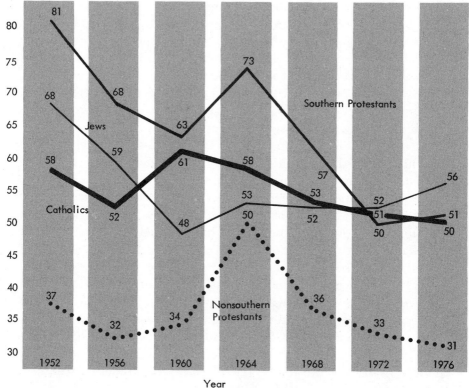

FIGURE 3.6
Trends in Democratic Partisanship among Religious Groups, 1952–1976*

Percentage strong and weak Democrats

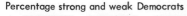

Year

* In this figure and the next, the complement of the reported percentages includes both Independents and Republicans. That is, the fact that 58 percent of the Catholics in 1952 were Democrats means that the other 42 percent were either Independents or Republicans.
Sources: SRC/CPS studies of 1952, 1956, 1960, 1964, 1968, 1972, and 1976.

Democratic identification might be due to the disappointment of black citizens, particularly in the South, who were mobilized into support for the Democrats in 1968, only to see their candidate lose. It is the case that most of the decline in black Democratic affiliation occurred in the South, where 91 percent Democratic loyalty in 1968 fell off to 66 percent in 1972; the comparable figures outside the South were 79 to 73 percent. Miller and his colleagues present an alternative explanation for erosion in black Democratic affiliation that is far more pregnant with implications for American politics and partisan realignment. They write (1973: 87):

The growth in Independents among blacks is apparently associated with an increased dissatisfaction with the perceived policies of the Democratic party, which are seen by blacks, on the average, as less liberal than their own policy preferences. For example, in 1970 nearly 24 percent of blacks placed themselves and the Democrats at the same policy position . . . but in 1972 only 15 percent did so. Coincidental with this increased dissatisfaction with the Democrats, there was stability in dissatisfaction with the Republicans but also a substantial increase in blacks saying they would support an independent black party if one were to form. . . . This increased support for an independent black party more than doubled among Independent blacks, rising from 21 percent in 1970 to 44 percent in 1972. Thus, while part of the decline in black Democratic identification may reflect a decrease in Democratic efforts to mobilize the black voters, another aspect . . . may be . . . disappointment and dissatisfaction with the performance of the Democratic party.

While this latter explanation is somewhat speculative and in need of additional supporting evidence, it does force us to question whether the black vote is as solid a pillar of Democratic strength as is often claimed. A final factor relevant to black Democratic loyalties, especially in the South, is the fact that since widespread attachments to the Democratic Party are of relatively recent vintage, these loyalties may be shaped more by contemporary events than by long-term influences. One potentially consequential event is the nomination of a candidate having a long-standing association with the civil rights movement. Hence, the decline in black Democratic loyalties in 1972 might in part be due to McGovern's being a less attractive candidate than was Humphrey in 1968.

Among southern and nonsouthern whites (see Figure 3.7), there has been less variability in partisan allegiances, although there has been a long-term decline in white southern support for the Democrats. The crucial datum about southern whites is that, despite the large drop in their Democratic identification (from 80 percent in 1952 to 47 percent in 1976), there has not been a corresponding gain for the Republicans. For example, only about 13 percent of southern whites were strong or weak Republicans in 1952; by 1972, this figure had risen only to 18 percent. Thus, despite the enormous Republican victories in the South in 1968 and 1972, the South is still Democratic with respect to partisan attachments. And these Democratic loyalties certainly contributed to Carter's near sweep of the South in 1976, although it should be noted that Carter did not win a majority of the southern

FIGURE 3.7
Trends in Democratic Partisanship among Racial Groups, 1952–1976

Percentage strong and weak Democrats

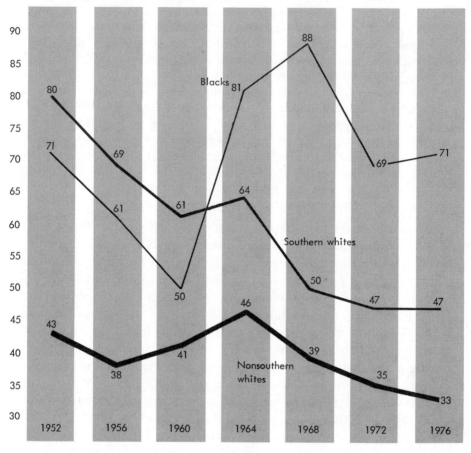

Sources: SRC/CPS studies of 1952, 1956, 1960, 1964, 1968, 1972, and 1976.

white vote despite being a native son of the region. Overwhelming support from southern blacks was crucial to Carter's success.

Among status groups, as measured by income, occupation, union membership, and citizens' perceptions of their social class, the trends in Democratic identification have not been as consistent or clear-cut. It was generally the case that Democratic identification dropped noticeably in 1972; this was particularly evident among union members, blue-collar workers, and people who call themselves working class. Fewer than half of each group were classified as strong and weak

Democrats in 1972; and while the Democrats still have a clear advantage over Republicans in the loyalties of these groups, erosion has occurred in such traditional pillars of Democratic support. Among occupational categories, persons in farm-related jobs exhibited the widest fluctuation in party affiliations, in part because of their great sensitivity to their economic situation which can fluctuate widely in response to actions of the federal government.

The previous analysis investigated trends in the partisanship of various social groups defined according to one or two characteristics. For an overall portrait of the partisan loyalties of social groups defined according to a number of characteristics simultaneously, see Figure 3.8. Note that the Democrats are strongest among southern and

FIGURE 3.8
The Partisan Allegiances in 1976 for Social Groups Defined According to Region, Race, Religion, and Occupation

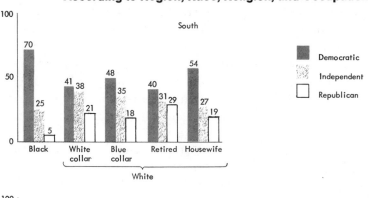

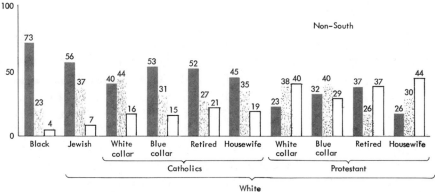

Source: CPS 1976 study. The format of the figure is based on one presented by William Flanigan, *Political Behavior of the American Electorate* (Boston: Allyn & Bacon, Inc., 1972), fig. 3.1, p. 53. Certain configurations of characteristics are not included since too few citizens fall into these categories.

nonsouthern blacks, nonsouthern retired and blue-collar Catholics, and Jews, while the Republicans claim the greatest loyalties among nonsouthern, Protestant, white-collar, housewives, and retired citizens. Republican loyalties drop below 10 percent in a number of categories, while Democratic affiliation falls below 30 percent only for nonsouthern, white-collar Protestants. The results of Figure 3.8 correspond quite closely to similar research conducted on the 1968 and 1972 electorates.

Our analysis thus far has focused on the partisan makeup of various social groups; we could also examine the social composition of various partisan groups. This latter topic is treated in Chapter 11 in our discussion of the strategies that political elites employ to put together majority electoral coalitions. We will conclude this section by examining the actual voting behavior as opposed to the partisanship of various politically relevant social groupings.

Robert Axelrod (1972) has described broad electoral coalitions for each party and determined the contribution that each coalitional component has made to each party's vote at each election since 1952. The Democratic coalition, according to Axelrod, consists of the poor, blacks, southerners, union members, Catholics, and residents of central cities, while the Republican coalition is practically the mirror image of the Democratic. Table 3.7 presents the voting loyalty rates of each element of both party coalitions.

Note that among union members, Catholics, and southerners, three pillars of the New Deal Democratic coalition, vote loyalty was lowest in 1972 and fairly low in 1968. In 1976, these groups returned to the Democratic nominee, although their support levels were not as high as in previous elections. Among blacks and central city residents, two groups with substantial overlap, Democratic support was still quite high in 1976, though not as high as in previous years.

Within the Republican coalition, the GOP showed the greatest strength in all groups in 1972. Of particular interest is the two thirds of the white vote claimed by the GOP in 1972 and the 60 percent of the northern vote, which is actually less than the GOP received in the South. These figures suggest that the traditional Democratic vote coalition disintegrated badly in 1972, with the Republicans doing surprisingly well among both their traditional suppporters and those of the Democrats. In 1976, the Republican support coalition reverted to its traditional composition, with the GOP winning slight majorities

TABLE 3.7
Loyalty Rates among Components of the Democratic
and Republican Electoral Coalitions, 1952–1976*

Party and Groups	Year						
	1952	1956	1960	1964	1968	1972	1976
Democrats							
Poor (income under $3,000)	47	47	48	69	44	45	67
Black (and other nonwhite)	83	68	72	99	92	86	88
Union member (or union member							
in family)	59	55	66	80	51	45	63
Catholic (and other non-Protestant) ...	57	53	82	75	61	43	57
South (including border states)	55	52	52	58	39	36	53
Central cities (or 12 largest							
metropolitan areas)	51	55	65	74	58	61	61
Republicans							
Nonpoor	56	59	50	40	44	61	49
White	57	59	51	42	47	66	52
Nonunion	61	63	55	45	46	63	52
Protestant	61	62	63	44	49	64	53
Northern	57	60	50	38	47	60	49
Not in central cities	57	60	52	40	45	63	49

* The table entries are the percentages of each party's coalition components remaining loyal to the party in the presidential election.
Source: Extracted from figures presented by Robert Axelrod, "Communications," *American Political Science Review* 72 (June 1978), pp. 622–24.

of the white and nonunion vote, but falling below normal Republican support among Protestants and non-central city residents.

TURNOUT AND DEFECTION AMONG PARTISANS AND INDEPENDENTS

We will conclude Chapter 3 by examining the relationship of party identification to turnout and vote defection over time, commenting on the implications of the observed trends for our analysis of presidential elections. Table 3.8 presents the turnout rate of partisans and independents since 1952. There are three important points to be made about the table. First, as expected, turnout is highest among the strong identifiers, while the difference in turnout rates of weak versus independent partisans is often small and inconsistent. Second, Republicans have higher turnout rates than Democrats, no matter the year or type of partisan identifier. Thus, the numerical advantage which the Democratic Party enjoys in terms of allegiances is partially offset by the

TABLE 3.8
Turnout Rates of Partisans and Independents, 1952–1976*

	Year						
	1952	1956	1960	1964	1968	1972	1976
Strong Democrats	75	79	78	82	83	75	81
Strong Republicans	93	81	85	92	86	87	92
Weak Democrats	70	68	72	73	72	71	68
Weak Republicans	76	79	81	86	81	79	74
Independent Democrats	74	73	69	71	71	72	72
Independent Republicans	78	74	84	84	81	76	74
Independents	76	77	65	62	65	53	57

* The table entries are turnout rates expressed in percentages.
Source: SRC/CPS studies of 1952, 1956, 1960, 1964, 1968, 1972, and 1976.

higher GOP turnout rate. In certain cases, the difference in turnout rate is small, but it does exceed 10 percent in many instances. The differential turnout rate of Democrats and Republican partisans and the numerical advantage that the Democrats enjoy help explain the oft-cited political strategy that asserts that the Democrats must get their supporters to the polls, while Republicans must do the same and also attract a heavy share of the Independent vote and some Democratic defectors.

The third significant point to note in Table 3.8 is that the turnout rate of pure Independents has dropped tremendously in the three most recent elections. One cause of the very low 1972 rate was the heavy influx of new voters (both newly enfranchised 18-year-olds and citizens who turned 21 since the previous election) who are disproportionately Independent and who traditionally have the lowest turnout rates. Yet while the Independent turnout was extremely low in 1972, this does not imply that the contribution of Independents to the total vote cast had declined. To the contrary, the lower turnout of Independents was more than compensated for by their greater numbers in 1972 so that the Independent proportion of the presidential vote (including pure and leaning Independents) was the highest it had been. This is illustrated in Table 3.9, which is similar to Table 3.8 except that it is percentaged to show the proportion of the vote cast by different classes of party identifiers. Note that in 1976 the proportion of the vote cast by Independents increased once again.

Between 1964 and 1976, the proportion of the vote cast by strong identifiers declined about 14 percent while the share of the vote due to Independents (both pure and leaners) increased by 14 percent. These

TABLE 3.9
The Proportion of the Vote Cast by Partisans
and Independents, 1952–1976*

	Year						
	1952	1956	1960	1964	1968	1972	1976
Strong Democrats	23	23	21	29	22	16	16
Strong Republicans	17	17	18	13	11	13	12
Weak Democrats	23	21	24	24	24	25	23
Weak Republicans	14	15	15	15	16	15	15
Independent Democrats	10	6	6	8	9	10	12
Independent Republicans	8	9	8	6	10	11	11
Independents	5	9	9	6	9	9	11

* The table entries represent the percentage of the vote for President in a certain year cast by a specific partisan category.
Sources: SRC/CPS studies of 1952, 1956, 1960, 1964, 1968, 1972, and 1976.

are significant changes reflecting millions of votes, with major implications for the conduct of politics. If a greater proportion of the vote is cast by citizens without strong partisan ties, then we can expect electoral outcomes to fluctuate more widely in the future, with landslide elections possibly becoming a common occurrence. Furthermore, as more votes are cast by Independents, it is likely that candidates will appeal to citizens on grounds other than traditional party loyalties and party issues; an electorally profitable strategy would be to seize upon those issues that would mobilize the Independent vote, assuming one did not frighten off one's partisan adherents. If the turnout rate of Independents was comparable to that of partisans, then the influence of the Independent vote on election outcomes would be even more striking.

An examination of the relationship between party identification and loyalty to one's party in presidential elections provides our final piece of evidence about the weakening of party ties. The defection rates of Democrats and Republicans and the voting behavior of Independents are given in Figures 3.9–3.11. Note that the only party identifiers who consistently exhibited great loyalty to their party's nominees were strong Republicans who even in the Democratic landslide of 1964 gave Barry Goldwater more than 90 percent of their vote. Among strong Democrats, the pattern of support for Democratic presidential candidates fluctuated more widely, reaching a peak in 1964 and a low point in 1972 when fewer than three fourths of the strong Democrats supported McGovern. In 1976, strong Democrats and strong Republi-

FIGURE 3.9
Presidential Voting of Democratic Identifiers, 1952–1976

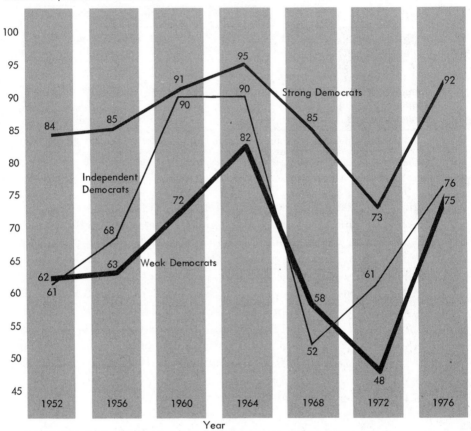

Percentage voting for
Democratic presidential candidate

Year

Source: SRC/CPS studies of 1952, 1956, 1960, 1964, 1968, 1972, and 1976.

cans overwhelmingly supported their party's nominee, the former giving Carter 92 percent of their vote and the latter giving Ford 97 percent.

The voting behavior of weak and independent Democrats and Republicans exhibit greater defection from one's party to the extent that slightly less than *half* of the weak Democrats in 1972 supported the McGovern candidacy and less than three fifths of the weak Republicans voted for Goldwater in 1964. Likewise, the support given to the Democratic nominees in 1968 and 1972 by independent Democrats

FIGURE 3.10
Presidential Voting of Republican Identifiers, 1952–1976

Percentage voting for Republican presidential candidate

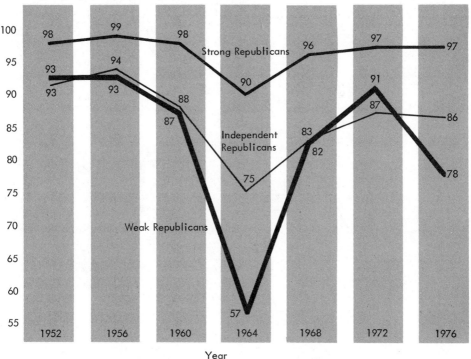

Year

Source: SRC/CPS studies of 1952, 1956, 1960, 1964, 1968, 1972, and 1976.

was low. Finally, the voting behavior of Independents from 1952–76 reveals the greatest variability, as one might expect given the absence of the anchoring effect of partisanship. Independent support for Democratic presidential candidates varied over 60 percent between 1952 and 1976.

Figures 3.9–3.11 indicate that while persons with partisan attachments are generally more likely to support their own party's nominees, there are numerous instances in which defection from one's party occurs. Hence, party identification takes us only part of the way in explaining why people vote as they do. To account for vote choices, particularly those of citizens who have deserted their party and those of Independents without any partisan inclinations, we must examine other influences. Moreover, despite the high levels of party loyalty

FIGURE 3.11
Presidential Voting of Pure Independents, 1952–1976

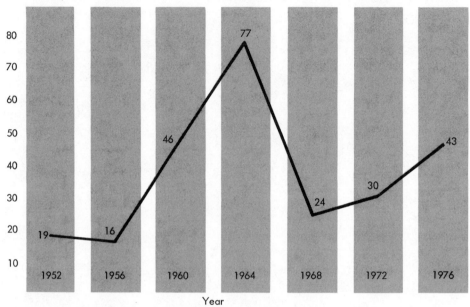

Percentage voting for
Democratic presidential candidate

Year

Source: SRC/CPS studies of 1952, 1956, 1960, 1964, 1968, 1972, and 1976.

observed in 1976, defection has become more common since the mid-1960s. This means that party identification is no longer as useful in accounting for why people vote for President as they do. The question becomes why. If party identification presently has a weaker effect on vote decisions, are there other factors today that might have a stronger effect on vote choice? In Chapters 4 through 7 we will examine the role of issues and candidates in presidential voting since 1952.

4

The Issue Voting Controversy

INTRODUCTION

According to the tenets of classical democratic theory, issues should play the decisive role in electoral choice. Classical democratic theory emphasized the importance of the rational citizen capable of choosing between alternatives on the basis of accurate information and sound reasoning. Democratic theory also stressed the need for a citizenry that was highly motivated to participate in public affairs and that had substantial interest and concern about such matters. The ideal citizen was deemed to be the independent who based his or her decisions on the issues at hand and did not rely upon mere group attachments or partisan affiliations or candidate attractiveness as bases for electoral choices.

In an early empirical study of voting behavior, Bernard Berelson and his associates (1954) discovered that the tenets of democratic theory did not hold in the electorate. Instead of being informed and interested, voters were found to be ignorant and apathetic. For example, on two hotly contested issues (the Taft-Hartley Law and price controls) which received extensive media coverage and on which Truman and Dewey took diametrically opposed positions in 1948, only 16 percent of a sample of citizens in Elmira, New York, knew the correct stances of both candidates on both issues, while over a third of the respondents knew only one position of one candidate correctly or none at all (Berelson et al., 1954: 227–28). These early findings were upsetting to scholars who worried about the viability of a democratic political system if the basic requirements of democratic theory could not be met. One response to the tension between classical democratic theory and the findings of empirical research was given by Bernard Berelson, who essentially redefined what were the necessary conditions for a democratic political system to endure.

Berelson (pp. 305–23) argued that classical theory focused too much on the individual citizen and that greater attention should be paid to the collective properties of the citizenry and the consequences of these properties for the political system at large. Thus, Berelson claimed that the presence of substantial apathy and ignorance in the electorate was actually beneficial since such citizens were unlikely to be highly concerned about politics and policies, thereby giving leaders greater independence and flexibility from popular pressures in making decisions. And, Berelson argued, elite decision making in the absence of mass pressures was likely to lead to wise choices that were conducive to the stability and maintenance of the political system. Thus, for Berelson, the stability of the political system and the ability of elites to govern became the overriding concerns, while the opinions of the citizenry became secondary. Berelson's reformulation of the conditions required for a democratic political system is often referred to as an example of an elitist theory of democracy. Obviously, conservative, status quo values are inherent in Berleson's reformulation, but the point is that his argument represented an attempt to reconcile empirical research and democratic theory by fundamentally altering the meaning of and conditions for democracy.

The work of Berelson and his associates was the first major study to call into question the competence of the average citizen to comprehend politics and make informed decisions at election time. Some years later, *The American Voter* presented further evidence about the shortcomings of the electorate. For example, Angus Campbell and his colleagues established three necessary conditions (discussed next) in order for issues to influence vote choice and found that these conditions were hardly met by the electorate. The authors of *The American Voter* also examined the manner in which citizens conceptualized or thought about politics and found that few citizens could be classified as ideologues with coherent sets of beliefs who employed broad principles in evaluating the elements of politics.

The American Voter focused on the electorate of the 1950s, and since that time research based upon more recent elections has challenged its findings. Thus, there is currently a controversy about the competence of the electorate to make informed voting decisions based upon issue-related considerations. The points of contention in this debate are both substantive and methodological and are important to understand to evaluate accurately the issue awareness of the contemporary electorate. Hence, in this chapter, we will discuss in detail the issue-voting controversy beginning with the earlier findings presented in *The American Voter* and other works from the Michigan Survey Research Center. Then we will examine some of the more recent research and conclude the chapter by offering a summary evaluation of the competence of the American electorate.

THE TRADITIONAL IMAGE OF THE VOTER

Issues

In *The American Voter* Campbell and his associates (pp. 169–71) presented a number of analyses related to the topic of issue voting. In the analysis most directly concerned with issue voting, the authors posited three conditions necessary for issue-oriented electoral choices and then determined how well the electorate satisfied these conditions. The authors cogently argued that for an issue to influence one's vote decision, the citizen must be aware of the issue in some form. Furthermore, the citizen must care at least minimally about the issue. And, finally, if the issue is to influence one's partisan choice, the citizen must perceive that one party represents his or her position on the issue better than the other party; otherwise the issue provides no reason to opt for one party over the other.

Thus, a national sample of citizens was presented with a series of 16 issues deemed important by the authors to ascertain the extent of citizen awareness on these issues. On the average, two thirds of the sample had an opinion on each issue and knew what the government was doing in the area. About a third of the respondents failed to exhibit any issue awareness on any of the 16 issues. The authors then examined the issue intensity of the two thirds of the sample that was informed about at least one issue and found that intensity varied widely across the issues; it was quite possible for people to be familiar with issues without being concerned about them (pp. 172–79).

Finally, the authors found that depending upon the specific issue in question only about 40 to 60 percent of the two thirds of the respondents with some issue awareness were able to perceive party differences on the issue and thereby see one party as closer to their own position than another. A summary of the results of the analysis (presented in Table 4.1) indicates that only between 18 and 36 percent of the electorate were able to meet the three conditions of issue voting on any specific issue. And these figures do not signify that issues actually influenced vote choice; they simply set an upper boundary on

TABLE 4.1
Perception of Partisan Differences on Issues
(in percentages)

Issue	Proportion of Respondents Who Perceive Party Differences on Issue, Having Fulfilled Prior Conditions
Foreign Policy	
Act tough toward Russia and China	36
U.S. international involvement ("stay home")	32
Friendliness toward other nations	32
Economic aid to foreign countries	23
Send soldiers abroad	22
Give aid to neutral countries	18
Domestic Policy	
Influence of big business in government	35
Influence of unions in government	31
Government guarantee of jobs	31
Segregation of schools	31
Cutting taxes	30
Racial equality in jobs and housing	28
Aid to education	27
Insure medical care	24
Firing of suspected communists	23
Leave electricity and housing to private industry	22

Source: Angus Campbell et al., *The American Voter* (New York: John Wiley & Sons, Inc., 1960), table 8–3, p. 182. Copyright © 1960 by John Wiley & Sons, Inc. Reprinted by permission of John Wiley & Sons, Inc.

the number of citizens whose electoral choices could have been affected by the issues in question.

It should be noted that the authors of *The American Voter* explicitly recognized that the political nature of the times could affect the degree to which citizens perceived party differences. That is, if the policy differences between the parties or the candidates, or both, were small in 1956, then there is little reason to expect that citizens should be able to perceive party differences. The converse of this is that perception of party differences by the citizenry should be greater when the parties and candidates take clear-cut, opposing positions on issues, an assertion that is reflected in the findings of some of the recent research on voting behavior, to be discussed shortly.

Ideology

A second analysis in *The American Voter* (pp. 216–65) relevant to issue voting concerns the way in which citizens conceptualize politics. Do citizens employ broad, overarching concepts such as liberal and conservative in thinking about politics or do they rely upon more specific and immediate frames of reference in interpreting political affairs? This is an important question since political elites, such as party activists and media commentators, often employ ideological terminology in discussing and analyzing politics. But if citizens are not conversant or comfortable with such terms as liberal and conservative, then there may be substantial slippage in the flow of communication from elites to citizens, which may affect the interpretation given to political events.

Citizen responses to a series of open-ended questions about their likes and dislikes of the candidates and the parties were analyzed, resulting in a four-category classification of conceptualization of politics ranging from the use of ideology at the most sophisticated end to no issue content at the least sophisticated. By an ideology was meant an elaborate set of interrelated attitudes organized according to some underlying continuum. One would expect issue voting to be more prevalent among citizens classified as ideological since such citizens do employ a more general frame of reference in evaluating politics under which could be subsumed opinions on specific issues. This notion is given some credence by the fact that the only empirically common ideological perspective used by citizens was the liberal-conservative continuum, which is undoubtedly the one general dimension used most often in discussing American politics. While the specific meaning of a liberal or conservative position may vary at different times, depending upon the immediate political circumstances, it nevertheless is the case that reliance upon such an abstraction in evaluating politics will facilitate the comprehension of issues and their relationship to partisan and candidate choices. The absence of an ideological perspective does not mean that issues will be irrelevant to vote choice, but it does mean that additional information about the issue will be required to place it in a meaningful political context so that it might influence vote decisions.

This distribution of the 1956 electorate into the four levels of conceptualization is shown in Table 4.2. Note that more citizens are

TABLE 4.2
The Levels of Conceptualization in 1956
for the Total Sample and Voters
(in percentages)

	Proportion of Total Sample	Proportion of Voters
A. Ideology		
I. Ideology	2½	3½
II. Near-ideology	9	12
B. Group benefits		
I. Perception of conflict	14	16
Single-group interest	17	18
II. Shallow group benefit responses	11	11
C. Nature of times	24	23
D. No issue content		
I. Party orientation	4	3½
II. Candidate orientation	9	7
III. No content	5	3
IV. Unclassified	4½	4
	100	100

Source: Angus Campbell et al., *The American Voter* (New York: John Wiley & Sons, Inc., 1960), table 10–1, p. 249. Copyright © 1960, John Wiley & Sons, Inc. Reprinted by permission of John Wiley & Sons, Inc.

placed in the no-issue content category than in the ideology classification. It should be noted that in order to be considered an ideologue, a citizen need not have given highly sophisticated responses to questions about his or her likes and dislikes of the parties and candidates. For example, the following replies given by a woman from a Chicago suburb sufficed to have her assigned to the category of ideology (*The American Voter:* pp. 228–29).

(Like about Democrats?) No. (Is there anything at all you like about the Democratic Party?) No, nothing at all.

(Dislike about Democrats?) From being raised in a notoriously Republican section—a small town downstate—there were things I didn't like. There was family influence that way. (What in particular was there you didn't like about the Democratic Party?) Well, the Democratic Party tends to favor socialized medicine—and I'm being influenced in that because I came from a doctor's family.

(Like about Republicans?) Well, I think they're more middle-of-the-road—more conservative. (How do you mean, "conservative"?) They are not so subject to radical change. (Is there anything else in particular that you like about the Republican Party?) Oh, I like their foreign policy—and the segregation business, that's a middle-of-the-road policy. You can't push it too fast. You can instigate things, but you have to let them take their course slowly. . . .

The authors of *The American Voter* asserted that the replies just quoted indicated that the "respondent operates with a fairly clear sense of the liberal-conservative distinction and uses it to locate both the major parties and the more specific policy positions espoused" (p. 229). Thus, relatively few citizens relied upon the liberal-conservative continuum or any other overarching dimension in framing their responses about likes and dislikes of the parties and candidates.

The low frequency of ideological conceptualization should not be construed as implying that citizens who are not assigned to the ideology category are somehow deficient or irrational; many of the citizens who are classified in other categories would be recognized as acting in their own rational self-interest, that is, voting for the candidate or party that espouses policies of immediate benefit to the individual. For example, the quotation on page 37 from the Ohio farm woman indicates a preference for the Democratic Party since that party is perceived as being good for farmers while the Republicans are seen as favoring "the richer folks." Even citizens who simply cite the nature of the times in response to questions about party and candidate likes and dislikes might be viewed as behaving according to rational self-interest. If times are good, vote for the incumbents; if times are bad, reject the incumbents. Citizens in the nature of the times category may not have a lot of specific information about politics organized in a coherent fashion, but they are aware in a vague, more general sense of their own and the country's condition. The following comments from a woman in New York City represent a nature of the times response (p. 243):

(Like about Democrats?) What was in all the papers last week. Stevenson will see to it that they stop testing the bomb and I'm in favor of that. I don't want them to explode any more of those bombs. (Is there anything that you like about the Democratic Party?) I don't know anything about the party, really. I just want them to stop testing the bomb.

(Dislike about Democrats?) I don't know much about the parties. (Is there anything you don't like about the Democratic Party?) No—I don't know much about the whole thing.

(Like about Republicans?) My husband's job is better. (Laughed.) (How do you mean?) Well, his investments in stocks are up. They go up when the Republicans are in. My husband is a furrier and when people get money they buy furs.

(Dislike about Republicans?) No. (Is there anything at all you don't like about the Republican Party?) No—I don't know that much about the parties.

(Like about Stevenson?) As I mentioned before, he's saying stop testing the bomb because it can do so much damage. My husband says that's such a minor point, but I don't think so.

(Dislike about Stevenson?) Nothing, nothing at all.

(Like about Eisenhower?) No, nothing in particular. (Is there any-anything at all?) No.

(Dislike about Eisenhower?) That he might die and Nixon would be President and I don't care for Nixon. He might not have his four-year term. There's a lot said about the other sickness that he had—not the heart attack.

It is in the no issue content category that we literally find no issues cited in support of one's party and candidate preferences. One might argue that issue concerns are present even in this category, but that the question asked of citizens simply did not ask directly about issues. For some respondents, their support of a party may rest in generalized, long-standing images that they have of the party, such as one party being the party of the common man or the party of prosperity or the party of peace. Thus, when such citizens claim to vote on the basis of party, there may actually be some underlying issue rationale for electoral choice. However, an examination of the responses that get one assigned to the no issue content category indicates quite convincingly that citizens in the category have little awareness of the issue stances of the parties and candidates at the specific election. Most of the responses in this category are rather unelaborated references to parties and candidates. An example of a party-oriented reply is given by a North Carolina man (p. 246):

(Like about Democrats?) No, Ma'am, not that I know of.

(Dislike about Democrats?) No, Ma'am, but I've always been a Democrat just like my daddy.

(Like about Republicans?) No.

(Dislike about Republicans?) No.

(Like about Stevenson?) No'm.

(Dislike about Stevenson?) No, Ma'am.

(Like about Eisenhower?) Not as I know of.

(Dislike about Eisenhower?) No, Ma'am.

A Texas woman provides an illustration of a candidate-oriented response (pp. 247–48):

(Like about Democrats?) No, I don't know anything about political parties. I'm not interested in them at all.

(Dislike about Democrats?) No, nothing.

(Like about Republicans?) No, I don't know about the *party*. I like Ike.

(Dislike about Republicans?) No, nothing I can put my finger on.

(Like about Stevenson?) Right now I can't think of anything I like well enough to vote for him.

(Dislike about Stevenson?) No, I just have my choice and it is not Stevenson. It is Ike.

(Like about Eisenhower?) I just like him, the way things have gone. (How do you mean?) That's really all I know.

(Dislike about Eisenhower?) No.

In summary, we can conclude that issue voting could occur at all levels of conceptualization except the no issue content category, which includes 22.5 percent of the sample and 17.5 percent of the voters. This does not mean that issue voting does occur in the first three levels of conceptualization; other conditions would have to be satisfied, including citizen concern about the issue and the perception that the election does offer a choice.

The questions used to measure the levels of conceptualization required citizens to mention spontaneously an ideological perspective if they were to be classified as ideologues. Hence, Converse (1974) argued that if citizens were asked directly about the terms liberal and conservative, there would be a higher level of recognition of the terms than one might expect, given the small number of citizens found to conceptualize politics ideologically. Therefore, a sample of citizens was asked in 1960 whether they thought one of the two political parties was more conservative than the other and what they meant by the terms.

Converse found (pp. 318–19) that at best about half of the sample had a reasonable recognition of the terms liberal and conservative. He further subdivided the recognition exhibited into broad versus narrow comprehension of the terms. Many of the narrow understandings focused on questions of spending and saving which, according to Converse, do not begin to tap the richness of the liberal-conservative dimension. Overall, only about 17 percent of the respondents had a broad understanding of liberal-conservative differences, while an additional 33 percent had a more narrow comprehension that was accurately linked to the positions of the political parties.

Converse (pp. 321–23) constructed a fivefold classification based upon recognition and understanding of the terms liberal and conservative and related it to the levels of conceptualization discussed previously. As expected, ideologues exhibited the greatest awareness of the terms, while no issue content citizens had the lowest levels of comprehension. (See Table 4.3.) In general, it was found that citizens at the higher levels of conceptualization and recognition tended to be more educated and more politically active.

Converse carried his analysis a step further by investigating the coherence of the issue positions of a sample of citizens and a sample

TABLE 4.3
The Relationship between Levels of Conceptualization and Recognition and Understanding of the Terms Liberal and Conservative
(in percentages)

Recognition and Understanding Stratum*	Levels of Conceptualization				
	Ideologue	Near Ideologue	Group Interest	Nature of the Times	No Issue Content
I.	51	29	13	16	10
II.	43	46	42	40	22
III.	2	10	14	7	7
IV.	2	5	6	7	12
V.	2	10	25	30	49
Total	100	100	100	100	100
Number of cases	45	122	580	288	290

* The definitions of the strata are: I. recognition and proper matching of label, meaning and party and a broad understanding of the terms "conservative" and "liberal"; II. recognition and proper matching but a narrow definition of terms (like "spend-save"); III. recognition but some error in matching; IV. recognition and an attempt at matching but inability to give any meaning for terms; V. no apparent recognition of terms (does not know if parties differ in liberal-conservative terms and does not know if anybody else sees them as differing).

Source: Adapted with permission of Macmillan Co., Inc., from "The Nature of Belief Systems in Mass Politics," by Philip E. Converse in *Ideology and Discontent,* by David E. Apter. Copyright © 1964 by The Free Press of Glencoe, a Division of the Macmillan Company.

of elites—congressional candidates. This analysis was conducted to check on the possibility that citizens might have organized beliefs on specific issues that reflect an underlying liberal-conservative continuum, even though citizens are unable to articulate ideological utterances in response to open-ended questions in an interview situation. Thus, Converse turns his attention to mass belief systems, which are defined as configurations "of ideas and attitudes in which the elements are bound together by some form of constraint . . ." (p. 302). Or in simpler terms, a belief system is a set of interrelated attitudes that exhibit constraint.

Converse discusses constraint in the static and the dynamic case. In the static situation, constraint refers to how well we can predict a person's position on an issue, given knowledge of his or her stance on another issue. For example, if we know that a person favors using all available force to solve the problem of urban riots, we might also expect the person to be supportive of capital punishment. Constraint in the dynamic case refers to the extent to which a change in one element of a belief system leads to changes in other elements (p. 302).

Converse examines the static constraint exhibited by citizens and congressional candidates on a series of specific issues; the results are presented in Table 4.4. The entries in the table are correlation coefficients (tau-gammas), which give an indication of how related issue positions are on pairs of issues. The closer the value of the coefficient is to 1.0, the more closely related are the two issue positions. Another way of interpreting the coefficients is to say that the higher their value, the more able we are to predict to an individual's position on the issue, given information about his stance on the other issue.

The figures of Table 4.4 indicate that constraint is higher among the congressional candidates than the average citizens. The average correlation between pairs of domestic issues is .53 for congressional candidates and only .23 for citizens, while the comparable correlations on foreign affairs issues are .25 and .11. Finally, the average relationship between issue position and party preference is a moderate .38 for candidates and a rather weak .11 for citizens.

The implications of these findings are threefold. The first is that yet another analysis has failed to uncover any substantial coherence in the issue beliefs held by citizens. With respect to the issues investigated, there was no underlying organization to the responses, such as the liberal-conservative dimension. Second, the fact that citizens' issue beliefs were only weakly related to their partisan affiliation indicates

TABLE 4.4

The Constraint on Issue Opinions for a Sample of 1958 Congressional Candidates and for a Sample of Citizens*

	Employment	Education	Housing	FEPC	Economic	Military	Isolationism	Party Preference
Congressional Candidates								
Employment	—	.62	.59	.35	.26	.06	.17	.68
Aid to education		—	.61	.53	.50	.06	.35	.55
Federal housing			—	.47	.41	−.03	.30	.68
FEPC				—	.47	.11	.23	.34
Economic aid					—	.19	.59	.25
Military aid						—	.32	−.18
Isolationism							—	.05
Party preference								—
Cross-Section Sample								
Employment	—	.45	.08	.34	−.04	.10	−.22	.20
Aid to education		—	.12	.29	.06	.14	−.17	.16
Federal housing			—	.08	−.06	.02	.07	.18
FEPC				—	.24	.13	.01	−.04
Economic aid					—	.16	.33	−.07
Soldiers abroad						—	.21	.12
Isolationism							—	−.03
Party preference								—

* The table entries are tau-gamma coefficients. The greater the value of the coefficient, the greater the constraint between pairs of issues.

Source: Adapted with permission of Macmillan Co., Inc. from "The Nature of Belief Systems in Mass Politics," by Philip E. Converse in *Ideology and Discontent*, by David E. Apter. Copyright © 1964 by The Free Press of Glencoe, a Division of The Macmillan Company.

that issue positions cannot be accounted for by adherence to well-defined party programs and that citizen perceptions of distinct party differences were minimal. Finally, the findings suggest the importance of distinguishing between political discourse at the elite versus the mass level; interpretations of politics based upon such terminology as liberal and conservative may be more appropriate for political elites than for average citizens.

Nonattitudes

The final piece of research from the Michigan Survey Research Center contributing to the traditional view of the electorate is an analysis by Converse (1970) of the phenomenon of nonattitudes. Converse argues that the survey approach to the study of citizen opinions introduces the danger that one will measure attitudes that do not really exist. That is, the very act of asking people about issues may create responses that do not represent any genuinely held attitudes about the topic at hand but simply reflect a desire on the part of the respondents in an interview situation to appear cooperative and informed about current issues. No matter how socially acceptable one makes it for the citizen to respond "I don't know" to a question, or no matter how carefully one tries to screen out citizens who have no opinion on an issue, respondents still give replies to queries about which they know and care very little. It is these replies that are labeled "nonattitudes."

To study nonattitudes, Converse examined the stability of responses to a series of issue questions asked of the same individuals over time. The results indicated that for many issues there was little stability in responses; persons who at one time point claimed to favor a certain program expressed opposition to it at a later time and support for it at an even later point. This instability of responses is, for Converse, evidence that nonattitudes have been measured.

This simple finding of response instability is potentially the most damaging to any claim that issue-related voting is widespread, for it suggests that on many issues the citizen's position does not reflect any firmly held preferences but is instead an artifact of the interview situation. It also suggests the ease with which citizens might change their issue opinions, perhaps to bring them in line with the positions of their preferred party or candidate, or both. Of course, all that is required for issue voting is one issue about which the citizen cares sufficiently so that the issue influences vote choice; if such an issue exists, then instability or nonattitudes on other issues is not as worrisome.

Summary of the Traditional Image

In summary, the traditional description of the voter's competence states that on many issues citizens have no genuine, consistently held opinions, and that on other issues citizen concern is minimal and their perceptions of party differences weak to nonexistent. Furthermore, it was found that citizens do not employ broad frameworks in organizing the elements of politics, that their beliefs are not integrated into a more coherent whole, and that they have a limited awareness of the terms liberal and conservative, terms which figure prominently in contemporary debates about politics. Thus, the image of the average citizen presented in the traditional literature is a rather negative one, which suggests that issue concerns are not likely to play a prominent role in electoral choice and that classical democratic theory may impose too severe demands on the contemporary electorate. It should be pointed out that the conclusions of the traditional research cited were carefully qualified; there was no suggestion that the results presented held for all time and under all conditions. In fact, the conclusions were often phrased in a conditional sense, and it is a consideration of these conditions that will help us partially reconcile the traditional and the revisionist literature on the voter's competence.

THE REVISIONIST IMAGE OF THE VOTER

Introduction

The revisionist literature criticizes the traditional description of the citizen's issue and ideological awareness on methodological and substantive grounds. In this section, we will discuss a sample of this literature that illustrates the kinds of concerns guiding current research; no attempt will be made to provide an exhaustive account of the more recent research. Much of the revisionist literature itself has come under attack, mainly on methodological grounds; we will highlight some of the more important criticisms being made.

The most prominent early revisionist work was *The Responsible Electorate* by V. O. Key, Jr., who argued that "voters are not fools"

(p. 7). Key examined voters who voted for the same (standpatters) and different (switchers) parties in successive presidential elections and found that switchers tended to move to the party closest to the voter's own position on some important issue. This, for Key, was evidence confirming the voter's rationality. Particularly interesting about his work is that it spans the 1936–60 era and suggests that issues were more important than *The American Voter* study of the 1952 and 1956 elections found. Unfortunately, Key's analysis, while quite insightful, suffered from data problems over which he had no control. The major problems were reliance on limited data sets that restricted the types of analyses that could be performed and reliance on recall data for past voting behavior. Furthermore, Key had no way of determining whether voters were engaging in rationalization, that is, changing their issue positions to bring them in line with those of the candidate for whom they had decided to vote. Hence, our examination of the revisionist literature will concentrate more on recent research based upon more extensive data resources.

Issues

Some Methodological Innovations. *The American Voter* has been criticized for the way in which the 16 issues investigated were chosen. The issues were selected by the authors, who deemed them important on a priori grounds. David RePass (1971), among others, has argued that the use of a list of predetermined issues may not include those issues that are actually of greatest importance to the voter, no matter how carefully one tries to identify all the major issues. A better strategy, RePass argued, is to allow the respondents themselves to define the issues that are of importance to them. These salient issues are the ones that are most likely to influence vote choice.

Thus, a prominent strategy in recent research is to identify groups of citizens who express concern about specific issues and to focus on their voting behavior. This type of analysis is facilitated by the inclusion (since 1960) of questions on the SRC/CPS election studies that ask respondents to name the most important problems that they think government should address. This approach generally results in more positive assessments of citizen competence, in part because it focuses on those subsets of citizens that are more likely to be issue motivated, while *The American Voter* analyzes the entire electorate as a whole. Analysis of such subsets helps delineate the conditions under which issue voting is likely to occur, but the results obtained may pertain to only a very small segment of the entire electorate. Some examples should suffice to give the reader the gist of this type of research.

RePass examined the responses to the "most important problems" questions asked by SRC/CPS in the 1960 and 1964 presidential elections. He found that more than 25 issues were cited with some frequency in each year, with no single issue dominating in mentions. Moreover, the kinds of issues mentioned at each election differed dramatically: in 1960 foreign affairs were cited most often, while in 1964 domestic concerns, particularly civil rights related matters, were of paramount concern (pp. 391–92). These findings suggested to Re-Pass the difficulty of constructing a comprehensive list of issues, as was done in *The American Voter,* and led him to conclude that one reason for the low level of issue awareness described in *The American Voter* was the type of questions used.

RePass discovered that on 19 of 25 issues mentioned in 1964 more than 60 percent of the people were able to perceive party differences, leading him to conclude that "the public does perceive party differences on those issues that are salient to them" (p. 394). This finding appears to contradict *The American Voter* assertion about minimal perceptions of party differences; in fact, the finding is not directly comparable since RePass examined only those citizens for whom the issue was salient. For example, RePass stated that over 80 percent of the citizens for whom medical care for the aged was a major concern were able to perceive party differences on the issue. However, less than 5 percent of the sample considered medical care to be an important problem (p. 396).

Two additional examples of research that identified subsets of citizens more likely to be influenced by issues were conducted by Natchez and Bupp (1970) on the 1964 election and by Kirkpatrick and Jones (1974) on the 1964 and 1968 elections. Natchez and Bupp believed that the traditional way of studying issues underestimated the impact of the issues on the vote; they therefore proposed placing citizens into issue publics on the basis of issues important to them and then examining the relationship between issue position and vote. They found that issues were important in vote choice among issue publics; for example, "seven out of ten pro-Goldwater voters who were not concerned that the government actively promote civil rights voted Republican. Within the issue public, the relationship is reversed; seven out of ten pro-Goldwater voters voted Democratic" (p.

449). Similarly, Kirkpatrick and Jones found that change and constancy in partisan vote over two presidential elections were strongly related to issue position within issue publics.

A very straightforward way of demonstrating the impact that issues can have on vote is to isolate those individuals whose partisanship and issue preferences conflict. That is, when a person's party identification and his or her perception of which party will better handle an issue are not congruent, one can observe whether the citizen voted according to party or to issue. Where partisanship and issue positions are in harmony, it is difficult to disentangle the impact of each on vote. Hence, in Table 4.5 we have related party identification to vote in 1964, 1968, 1972, and 1976 for three groups of citizens—those who named the GOP as the preferred party on their most important problem, those who named the Democrats, and those who preferred neither party on the issue.

For our purposes, the most interesting cells in the table are those in which partisanship and issue position conflict for they enable us to see directly how citizens reacted to the conflict. Note that among Democratic identifiers in 1976 who preferred the GOP on their most important issue, fully 86 percent defected from Carter. Among Republicans who thought the Democratic Party better on their key issue, only 48 percent remained loyal to Ford. Thus, there is substantial vote defection where issue stance and partisanship are incongruent on an important issue, thereby providing some evidence of the impact of issues on vote. However, very few respondents exhibit these incongruent preferences, indicating that issue-based defection (at least on the issue cited as most important by the respondent) is not all that common. The relative infrequency of incongruence is to be expected, given the tendency to bring issue stance into line with partisanship and given the likelihood that in some instances partisanship itself has an issue basis. Of course, the tendency to rationalize issue positions so that they are harmonious with party identification is probably much less for issues that are of great importance to the citizen.

Where issue stance and party identification coincided in Table 4.5, loyalty to the candidate of one's party was extremely high; for example, 99 percent of the consistent Republicans voted for Ford in 1976, while 96 percent of the congruent Democrats supported Carter. Citizens who expressed no party preference on the issue most important to them in 1976 tended to support their own party's nominee, with the Independents going heavily for Ford. The 1964, 1968, and 1972 results

TABLE 4.5
The Relationship between Party Identification and Vote for Three Categories of Issue Partisanship in 1964, 1968, 1972, and 1976
(in percentages)

Year and Vote	Republicans*			Neither*			Democrats*		
	Dem.†	Ind.†	Rep.†	Dem.†	Ind.†	Rep.†	Dem.†	Ind.†	Rep.†
1976									
Ford	86	94	99	33	70	88	4	14	48
Carter	14	6	1	67	30	12	96	86	52
Total	100	100	100	100	100	100	100	100	100
Number of cases	29	65	140	191	272	212	367	147	48
1972									
Nixon	81	94	99	51	71	92	21	21	67
McGovern	19	6	1	49	29	8	79	79	33
Total	100	100	100	100	100	100	100	100	100
Number of cases	37	64	105	111	92	72	118	47	15
1968									
Nixon	49	77	94	18	52	84	4	20	50
Humphrey	34	6	4	66	32	9	92	80	50
Wallace	17	17	2	16	16	7	4	0	0
Total	100	100	100	100	100	100	100	100	100
Number of cases	67	108	163	156	106	70	180	30	8
1964									
Goldwater	61	89	94	14	27	66	3	7	20
Johnson	39	11	6	86	73	34	97	93	80
Total	100	100	100	100	100	100	100	100	100
Number of cases	33	47	145	105	59	67	295	68	45

* Party preferred on most important issue.
† Party identification: Democratic and Republican identifiers include strong and weak partisans, while Independents include pure Independents and leaners.
Source: SRC/CPS studies of 1964, 1968, 1972, and 1976.

closely resemble the 1976 findings. For example, Democrats who preferred the GOP on their most important problem cast 61 percent of
their vote for Goldwater despite the Johnson landslide of 1964. Similarly, Republican party identifiers with a Democratic issue partisanship cast 80 percent of their votes for Johnson. Hence, issue concerns
can and do deflect citizens from their party identification in voting.

In summary, methodological innovations (including one to be discussed in the next section) lead to findings of greater issue awareness,
clearer perceptions of party differences, and greater impact of issues
on vote. The procedure of allowing the respondents themselves to
determine the salient issues, and of analyzing issue publics, guarantees
that the issues investigated will be ones about which the citizen is
more concerned and often has more information. Yet developments
in the measurement of issues are not the only factors cited in the
literature to account for the increased importance of issues and the
greater frequency of issue voting.

The Nature of the Times.   Much of revisionist literature claims
that the findings of *The American Voter* are time-bound: that they
refer to the relatively tranquil era of the 1950s in which conflict between the parties and candidates was at a minimum and in which
many of the divisive issues of the 1960s and 1970s had not yet emerged.
In more turbulent times, when the parties take more distinctive positions, it is argued, both perceptions of partisan differences on issues
and issue voting itself will be higher. For example, in addition to the
methodological innovations he employed, RePass (1971: 392–93)
claimed that an additional source of the higher levels of perceived
party differences and issue awareness that he found was the presidential campaign of 1964, particularly the ideological candidacy of Barry
Goldwater that acted to sharpen party differences. Thus, the specific
candidates and the kinds of campaigns they wage can have a direct
effect on the extent of issue awareness and perceptions of party differences. These contextual considerations are cited in a number of places
in the revisionist literature.

Gerald Pomper (1972) analyzed six issues for which comparable
information was available in the four presidential elections between
1956 and 1968. He found that the relationship between party identification and issue position was stronger in more recent presidential
elections, as evidenced in Table 4.6. Note that the maximum relationship between partisanship and policy preference generally occurred
in 1964. Note also that the relationships were strongest for social wel-

TABLE 4.6
The Correlation (Gamma) between Party Identification
and Policy Position on Six Issues, 1956–1968

	Year			
Issue	1956	1960	1964	1968
Aid to education	.15	.20	.34	.36
Medical care	.24	.18	.45	.41
Job guarantee................	.19	.16	.31	.25
Fair employment	.04	—.02	.22	.24
School integration	.04	—.01	.08	.43
Foreign aid	.01	—.03	.08	.04

Source: Extracted from Gerald Pomper, "From Confusion to Clarity: Issues and American Voters, 1956–1968," *American Political Science Review* 66 (June 1972), table 1, p. 417. The greater the correlation, the more distinctive are the policy positions taken by Democrats versus Republicans.

fare and civil rights policies and weakest for foreign aid, which was not as strong a point of conflict between the parties nor as likely to arouse popular passions. Pomper also measured the extent of perceptions of party differences on issues for those citizens who had an opinion on the issues; these results are presented in Figure 4.1. Note that the highest level of perceived party differences also occurred in 1964, a figure that easily exceeded the levels cited in *The American Voter*. Since Pomper utilized questions identical to those employed in *The American Voter*, methodological differences could not account for the differences between his and the SRC's work. Instead, Pomper cites the presidential candidacy of Barry Goldwater as responsible for increasing the levels of issue awareness and perception of party differences. Thus, Pomper supports RePass with respect to the potential impact of the political context on observed levels of issue voting.

Pomper's findings have been criticized on methodological grounds by Margolis (1977), who argues that much of the evidence supporting increased issue awareness is based on small subsets of the total sample. Margolis reanalyzes the data calculating percentages based on the entire sample and finds much less impressive increases in issue awareness over time. Moreover, he extends Pomper's work to the 1972 election and finds that the 1964–68 patterns do not hold in 1972; in fact, the 1972 figures more closely resembled those from the 1950s than the 1968 results. One implication of Margolis's work is to be sensitive to what proportion of the American electorate a finding applies: high levels of issue awareness and issue voting among a small segment of the

FIGURE 4.1
The Proportion of Citizens with Opinions on Six Issues Who Perceive Party Differences on These Issues, 1956–1968

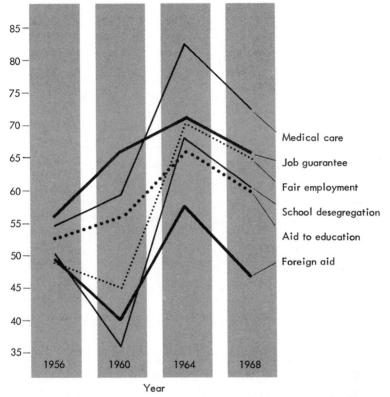

Percentage of citizens perceiving party differences

Medical care
Job guarantee
Fair employment
School desegregation
Aid to education
Foreign aid

Year

Source: Extracted from Gerald Pomper, "From Confusion to Clarity: Issues and American Voters, 1956–1968," *American Political Science Review* 66 (June 1972), table 2, p. 418.

electorate may not be generalizable to the entire population. Moreover, his work indirectly sensitizes us to the possibility that the supposedly atypical quiescent 1950s may have been no more atypical than the turbulent 1960s.

The importance of the specific political context in affecting issue awareness is also illustrated in the work of Page and Brody (1972), who examined the impact of the Vietnam War on vote choice in 1968. Despite the fact that Vietnam was mentioned by more than 50 percent of Americans as the most important problem facing the United States in 1968, Page and Brody found "that Vietnam policy preferences did not have a great effect on voting for the major party candidates in 1968" (p. 982). Support for Nixon varied little between citizens who favored escalating the war, maintaining the same policy, and pulling out of Vietnam entirely. The minimal effect of Vietnam on vote choice might seem surprising, given how often it was mentioned as a major problem. The authors explain this apparent paradox by asserting that the public saw very little difference between Humphrey and Nixon on the war. If the candidates offered little choice on the issue, then the issue could not have a great impact on vote decisions.

The interesting question becomes why did people fail to perceive any substantial differences between Humphrey and Nixon on Vietnam. Was it because of some deficiency or lack of information on the part of the electorate, or might there be another explanation? Page and Brody suggest an alternative explanation—namely, that Nixon and Humphrey did not take distinct stands on Vietnam and that citizens were simply responding to what the candidates offered. The authors based their conclusion on a systematic analysis of the speeches and statements of the candidates, which yielded few differences between Humphrey and Nixon (pp. 987–90). Thus, a political campaign variable—the respective positions of the candidates—must be taken into account in evaluating citizen awareness. Where the candidates or parties emit ambiguous signals by taking indistinct positions on issues, it is unreasonable to blame the electorate for its inability to recognize party or candidate differences.

The methodological implication of the Page and Brody work is that it is not sufficient simply to relate the voter's own position on an issue to his vote choice. We must also determine where the voter perceives the candidate to stand on the issue. For example, if one citizen claimed to be a hawk on Vietnam while another was a dove, yet both voted for Nixon, we might be tempted to conclude that issue position did not influence vote choice. This could be a faulty inference if the hawkish citizen thought Nixon was a hawk and thus voted for him, while the dovish voter saw Nixon as a dove and voted for him on that basis. In this hypothetical situation, the Vietnam issue directly influenced both citizens' votes for Nixon despite their own differing policy positions. Thus, a methodological innovation in the study of issue voting has been the development of proximity variables, which measure the distance between the citizen's own issue position and his perception of the candidate's or party's stance.[1]

---

[1] The power of proximity measures is shown in the following example. The corre-

However, even if citizens vote for the candidate closest to their own issue position on an issue or issues, this may not be definitive evidence that issues actually affected vote choice. Brody and Page (1972) discuss three processes that can result in voters selecting candidates nearest them on issues; but only the first process, in which the citizen evaluates the candidates' positions and votes accordingly, could be called issue voting. The second process, labeled "projection," involves the voter seeing "a candidate as close to himself on an issue because he otherwise felt positive about the candidate" (p. 457). That is, a person who likes a candidate for whatever reason (personality, party identification) may distort the candidate's policy position on an issue so that it corresponds with the voter's own. Persuasion is the third process that can lead to proximity between citizen and candidate; here a preferred candidate moves the voter's own issue position toward that of the candidate's. That these processes occur is documented by Page and Brody, who write with respect to Humphrey and Nixon's Vietnam positions in 1968 (1972: 987):

> Those who saw a big difference between Humphrey and Nixon—a difference in either direction—were generally perceiving each candidate as standing wherever they wanted him to stand. They projected their own opinions onto their favored candidate. Among Republicans, who mostly favored Nixon, extreme hawks thought that Nixon was an extreme hawk; extreme doves thought that he was an extreme dove; and those in the middle thought that Nixon stood in the middle. . . . Similarly, among Democrats, extreme hawks tended to think Humphey was an extreme hawk; extreme doves thought Humphrey was an extreme dove; and those in the middle thought he stood in the middle. . . .
>
> Many of those who saw a big difference between Nixon and Humphrey, in other words, were responding to their own wishes. Their perceptions were the result of intended vote, not the cause. These people were not engaged in policy voting.

The assessment of the impact of issues on vote becomes even more complex if we introduce the notion of *rationality,* a term we have heretofore shunned because of its many meanings. RePass (1974) presents one definition of a rational vote, which asserts that voter concern

---

lations between the respondents' own positions on Vietnam and the vote (as measured by Nixon vote versus non-Nixon vote, Humphrey vote versus non-Humphrey vote, and Wallace vote versus non-Wallace vote) were only —.03, .05, and —.03 respectively. When proximity items that measure the distance between the citizen's position and his perception of the candidates' positions are used, the correlations jump to .40, .43, and .36 respectively. See Beardsley (1973).

about an issue is not sufficient to guarantee a rational vote; rationality also requires that citizens be able to "correctly name the party which supports their position on that issue" (p. 3). While this is only one possible meaning of rationality, it is an interesting one since it raises the possibility that an issue vote may not be a rational vote if it is based upon faulty information. For example, the citizen who in 1972 voted for Nixon over McGovern because he believed that Nixon was more likely to grant amnesty to draft evaders could be classified as an issue voter but not as a rational one since his perception of Nixon's position seems to be incorrect.

While RePass finds that almost two fifths of the voters were solidly rational in 1964 and only 25 percent irrational or nonrational, it nevertheless remains the case that assessing the amount of issue voting (yet alone rational issue voting) is a very difficult task which, ideally, requires information about the temporal sequence linking a person's own issue positions, his perceptions of the candidates' stances, and his evaluations of the candidates. If the citizen's position and his perceptions of the candidates are temporally prior to his candidate evaluation and vote intention, then we are on firmer ground in concluding that issue voting occurred. But information about the temporal ordering is costly to come by, requiring a panel design with repeated interviews with the same respondents conducted periodically throughout the campaign. And deciding whether a vote is rational or not requires the ability to determine whether citizen perceptions of candidates are correct or not, a problematic task on issues in which candidate positions are vague. Thus, rather than attempt to measure the precise amount of issue voting that occurs at any specific election, we will instead in the conclusion of this chapter specify some general conditions that facilitate and depress the levels of issue voting and ideological awareness. But first we shall examine the revisionist literature on ideology and belief systems.

Ideology

Conceptualization. The revisionist literature on ideological awareness reaches conclusions similar to the issue voting literature—namely, that the level of ideological sophistication is higher than that found in *The American Voter.* This higher level is attributed to both measurement differences, including alternative definitions of an ideologue, and to changes in the political environment that have led to genuine increases in ideological awareness. For example, Field and Anderson (1970) questioned whether the amount of ideological conceptualization of politics might not be higher than reported in *The American Voter* in elections characterized by ideological conflict at the elite level. Thus, they investigated the 1964 election in which Barry Goldwater flaunted the fact that he was offering an ideological choice. Using a somewhat more lenient scheme for classifying citizens as ideologues, Field and Anderson found that the proportion of ideologues in the 1956, 1960, and 1964 electorates was 21 (*The American Voter* said 15), 27, and 35 percent. Since their more lenient coding system was used across all three elections, they appropriately concluded that the specific election context does indeed influence the extent of ideological awareness. They argued that *The American Voter* may have emphasized too strongly the importance of individual characteristics, such as education, information, and political involvement, to ideological sophistication; their research indicates that the political context exercises an independent influence. Of course, as Field and Anderson note, even in the ideological election of 1964, only 35 percent of the electorate could be classified as ideologues, suggesting there are some upper limits to the proportion of ideologues one might uncover in any election, perhaps because of the cognitive limitations of the electorate cited in *The American Voter* (p. 345).

An analysis (Klingemann, 1973) of citizens' likes and dislikes about the candidates and parties in 1968 provides a more appropriate comparison to the 1956 levels of conceptualization presented in Table 4.2. Whereas in 1956 ideologues comprised 11.5 percent of the sample and 15.5 percent of voters, the comparable figures for 1968 were 23 and 27 percent. This increase in the number of ideologues was not due to the rise in educational levels between 1956 and 1968. Note in Figure 4.2 that while the proportion of ideologues increases at higher levels of education, there are more ideologues in 1968 than in 1956 at *all* levels of education. This means that even after the effects of education are removed, the proportion of ideologues is higher in 1968 than 1956. This again suggests the importance of the political stimuli impinging upon the electorate as a determinant of ideological conceptualization.[2]

---

[2] Note that the argument claims only that rising education does not account for the increase in ideological conceptualization between 1956 and 1968. It does not negate the important influence of educational attainment on one's level of conceptualization, as evidenced by the fact that people with higher levels of education are much more likely to be ideologues.

120

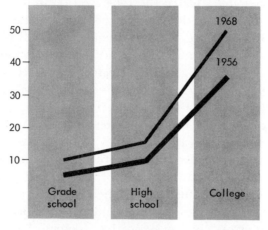

FIGURE 4.2
The Proportion of Ideologues at Three
Educational Levels for the 1956 and 1968
Electorates

Proportion of ideologues in educational group

Education

Source: Extracted from Angus Campbell et al., *The American Voter* (New York: John Wiley & Sons, Inc., 1960), table 10–2, p. 250; and a table from a handout by Hans Klingemann entitled "Dimensions of Political Belief Systems: 'Levels of Conceptualization' as a Variable. Some Results for USA and FRG 1968/69," preliminary handout prepared for the E.C.P.R. Workshop on Political Behavior, Dissatisfaction and Protest, April 12–18, 1973, Universitat Mannheim.

Constraint. With respect to the topic of belief system constraint, the most far-reaching revisionist research is that of Nie and Andersen (1974) and Nie, Verba, and Petrocik (1976) who examined the linkages among citizen issue opinions over time for an identical set of issues. Nie and Andersen determined the correlation between pairs of issue positions and used as their measure of constraint the average correlation for sets of issues. Figure 4.3 shows the average level of constraint on domestic and foreign issues over time; quite clearly, the consistency of responses in the post-1964 era far exceeds that of the 1956–60 period. The authors summarize (p. 559):

> . . . From 1964 onward, attitudes in the mass public on the issues of social welfare, welfare measures specific for blacks, racial integration in the schools, and positions on the cold war are substantially inter-

FIGURE 4.3
Changes in Constraint on Domestic and Foreign Issues, 1956–1972

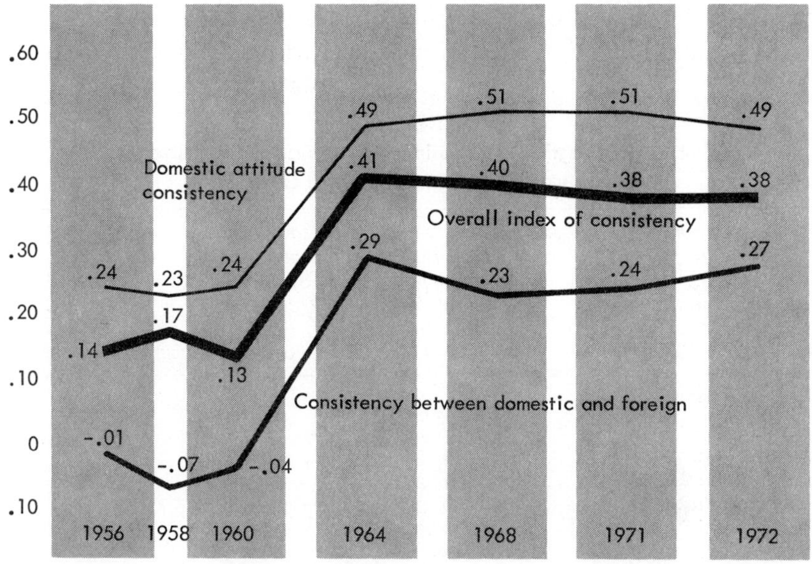

Source: Norman H. Nie and Kristi Andersen, "Mass Belief Systems Revisited: Political Change and Attitude Structure," *The Journal of Politics* 36 (August 1974), fig. 4, p. 558. Nie and Andersen examine five issues asked over time. Four of the issues are domestic in nature, dealing with questions of welfare, black welfare, integration, and size of government, while the fifth issue concerns the cold war. With five issues, one can calculate ten correlations between pairs of issues. It is the average of these ten correlations that is represented by the overall index consistency, while the domestic attitude consistency is the average of the pairwise correlations among the four domestic issues. The domestic-foreign consistency is simply the average of the correlations between the four domestic issues and the cold war item.

correlated. That is, those who are liberal in one of these issue-areas tend to take liberal positions on the others, and the same is true for those at the conservative end of the attitude continuum. . . .

Moreover, Nie and Andersen find that new issues, such as amnesty, the rights of radicals, and others, are somewhat correlated with the more traditional issues, suggesting the presence of a general liberal-conservative ideology or, more accurately, constraint across a number of issues that fit a liberal-conservative pattern (pp. 562–63).

As did Converse, Nie and Andersen compared the level of constraint at the mass and elite levels. They found that the mass public of 1972 exhibited more constraint (see Table 4.7) than did the sample of 1958 congressional candidates examined by Converse; unfortunately, more recent elite samples were not available.

The question arises as to the causes of the observed higher levels of constraint in mass belief systems. Nie and Andersen rule out rising educational levels as the explanation since there is increased constraint for citizens at all levels of education. The authors finally conclude that

TABLE 4.7
Issue Constraint for 1958 Congressional Candidates
Compared to the Mass Public Over Time

	Index of Attitude Consistency within Domestic Issues	Index of Consistency between Domestic and Foreign	Overall Index of Attitude Consistency
Congressional candidates 1958	.38	.25	.31
Mass public 1956	.24	—.01	.14
Mass public 1960	.24	—.04	.13
Mass public 1964	.49	.29	.41
Mass public 1968	.51	.23	.40
Mass public 1972	.49	.27	.38

Source: Extracted from Norman H. Nie and Kristi Andersen, "Mass Belief Systems Revisited: Political Change and Attitude Structure," *The Journal of Politics* 36 (August 1974), table 4, p. 566.

the explanation rests in the changed salience of politics itself, that the 1960s and 1970s were more exciting, dramatic, issue-oriented times than the 1950s. They write (p. 580):

> ... The pattern of attitudes found among Americans in the 1950s was a transient phenomenon and not an inevitable characteristic of mass politics. Of course, the pattern that emerged in the 1960s may be transient as well, but that does not change our argument about the lack of inevitability of the earlier pattern. Indeed, our data suggests that not only specific political attitudes but the *structure* of mass attitudes may be affected by politics in the real world. The average citizen may not be as apolitical as has been thought.

As plausible as the Nie and Andersen finding about increased issue constraint in the 1960s seems to be, it has come under serious challenge on methodological grounds. Numerous investigators (Sullivan et al., 1978; Bishop et al., 1978a, 1978b, 1978c) have argued that the increase in issue constraint attributed by Nie and his associates to the more politicized nature of the 1960s is in reality due to changes in the wording of the issue questions asked by the Center for Political Studies in 1964, changes that have been shown to result in higher constraint.[3]

If question wording accounts for the rise in issue constraint, then where does this leave the revisionist literature about the competence of the average citizen? One answer is to downplay the constraint evidence and rely more heavily on the ideological conceptualization research which, as discussed earlier, indicates increased ideological sophistication with identical measurement strategies. Moreover, two analyses of the 1972 election provide evidence of an electorate more attuned to ideological considerations than depicted in the traditional literature. Stimson (1975) found that constraint was highest over a set of issues for citizens with the greatest cognitive abilities, as measured by level of education and amount of political information. Although agreeing with Converse's definition of constraint, Stimson found that the amount of belief structuring was greater than estimated by Converse and attributed this to the changed nature of the times. In the CPS report on the 1972 election, Miller and his associates declare (1976: 754): "Ideology and issue voting . . . provide a means for better explaining the unique elements of the contest than do the voters' social characteristics, the nature of candidates, the events of the campaign, political alienation, cultural orientations, or partisan identification." They find a strong relationship between a liberal-conservative

[3] Prior to 1964, SRC/CPS issue questions presented respondents a single position on an issue and determined support or opposition for the position along a five-point agree-disagree scale. For example, in 1960 the question on medical welfare was worded: "The government ought to help people get doctors and hospital care at low cost. Do you have an opinion on this or not? (If yes): Do you think the government should do this?" In 1964 SRC/CPS presented respondents with competing alternatives on an issue and asked them to choose between them. Hence, in 1964 the medical welfare question was worded: "Some say the government in Washington ought to help people get doctors and hospital care at low cost; others say the government should not get into this." Have you been interested enough in this to favor one side over the other? (If yes): "What is your position? Should the government in Washington help people get doctors and hospital care at low cost or stay out of this?" In 1968, these dichotomous choice items were expanded into seven category measures with labelled end points. Hence, the issue questions have been changed in major ways, mainly because the respondents' answers would be more valid when they were faced with a choice among alternatives. Because of the concern about measuring non-attitudes, issue items have been preceded by filter questions (e.g., do you have an opinion. . . , have you been interested. . . .) designed to screen out people without genuine attitudes. These filter questions have also changed over the years and Bishop et al. (1979) have shown that different filters result in substantially different numbers of people being included in the analysis. Hence, studies of issue consistency may not be truly comparable because of differently defined sets of respondents.

proximity measure and the citizen's vote. Moreover, they observe fairly high correlations within clusters of issues, which is viewed as evidence of constraint as well as substantial correlations between specific issues and one's position on a liberal-conservative scale. The authors conclude that ideology is much more relevant today in influencing vote and attribute this to the more distinctive alternatives offered by candidates in response to the social and political crises of the 1960s and 1970s. And in the CPS report on the 1976 election, Miller and Miller (1977) found that while the impact of party identification on vote choice had increased and the effect of issues declined, the levels of issue consistency and ideological thinking remained essentially unchanged from 1972.

Finally, there is additional research that suggests that citizens' opinions exhibit constraint, at least within specific issue areas. For example, Sheatsley has shown that generalized racial attitudes are closely related to opinions on specific race-related matters. Similarly, Page and Brody (1972) found a clear structure in citizens' responses to a series of questions about the Vietnam War. Other research (e.g., Lane, 1962) relying upon more in-depth, intensive interviewing techniques has revealed greater consistency and coherence in citizens' attitudes, raising the possibility that the sample survey approach may not be the optimal one for investigating constraint, mainly because people may not be able to articulate in a brief interview the kinds of considerations that enter into their evaluations of politics and because there may be insufficient probing to determine why people believe what they do. One should keep in mind, however, that in-depth approaches may be suitable for answering questions different than those raised in the issue-voting controversy; given that political stimuli and communications in the real world are not presented to voters in an in-depth fashion, the sample survey may be the more appropriate way to study citizen responses to an election campaign.

THE COMPETENCE OF THE INDEPENDENT AND THE FLOATING VOTER

It is clear that elections are won and lost in large part according to the behavior of Independents who, without the anchoring ties of partisanship, are the citizens most volatile in their partisan choice over successive elections, as shown in Figure 3.11. This volatility in conjunction with the increase in the number of Independents discussed in Chapter 3 makes the Independent citizenry a critical battleground for campaign strategists. It therefore becomes important to ascertain how informed and concerned Independents are; it would be extremely upsetting to many observers of American politics if election outcomes largely depended on blocs of uninformed voters.

As with the issue-voting literature, there is both a traditional and a revisionist portrait of the Independent voter. Before turning to these descriptions, it should be noted that the relevant literature discusses different yet interrelated groups of voters. Some analyses focus on partisans versus Independents, while others concentrate on stand-patters versus switchers, or floaters—that is, citizens who are consistent versus inconsistent in their partisan choice over successive elections. While Independents are more likely to be switchers and partisans standpatters, there is certainly not a perfect overlap between the categories. For example, the partisan who temporarily defects from his party's nominee but returns to the fold at the next election is clearly a switcher, but certainly not an Independent. The reader should keep the distinction between switchers and Independents in mind as the relevant literature is discussed.

The traditional view of the Independent can be summarized very briefly by the following passage from *The American Voter* (p. 143):

> Far from being more attentive, interested, and informed, Independents tend as a group to be somewhat less involved in politics. They have somewhat poorer knowledge of the issues, their image of the candidates is fainter, their interest in the campaign is less, their concern over the outcome is relatively slight, and their choice between competing candidates, although it is indeed made later in the campaign, seem much less to spring from discoverable evaluations of the elements of national politics.

And concerning the floating voter, Converse (1970) found that citizens who voted for different parties in 1956 and 1960 had lower levels of information than the stable voters. Thus, the standard image of the Independent and the floater is not a very positive one.

RePass (1971) has challenged *The American Voter* description of the issue awareness of the Independent. He discovered (p. 398) that Independents ranked between Republicans and Democrats with respect to the extent of their issue concerns; for example, 30 percent of the Independents mentioned four to six issues about which they were concerned compared to only 15 percent of the strong Democrats. RePass's findings did not challenge *The American Voter* findings about involvement and participation.

RePass explained his findings of high issue concern among Independents by arguing that *The American Voter* may have used inappropriate measures (pp. 398–99):

> Conclusions about the Independent voter . . . were based upon responses to the open-ended questions that measured attitudes toward parties and candidates, not toward issues. The Independent is placed at a disadvantage in answering these questions—especially the questions about parties . . . responses to these questions frequently reflect long-term cognitive elements of party identification. Since most Independents have received few cues about parties in their socialization process, it is understandable that their references to parties would be deficient.

Furthermore, there is evidence (Converse, 1974: 324, fn. 20) that if one excludes from analysis those Independents who are habitual nonvoters and therefore cannot influence election outcomes, the remaining Independents are just as involved and informed, if not more so, than the partisans.

A more telling criticism of *The American Voter* description of the Independent is the failure to distinguish between independent leaners and pure Independents. In Chapter 3 we noted that independent leaners tend to vote like the partisans of the party to which they lean rather than mirroring the pure Independents. In a similar vein, there is a growing body of literature (Miller and Miller, 1977; Keith et al., 1976) which shows, among other things, that independent leaners more closely resemble partisans than Independents in such areas as turnout, campaign attentiveness, civic involvement, and political knowledge. And concerning the conceptualization of politics, Table 4.8 demonstrates that leaning Independents differ dramatically from pure Independents.

Note that only 10 percent of the pure Independents are classified as ideologues, compared to 26 and 44 percent of the independent Democrats and Republicans. And fully 38 percent of the pure Independents are in the no-issue content category, compared to only 20 and 13 percent for the leaning Democrats and Republicans. Perhaps pure Independents are penalized (see the RePass argument earlier) by a classification scheme based on evaluations of the political parties and candidates, but parties and candidates are the major actors in presi-

TABLE 4.8

The Relationship between Party Identification and Levels of Conceptualization, 1968

(in percentages)

Level of Conceptualization	Party Identification						
	Strong Democrat	Weak Democrat	Independent Democrat	Independent	Independent Republican	Weak Republican	Strong Republican
Ideology	15	17	26	10	44	28	40
Group benefits	56	40	33	21	15	16	16
Nature of times	17	22	22	31	28	30	31
No issue content	12	21	20	38	13	26	13
Total	100	100	100	100	100	100	100
Number of cases	296	336	137	128	122	206	143

Source: Calculated from a table in a handout by Hans Klingemann, "Dimensions of Political Belief Systems: 'Levels of Conceptualization' as a Variable. Some Results for USA and FRG 1968/69," prepared for the E.C.P.R. Workshop on Political Behavior, Dissatisfaction and Protest, April 12–18, 1973, Universitat Mannheim.

dential elections. Finally, note that a higher proportion of leaners than strong partisans of each party are categorized as ideologues.[4]

Hence, the leaning Independents who comprised about three fifths of all Independents in 1976 (see Table 2.1) are not the uninformed, uninvolved group depicted in *The American Voter,* although the pure Independents still bear a strong resemblance to the traditional portrayal. For example (as shown in Table 4.9) 39 and 45 percent of the

TABLE 4.9

The Percentage of Various Categories of Independents with at Least Some College Education, 1956 and 1976

	1956	1976	Percent Increase
Pure independents	28	29	1
Leaning independents	39	45	6
Leaning independent under 30	40	51	11
All partisans and independents	32	34	2

Source: 1956 and 1976 SRC/CPS election studies.

leaners in 1956 and 1976 had at least some college education, levels 7 and 11 percent higher than the figures for all citizens in those years. In contrast, only 28 and 29 percent of the pure Independents had some college experience. More important, among leaners between the ages of 18 and 30 in 1976, a slight majority had at least some college education, a figure about 17 percent higher than the overall population total and a full 11 percent higher than the comparable figure for young leaners in 1956. Hence, the Independent leaner is likely to be as competent a voter as the partisan.

Returning to the floating voters, there is an ever-growing body of evidence that indicates the switching voters tend to move in response to genuine issue concerns and do not simply float randomly back and

---

4 As an aside, note that Republicans are much more likely to have an ideological orientation to politics, while Democrats are more oriented to group benefits. This may help explain why the GOP has problems expanding its base of support. One can speculate that Republicans' attachments to their party are more likely to be based on general agreement with philosophical principles that are not readily modified or compromised. Hence, attempts to broaden the base may be seen as threats to the purity of the party's traditional stances. But for Democrats, developing and maintaining a broad base is made easier by a dominant group-benefits outlook which enables political differences to be resolved by the provision of tangible (and symbolic) benefits to the groups comprising the Democratic coalition.

forth between the parties. In addition to the Key work cited earlier, Natchez and Bupp (1970: 436–43) found that citizens who belonged to an issue public were more likely to change their partisan choice between 1960 and 1964. A similar conclusion was reached by Kirkpatrick and Jones (1974: 544–55) for 1964–68 switchers *and* standpatters. That is, both stable and moving voters appeared to behave according to well-founded policy preferences. The SRC/CPS work on the 1968 election showed that 1964–68 switchers, particularly 1968 Wallace voters were clearly policy motivated (Converse et al., 1969: 1095–1101). Finally, the research on vote defection suggests a similar conclusion—namely, that defectors can be guided by policy concerns (Boyd, 1969).

In summary, the contemporary research indicates that the floating voter can respond to issue considerations and that the leaning Independent is capable of making informed decisions. This is presumably good news for those who worry about elections being decided by blocs of uninformed, unconcerned voters. A more interesting implication is that the potentiality for issue-based politics is greater than previously thought, particularly given the weakening of partisan ties. It may be that the opportunity for an issue-oriented third party or for a realignment of the existing parties on the basis of issue appeals is better than it has been since the 1930s, even if the actual likelihood of a realignment is low.

SUMMARY AND CONCLUSION

The revisionist literature surveyed in this chapter generally revealed higher levels of issue awareness and ideological conceptualization. This was attributed to both methodological innovations and to genuine changes in the electorate brought on in part by the changed nature of politics in the 1960s and 1970s. However, any attempt to estimate the precise amount of issue voting or ideological sophistication must take into account a variety of conditions that can affect issue and ideological awareness. Hence we will conclude this chapter by specifying some general conditions that influence the amount of issue voting.

Issue voting requires information, and the acquisition of information involves costs for the citizen. These costs are probably less for citizens with the cognitive skills (e.g., education) that facilitate the collection and evaluation of information. Thus, one might expect that the increase in American education levels may gradually lead to a citizenry better able to be informed about politics and elections.

The impact of educational trends, however, seems marginal at best. Probably the quickest way for the information costs of citizens to be reduced is for the parties and candidates to take distinct positions on issues and to campaign on the basis of those positions. One might further argue that where parties offer meaningful choices on issues relevant to the population, citizens themselves will be more willing to incur the costs of being informed.

However, the incentives for the parties to take distinctive positions may not exist, even for issues that are points of contention at the elite level and among segments of the electorate. As Anthony Downs (1957: 117–22) argues, in a two-party system where most of the voters fall in the middle of the political spectrum, the wisest electoral strategy for the parties is to converge toward the center. If new issues arise that do not coincide with the existing lines of party cleavage or if the existing issues that divide the parties assume new forms, then the parties may respond in a number of ways.

In one scenario, the parties will move to incorporate the new or revised issues without upsetting the existing bases of party support. However, it may be impossible for the parties to handle these new issues without alienating some substantial segment of their existing support. In such a situation, the parties may try to straddle or avoid issues, thereby making the information costs of voters very high.

Of course, where parties straddle an issue, a vacuum may exist which can encourage the emergence of a third-party candidacy directed toward voters on the basis of issues, thereby reducing information costs and facilitating issue voting. Evidence for this scenario is provided by the formal work of Anthony Downs, who argues that (pp. 125–27) parties in a multiparty system are more likely to take distinctive positions, and by the empirical work of Weisberg and Rusk (1970) and Converse et al. (1969). Weisberg and Rusk (pp. 1177–83) analyzed popular evaluations of the potential presidential nominees in 1968 and found that a multiplicity of candidates seemed to facilitate issue-based evaluations, particularly for such would-be nominees as Robert Kennedy, Eugene McCarthy, Nelson Rockefeller, and George Romney, all of whom challenged establishment candidates within their parties largely on the basis of issues.

Converse and his colleagues (1969: 1097) found that support for the third-party candidacy of George Wallace in 1968 was largely issue based, while the Nixon and Humphrey vote was primarily a party vote. Almost half of the citizens questioned said they liked Wallace because of his issue stands; only about a fourth of the replies dealing with Nixon and Humphrey exhibited issue content. More specifically, Converse and his colleagues found that Wallace voters were far more uniformly hawkish, pro-segregation, pro-police, and the like. In short, the authors argued (p. 1097) that "Wallace was a 'backlash' candidate, and there is no question but that the positions communicated to the public accounted for his electoral support in a very primary sense." The Wallace candidacy well illustrates the situation of an issue-based third party that makes it easy for voters to be informed on issues.

In conclusion, while the amount of issue voting may still not be impressively high, particularly with respect to the tenets of classical democratic theory, the important thrust of the revisionist literature is that the electorate is capable of making issue-related decisions, especially when the candidates and parties fashion issue appeals to the electorate. As Key, Page and Brody, and others have argued, it is unreasonable to demand issue voting from citizens when the parties themselves do not offer meaningful, clearly stated choices. The decisions made by the electorate can be no better than the choices offered by the parties and candidates.

5

Issues and Candidates, 1952–1960

INTRODUCTION

As discussed in Chapter 2, *The American Voter* identified six partisan attitudes that influenced citizens' vote decisions—attitudes toward the Democratic and Republican candidates, attitudes toward the issues of domestic and foreign policy, attitudes toward the political parties as managers of government, and attitudes toward the groups involved in politics. These six attitudes have achieved varying degrees of importance in the elections between 1952 and 1976, and thus our first task in this chapter is simply to assess their impact on the parties' electoral fortunes over time. Then we will examine the specific content of these attitudes, focusing in particular on candidate and issue attitudes. For example, to say that foreign policy attitudes were more important in 1972 than in previous elections and that they tended to favor the Republicans is an incomplete statement; it is also important to know which specific aspects of foreign policy were uppermost in citizens' minds as they arrived at vote decisions. Thus, the second part of this chapter and all of Chapters 6 and 7 will focus on the crucial candidate and issue considerations that have dominated presidential campaigns since 1952.

THE SIX PARTISAN ATTITUDES OVER TIME

Candidate Attitudes

Of the six partisan attitudes, it is attitudes toward the candidates that have exhibited the greatest fluctuations in their contribution to Democratic and Republican electoral fortunes since 1952. That candidate attitudes have varied the most is not surprising, given that the candidates are likely to be the elements unique and new to any election. What is surprising is the fact that the parties have at times offered presidential candidates who were not highly evaluated by their own party members, yet alone by Independents and the opposition. Figure 5.1 presents the mean evaluations of the major party presidential candidates since 1952, as measured by the frequency of positive and negative comments offered about the candidates.

Note that for all citizens the mean evaluations of the Democratic candidates were positive through 1964, slightly negative in 1968, very much so in 1972, and slightly positive in 1976. Even more telling is that the evaluation of McGovern in 1972 by Democratic identifiers was not positive but instead neutral, certainly a revealing comment on the weakness of the McGovern candidacy, while Carter was viewed quite positively by Democrats in 1976. Throughout this period, Independents assessed four Democratic candidates positively (Stevenson in 1952, Kennedy in 1960, Johnson in 1964, and Carter in 1976) and three negatively, while Republican loyalists were consistently negative toward the Democratic nominees as expected, with Lyndon Johnson being the least unpopular Democratic candidate in Republican eyes.

Reactions to the Republican candidates by the entire citizenry and by Independents were uniformly favorable, with the major exception of Goldwater in 1964; Ford's ratings in 1976, while positive, were not strongly so. Democratic assessments of GOP presidential candidates have generally been more favorable than Republican evaluations of Democratic candidates; only in 1964 and 1968 were Democrats sub-

FIGURE 5.1
Evaluations of the Democratic and Republican Candidates, 1952–1976

A. Affect toward Democratic candidates, 1952–1976

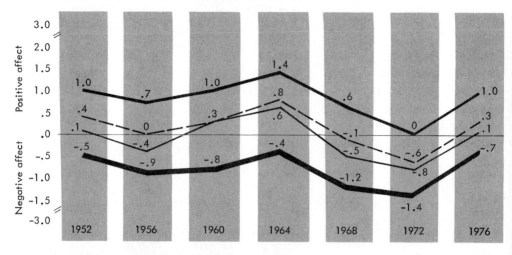

B. Affect toward Republican candidates, 1952–1976

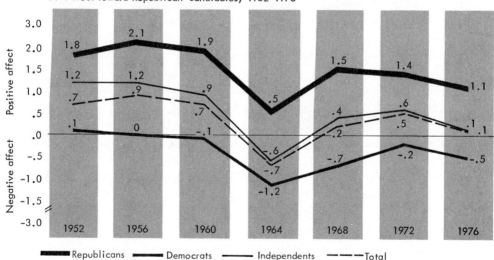

Sources: Arthur Miller et al., "A Majority Party in Disarray: Policy Polarization in the 1972 Election," *American Political Science Review*, fig. 6, pp. 55, in revised mimeo version and 1976 CPS election study.

stantially negative toward the Republican nominees. Republican partisans, as expected, have always ranked their candidates highly, with Goldwater receiving the weakest of these positive endorsements and Eisenhower in 1956 the strongest.

Thus we see that evaluations of the major party candidates have varied markedly, and the interesting question becomes how these assessments translate into vote outcomes. Some research by Donald Stokes (1966) supplemented by findings presented by Michael Kagay and Greg Caldeira, help address this question. Figure 5.2 shows the contribution to the Democratic and Republican vote totals due to the impact of candidate attitudes, while Figure 5.3 summarizes the net impact of candidate attitudes on the vote division. Note that with the

FIGURE 5.2
The Electoral Impact of the Democratic and Republican Candidates, 1952–1976*

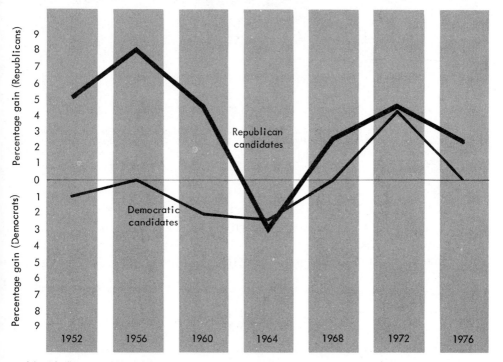

* In this figure and Figures 5.3, 5.5, and 5.6, what is being measured is the effect on the two-party vote attributable to the attitudinal component in question. For example, the 1956 entry in the above figure for Republican candidates should be interpreted as indicating that the GOP received an advantage of about 8 percent in the popular vote due to attitudes toward Eisenhower.

Sources: Donald E. Stokes, "Some Dynamic Elements of Contests for the Presidency," *American Political Science Review* 60 (March 1966), fig. 3, p. 22; Michael Kagay and Greg Caldeira, "Public Policy Issues and the American Voter, 1952–1972," unpublished paper; and communication from Michael Kagay.

FIGURE 5.3
The Net Electoral Impact of the Candidates, 1952–1976

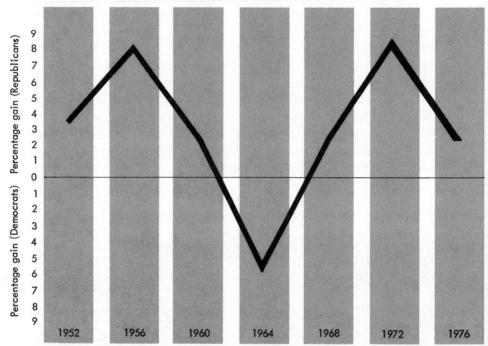

Sources: Donald E. Stokes, "Some Dynamic Elements of Contests for the Presidency," *American Political Science Review* 60 (March 1966), fig. 4, p. 23; Michael Kagay and Greg Caldeira, "Public Policy Issues and the American Voter, 1952–1972," unpublished paper; and communication from Michael Kagay.

exception of 1964, attitudes towards the Republican presidential candidates always made a positive contribution to Republican vote totals, reaching a peak in 1956 when the Eisenhower candidacy led to an almost 8 percent advantage for the GOP. Attitudes toward the Democratic candidates have not provided the same advantage to the Democrats as have attitudes toward the Republican candidates for the GOP; in fact, in three elections—1956, 1968, and 1972—the net effect of assessments of the Democratic candidates was a gain in votes for the GOP. While this Republican gain was tiny in 1956 and 1968, it exceeded 4 percent in 1972 and, in conjunction with the over 4 percent advantage accruing to the GOP because of its own candidate, resulted in a net gain of over 8 percent—the greatest net impact of candidates in the seven elections under investigation. The elections characterized by the weakest net impact of candidates were 1952, 1960, and

1976; in the first two cases both parties' nominees were evaluated positively and aided their own party's electoral prospects. In 1976, attitudes toward Carter provided the Democrats hardly any advantage at all, while attitudes toward Ford gave the GOP about a 2½ percent gain, resulting in a net gain for the Republicans of about 2.4 percent.

In summary, we observe that candidate evaluations have generally been a plus to Republican electoral fortunes. We further observe (in Figure 5.1) that Democratic Party identifiers have generally been less enthusiastic toward their party's candidates than Republican loyalists have been toward theirs. This raises the question of why. One speculative but plausible answer is that the Democratic Party is a more diverse, heterogeneous party, thereby making it difficult to nominate a candidate with as widespread appeal to Democratic loyalists as GOP nominees have to Republican followers. Perhaps there was no candidate that the Democrats could have nominated in 1972 who could have approached the popularity of Richard Nixon in the electorate at large, although there were probably Democratic candidates who would have been more attractive than McGovern to the Democratic rank and file.

Another reason for the GOP advantage in candidate evaluations might simply rest in the chance elements of politics, resulting in the Republicans nominating the more attractive, popular candidates. For example, had Robert Kennedy not been assassinated in 1968, perhaps the Democratic Party would have emerged from the Chicago convention with a stronger ticket. Likewise, had Hubert Humphrey won the California primary over McGovern in 1972, perhaps a compromise or dark horse nominee would have resulted and enabled the Democrats to wage a more effective campaign. On the Republican side, one can argue that had Rockefeller's narrow defeat at the hand of Goldwater in the California primary in 1964 been reversed, the GOP would likely have nominated a compromise candidate such as Scranton, Lodge, or Nixon who would have been more popular with the various wings of the GOP. In a political world dominated with winning elections, the GOP as the minority party should be especially concerned with nominating attractive candidates if it hopes to fashion an electoral victory. That the parties have on occasions ignored such rational concerns is evidenced by their nomination of candidates (Goldwater in 1964 and McGovern in 1972) who were relatively unpopular among their own party's adherents. The features of the presidential nomination process that permit relatively weak nominees to emerge will be discussed in Chapter 11.

Yet a third explanation for the Republican advantage in candidate evaluation at all elections except 1964 refers to the nature of the times and the impossibility of divorcing perceptions of the candidates from the political context in which nominees must compete. For example, twice—in 1952 and 1968—the Democratic Party entered the election as the incumbent party under attack for a variety of reasons, including the state of the economy and unpopular land wars in Asia. While the Democrats were the incumbent party at these elections, their nominee was not the incumbent President, who in both cases chose not to seek reelection, but nonincumbents who were saddled with the legacy of unpopular administrations. Under such circumstances, it is difficult for the nominee to be perceived very favorably since in many voters' minds he is linked to the unpopular policies of the previous administration. Furthermore, in 1956 and 1972, the Democratic candidates (Stevenson and McGovern) had the unenviable task of challenging Republican incumbents (Eisenhower and Nixon) who were campaigning for reelection in part on the basis that they had solved many of the problems inherited from the previous Democratic administration. Given the immense personal popularity of Eisenhower in 1956, perhaps there was no Democratic candidate who would not have suffered in popular evaluations. While Nixon's reelection did not seem foreordained in the middle of his first term, by the time 1972 arrived he was in a secure electoral position, not only because of the Democratic nomination of McGovern but also because of the ability of an incumbent President to structure situations for maximum political advantage, such as by well-timed and well-publicized journeys to China and the Soviet Union and by the stimulation of the economy through release of massive funds in the period prior to the election.

One thrust of the above discussion is that much more enters into citizens' assessments of candidates than simply the candidate's personality, speaking style, and the like. Voters may like a candidate because of his personal characteristics or because of his policy views or because of his association with other positively evaluated elements of politics. It is useful to know which of these basic factors most influence citizen evaluations of candidates for there are some important strategic considerations involved. If feelings toward the candidates are mainly personality based, then it behooves parties to nominate personally attractive candidates. But if policy considerations are also important components of candidate evaluations, then the candidates and parties must be concerned with fashioning optimal policy appeals as well as generating attractive candidate images. Of course, both policy and personal factors affect candidate evaluations, and certainly the two elements are not independent, given the ample opportunity for citizens to engage in rationalization and perceptual distortion. Furthermore, a variety of situational factors, such as the kinds of appeals a candidate makes, affect whether people respond to the candidates primarily in personal or policy terms.[1] Still, we would like to know how the personal versus policy component of candidate evaluations have varied over time; our expectation is that the personality aspect of candidate ratings will exhibit the widest fluctuations since these are the most idiosyncratic factors.

Some research by Sam Kirkpatrick and his associates (1974) examined the components of candidate evaluation. Kirkpatrick analyzed the responses to the SRC/CPS open-ended questions about candidate likes and dislikes and classified citizens' comments according to which aspect of the candidate they mentioned—personality, domestic policy stances, foreign policy positions, or suitability as an administrator of government. As shown in Figure 5.4, the personality component of candidate rankings has varied the most over time, while the domestic policy aspect has always been pro-Democratic, even in 1972 when McGovern himself received highly negative ratings. This means that for many voters the issue positions they associated with McGovern were more popular than McGovern himself. Undoubtedly, this reflects a long-standing Democratic advantage in the electorate with respect to certain domestic policy programs, particularly matters of social welfare, an advantage that the economic crises of the 1970s may serve to increase. The foreign policy component of candidate assessment favored the Republicans in all years except 1964, while the management component has been more evenly divided. We will say more in Chapter 8 about the conceptual difficulties in sorting out the impact of candidate and issue attitudes. In summary, it appears that different elements do enter into evaluations of a candidate and that it is the personal characteristics of the nominee that have the greatest potentiality for affecting election outcomes. Certainly, the very nomination of one candidate over another strongly determines the kind of campaign that will be conducted.

---

1 Shabad and Andersen (1979) show that women are not more personality-oriented and less issue-oriented than men in their evaluations of the presidential candidates.

FIGURE 5.4
Mean Partisan Advantage of Candidate Attitude Components
for All Citizens, 1952–1972

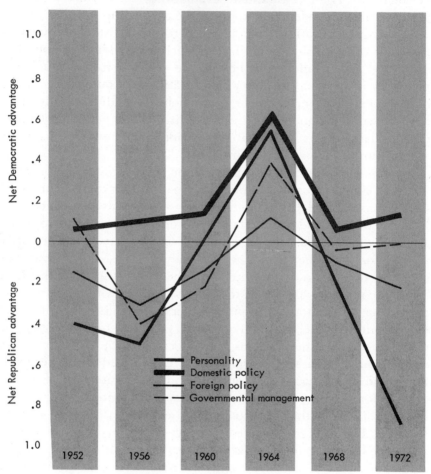

Source: Samuel Kirkpatrick, William Lyons, and Michael R. Fitzgerald, "Candidate and Party Images in the American Electorate: A Longitudinal Analysis," paper presented at the annual meeting of the Southwestern Political Science Association, Dallas, Tex., March 28–30, 1974, modified from fig. 4.

Domestic and Foreign Policy Issue Attitudes

The electoral impact of domestic and foreign policy attitudes between 1952 and 1976 is shown in Figure 5.5. Note that the era began and ended with a Republican advantage in the realm of foreign affairs, an advantage that disappeared only in the 1964 election due to the "collapse of the belief that the party under Goldwater was more

FIGURE 5.5
**The Electoral Impact of Domestic and Foreign Policy
Issue Attitudes, 1952–1976**

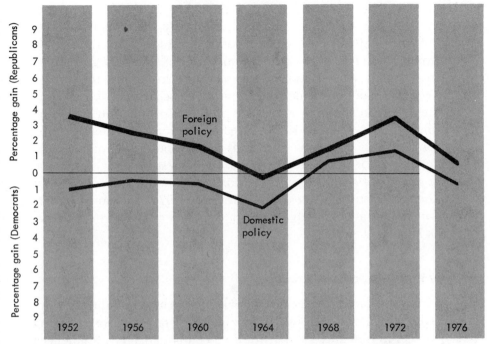

Sources: Donald E. Stokes, "Some Dynamic Elements of Contests for the Presidency," *American Political Science Review* 60 (March 1966), figs. 1 and 2, pp. 20–21; Michael Kagay and Greg Caldeira, "Public Policy Issues and the American Voter, 1952–1972," unpublished paper; and communication from Michael Kagay.

likely to bring peace than were the Democrats under Johnson" (Stokes, 1966: 21). This is a prime example of a situation in which the choice of a specific candidate can upset long-standing images of the parties. By 1968 the Republican advantage in foreign affairs had returned due to Democratic responsibility for the Vietnam War, and by 1972 the GOP advantage returned to the peak achieved before in 1952. Note that in 1976 foreign policy provided only a very small advantage for the Republicans.

The domestic policy curve reveals a small but consistent advantage for the Democrats through 1964, and a lead for Republicans in 1968 and 1972, as traditional New Deal social welfare issues gave way in part to new issues dealing with race, law and order, and other matters labeled under the rubric of social issues. Until 1964, the predominant domestic policy image of the parties was the association of Democrats with prosperity and the Republicans with hard times. Stokes (1966: 21) writes that this association weakened with the prosperity of Eisenhower's first term, which convinced many voters that the GOP was not inexorably linked with economic depression. But the Republican recession of 1958 in conjunction with the relatively good times of the Kennedy/early-Johnson years served to strengthen the linkage between bad economic times and Republican occupancy of the White House. One can conjecture that the problems of inflation and recession in the early and mid-1970s served to further strengthen the association between economic hardships and Republican incumbency, although the Democratic advantage on domestic policy issues was quite small in 1976. And with continuing economic difficulties after Democratic capture of the White House in 1976, one can speculate that the domestic policy advantage traditionally enjoyed by the Democratic Party will erode.

Party Performance and Groups

With respect to attitudes toward party performance and the groups involved in politics, we observe in Figure 5.6 fairly consistent party differences in how these two attitudinal components have influenced vote outcomes between 1952 and 1976. With the exception of the 1964 election, attitudes toward the parties' performance have favored the Republicans, although only in 1952 was this effect particularly strong. Attitudes toward groups, on the contrary, have consistently favored the Democratic Party, with the most frequent positive comment referring to the Democrats as the party of the common man, in contrast to images of the GOP as the party of the more privileged elements of society. Stokes (1966: 20–21) suggests that one reason for the decline in the Democratic advantage on this dimension in 1960 and 1964 was the association of the Democratic Party with groups less popular than the common man, such as racial (blacks in 1964) and religious (Catholics in 1960) groups. But even in 1968 and 1972, when racial themes were underlying currents in the campaigns and white resistance to black demands in a number of areas was increasing, the Democratic Party maintained its favorable position along the group benefits dimensions. And in 1976, group benefits was the attitudinal component that most helped the Democrats.

FIGURE 5.6
The Electoral Impact of Party Performance and Group Attitudes, 1952–1976

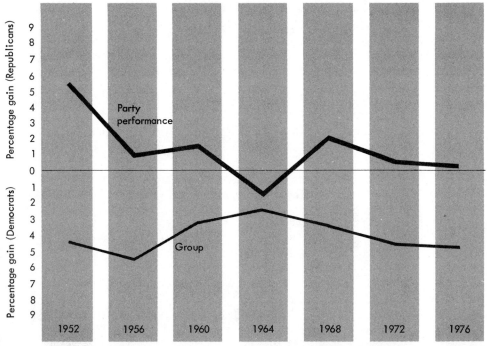

Sources: Donald E. Stokes, "Some Dynamic Elements of Contests for the Presidency," *American Political Science Review* 60 (March 1966), figs. 1 and 2, pp. 20–21; Michael Kagay and Greg Caldeira, "Public Policy Issues and the American Voter, 1952–1972," unpublished paper; and communication from Michael Kagay.

THE CANDIDATES AND ISSUES, 1952–1960

We have seen in the previous section that the six partisan attitudes fluctuate in response to the conduct and content of campaigns, and that the attitudes represent those short-term forces at each election that help account for why the majority Democratic Party was not victorious at each of the elections. Now we will turn to a more explicitly political discussion of each election, endeavoring to make more politically meaningful the content of the six partisan attitudes. We will consider each election sequentially, beginning each discussion with a chart summarizing the effects of the six partisan attitudes, followed by an analysis of the issues, events, and candidates that gave meaning and shape to the partisan attitudes. In the remainder of this chapter, we will analyze the presidential elections from 1952 to 1960, an era of electoral stability, while in the next chapter we will discuss the 1964 to 1972 period, an era dominated by speculation about partisan change and realignment. Finally, in Chapter 7, we will discuss the 1976 election, which includes elements of stability and change.

1952 and 1956

The 1952 and 1956 elections will be considered together in order to facilitate comparisons across elections in which the major party candidate choices were identical. Figure 5.7 summarizes the impact

FIGURE 5.7
The Effects of the Six Partisan Attitudes
on the 1952 and 1956 Presidential Elections

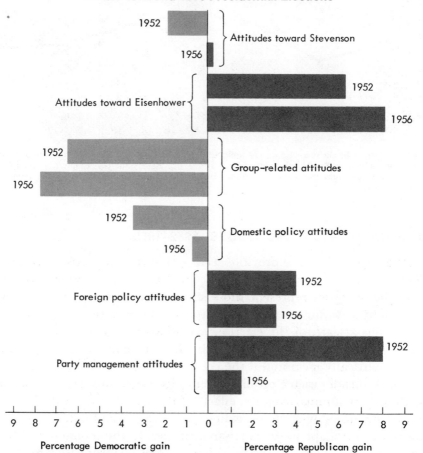

Source: Donald E. Stokes, Angus Campbell, and Warren E. Miller, "Components of Electoral Decision," *American Political Science Review* 52 (June 1958), fig. 3.

of the six partisan attitudes across the two elections. Stokes and his colleagues describe Figure 5.7 as indicating (1958: 382):

> . . . the Republican victory of 1952 resulted from the great appeal of Eisenhower, from a pro-Republican attitude toward foreign issues, and from a strongly anti-Democratic response to the parties as managers of government. This combination of forces appears to have overwhelmed the favorable response to Stevenson, the substantial Democratic group appeal, and a pro-Democratic attitude on domestic issues. The Republican victory of 1956 seems to have resulted from somewhat different components. In the latter election, the force of Eisenhower's appeal seemed of paramount important. The Republican cause was again aided by a favorable response to foreign issues. But with the corruption issue spent, the public's attitude toward the parties as managers of government contributed much less to the Republican majority. On the Democratic side, the appeal of Stevenson apparently was no longer more an asset than a liability to his party, and the party's advantage in domestic issues was greatly diminished. Only a strong Democratic group appeal appeared to reduce the size of the Republican majority in the latter year.

The importance of party management and foreign policy concerns to the 1952 election outcome is reflected in the GOP's campaign theme that tagged the Democratic Party as the party of "Corruption, Korea, and Communism." The issue of corruption and the extent to which it hurt the Democrats in 1952 may seem perplexing in retrospect, given that Stevenson and not Truman was the Democratic candidate in 1952. Nevertheless, the Republicans emphasized in the 1952 campaign the "mess in Washington" under the Truman administration, even though Truman himself was in no way implicated in the misdeeds of his aides. The misdeeds themselves pale in comparison to the Watergate-related offenses, but the repeated pattern of publicized misdeeds created the image of the Democrats as the party of mismanagement and corruption. This was exploited by Republicans in speeches, campaign literature, and documents, such as the party's platform, which included the following statement (Bone, 1955: 656):

> The present Administration's sordid record of corruption has shocked and sickened the American people. Its leaders have forfeited any right to public faith by the way they transact the Federal Government's business.
> Fraud, bribery, graft, favoritism and influence-peddling have come to light. Immorality and unethical behavior have been found to exist among some who were entrusted with high policy-making positions,

and there have been disclosures of close alliances between the present Government and underworld characters.

That the electorate responded to Republican charges of corruption is evidenced by the fact that a sample of citizens made 546 pro-Republican comments about corruption in 1952 compared to no such pro-Democratic references (Campbell et al., 1960: 50). By 1956 as memory of Democratic misdeeds faded into the past and the incumbent Republican administration managed to maintain a clear reputation, the impact of party performance attitudes on vote outcome had declined substantially.

On the issue of war and peace, citizen comments favored the GOP by a ratio of more than 7 to 1 in 1952, an advantage that increased to more than 35 to 1 in 1956, undoubtedly because of successful Republican efforts to extricate the United States from Korea (Campbell et al., 1960: 49). Certainly the Korean War was the dominant force behind citizens' evaluations of the parties on the issue of war and peace in 1952. Republican advantage on this issue received a further boost when General Eisenhower said, in a campaign speech in Detroit less than two weeks before the election (Weisbord, 1966: 378):

> Where will a new Administration begin?
> It will begin with its President taking a simple, firm resolution. That resolution will be: To forego the diversions of politics and to concentrate on the job of ending the Korean war—until that job is honorably done.
> That job requires a personal trip to Korea.
> I shall make that trip. Only in that way could I learn how best to serve the American people in the cause of peace.
> I shall go to Korea.

This simple promise, despite the lack of any specific content as to how the war would actually be ended, and despite being made late in the campaign after most voters had made up their minds how to vote, served to bolster the image of the GOP and Eisenhower as competent to handle the nation's foreign affairs.

Unlike corruption and Korea, citizens made few comments about the problem of communism and the alleged Democratic responsibility for worldwide Communist gains and for domestic Communist subversion in response to questions about likes and dislikes of the parties and candidates. This suggests that "communism" was not a very central concern to most Americans in 1952, at least in comparison to other concerns. This may seem perplexing, given the tremendous amount of attention the issue received in the media and given how prominent the issue was in elite discourse about politics. For example, the 1952 Republican platform included such accusations (Bone, 1955: 647):

> We charge that the leaders of the Administration in power lost the peace so dearly earned by World War II.
> The moral incentives and hopes for a better world which sustained us through World War II were betrayed, and this has given Communist Russia a military and propaganda initiative which, if unstayed, will destroy us.
> They abandoned friendly nations such as Latvia, Lithuania, Estonia, Poland and Czechoslovakia to fend for themselves against the Communist aggression which soon swallowed them.

* * * * *

> In all these respects they flouted our peace-assuring pledges such as the Atlantic Charter, and did so in favor of despots, who, it was well known, consider that murder, terror, slavery, concentration camps, and the ruthless and brutal denial of human rights are legitimate means to their desired ends.

The failure of the "communism" issue to penetrate the consciousness of the mass electorate suggests the need to keep in mind that hard-hitting controversy at the elite level about apparently earth-shaking issues may not be reflected in the concerns expressed by average citizens who are often more attentive to issues of more immediate relevance to their own social and economic situations.

While such factors as Korea, corruption, and the personal appeal of Eisenhower led to an impressive Republican victory in 1952, there were forces favorable to the Democratic Party, namely perceptions of the Democrats as the party of lower status groups, the party of prosperity, and the party associated with the popular domestic policies of the New Deal and Fair Deal. According to Stokes and his associates (1958: 372), these three favorable images carried over to the 1956 campaign, although Democratic advantages with respect to prosperity and domestic programs declined markedly as the country remained prosperous under a Republican administration that did not try to repeal the New Deal and Fair Deal. Thus, the 1956 Republican platform boasted

> In four years we have achieved the highest economic level with the

most widely shared benefits that the world has ever seen. We of the Republican Party have fostered this prosperity and are dedicated to its expansion and to the preservation of the climate in which it has thrived.

and promised to

Continue and further perfect its programs of assistance to the millions of workers with special employment problems, such as older workers, handicapped workers, members of minority groups, and migratory workers;

* * * * *

Extend the protection of the Federal minimum wage laws to as many more workers as is possible and practicable. . . . (Porter and Johnson, eds., 1970: 545, 549).

Eisenhower's 1952 promise not to repeal the social gains of the previous decades was evidently quite credible in 1956. This suggests how even fairly enduring images of the parties are affected by more short-term political and economic conditions.

There probably have been few campaign slogans that have better expressed the sentiment of the electorate than the 1952 and 1956 theme of "I like Ike." While citizens' comments about both candidates were positive by a margin of about 2 to 1 in 1952, in 1956 references to Eisenhower were favorable by almost $2\frac{1}{2}$ to 1 and comments about Stevenson were overall slightly negative (Stokes et al., 1958: 376). As Figure 5.7 indicates, the only pro-Eisenhower attitudinal component to increase in importance between 1952 and 1956 was attitudes toward Eisenhower himself. As the authors of *The American Voter* argue (p. 56), Eisenhower's appeal, "already strongly personal in 1952, became overwhelmingly so in 1956." While references to Eisenhower's military accomplishments were quite common in 1952, by 1956 these comments were fewer replaced by positive assessments of his personal qualities. Stokes and his coauthors state (1958: 378):

It was the response to personal qualities—to his sincerity, his integrity and sense of duty, his virtue as a family man, his religious devotion, and his sheer likeableness—which rose sharply in the second campaign. These frequencies leave the strong impression that Eisenhower was honored not so much for his performance as President as for the quality of his person. . . .

Stevenson suffered in 1956 from evaluations of his personal qualities and his experience. Evidently, his impressive record as Governor of Illinois had faded from the public's memory by the 1956 campaign.

Thus, the 1956 election is commonly described as one dominated by the personality of Eisenhower, with issue concerns playing a minimal role. Stanley Kelley (1960) analyzed the content of the 1956 campaign speeches and concluded that, with the exception of farm policy and the testing of the hydrogen bomb, the candidates did not take clearly distinctive stands. Kelly wrote (p. 52):

> Much of the time, both candidates described their policy positions in terms so general that their statements lacked any clear relation to issues on which voters had to make decisions. Both were for peace, social welfare, full justice for farmers, honest government, a strong national defense, the expansion of civil liberties, full employment, the development of individual talents, a vigorous economy, a flourishing world trade, and a large number of other objectives of similarly general appeal. They voiced their allegiance to these ideals again and again. Sometimes they did so in slightly different words, and sometimes one mentioned goals that were not mentioned by the other, but at no time did either candidate declare himself to be opposed to any statement of fundamental belief that his opponent had advanced.

Evidence that the voters themselves did not differentiate the parties clearly across a wide range of issues is presented in Table 5.1. While the results reported in the table are not fully satisfactory, since they do not include the salience of the issue to the citizen nor the citizen's own position on the issue, they nevertheless indicate that policy discrimination between the parties in 1956 was weak, in part because of the similar stances taken by the candidates and in part because many of the issues were not crucial ones about which citizens were aroused. On 13 of the 16 issues, more than two fifths of the citizens saw no difference between the parties. Neither party was systematically advantaged on the ten domestic issues, while Republicans enjoyed a consistent advantage on the six foreign policy issues, although on four of them, a majority of citizens saw no difference between the parties. While the foreign policy crises of Suez and Hungary, which erupted shortly before the 1956 election, may have worked to the advantage of the incumbent Republican administration, which was perceived as more competent in foreign affairs and better able to maintain peace, it

TABLE 5.1
Preferred Party on 16 Issues, 1956

Issue	Party Closer to Respondent on Issue			Total Percent	No. of Cases	Democratic Advantage
	Democrats	No Difference	Republicans			
Foreign Policy						
Act tough toward Russia and China	21	41	38	100	1,093	−17
U.S. International Involvement ("stay home")	20	46	35	100	1,104	−15
Friendliness toward other nations	17	51	32	100	1,227	−15
Economic aid to foreign countries	21	50	28	99	1,003	−7
Send soldiers abroad	10	58	32	100	1,044	−22
Give aid to neutral countries	18	55	27	100	854	−9
Domestic Policy						
Influence of big business in government	51	25	25	101	891	26
Influence of unions in government	27	34	39	100	889	−12
Government guarantee of jobs	33	43	24	100	1,031	9
Segregation of schools	28	47	25	100	1,114	3
Cutting taxes	29	40	32	101	979	−3
Racial equality in jobs and housing	23	51	26	100	1,005	−3
Aid to education	29	48	22	99	1,006	7
Insure medical care	31	46	23	100	847	8
Firing of suspected Communists	17	54	29	100	981	−12
Leave electricity and housing to private industry	29	38	33	100	814	−4

Source: 1956 SRC Election study. The percentages are based upon only those respondents who cited a preference for one of the parties or saw no difference between them. The Democratic advantage in the last column is simply the difference between the percentage of people favoring the Democrats on the issue and the percentage of people favoring the Republicans. A minus sign indicates a Republican advantage. Percentages that do not sum to 100 are due to rounding error.

nevertheless remains the case that personality and not policy concerns were the more important determinants of the 1956 election outcome.

In summary, using our terminology from Chapter 1, the 1952 and 1956 elections represent deviating elections in which the minority Republican Party was twice successful in electing its presidential candidate. Yet throughout the period, the Democrats maintained their hold on the electorate's partisan loyalties, as shown in Table 2.1, and kept control of the Congress for six of the eight Eisenhower years as many of the Democrats who defected to Ike returned to their party for other contests. The major short-term forces that resulted in the departures from the normal vote in 1952 and 1956 were the immense popularity of Eisenhower in both elections and the government mismanagement issue in 1952. Between 1948 and 1952, the Republicans improved their presidential vote performance in almost all population groups and maintained and even increased these gains in 1956, with the major exception of the farm vote. Eisenhower's popularity was a short-term force that affected most segments of the population similarly. As we turn to the 1960 election, we observe an outcome that more closely reflects the normal vote, but one influenced by a short-term force that differentially affected religious groups—the Catholicism of John Kennedy.

1960

The most striking feature of the six partisan attitudes in 1960—depicted in Figure 5.8—is their almost perfect balance: three favored the Democrats and three the Republicans, with the net impact of the six a toss-up. This closeness is, of course, reflected in the 1960 election outcome in which Kennedy defeated Nixon by the very slim margin of 112,000 votes out of about 69 million votes cast. Because of the photofinish in the 1960 election, observers are prone to cite any of a number of factors as critical to the election outcome. Thus, commentators speculate about who would have won the election had Eisenhower begun campaigning for the Republican ticket sooner, or had Nixon instead of Kennedy expressed symbolic opposition to the jailing of Martin Luther King, or had Nixon been in better physical shape for the first of the televised Great Debates. While any of a number of influences might have tipped the election either way and thus might be labeled decisive, there were a few factors that merit particular attention. The first is simply the attitudes toward the candidates. In retro-

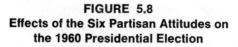

FIGURE 5.8
Effects of the Six Partisan Attitudes on the 1960 Presidential Election

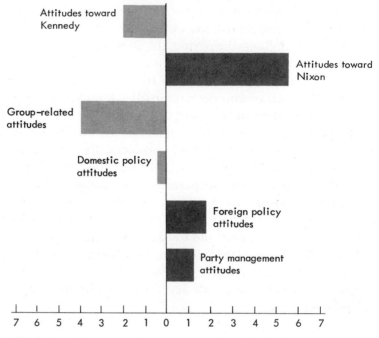

Percentage Democratic gain   Percentage Republican gain

Source: Constructed from figures presented by Michael Kagay and Greg Caldeira, "Public Policy Issues and the American Voter, 1952–1972," unpublished paper.

spect, it may surprise many readers that while attitudes toward both candidates were positive in 1960, it was Nixon who received the more favorable evaluations. A major factor influencing evaluations of Kennedy was his Catholicism, and it is the impact of the religious issue that is our first concern in discussing the 1960 election. Probably the most publicized feature of the 1960 campaign was the series of televised debates between the candidates; the effect of the Great Debates on the election outcome is our second major concern. Finally, we will detail some of the issue concerns of the 1960 electorate.

The Religious Issue in 1960. In 1928 the Democrats nominated as their presidential candidate Governor Al Smith of New York, a Catholic. Smith suffered an overwhelming defeat, losing many traditional Democratic states. His showing was cited as evidence that the American electorate was not ready for and would not accept a Catholic President. As Kennedy was contesting for the Democratic nomination in 1960, the impact of his religion became a central question, one which was presumably answered in the West Virginia primary where the Catholic Kennedy easily defeated the Protestant Hubert Humphrey in the overwhelmingly Protestant state. Unfortunately, the West Virignia primary did not end the religious issue; once Kennedy won the Democratic nomination, the religious issue arose again and again, often taking very ugly forms.

Most observers today agree, and the evidence seems quite convincing, that Kennedy's Catholicism hurt him substantially in the popular vote. Philip Converse et al. (1966: 92) estimated that throughout the nation the religious issue cost Kennedy about 2.2 percent of the popular vote, which translates into approximately $1\frac{1}{2}$ million votes. However, the effects of the religious issue were not uniform throughout the country; it is estimated that Kennedy's Catholicism cost him 16.5 percent of the two-party vote in the heavily Protestant South while it resulted in a 1.6 percent gain outside the South. Thus, one might plausibly speculate that while religion may have hurt Kennedy in the popular vote it did not hurt him and may actually have helped him in the Electoral College vote, which he won by the sizable margin of 303–219 despite his small popular vote margin.[2] For example, although Kennedy's Catholicism cost him many votes in the South, this area was so heavily Democratic that the reduced Democratic vote totals enabled the GOP to carry only three states—Florida, Tennessee, and Virginia. Outside the South, Kennedy scored narrow victories in many states with large numbers of electoral votes and large numbers of Catholic voters. For example, Kennedy carried Illinois and its 27 electoral votes by a margin of less than 9,000 votes, or approximately $\frac{2}{10}$ of 1 percent and New Jersey with 16 electoral votes by 22,000 votes or $\frac{8}{10}$ of 1 percent.

The assertion that religion was an issue in 1960 does not mean that the candidates or parties themselves took stands on the matter or made it a focal point of the campaign. To the contrary, Kennedy and Nixon exercised considerable restraint and care in trying to prevent religion from emerging as an ugly, divisive issue. Nevertheless, religion was an important concern, as evidenced in a number of ways. For example,

---

[2] This speculation is supported by the simulation work of Pool, Abelson, and Popkin who estimated that Kennedy's Catholicism gained him 22 electoral votes even as it was costing him about $1\frac{1}{2}$ million popular votes. See Pool, Abelson, and Popkin, 1965: 115–118.

Converse (1966: 112–113) reports that more than half of the Protestants interviewed in the 1960 Survey Research Center election study spontaneously introduced the Catholic question, mainly in a negative fashion, suggesting its salience to many citizens. Additional evidence attesting to the importance of religion is provided by an examination of the voting patterns of SRC respondents who voted in both 1956 and 1960; these figures are shown in Table 5.2. Note that 6 percent of

TABLE 5.2
The Voting Behavior of Citizens
Who Voted in Both 1956 and 1960
(in percentages)

1960 Vote / 1956 Vote	Stevenson	Eisenhower	Total
Kennedy	33	17	50
Nixon	6	44	50
Total	39	61	100

Source: Philip E. Converse et al., "Stability and Change in 1960: A Reinstating Election," in Angus Campbell et al., *Elections and the Political Order* (New York: John Wiley & Sons, Inc., 1966). Copyright © 1966, John Wiley & Sons, Inc. Reprinted by permission of the publisher.

the sample voted for Stevenson in 1956 and Nixon in 1960. One might ask which citizens could resist the popular appeal of Eisenhower in 1956, yet move to the GOP in 1960. The answer is Protestants; of the 6 percent who exhibited this vote pattern, 90 percent were Protestants and 8 percent Catholics. Likewise, among the 17 percent who moved from Eisenhower to Kennedy, about 60 percent were Catholic and 40 percent were Protestant (Converse et al., 1966: 84). This is certainly indirect evidence of the impact of religion on candidate choice.

More direct evidence is given by an analysis of the normal Democratic vote expected from Protestants and Catholics. While the normal Democratic vote among Catholics in 1960 was 63 percent, their actual Democratic vote was 80 percent. And the actual Democratic vote among white Protestants was about the same margin below normal. Finally, if we examine the voting behavior of Protestant Democrats and Protestant Independents of various degrees of religiosity, we observe that the greater the religiosity, the more marked are the departures from the expected Democratic vote. For example, Converse et al. (1966: 89) report that Protestant Independents who did not attend church split their vote almost 50–50 between Kennedy and Nixon as expected. Among seldom church attenders, Nixon received 61 percent of the vote; among often church goers, Nixon got 72 percent of the vote; and among regular church attenders, he received 83 percent of the vote.

Religion was an unusual issue in two respects—it had a substantial impact on vote choices and its impact did not depend upon skilled exploitation of the matter by candidates. Religion was one of those few salient concerns capable of arousing many citizens even as the candidates themselves tried to ignore the matter. The novelist James Michener wrote of his experiences as Democratic county chairman in Bucks County, Pennsylvania, in 1960 and gave some vivid illustrations of the grass-roots passions that religion could arouse. Numerous anti-Catholic pamphlets were circulated, some of which Michener described as follows (1961: 91–92):

> One of the most impressive carried a cover showing a fat and apparently venal bishop on his throne, with "The Rest of Us" kneeling abjectly and kissing his foot.

*   *   *   *   *

> One of the pamphlets . . . showed a trio of priests supervising the following tortures of Protestants: one victim was being crucified upside down; another was being hauled aloft by his hands twisted behind his back while weights were applied to his feet; a third was stretched prone while water was being forced into him. . . .

Michener reported the following experience that graphically illustrates the kinds of emotions and fears religion was capable of releasing (p. 293):

> In the bars in my district broken-hearted Republicans were saying, "In this election the decent people of American were swamped by the scum. It's really terrifying to contemplate the kind of people who are going to govern this nation." One man garnered a lot of laughs each Saturday by announcing, "Tomorrow attend the church of your choice . . . while you still have a choice."

At the national level, the renowned Reverend Norman Vincent Peale misguidedly lent his presence to a conference devoted to such matters as the fitness of a Catholic to be President, thereby giving respectability to much of the anti-Catholic activity. This event and the obvious snowballing of religious propaganda led Kennedy to speak before the Greater Houston Ministerial Association on September 12 to discuss his view of the Presidency and the relevance of his Catholicism. He said (White, 1961: 468):

> But because I am a Catholic, and no Catholic has ever been elected President, the real issues in this campaign have been obscured—perhaps deliberately in some quarters less responsible than this. So it is apparently necessary for me to state once again—not what kind of church I believe in, for that should be important only to me, but what kind of America I believe in.
>
> I believe in an America where the separation of church and state is absolute—where no Catholic prelate would tell the President (should he be a Catholic) how to act and no Protestant minister would tell his parishioners for whom to vote—where no church or church school is granted any public funds or political preference—and where no man is denied public office merely because his religion differs from the President who might appoint him or the people who might elect him.

While Kennedy's speech was received favorably from a previously skeptical if not hostile audience, it did not lead to the elimination of religious influences on citizens' candidate preferences. As we will see in the next section, a substantial proportion of the negative references to Kennedy center on his religion. But as shown in Figure 5.8, the overall response to both candidates was positive. Thus we will now discuss the images of the two candidates held by the electorate.

The Evaluations of Kennedy and Nixon. Tables 5.3 and 5.4 show the favorable and unfavorable comments made about Kennedy and Nixon. While the total number of positive references made about each candidate does not differ substantially, there are some noteworthy differences in the types of positive comments offered about each. About 10 percent more citizens said that Nixon was generally a good man and cited his political or other experience. Nixon received his greatest advantage in the area of foreign policy, where 17 percent more citizens made positive comments about him compared to Kennedy. Even among Democrats, a higher proportion viewed Nixon more favorably than Kennedy in the realm of foreign affairs. Kennedy's strongest characteristic vis à vis Nixon was his education and informedness; 8 percent more citizens offered this comment about Kennedy. These frequent references to Kennedy's being informed may be a consequence of the Great Debates, which established that Kennedy was not the uninformed, inexperienced, ill-equipped candidate that many viewers were expecting to see.

Among groups of party loyalists, we observe patterns of candidate evaluations that illustrate the importance of party identification as a perceptual screen through which the elements of politics are evaluated; Democrats are obviously more favorable to Kennedy and Republicans to Nixon. With respect to the more frequently mentioned characteristics (with the exception of education), positive assessments of Nixon by Democrats are more common than favorable evaluations of Kennedy by Republicans. On religion, Cathloics are more positive toward Kennedy and Protestants toward Nixon; of course, this pattern is closely related to the partisan differences since Catholics tend to be Democrats and Protestants Republicans. The only frequent favorable religious comment about the candidates was made by Catholics, 11.3 percent of whom said they liked Kennedy because of his religion.

It is when one turns to the unfavorable comments about the candidates that the importance of religion in evaluations of the candidates shows up most clearly. For example, among Protestants, the most frequent negative comments about Kennedy dealt with his Catholicism and the likelihood that the Catholic church would control him; fully one third of Protestants made such references, indicating the tremendous salience of religion to many citizens. Overall, more than one fourth of the respondents offered a negative comment about Kennedy's Catholicism; the next most frequent criticism, expressed by about 9 percent of the citizens, asserted that Kennedy was not a good man, that he was not qualified. There was also some feeling that Kennedy was too young and too rich.

An examination of the negative comments about Nixon reveals few directed to his qualifications and abilities and his personal qualities. Despite the nicknames, such as "Tricky Dick," given Nixon by political foes and the joking of critics who asked "whether one would buy a used car from him," only 4 percent of the electorate said that Nixon lacked integrity and 4 percent said that he was not likeable. In fact, the preponderance of unfavorable references to Nixon touched upon such matters as group attachments, issues, and party, with the most frequent criticism of Nixon being "He's a Republican." Thus, Richard Nixon was widely seen as a competent and personable individual, more so than Kennedy. Yet except for the matter of religion, the reactions to both candidates were clearly favorable.

The Issues in 1960. As shown in Tables 5.3 and 5.4, the number of issue-related comments about the candidates was quite low, thereby reemphasizing the results of Figure 5.8 which indicate that domestic and foreign policy issue concerns exercised relatively little influence

TABLE 5.3
The Favorable References to Kennedy and Nixon*
(in percentages)

Reference	Kennedy					Nixon				
	All	Dem.	Rep.	Prot.	Cath.	All	Dem.	Rep.	Prot.	Cath.
Generally a good man, capable, experienced	14	20	8	12	23	26	15	44	30	19
Record and Experience										
War or military experience	1	1	0	0	1	0	0	0	0	0
Political or other experience	6	8	6	5	10	16	11	24	18	9
Qualifications and Abilities										
Good leader, knows how to handle people	2	2	1	12	3	1	0	2	10	0
Good administrator	0	0	1	1	0	0	0	1	0	0
Strong, decisive, confident	6	9	3	4	14	2	1	5	3	2
Independent, own boss	1	1	0	0	2	1	0	1	1	0
Educated, well informed	18	23	13	15	28	9	6	16	10	8
Good speaker	3	3	4	3	4	1	1	2	1	1
Other	2	3	1	1	4	2	7	4	3	0
Personal Qualities										
Integrity, ideals	7	9	5	5	12	4	2	9	5	3
Sense of duty, patriotism	3	4	1	2	5	1	1	2	2	0

Religious	0	0	0	0	0	0	0	0	0	0
Church won't dictate to him	1	1	0	1	1	0	0	0	0	0
Catholic/Protestant, not a Catholic	4	5	3	2	11	4	4	3	6	0
From good family, good family life	1	2	1	1	2	1	0	3	2	1
Hard-working, full-time President	1	2	2	1	1	1	1	1	1	1
Likeable, nice personality	7	8	8	7	9	5	4	6	5	4
Kind, warm	0	1	0	1	1	0	0	1	0	0
Sincere	5	6	3	5	6	3	1	8	3	3
Age	8	11	4	7	14	2	3	3	3	3
Self-made man	0	0	0	0	0	3	2	6	4	2
Other	3	4	2	2	6	4	4	6	4	4
Issues and Policies										
Domestic policies	10	13	3	8	11	6	3	12	7	5
Foreign policies	4	6	1	3	11	22	10	39	25	13
General references	4	6	0	3	7	4	3	8	5	5
Association with groups (old people, farmers, blacks, common people, etc.)	8	13	1	6	14	3	1	5	4	1
Party References										
He's a Democrat/Republican	11	22	0	10	11	4	1	13	5	2
Other party references	6	8	2	4	7	10	6	18	11	8
Miscellaneous comments	6	7	3	4	12	4	2	8	5	2

* The table entries are the percentage of each group making the specific reference.
Source: SRC 1960 election study.

TABLE 5.4
The Unfavorable References to Kennedy and Nixon*
(in percentages)

Reference	Kennedy					Nixon				
	All	Dem.	Rep.	Prot.	Cath.	All	Dem.	Rep.	Prot.	Cath.
Not a good man, not qualified	9	4	16	10	4	2	3	2	2	3
Unsatisfactory experience	3	2	6	3	2	2	3	0	1	3
Qualifications and Abilities										
Not a leader, can't handle people	0	0	0	0	0	1	1	0	1	1
Poor administrator	0	0	1	1	0	0	0	2	0	0
Weak, indecisive	1	0	1	1	0	2	3	2	1	6
Not independent, not own boss	1	0	2	1	0	1	2	1	1	4
Poorly informed, stupid	2	2	4	2	2	1	2	0	1	2
Poor speaker	1	0	2	1	1	1	1	0	1	0
Other	0	0	1	0	0	0	0	0	0	0
Personal Qualities										
Lacks integrity	3	2	5	3	3	4	6	1	3	5
Unpatriotic	0	0	1	0	0	0	0	0	0	0
Catholic church would control him	6	5	7	8	0	0	0	0	0	0
He's a Catholic/Quaker	20	18	25	25	2	0	0	0	0	0
Dislikes family	1	1	2	1	1	0	0	0	0	0

Would be part-time President	0	0	0	0	0	0	0	0	0	0
Not likeable, unpopular	2	1	4	2	1	4	5	2	3	4
Cold, aloof	0	0	0	1	0	1	1	0	1	1
Insincere	0	0	0	1	0	1	1	0	0	1
Too young	6	4	10	7	3	0	0	2	0	0
Too rich	5	3	9	6	3	0	0	0	0	0
Doesn't think before he talks	2	1	4	3	1	1	1	0	1	0
Other	3	2	7	4	1	2	3	2	0	3
Issues and Policies										
Domestic policies	7	5	12	8	4	5	7	3	5	6
Foreign policies	5	2	7	5	4	6	9	2	5	8
General references	1	0	4	2	1	2	4	0	2	4
Unfavorable group references	2	1	3	2	1	5	9	0	4	8
Party References										
He's a Democrat/Republican	2	0	7	3	1	9	18	0	9	9
Other party references	8	4	15	8	6	6	9	2	4	15
Miscellaneous comments	5	5	7	6	2	8	5	1	7	10

* The table entries are the percentage of each group making the specific reference.
Source: SRC 1960 election study.

on the election outcome. In fact, there was no consensus in 1960 as to which specifically were the crucial issues. The five issues most frequently mentioned as the most important problem in 1960 are listed in Table 5.5, together with the party perceived as preferable on the issue and the proportion of respondents mentioning the problem.

Note first that no issue is mentioned by as many as 10 percent of the respondents. Even though four of the five problems mentioned deal directly or indirectly with foreign affairs and national defense, their cumulative total barely represents one fifth of the electorate. This contrasts sharply with the 1968 and 1972 elections where 43 and 25 percent of the citizens asserted that Vietnam was the most important national problem. Further observe that where foreign affairs is mentioned in 1960, it is cited in very general terms; there was no single, well-defined issue on which opinions had crystallized Thus, while overall more than half of the citizens cited some foreign policy related matter as most important in 1960, the election did not turn on such concerns to any great degree. This is not surprising, given the various appeals made by the candidates. For example, on the question of which party could better deal with Khrushchev and the Soviet Union, the Republicans would point to Nixon's famous kitchen debate with the Soviet leader, while the Democrats would charge that the GOP had allowed our military capability and economic growth to falter, thereby making it more difficult for the United States to meet the Soviet challenge. Both candidates did their best to demonstrate that they would be firmer in dealing with the Communist bloc. The Democrats even charged the Eisenhower administration with allowing a "missile gap" to develop that threatened American security; after Kennedy became President, the missile gap mysteriously and quickly vanished.

Overall, one must conclude that matters of genuine public policy (as opposed to the religious issue) had little impact on the vote division in 1960. The strongest pro-Democratic force indicated in Figure 5.8 was group-related attitudes and Kennedy on the campaign trail emphasized his ties to the Democrat Party and the Democrats as the party of the common man. It was not unusual for Kennedy to include in his speeches such statements as (Weisbord, 1966: 411–412):

> Mr. Nixon and I represent two wholly different parties, with wholly different records of the past, and wholly different views of the future. We disagree, and our parties disagree, on where we stand today and where we will stand tomorrow. . . . Mr. Nixon and the Republicans stand for the past. We stand for the future. Mr. Nixon

TABLE 5.5

The Five Problems Most Frequently Cited as Most Important in 1960

Problem	Party Preferred on Most Important Problem			Total Percent	No. of Cases	Percentage of Electorate Mentioning Problem
	Democrats	No Difference	Republicans			
Foreign affairs/keeping peace	18	33	49	100	125	8.4
Unemployment	72	24	4	100	102	6.8
Foreign affairs/no mention of peace	38	18	44	100	94	6.3
Keeping a position of strength	20	18	62	100	60	4.0
Negotiate with Russia	33	21	46	100	52	3.5

Source: SRC 1960 election study. The table presents those five problems most frequently mentioned as the most important problem facing the nation. The percentages in the last column of the table are based upon all respondents who cited the problem, regardless of whether they could answer the question about the most preferred party.

represents the Republican Party which has put up in recent years Mr. Dewey, Mr. Landon, Mr. Coolidge, Mr. Harding, Mr. Taft, Mr. McKinley. I represent the party which has run Woodrow Wilson and Franklin Roosevelt and Harry Truman and Adlai Stevenson.

Kennedy in general emphasized a mood, a need to sacrifice, a need to get the country moving again. As the candidate of the out party, he had greater leeway in going on the attack and challenging the GOP record of the previous eight years. As the Republican heir, Nixon defended the record of the Eisenhower administration at the same time that he promised to build upon it. Despite their efforts to exploit the differences that existed between them, the candidates (particularly Nixon in the first debate) often wound up in agreement on goals and therefore stressed differences in the means to be used to achieve those goals. Evidently, these latter differences were not very salient to the electorate, and in many eyes the two candidates were Tweedle-dee and Tweedle-dum. Thus, the election outcome basically reflected the impact of partisanship as modified by the religious issue. This resulted in a Democratic vote somewhat less than normal, but a Democratic victory nonetheless. Hence, we label the 1960 election as maintaining, one in which the party with the majority allegiance in the electorate captured the White House.

The Great Debates. The Great Debates probably represent the high point in the use of television to bring the campaign to the electorate. The debates today have become almost mythologized as the factor that led to Kennedy's victory; Kennedy himself is reported as saying that "It was TV more than anything else that turned the tide" (White, 1961: 353). Yet most of the research available indicates that the debates had little impact on vote choice, although little impact may have been sufficient to swing an election as close as 1960.

On the debates, Kennedy and Nixon confronted one another, usually from the same studio, responding to questions from reporters and commenting on each other's answers. This format reduced the opportunity for citizens to be highly selective in their attentiveness to the candidates; it took great effort to tune in one's preferred candidate and tune out the other. There were four debates, each devoted to various topics. The occurrence of the debates was facilitated by Congress, which waived Section 315 of the Federal Communication Act—the equal time provision; this action allowed the networks to give free time to the major party candidates without having to grant such time to the numerous minor party contenders. Between 1964 and 1972, there were no such debates because of political and strategic reasons. In 1964, Johnson as the incumbent President heavily favored to win the election was loath to risk his future in debates; thus, the Democrats in Congress obligingly failed to suspend the equal time provision. In 1968, Nixon, perhaps remembering his 1960 experience and not wishing to risk his preelection advantage, refused to debate and instead relied upon a more controlled use of television (described in Chapter 9). A similar situation held in 1972 as in 1964, in which a heavily favored incumbent did not want to chance televised debates and even disdained extensive formal campaigning, claiming that affairs of state had to take precedence. In 1976, debates were held as the unelected incumbent challenged his opponent to debate. Ford did this in part because the polls showed him trailing badly; hence, he risked little by participating in debates. The 1976 debates were sponsored by the League of Women Voters and hence were treated by the television networks as a news event to be covered, rather than as a network-generated program. This was a subterfuge designed to exclude minor party participation in the debates.

An examination of the Gallup Poll results just before and after the first 1960 debate indicate little net change in vote preferences. Just before the first debate, Gallup reported that Nixon was favored over Kennedy by a margin of 47 to 46 percent, with 7 percent undecided. After the first debate, Gallup found Kennedy favored by a margin of 49 to 46 percent, with 5 percent undecided (Katz and Feldman, 1962: 211). Thus, one might be tempted to conclude that Kennedy gained 3 percentage points because of his first debate performance, but such a conclusion is risky since the observed changes could easily be accounted for by sampling error as well as by other political factors. The studies of the debates generally indicate that Kennedy "won," particularly the first debate, not because he won over many former Nixon partisans, but because he established himself as a credible, competent candidate to many citizens, including Democrats, who worried about his youth and supposed inexperience. Theodore White (1961: 349) reports that after the first debate, Kennedy's crowds, already growing in size, became much larger and far more enthusiastic "as if the sight of him, in their home or on the video box, had given him a 'star quality' reserved only for heros and movie idols." At the local level, Michener (1961: 127–28) reports that immediately after the first debate money and volunteers began streaming into campaign headquarters. Thus, one important effect of the debate may have been to rally the faithful, to increase the enthusiasm of Democrats toward the Democratic ticket.

Katz and Feldman (1962) reviewed numerous studies of the effects of the Great Debates and concluded that the first debate was won by Kennedy, the third by Nixon, and the second and fourth even. They found that partisans tended to claim that their candidate had won the debate, although Republicans were more likely to say that Kennedy had won than Democrats were to say Nixon. The most ambitious research on the debates reviewed by Katz and Feldman was the four-wave panel investigation of the nation conducted by the Opinion Research Center. These surveys found that the primary effect of the debates, especially the first, was to strengthen the commitment of partisans to their own party and its candidates. This was especially true of Democrats who had been less enthusiastic and convinced about Kennedy earlier in the campaign. Table 5.6 presents the results of the ORC surveys.

Note that only after the first debate was there a sizable advantage for either candidate. Also observe that nonviewers of the debates tended to be *less* stable in their evaluations than viewers. Katz and Feldman wrote (1962: 209):

> This is not as surprising as it sounds considering the fact that the non-viewers were far less interested in the election and far less committed to a candidate than the viewers. Previous election studies have shown that these are the people who are most open to influence, who are least likely to vote, and whose responses, in any case, are of dubious reliability.

The relationship between stability of vote intention and viewing of the debates is made more complex by the research of Converse (1970), who found that voters who missed *all four* debates exhibited the highest stability in vote intentions over the course of the campaign. While this finding may appear to contradict the ORC studies, the two can be reconciled by noting that Converse is talking about citizens who missed all four debates, while the ORC surveys are referring to citizens who happened to miss the particular debate in question. Converse has likely isolated those citizens who were the least interested in politics and received little if any political communications through the media or personal contact. Since such citizens receive little or no political cues or information, there is no impetus toward attitude change, resulting in high stability of vote intentions. Individuals who missed one debate (but not all) may not be highly interested in politics but do receive political communications that may lead to attitude change, especially

TABLE 5.6
The Great Debates and the Stability of Attitudes toward the Candidates, by Viewer and Nonviewer
(in percentages)

	First Debate		Second Debate		Third Debate		Fourth Debate	
	Viewers	Nonviewers	Viewers	Nonviewers	Viewers	Nonviewers	Viewers	Nonviewers
Unchanged	58	52	65	66	73	69	70	67
Change to Kennedy	25	25	17	17	14	15	16	16
Change to Nixon	17	23	18	17	13	16	14	17
Net gain for Kennedy	+8	+2	−1	0	+1	−1	+2	−1

Source: Elihu Katz and Jacob J. Feldman, "The Debates of the Light of Research: A Survey of Surveys," table 11–7, p. 210. From *The Great Debates*, edited by Sidney Kraus. Copyright © 1962 by Indiana University Press, Bloomington. Reprinted by permission of the publisher. The table entries represent the percentage of viewers and nonviewers whose attitudes toward the candidates changed or remained stable as measured along a nine-point scale.

given their weaker initial predispositions. The point is that the relationship between the amount of political cues received and the stability of attitudes may be more complex than anticipated.[3]

In summary, most of the empirical research on the Great Debates argues that they changed few votes. Yet as Katz and Feldman (pp. 211–13) point out, if you ask people whether the debates helped them make their candidate choice, they readily say yes. It is likely that most of this "help" is in the reinforcement of existing predispositions, and this may have been just what Kennedy needed to convince a sufficient number of Democrats that he was indeed a serious, legitimate candidate for the Presidency. Perhaps, then, Kennedy was correct in his assertion that he could not have won without television.

CONCLUSION

While the GOP won two of the three presidential elections between 1952 and 1960, there was little interpretation of the results as indicating that a pro-Republican realignment was imminent. The two Eisenhower victories were viewed primarily as tributes to a very popular individual, and the Democratic recapture of the White House in 1960 was largely seen as a return to the traditional pattern of Democratic domination of presidential politics. From the perspective of 1960, the Democratic New Deal coalition seemed very much alive.

---

[3] Research by Edward Dreyer (1971–72) fails to confirm Converse's more general notion that the relationship between media exposure and attitude stability is curvilinear, with the highest levels of stability observed among the lowest media users and high media users.

6

Issues and Candidates, 1964–1972

INTRODUCTION

While the Republicans won two of the three presidential elections between 1964 and 1972 just as they had won two or three between 1952 and 1960, the similarity ends there. The 1964–72 era concluded with speculation rampant about the emergence of the GOP as the majority party. The elections in this period exhibited tremendous volatility, with the Democrats scoring a massive landslide in 1964 and the GOP an equally impressive presidential victory in 1972. The era itself witnessed the emergence of the civil rights revolution and the war in Vietnam as major questions of public policy, and the controversy surrounding these issues added great drama to electoral politics.

1964

The landslide victory won by the Democrats in 1964 is readily understandable, given the effects of the six attitudinal components depicted in Figure 6.1. The Democrats were preferred on all six

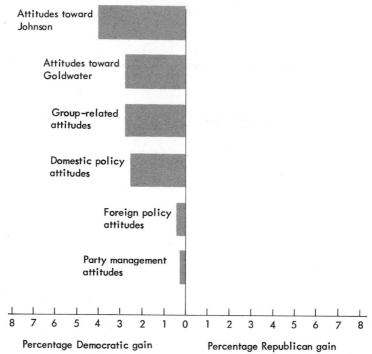

FIGURE 6.1
Effects of the Six Partisan Attitudes on
the 1964 Presidential Election

Percentage Democratic gain   Percentage Republican gain

Source: Constructed from figures presented by Michael Kagay and Greg Caldeira, "Public Policy Issues and the American Voters, 1952–1972," unpublished paper.

components, including such traditional Republican strengths as foreign affairs and government management. To run against the popular incumbent President who had reassured the nation with his steady performance after the assassination of President Kennedy, the Republicans chose Senator Barry Goldwater after a hotly contested, relatively inconclusive series of primary battles that split the GOP along ideological grounds. With the massive Republican defection from the Goldwater candidacy, it is no wonder that Lyndon Johnson won in a landslide.

What is surprising about the 1964 election is the uncertainty in classifying it as either a maintaining or converting or realigning election. On the one hand, the majority Democratic Party was victorious, and thus the election might be termed maintaining. On the other hand, the 1964 vote patterns differed dramatically from the results of the three previous presidential contests, raising the possibility that significant shifts in partisan allegiances were occurring. Thus, our analysis of the 1964 election will focus on the candidates and issues and the various interpretations of the election outcome.

The Candidates and Issues

Any discussion of the candidates and issues in 1964 must link the two since Goldwater himself gave special meaning to many of the issue positions he espoused. The election outcome might be summarized by two campaign themes associated with Goldwater. The first was his promise to offer "a choice, not an echo." That is, Goldwater sought to stress his differences with the incumbent Democratic administration (as well as with previous GOP "me-too" candidates) on matters of general philosophy of government and specific issues. With respect to the former, Goldwater warned against the encroachment of government and the concomitant loss of freedom. Thus, he proposed to roll back the trend toward government intervention in the society, and in offering specific suggestions uttered some careless comments about such possibilities as making social security voluntary and selling the Tennessee Valley Authority to private interests. Hence, Goldwater, like previous Republican candidates, railed against the growth of the federal government, but, unlike his precursors, he gave the impression that if he were elected many of the social programs of the New Deal and the Fair Deal would be repealed. These positions, together with some careless statements about the use of nuclear weaponry led many to revise the Goldwater slogan "In your heart you know he's right" to "In your heart you know he's right—far right." Goldwater was perceived as a reactionary by some and by others as a radical who would fundamentally alter the existing political and social arrangements between the people and the government. Undoubtedly, many of his issue positions, if they had been stated more carefully by another candidate, would not have been as frightening to so many voters.

Goldwater's difficulties did not begin with the general election campaign, but in fact were a legacy of the Republican primaries and the GOP National Convention. The Republican primaries in 1964 were indecisive, with no contender having a consistently strong track record. In the first primary (New Hampshire), a write-in candidate, Henry Cabot Lodge, defeated both Goldwater and Rockefeller, the two major contenders who represented the conservative and liberal wings of the GOP. In the last two primaries before the nominating convention, Rockefeller carried Oregon while Goldwater narrowly defeated Rockefeller in the climactic California primary. But despite Goldwater's less than impressive showing in the primaries, he and his supporters were in a dominant position at the convention, in part because of superior groundwork and organization in the nonprimary states, which resulted in solid blocs of delegates for Goldwater, especially from the South. With Goldwater's nomination all but assured, the battle turned to the GOP platform, a highly conservative document that moderate and liberal Republicans wanted to modify. They proposed compromise planks on three key issues: a stronger, pro-civil rights plank (Goldwater had voted against the 1964 Civil Rights Act); a condemnation of extremist groups, such as the Ku Klux Klan, the Communist party, and the John Birch Society (the leader of which had called President Eisenhower a Communist dupe); and a statement that the President and not military field commanders should control the use of nuclear weapons (Goldwater had talked of giving field commanders discretion in the use of tactical or conventional nuclear weapons).

The moderates lost on all three issues, Goldwater won the nomination, and the stage was set for his acceptance speech, usually a statement that among other things is designed to bind up the wounds of a divisive nomination battle. Goldwater, however, did not mollify the moderates and instead exacerbated the split with his now famous lines (Weisbord, 1966: 421):

> Anyone who joins us in all sincerity we welcome. Those, those who do not care for our cause, we don't expect to enter our ranks in any case. And let our Republicanism so focused and so dedicated not be made fuzzy and futile by unthinking and stupid labels.
>
> I would remind you that extremism in the defense of liberty is no vice!
>
> And let me remind you also that moderation in the pursuit of justice is no virtue!

In the context of the convention, this was a direct slap at the Republican moderates and liberals, mostly from the Northeast, who in large part sat out the presidential campaign.

Thus, the Republicans entered the general election campaign highly split, and these divisions were never healed despite later attempts under the auspices of General Eisenhower. This, in conjunction with the fact that fewer than "20 percent of all Republicans recalled having preferred Goldwater at the time of the convention" (Converse et al., 1965: 325), resulted in huge Republican defections from the Goldwater candidacy (see Figure 3.10)—obviously the kiss of death for a party that was already in the minority. The agony experienced by many Republicans in making their vote decision is illustrated in the following comments (Kessel, 1968: 266):

(Like about Democrats?) The Democratic party is more for human rights, I believe. (Anything else?) No.

(Dislike about Democrats?) Yes, their foreign policy. The Vietnam situation for one thing. They take more rights away from the individual person, but give more rights to all people. One morality. I guess that is right.

(Like about Republicans?) I believe in less central government. Things like medicare. All this welfare. I think people should help themselves more. The Republicans believe that also. They believe in more states' rights.

(Dislike about Republicans?) As far as the Republican platform itself, there was nothing I did like. (Anything at all?) No.

(Like about Johnson?) I think his role in civil rights in general, especially since he is a Southern man. The feeling he gives you. He has a warm feeling for people, and you feel he is a fair man.

(Dislike about Johnson?) I don't know anything about his personal life. If some things could be hidden like the Bobby Baker case. (Anything else?) Not against him personally, but since I am a registered Republican I wanted to vote that way. Now I really don't know.

(Like about Goldwater?) Yes, he would do a better job in handling foreign policy. His concern for communism in this country. (Anything else?) No.

(Dislike about Goldwater?) He is too impulsive. His stand on civil rights. He would not do a good job in enforcing the civil rights bill and that would lead to more trouble. He seems to be a cold hard man.

What further hurt Goldwater was that many of the disgruntled Republicans did have some place else to go—to Lyndon Johnson. Unlike 1960 when Kennedy stressed that he was the nominee of the Democratic Party, Johnson in 1964 submerged partisanship to some extent as he tried to win over Independents and Republicans to fashion an overwhelming victory. It was not uncommon for Johnson to make such statements as (Kelley, 1966: 59):

I am proud that I have always been the kind of Democrat who could work with my fellow Americans of the party of Lincoln and McKinley, Herbert Hoover and Dwight Eisenhower, Robert Taft and Everett Dirksen.

Moreover, the Democratic platform, written after the GOP fracas, included the following planks designed to have widespread appeal to dissatisfied Republicans and worried Independents (Porter and Johnson, 1970: 642, 644–45, 649):

Control of the use of nuclear weapons must remain solely with the highest elected official in the country—the President of the United States.

*　*　*　*　*

The Civil Rights Act of 1964 deserves and requires full observance by every American and fair, effective enforcement if there is any default.

Resting upon a national consensus expressed by the overwhelming support of both parties, this new law impairs the rights of no Americans; it affirm the rights of all Americans.

We condemn extremism, whether from the Right or Left, including the extreme tactics of such organizations as the Communist Party, the Ku Klux Klan and the John Birch Society.

A detailing of the images of the candidates as ascertained in the SRC 1964 election study reveals that the controversies surrounding Goldwater were widely visible to the mass public. Angust Campbell (1966: 259–60) reported that overall the negative comments about Goldwater outnumbered the positive by a margin of two to one, while for Johnson the pattern was just the reverse. Summarizing citizens' perceptions of the candidates, Campbell wrote (1966: 260, 263):

. . . while Mr. Johnson's personal attributes did not stir unusual favor among the electorate, he profited greatly from his long experience and record as a public official. He also drew favorable comment because of his association with the Democratic party and with the Kennedy administration. He was criticized as a "politician," "lacking in integrity," and associated with "immorality in government," these criticisms coming very heavily from the Republican partisans. . . . Mr. Johnson's stands on issues . . . were more frequently referred to than those of either candidate in 1960 and they were more commonly seen favorably than unfavorably.

. . . Mr. Goldwater was much more commonly spoken of unfavorably than favorably. While he was more often referred to as a man of integrity than Mr. Johnson, and less commonly as a "politician," in most other respects he suffered from the comparison. He was especially weak in the public assessment of his past record and experience. . . . His policy positions . . . drew an exceptional number of comments, most of them unfavorable.

Some of the more specific comments shed further light on the candidates' images. For example, 192 respondents said that Goldwater was impulsive, that he didn't think before he talked; only 1 person made this comment about Johnson. Similarly, 107 citizens thought that Goldwater was a fanatic or unstable; 1 individual thought the same of Johnson. With respect to the issue of social security, 177 people said they disliked Goldwater's stand; only 5 disliked Johnson's. More than 200 citizens said that Goldwater was too militaristic; 2 citizens offered that comment about Johnson (Campbell, 1966, 261–62). The issue of civil rights strongly influenced citizens' likes and dislikes about the candidates as shown in Table 6.1.

TABLE 6.1
The Frequency of Civil Rights Comments
as Related to Likes and Dislikes of Johnson and Goldwater

	Reason	
	Because He Is Pro Civil Rights	Because He Is Anti-Civil Rights
Like		
Johnson	101	1
Goldwater	3	55
Dislike		
Johnson	72	18
Goldwater	6	81

Source: Constructed from data presented by Angus Campbell, "Interpreting the Presidential Victory," tables 8.2 and 8.3, pp. 261–62, in *The National Election of 1964*, Milton C. Cummings, Jr., ed. Copyright 1966 by The Brookings Institution, Washington, D.C.

Note that there were few cases of misperception, that is, people liking Johnson because he was against civil rights or people disliking Goldwater because he was pro-civil rights. Civil rights was obviously a salient issue to many citizens, especially in the South, and moved both Republicans and Democrats to desert their party's nominee. For example, about one fourth of the strong and weak Democrats in the South who thought the civil rights movement was being pushed too fast voted for Goldwater; these defections constituted almost a fifth of all Southern Democrats (Campbell, 1966: 272–73). This is not to say that civil rights was the only issue affecting the South; Converse, Clausen, and Miller assert (1965: 330):

> Beyond civil rights, Southerners reacted negatively to the Goldwater positions much as their fellow citizens elsewhere. Many Southern white respondents said in effect: "Goldwater is right on the black man, and that is very important. But he is so wrong on everything else I can't bring myself to vote for him." From this point of view, the civil rights issue did indeed have a powerful impact in the South; without it, the 1964 Goldwater vote probably would not only have slipped to normal Republican levels, but would have veered as elsewhere to the pro-Democratic side. The more general ideological appeal to what Goldwater saw as Southern "conservatism" aside from the Negro question did not have major impact.

Even more dramatic than the movement of many white southerners to the Republicans was the almost unanimous support given Johnson by black citizens. While Goldwater certainly did not seek racist support, his vote against the Civil Rights Act attracted many unreconstructed segregationists to his cause and repelled most black voters. There was substantial concern among Democrats about the potential problem of backlash—the negative reactions of white citizens to the social and economic gains made by blacks—and how it might affect the ticket's chances in November. Evidence for the existence of backlash had been provided by the strong showings made by Alabama Governor George Wallace who entered three northern Democratic primaries—Wisconsin, Indiana, and Maryland—where he won 34, 30, and 43 percent of the vote. Wallace ran well in traditionally Democratic, white working-class neighborhoods, which raised the possibility that Goldwater might be able to fashion a majority by appealing to the South and West as well as to disgruntled urban workers—a coalition very similar in composition to that envisaged by Democratic candidate William Jennings Bryan in 1896. The outbreak of riots in major urban areas added further fuel to the potentiality of backlash. But backlash never developed to any great extent because of the unwillingness of Goldwater to exploit an overtly racial issue, the lessening of urban disorders as the presidential campaign began in earnest, and the cessation of black civil rights activities (partially under White House pressure) so as not to threaten the election of Johnson. Shortly after the Republican convention, Wallace decided not to run for President as a third-party candidate, leaving the field to Goldwater and Johnson.

In summary, there was little working for the Republicans in 1964, with the major exception of the race issue in the South, particularly the Deep South. Johnson and the Democrats, and it must be added, Goldwater himself, were successful in portraying Goldwater as outside the mainstream of American politics. Even when it appeared that a personal scandal involving a top-ranking Johnson aide might hurt the Democrats, two major international events occurred—the resignation of Khrushchev and the explosion of an atomic bomb by China—which served to turn the nation's attention away from thoughts of impropriety to the importance of firm, but unimpulsive leadership in a dangerous nuclear age. The conservative majority was not to be in 1964.

Interpreting the 1964 Election

Classifying the 1964 election is not as straightforward as one might think. One might argue that since the majority party won the election, it is by definition a maintaining election. But the actual vote patterns in 1964 differed substantially from previous elections that are classified as maintaining (1948 and 1960) and deviating (1952 and 1956). Of particular importance is the fact that the GOP ran best in the South in 1964 and worst in the Northeast, a pattern opposite that of past elections. And within the South, the Republicans ran best in the states that they had traditionally been the weakest—the Deep South. Goldwater carried Mississippi, Alabama, South Carolina, Louisiana, and Georgia with margins ranging from 87 to 54 percent even as he was polling less than 40 percent of the vote throughout the nation. Moreover, the phenomenon of the South being more Republican in presidential voting than the non-South continued through the 1968 and 1972 elections but not in 1976.

This reversal in traditional patterns has led some observers to argue that the 1964 election was a critical or realigning election. This argument is stated most directly by Gerald Pomper, who writes (1972: 424–25):

> . . . the central importance of the 1964 campaign lends support to the supposition that this election was a critical election, initiating a new political era in the United States, rather than the aberrant event it appeared at the time. A critical election, such as that of the New

Deal, is one in which a deep and enduring cleavage in the electorate becomes evident. Characteristic of such elections is increased voter consciousness of policy questions, and the later electoral persistence of group divisions based on the policy questions raised in the critical election. These hallmarks of a critical period are evident in the upsurge of mass perceptions of party differences in 1964 and the persistence of these perceptions in 1968.

Yet Pomper himself recognizes that additional evidence, such as substantial shifts in party identification and the emergence of new issues, is needed to determine whether the 1964 election was indeed realigning. And the evidence relevant to party identification suggests that no major realignment took place. For example, a comparison of the distribution of party identification in 1964 and 1966 (see Table 2.1) indicates a net drop of 6 percent in Democratic identification and a net increase of 1 percent in Republican identification. While these net figures may conceal additional gross change, they do not indicate any substantial shifts in partisan loyalties. A comparison of the 1964 and 1968 distributions of partisanship leads to the same conclusions.

One might object to an examination of the distribution of party identification nationally since important regional differences may be concealed. But even when we examine the South and non-South separately, there is little evidence of any large number of changes in party affiliation. We do observe that the proportion of Democratic identifiers dropped more in the South than the non-South—10 percentage points versus 6; the net result however was an increase in the number of Independents as the proportion of Republicans in both regions remained virtually unchanged. Additional evidence of stability (and hence no realignment) is provided by the 1966 election returns for gubernatorial and congressional races, which closely resembled the pre-1964, traditional voting patterns (Cosman and Huckshorn, 1968: 234–39).

The decline in Democratic identification in the South continued in 1972, with slightly more than half of all Southerners claiming to be Democrats. Yet the proportion of Republican identifiers in the South in 1972 was still only 16 percent. Outside the South, the Democratic Party suffered further losses, although not as great as within the South. Again, however, the Independents and not the Republicans have been the beneficiaries of the Democratic decline.

While there have been no major Republican gains in party identification, there have been other changes occurring, especially in the South. Black and Rabinowitz (1974: 11–12) show that the image of the Democratic Party held by white southerners became more negative between 1956 and 1968, with the greatest drop occurring between 1964 and 1968. At the same time, the image of the GOP has not improved except for a positive evaluation in 1972. Furthermore, Black and Rabinowitz (p. 42) show that in issue preferences on nine broad classes of issues, the Democratic Party has lost strength in the South and the GOP has gained. Yet even with this trend, Black and Rabinowitz find that southern whites are becoming more like nonsouthern counterparts in their tendency to express *no* party preference on the issues most important to them.

What then might we conclude about the 1964 election? In the nation at large there was no major change in the strength of the parties; thus we might classify the election as maintaining. In the South, however, there was a major change in voting behavior, though not in partisan affiliations. The changes in voting behavior have continued at the presidential level, resulting in presidential Republicanism in the South. But at the state and local level the South is still predominantly Democratic just as it is with respect to party identification. It is still not clear whether the 1964 election in the South should be considered deviating or realigning; whatever the interpretation, the 1964 outcome demonstrates how an issue—race—can dramatically upset traditional voting patterns when the parties offer distinctive choices on the issue. As Walter Dean Burnham asserted (1968: 38):

> It is not argued here that 1964 was a realigning election in the classic sense, such as the election of the 1850's, the 1890's and the 1930's. It did however . . . produce massive deviations from "standing decisions" in many parts of the country and was otherwise associated with much the same kind of complex value and policy polarization which has been conspicuous in such elections. The areas of maximum displacement from the norm in 1964, as in earlier elections marked by similarly massive electoral shifts, were in all probability areas which were marked by an abnormally high level of public consciousness about issues, related in some way to the defense of threatened local values against external attack.

The potential of issues for producing realignment and the importance of party and candidate positioning on the issues will be further discussed in Chapter 12.

1968

The effects of the six partisan attitudes shown in Figure 6.2 reveal that in a two-party, two-candidate comparison, citizens gave a sizable advantage to the GOP. The Republicans enjoyed a slight to moderate advantage on all the partisan attitudes except for the group-benefits component. The figure tells only a part of the 1968 election story since

FIGURE 6.2
Effects of the Six Partisan Attitudes on
the 1968 Presidential Election

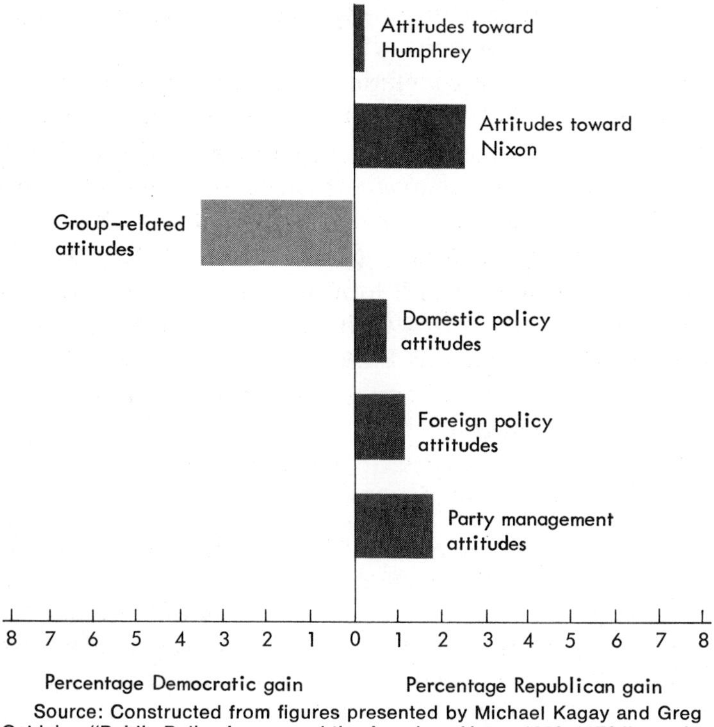

Percentage Democratic gain   Percentage Republican gain

Source: Constructed from figures presented by Michael Kagay and Greg Caldeira, "Public Policy Issues and the American Voter, 1952–1972," unpublished paper.

the race was a three-candidate contest, with George Wallace of the American Independent Party challenging the major party candidates, Hubert Humphrey and Richard Nixon. Wallace's candidacy was certainly the preeminent feature of the campaign, and his presence contributed to a second important aspect of the election, namely, the closeness of the outcome, given the huge early Republican lead. These two features along with a discussion of issues are the primary foci in our consideration of the 1968 election.

The Resurgence of the Democrats

The Democrats left their 1968 nominating convention in Chicago bitterly divided over the Vietnam War as well as the conduct of the convention itself. Hubert Humphrey, closely tied to the war policies of the Johnson administration, won the nomination over antiwar candidates in a strenuously fought struggle. The party was hurt further by the fact that its convention was held late in August; this occurred since the convention was scheduled when it was assumed that President Johnson would be the nominee. Hence, the Democrats had little time to heal their wounds and map strategies prior to the traditional Labor Day start of the campaign.

At one stage early in the campaign, Wallace was running a fairly close third to Humphrey in the public opinion polls and there was much conjecture that Humphrey might even finish third in the Electoral College vote, given Wallace's presumed solid base of southern support. The standing of the three candidates over the course of the campaign as measured by Gallup Poll reports is presented in Table 6.2. Note that Nixon enjoyed a sizable lead well into the last weeks of the campaign.

TABLE 6.2
**The Standing of Humphrey, Nixon, and Wallace
over the Course of the Campaign**
(in percentages)

Date	Nixon	Humphrey	Wallace	Undecided	Total
September 3–7	43	31	19	7	100
September 20–22	43	28	21	8	100
September 27–30	44	29	20	7	100
October 3–12	43	31	20	6	100
October 17–21	44	36	15	5	100
October 31–November 2 ..	42	40	14	4	100

Source: Gallup Polls.

Humphrey's resurgence has been attributed to a number of sources. One is that many Democrats after toying with a Nixon or a Wallace vote returned to the fold. This return was facilitated in the North by the activities of labor union leaders and Democratic Party officials in portraying Wallace as an enemy of the working man. For example, the Democratic State Central Committee in Michigan distributed numerous leaflets charging Wallace with fostering policies detrimental to the common man, such as:

> Out of their low incomes, Alabamians pay a 6% sales tax. It's the nation's highest. It applies to everything, even food and clothing. If applied nationally, the tax would take $450 a year out of the average wage earner's pocket.

Chester, Hodgson, and Page (1969) believe that it was Humphrey's September 30 Salt Lake City speech on Vietnam that marked the turning point in his campaign. After much debate among his aides, Humphrey carved out a position on Vietnam somewhat distinctive from that of President Johnson, the key provisions being (Chester, Hodgson, and Page, 1969: 726):

> As President, I would be willing to stop the bombing of North Vietnam as an acceptable risk for peace, because I believe that it could lead to success in the negotiations and a shorter war. This would be the best protection for our troops.
>
> In weighing that risk—and before taking action—I would place key importance on evidence, direct or indirect, by deed or word, of Communist willingness to restore the Demilitarized Zone between North and South Vietnam.
>
> If the Government of North Vietnam were to show bad faith, I would reserve the right to resume the bombing.

This speech helped Humphrey establish his independence from Johnson, encouraged some Democratic doves to return to the ticket, and brought in badly needed campaign contributions.

The surge of Humphrey and the decline of Wallace were also facilitated by the vice presidential candidates of the three parties. Wallace chose as his running mate General Curtis LeMay, former Air Force chief of staff. At the news conference announcing his candidacy, LeMay gave a series of responses to reporters' questions that indicated his readiness to use nuclear weaponry. Despite the effort of Wallace to minimize the impact of LeMay's statements, their effect was similar to similar statements made by Goldwater in 1964.

Nixon chose as his running mate Governor Spiro Agnew of Maryland, while the Democratic vice presidential nominee was Senator Edmund Muskie of Maine. Almost immediately, the competence and caliber of the two nominees became a campaign issue. Muskie was widely praised for his calm, forthright approach; his ability to handle protesters; and his overall performance. Agnew, however, became something of a campaign joke to many citizens, with his use of ethnic slurs and his assertions that "when you have seen one slum, you have seen them all" and "Hubert Humphrey is squishy soft on Communism." The Democrats did their best to exploit the vice presidential issue, such as by taking out full-page ads in newspapers that simply stated: "President Agnew?" That the public responded differentially to the vice presidential candidates is demonstrated by the mean thermometer rating given each: Muskie received a mean rating of 61; Agnew an evaluation of 50; and LeMay a rating of 35 (Weisberg and Rusk, 1970: 1169). Furthermore, a Harris Survey conducted about a month before the election showed Muskie preferred over Agnew by a margin of 17 percent, even as Nixon was heavily preferred over Humphrey. In fact, only about half of the citizens who preferred Nixon also preferred Agnew, according to a Louis Harris Poll. Fortunately for Agnew, citizens could not cast separate votes for President and Vice President. Yet strategically Agnew may have been an excellent choice to appeal to southern conservative voters, thereby allowing Nixon to avoid blatant regional and ideological appeals.

Finally, on October 31, about one week before the election, President Johnson announced a halt to the bombing of North Vietnam and the commencement of peace talks the following week. Unfortunately for the Democrats, the South Vietnamese balked at this arrangement and Humphrey did not profit as much as he might have by the cessation of bombing. Theodore White (1969: 383), among others, believes that, had these last-minute developments clearly indicated peace was at hand, Humphrey would have won the election. Four years later Henry Kissinger would announce somewhat prematurely before the 1972 election that "peace was at hand" in Vietnam.

Our discussion of the ebb and flow of the 1968 campaign has thus far focused mainly on Humphrey and Wallace and largely ignored Nixon. In part this is because the Nixon campaign was primarily a holding action designed to protect the lead the Republicans enjoyed at the outset of the campaign; this description is supported by the fact that Nixon began the campaign with 43 percent of the vote in the polls and two months later received just that proportion from the voters. Political satirist Art Buchwald (1968) described a conversation between the "old" Nixon and the "new" Nixon that humorously reflected the GOP campaign:

The "New" Nixon said, "Sit down, Dick, and listen carefully. This is a unique election situation. We don't have to attack the Democrats because they're going to make mincemeat out of each other. In order for Humphrey to get anywhere in the election he's going to have to attack Lyndon Johnson's policies in Vietnam. Then to defend himself Lyndon Johnson is going to have to attack Hubert Humphrey. Gene McCarthy will attack both of them, and all we have to do is sit back and talk about crabgrass in the United States."

In a more serious vein, *New York Times* journalist James Reston (1968) criticized Nixon for evading the issues. Reston wrote:

The Vietnam issue is probably the best illustration of the point. Mr. Nixon is exploiting it very shrewdly. He is simply saying it's a mess, which it obviously is, and holding Vice President Humphrey and the Democrats responsible for it.

He is certainly not telling us how to get out of it. He is merely refusing to discuss it on the ground that this might interfere with the Paris peace talks, and meanwhile putting out campaign TV ads showing dead American soldiers on the battlefield while a voice cries it is time for new leadership.

As the campaign drew to a close, there was increasing evidence that Nixon's campaign performance was hurting him among voters; Evans and Novak (1968) reported that, based upon polling conducted by the Oliver Quayle organization, "the caution with which Richard M. Nixon has pursued his meticulously planned campaign has backfired into a deepseated and probably ineradicable public belief that he is ducking the issues."

On election day, the Republicans held on to eke out a narrow victory. Wallace carried only Alabama, Mississippi, Georgia, Louisiana, and Arkansas, while Nixon comfortably carried the Electoral College vote even as he and Humphrey almost evenly shared the popular vote. The only southern state carried by the Democrats was Texas as a three-way split in the vote enabled Humphrey to squeak through. As in 1964, the Democrats ran best in the Northeast.

The Wallace Candidacy and the Issues

The presence of George Wallace in the 1968 presidential contest marked the first serious third-party challenge since the four-candidate race of 1948. While Wallace ultimately received only 13.5 percent of the popular vote and 46 electoral votes, these figures should not detract from the importance of his candidacy. Certainly Wallace's presence hurt the Republican ticket, resulting in an election closer than it otherwise would have been. Evidence for this assertion is provided by a survey cited by Daniel Mazmanian (1974: 71), which found that "Wallace supporters overwhelmingly favored Nixon when forced to decide between the two major-party candidates; 58 percent chose Nixon and 22 percent Humphrey. . . ." Converse and his colleagues (1969: 1090–92) found that while Wallace voters tended to be Democrats (68 percent in the South and 46 percent outside the South), many of these Democrats preferred Nixon over Humphrey and would probably have so voted had Wallace not been running. They concluded that in a two-candidate contest Nixon would have run somewhat stronger.

As mentioned in Chapter 4, the Wallace vote, in contrast to that for Humphrey and Nixon, was largely issue based: the crucial issues being Vietnam, law and order, and civil rights. In contrast to the case of Humphrey and Nixon, evaluations of Wallace by citizens were fairly closely related to their own issue stances. One reason for this was that there was far less ambiguity in citizens' eyes as to where Wallace stood on the issues. For example, Table 6.3 shows perceptions of the positions of Humphrey, Nixon, and Wallace on the issues of Vietnam and urban unrest as measured along a seven-point categorization. Note the homogeneity of the perceptions of Wallace's positions. More than two thirds of the citizens saw Wallace as favoring the use of all available force to solve the problem of urban unrest, while almost half saw Wallace favoring complete military victory in Vietnam. Assessments of the positions of Humphrey and Nixon on urban unrest ranged over the spectrum of alternatives, with Humphrey viewed more toward the "liberal" end of the continuum and Nixon the "conservative." On Vietnam there were scant differences in popular perceptions of the stands of Humphrey and Nixon, in part because (as discussed in Chapter 4) the two candidates took very similar stands.

The widespread agreement on Wallace's issue stances obviously reflects the clarity of his stands. For example, the American Independent Party platform was unusually straightforward as far as party platforms go on a number of issues, as indicated in the following passages (Porter and Johnson, 1970: 702, 715–16):

> We have seen them (the courts), in their solicitude for the criminal and lawless element of our society, shackle the police and other law enforcement agencies; and, as a result, they have made it increasingly

TABLE 6.3
Citizen Perceptions of the Stands of Humphrey, Nixon, and
Wallace on the Issues of Vietnam and Urban Unrest
(in percentages)

Issue	Solution	Perception of Humphrey	Perception of Nixon	Perception of Wallace
Urban unrest	Solve problems of poverty and unemployment	25	9	3
	————	24	10	2
	————	19	14	3
	————	19	31	4
	————	6	19	4
	————	4	11	13
	Use all available force	3	6	71
	Total	100	100	100
Vietnam	Immediate withdrawal	5	4	7
	————	8	6	3
	————	16	12	5
	————	37	31	9
	————	15	23	7
	————	9	14	18
	Complete military victory	9	9	51
	Total	99	99	100

Source: 1968 SRC study. The table entries are the percentages of respondents who placed each candidate at each position on each issue.

difficult to protect the law-abiding citizen from crime and criminals. This is one of the principal reasons for the turmoil and the near revolutionary conditions which prevail in our country today. . . .

* * * * *

We will then require the establishment of firm objectives in Vietnam. Should negotiations fail, and we pray that they will not fail, these objectives must provide for a military conclusion to the war. This would require the military defeat of the Vietcong in the South and the destruction of the will to fight or resist on the part of the government of North Vietnam. . . .

And Wallace himself uttered a number of graphic campaign statements that left absolutely no doubt where he stood; for example, demonstrators, protesters, and the like received the following warning from Wallace: "The first anarchist who lies down in front of my automobile when I become President, that's the last automobile he'll ever want to lie down in front of."

Overall, there was substantial agreement in the electorate about what constituted the most important issues, although there was much less agreement as to the party best able to handle the problem. Note that in Table 6.4 only five issues account for almost two thirds of the

TABLE 6.4
The Five Problems Most Frequently Cited as Most Important in 1968

Problem	Party Preferred on Most Important Problem						Percentage of Electorate
	Dem.	No Diff.	Rep.	Wallace	Total Percent	No. of Cases	Mentioning Problem
Vietnam	23	40	35	2	100	584	43
Public disorder ..	11	41	44	4	100	117	8
Civil rights/ general	39	34	22	5	100	67	5
Poverty	49	30	19	2	100	59	4
Negro riots	17	26	40	17	100	47	3

Source: SRC 1968 election study. The table presents those five problems most frequently mentioned as the most important problem facing the nation. The percentages in the last column of the table are based upon all respondents who cited the problem, regardless of whether they could answer the question about the most preferred party.

problems mentioned as most important, a situation that differs dramatically from the previous elections we have discussed. The Democrats enjoyed an advantage on civil rights and poverty, while the GOP was preferred on Vietnam, public disorder, and Negro riots. Note that among those respondents who mentioned the specific problem of Negro riots, rather than the more general problem of public disorder, preference for Wallace rose to 17 percent. A poll reported by Theodore White (1969: 364) showed that more than half of all Americans thought that Wallace would handle the problem of law and order the way it was supposed to be handled.

The racial overtones to many of the issues cannot be ignored and are reflected in the 1968 voting patterns. For example, about 97 percent of black citizens voted for Humphrey and the remaining 3 percent for Nixon. Among whites, the Democrats received about 35 percent of the vote, the Republicans 52 percent, and Wallace 14 percent. This 62 percent difference (97 – 35) in support for Humphrey by racial groups is a much greater cleavage than that associated with social class (Converse et al., 1969: 1085, fn. 4).

Beyond the obvious racial differences in support for Wallace, there were some noteworthy patterns among other demographic groups. Most surprising was the fact that Wallace ran best among the youngest age groups. Converse and his associates (1969: 1103) report that Wallace received 13 percent of the vote cast by citizens under 30 years of age and only 3 percent from citizens over 70, with a regular decline in support from the intermediate age groups. The explanation given for this finding was that young people have weaker attachments to the party system and therefore are more susceptible to the appeals of a third-party candidate. Furthermore, the authors point out the fallacy in assuming that the young age group is a homogeneous, politically liberal, college-educated collection of citizens. Certainly one implication in the age-level differences in support for Wallace is that prospective third-party candidates might look to the large bloc of uncommitted, Independent young citizens as the most likely sources of support.

As expected, Wallace ran best in rural areas and in the South where he garnered more than half his popular vote and all of his electoral votes. Among religious groups, Wallace ran best among Protestants; among partisan groups, he ran best among Independents and weakest among Republicans. There was a tendency for males to be more supportive of Wallace than females, just as there was a pattern of greater Wallace strength among less-educated citizens. Finally, Wallace received greater support among union members than nonunion members; in particular, his poorest showing among occupational groups came in the professional and businessman category (Converse et al., 1969: 1101–02; *Gallup Opinion Index*, December 1968, p. 5).

Popular evaluations of Wallace clearly reflect his greater attractiveness to southern whites and Independents and his lesser appeal to nonsouthern whites and blacks and partisans. For example, the most frequent reason given for liking Wallace was his stand on the law and order issue, which was mentioned by almost one fifth of Independents and 16 percent of white citizens but only 1 percent of blacks. The personal characteristics of Wallace most frequently commended were his integrity and outspokenness, each of which was cited by 5 percent of all citizens and even by 2 percent of the black respondents.

Yet the preponderant image of Wallace was a negative one, particularly among blacks. The most common hostile comments offered by blacks about Wallace centered not on his personal attributes but on his issue stances. More than a fourth of all blacks disliked Wallace's civil rights stand and his general association with blacks; many less blacks expressed dissatisfaction with his law and order stand. Almost a third of black citizens said there was nothing at all about Wallace that they liked. Overall, about 10 percent of all citizens volunteered that Wallace was a bigot and racist, and at least 5 percent of the population said that Wallace was impulsive, fanatical, and dictatorial and lacked integrity.

Interpreting the 1968 Election

Like the 1964 election, the interpretation of the 1968 election is problemmatical. Even though most of Wallace's 1968 supporters voted for Nixon in 1972, this does not mean that realignment occurred or that the Wallace party served as a way station for Democrats in the process of becoming Republicans. The off-year congressional elections of 1970 and 1974 as well as our ongoing surveys of party identification indicate that the Democrats are still the majority party. Still the question remains as to how the Wallace voters (or for that matter, the cynics of the left discussed in Chapter 1) will respond to future events and political alternatives.

The Wallace candidacy was significant because of what it had to say about the possibilities of realignment. It demonstrated that millions of voters can be attracted to a third party when the two major parties are perceived as offering unsatisfactory alternatives on important issues. Yet it also suggests the vulnerability of a third-party candidate to attempts by a major party to co-opt its positions. To illustrate, one might argue that an independent candidacy by Wallace in 1964 would not have been nearly as successful since Goldwater offered a distinctive alternative to Johnson on the issues of race and law and order. Furthermore, while Wallace attracted many voters because of clarity and extremity of his positions, he also repelled many voters. As discussed previously, a candidate may be "right" on one issue but wrong on many others. This is especially critical for a third-party candidacy that does not have a natural partisan source of support to rely upon. As an attempt to win the Presidency, the Wallace candidacy fell far short. As an effort to serve as a broker resolving an Electoral College deadlock in favor of the candidate who promised the most, Wallace came a lot closer than many observers realize.

1972

The reasons for the Nixon landslide in 1972 are clearly evidenced by the effects of the six partisan attitudes shown in Figure 6.3; the Democrats enjoy an advantage only for group-related attitudes. Perhaps the surprising feature of the 1972 election is the shallowness of the GOP victory: even as Nixon was capturing the White House, the Democrats gained two Senate seats, one governorship, and lost only a scattering of House seats. This suggests that the presidential election

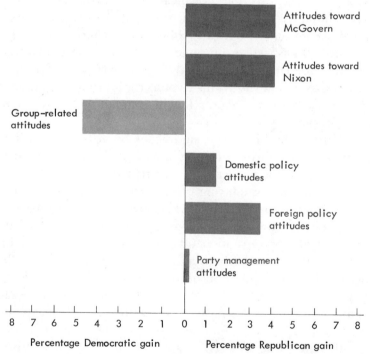

FIGURE 6.3
Effects of the Six Partisan Attitudes on
the 1972 Presidential Election

Attitudes toward McGovern

Attitudes toward Nixon

Group-related attitudes

Domestic policy attitudes

Foreign policy attitudes

Party management attitudes

8 7 6 5 4 3 2 1 0 1 2 3 4 5 6 7 8

Percentage Democratic gain   Percentage Republican gain

Source: Constructed from figures presented by Michael Kagay and Greg Caldeira, "Public Policy Issues and the American Voter, 1952–1972," unpublished paper.

was more a rejection of McGovern than an endorsement of the GOP. The very low voter turnout in 1972 further suggests that the electorate was not wildly enthusiastic about the choices available to them.

The Nixon landslide is all the more surprising since, throughout 1971 and even into 1972, it appeared that Nixon would face a tough battle for reelection because of the nation's economic difficulties and the continued American involvement in Vietnam, albeit at a sharply reduced level. For example, in a trial run between Nixon, Muskie, and Wallace in February of 1972, Gallup found that Nixon held a scant 43–42 percent advantage over Muskie among registered voters, with 10 percent for Wallace and 5 percent undecided. Hence, our major focus on the 1972 election concerns how the minority party won an overwhelming victory.

The Campaign

McGovern began the campaign even further behind than Humphrey in 1968, but unlike Humphrey was never able to close the gap substantially. The first Gallup survey after the conventions showed Nixon leading McGovern 57 to 31, with 12 percent undecided and the actual November vote of 61–39 did not differ much from the early poll results. Some observers argue that the Democratic ticket—in fact, any Democratic ticket—was doomed once the crippling of Governor Wallace prevented even his consideration of a third-party candidacy. The effect of Wallace on the parties' fortunes is demonstrated by what happens in the hypothetical Nixon-Muskie race cited previously when Wallace is not a third-party candidate; in such a contest, Nixon easily defeated Muskie by a margin of 52 to 41, with 7 percent undecided.

Like 1968, the Democrats left their 1972 convention as divided party. Many traditional sources of Democratic support, such as labor, were alienated by the McGovern nomination and the proceedings surrounding it. And later, when he tried to make peace with disenchanted Democrats, such as Chicago Mayor Richard Daley, McGovern received flak from his ardent supporters who saw him behaving like the traditional politicians that they had opposed.

In the post-convention period when the candidates should be gearing up for the general election, the McGovern candidacy suffered two serious jolts from which it never recovered. The first was the disclosure that the Democratic vice presidential nominee, Senator Thomas

Eagleton of Missouri, had been treated for mental exhaustion on a number of occasions. McGovern compounded the problem by his vacillation on the issue; his statement of 1,000 percent support for Eagleton was soon followed by the dropping of Eagleton from the ticket. The other incident that lessened McGovern's credibility was the Salinger affair. Pierre Salinger had talked with North Vietnamese peace negotiators in Paris at McGovern's request only to have conflicting public statements issued by McGovern and Salinger upon the latter's return as to whether McGovern had actually suggested the meeting.

McGovern was further hurt by the openness of his campaign and the accessibility of him and his staff to the press, thereby guaranteeing that all quarrels and disputes within his organization would eventually be made public. This resulted in the appearance of the McGovern organization as fragmented and McGovern as an ineffective leader. The accessibility was so great that newspaperman Timothy Crouse, upset by the isolation of the Nixon campaign, complained about the McGovern organization (1973: 361–62):

> It is one thing for a candidate to see the press frequently and answer their questions honestly, which McGovern tried to do, thereby providing an admirable contrast to the reclusive Nixon. However, it is another thing for a campaign staff to talk openly about its problems, feuds, and discontents. That is the political equivalent of indecent exposure, and the McGovern staffers indulged in it with a relish that bordered on wantonness. While the Nixon people, by keeping their mouths tightly shut, managed to keep the lid on the largest political scandal in American history, the McGovern people, by blabbing, succeeded in making their campaign look hopelessly disorganized and irresponsible.

Meanwhile, the Republican campaign was running smoothly (with the exception of the Watergate arrests) according to plans laid out months earlier. Nixon ran as the incumbent President and not as the candidate of the Republican Party; in fact, his campaign was run not by any GOP committee but by his own specially created organization, the now infamous Committee for the Reelection of the President (CREEP). Nixon kept his overt campaign activities to a minimum and relied heavily on surrogate campaigners to bring the attack to McGovern. And since the McGovern campaign never got off the ground, Nixon was never forced to step down from his "above the battle" posture.

The Issues

The five issues most frequently cited as the most important problems confronting the nation are shown in Table 6.5. Vietnam and inflation are obviously the most important concerns, with the GOP enjoying an advantage on each. Yet an average of almost half of the citizens saw no difference between the parties on the five issues, which may seem surprising, given that the 1972 election is commonly described as one in which one candidate (McGovern) regularly took extreme issue positions. This apparent paradox is readily resolved when one distinguishes between the candidate's and the party's position.

TABLE 6.5
The Five Problems Most Frequently Cited as Most Important in 1972

Problem	Party Preferred on Most Important Problem					Percentage of Electorate Mentioning Problem
	Dem.	Diff.	Rep.	Total Percent	No. of Cases	
Vietnam	21	39	40	100	201	26
Inflation	24	44	32	100	104	14
Drugs	14	59	27	100	44	6
Crime	17	55	29	101	42	6
Civil rights/general	31	44	26	101	39	5

Source: CPS 1972 election study. The table presents those five problems most frequently mentioned as the most important problem facing the nation. The percentages in the last column of the table are based upon all respondents who cited the problem, regardless of whether they could answer the question about the most preferred party.

George McGovern was widely perceived as being to the far left of the political spectrum. These perceptions probably were encouraged by the California primary debates in which Humphrey aggressively attacked McGovern's issue positions, particularly his plans for defense cutbacks and his $1,000 a person welfare program. While McGovern did not unqualifiedly endorse "amnesty, acid, and abortion," as charged by his political opponents, his campaign rhetoric—his comparison of Nixon to Hitler, his offer to beg the North Vietnamese for the return of American prisoners of war, and the like—helped create the image of McGovern as an extremist. Evidence for this is provided by Miller and his associates who found that citizens saw Nixon as closer to their own preferred issue positions than McGovern on 11 out of 14 issues studied. Only on the questions of urban unrest, inflation, and ecological pollution was McGovern seen as closer to the voters' positions, while on such issues as Vietnam, amnesty, campus unrest, marijuana, desegregation, and others Nixon was viewed as closer to the citizens' preferences.

A normal vote analysis conducted by Miller and his colleagues (1973) showed how voters' stances on issues related to their vote decisions. For example, among voters who opposed amnesty, McGovern received only 22 percent of the vote, a full 28 percent below the normal Democratic vote. Similarly, among citizens who favored a military victory in Vietnam, the normal Democratic vote was 49 percent, yet McGovern received only a scant 15 percent of their vote. And among citizens who favored heavy penalties for marijuana usage, McGovern's 30 percent of the vote was fully 24 percent lower than the normal Democratic vote (p. 21). While McGovern received slightly more than the normal Democratic vote among citizens who favored amnesty, the legalization of marijuana, and immediate withdrawal from Vietnam, the number of citizens who took the extreme liberal position on these and other issues was usually small, which meant that the gains that McGovern received from citizens in these categories did not begin to balance the losses he suffered from more conservative citizens. Miller and his associates further show that the effects of issues on vote choices are even more pronounced when one directly incorporates citizen perceptions of the candidates' stances (pp. 24–28). Peter Natchez summarized the issue difficulties that McGovern encountered and how these problems interacted with his more general image problem; he wrote (1974: 5):

> People—75 percent of them—thought that McGovern's ideas were "far out" and "impractical." He was thought to be a liberal by 31 percent; another 31 percent took him for a radical. (In contrast, only 17 percent of the electorate described themselves as liberal, and only 1 percent as radical.) The two weaknesses of George McGovern's candidacy, his "indecisiveness" and "extremism," fed on each other; his indecisiveness created an aura of impracticality around the issue positions he was trying to develop; his search for the right issues made him seem indecisive.

Watergate

The notable point about the issues listed in Table 6.5 is the one that does not appear there—Watergate. For a variety of reasons,

McGovern was unable to exploit Watergate as an issue damaging to the GOP. One reason for this is that the full dimensions of Watergate, especially the cover-up, were not yet clear by election day. Much of the Watergate story, however, had been reported prior to the election. *Washington Post* reporters Carl Bernstein and Bob Woodward wrote numerous stories about illegal or questionable activities of high-level Nixon aides. For example, they wrote in early October of 1972 that the Watergate breakin was only a small part of a Republican plan of sabotage and spying headed by Donald Segretti. It was also reported that the President's personal attorney, Herbert Kalmbach, was one of five persons authorized to make payments to Segretti out of a secret fund. And shortly before the election, it was charged that the President's closest and most powerful aide, H. R. Haldeman, controlled a secret fund for political espionage and sabotage.

Thus, a significant part of the Watergate story was known prior to the election, and the question arises as to why the scandal had so little effect. One compelling explanation is that the sources of the Watergate news, such as the *Washington Post, New York Times,* and George McGovern, were not viewed as impartial, trustworthy sources, but instead were seen as biased, as out to get the President with innuendoes and unproven charges. Presidential press secretary Ron Ziegler repeatedly referred to the Watergate stories as character assassination, guilt by association, shabby journalism, and the like, and even characterized the *Post* as an agent of the McGovern campaign. Evidently many citizens agreed with Zeigler's characterizations, and thus the sources of most of the Watergate information were not credible to many citizens. The administration did its best to portray the *Post* as a part of the liberal Eastern establishment that was not to be believed. And McGovern himself was seen as a biased source since he had a direct interest in the election outcome as well as severe credibility problems of his own.

Other reasons given for the minimal impact of Watergate were that citizens viewed the matter as politics as usual, that the Republicans had not done anything that the Democrats had not done in the past. Perhaps the partial exposure of the Watergate scandals led to this view; perhaps if the full story had been disclosed by election day, citizens might have responded differently. The Watergate story, however, was still unfolding as the election drew near, and it was submerged by the developments in the Vietnam peace negotiations and Henry Kissinger's dramatic statement that peace was at hand.

The Images of the Candidates

Overall, McGovern was not a very popular candidate. His mean thermometer rating was a cool 49 compared to a relatively warm 66 for Nixon. His presumed major advantage—a reputation for integrity and honesty—was quickly eroded by the Eagleton and Salinger fiascos. A poll reported in *Newsweek* and summarized in part in Table 6.6 shows the image problems that McGovern faced.

TABLE 6.6
Evaluations of Nixon and McGovern as President
(in percentages)

Which of these words or phrases describe Richard Nixon's conduct of the Presidency? Which would describe George McGovern's?	Nixon	McGovern
Sticks to principles	40	17
Strong, forceful	34	17
Thinks things out slowly	34	8
Tries to be fair	30	22
Good judgment	30	11
Forward-looking	29	26
A moderate	24	9
Puts country's interest ahead of politics	27	13
Too much of an opportunist	12	14
Weak, uncertain	7	10
Makes snap decisions	9	18
Biased, unfair	6	5
Poor judgment	11	17
An extremist	3	20
Too much of a politician	24	19

Source: *Newsweek,* August 28, 1972, pp. 17–18. Copyright 1972 by Newsweek, Inc. All rights reserved. Reprinted by permission.

It is ironic that 40 percent of citizens would use the phrase "sticks to principles" to describe the Nixon Presidency after Nixon established peacetime wage and price controls, pursued a policy of detente with the Soviet Union, and established diplomatic contacts with the People's Republic of China. All of these policies were pursued in clear contradiction to Nixon's previous record and promises in these areas. Yet it was McGovern that few people saw as sticking to principles, because the issues on which McGovern vacillated, such as Eagleton, Salinger, and welfare reform, were simpler to comprehend, especially as the media were able to show clearly conflicting statements uttered by George McGovern within a relatively short time. Certainly the media's coverage of Nixon's foreign policy initiatives did not focus on the inconsistency of the present policies with past Nixon stands, but instead emphasized the boldness and imagination of the Nixon foreign policy maneuvers. The role that the media play in structuring the public's perceptions of events will be discussed in Chapter 9.

Interpreting the 1972 Election

Some observers have claimed that the 1972 vote marked the end of the Democratic coalition of the New Deal era. There is evidence to support and refute this assertion, depending upon the perspective one takes. On the one hand, it is clear that McGovern ran poorly among traditional sources of Democratic strength. For example, he received less than a majority of the vote from manual workers, members of labor union families, and Catholics; among southerners, he received less than a third of the vote. He ran strongest among blacks and Jews, although his percentages here (about 87 and 67 percent) were lower than the comparable figures for Humphrey in 1968 (*Gallup Opinion Index,* December 1972, pp. 8–10). Thus, it does appear that the New Deal coalition fell apart. From another perspective, however, Mc-Govern ran better among components of the New Deal alliance (except for the South) than he did among groupings not considered a part of the Roosevelt coalition. The problem for McGovern was that he ran poorly among all population segments—so that even as his support coalition resembled the New Deal alliance, his level of support was so much lower than that given to previous Democratic candidates that he suffered a lopsided defeat.

Miller and his colleagues (1973: 35) have argued that the 1972 outcome is best explained by recourse to ideology and issues and that the "effects of party identification [were] for the first time in at least 20 years slightly less potent in determining voting behavior than [were] issue attitudes." Without claiming that a realignment occurred in 1972, they point out that the potential for realignment is great so long as citizens' issue preferences and the parties' issue positions do not coincide. Yet as we examine the 1972 results, the evidence for realignment is at best spotty. As mentioned earlier, the outcomes of the non-presidential races were generally favorable to the Democrats. An examination of the 1972 congressional and gubernatorial voting by elements of the New Deal coalition shows solid Democratic support. To illustrate, Catholics cast 65 percent of their vote for Democratic

House candidates, 55 percent for Democratic Senate candidates, and 60 percent for Democratic gubernatorial candidates. The comparable figures for labor union families were 62, 53, and 67 percent, and for Southerners 69, 60, and 59 percent. Thus, there were substantial differences in support for the Democratic Party from the top to the bottom of the ticket.

Any pro-Republican realigning effects that the 1972 election may have had have likely been canceled by the Watergate revelations and the ongoing economic difficulties since 1972. As these issues occupied centerstage, the concerns about social issues many voters associated with the McGovern candidacy receded. The 1974 election was a Democratic sweep, and particularly notable was the strong showing the party made in the South where many of the GOP gains of previous elections were wiped out. And, as mentioned earlier, the South was the strongest region for the Democrats in 1976, in large part because of the candidacy of a native son. Hence, we now turn to the 1976 election, which in many ways represents a stark contrast to the 1964, 1968, and 1972 election outcomes.

7

The 1976 Election

INTRODUCTION

Had any political analysts predicted in 1972 that Gerald Ford and Jimmy Carter would be the 1976 presidential nominees and that Ford would be running as the incumbent President, they likely would have had their credentials (as well as their sanity) challenged. 1972 had witnessed a landslide Republican victory, one that many observers thought foretold the emergence of the Republican majority. But the era of Republican dominance was not to be—as Richard Nixon and Spiro Agnew left office in disgrace and the unelected incumbent Ford failed in his bid to keep the Presidency in Republican hands. The 1976 election evidenced continuity and change, the continuity arising from the restoration of a Democratic voting majority similar to the New Deal coalition, and the change represented by the dramatic alterations in the presidential selection process—the increased importance of the primaries and the mass media and the advent of public financing of presidential campaigns—which enabled an unknown candidate, such as Carter, to capture the nomination in the first place. The paths by which Carter and Ford secured their respective nominations will be detailed in Chapters 9 and 10; for the remainder of this chapter, the focus will primarily be on the general election campaign in 1976.

THE COURSE OF THE CAMPAIGN

Unlike the situation in 1968 and 1972, the Democratic convention in 1976 was characterized by harmony and unity while the GOP gathering was marked by rancor and divisiveness. Carter had clinched his nomination early, thereby allowing the Democrats to stage a very orderly convention, which was viewed positively by the television audience. In contrast, the Republican contest between Ford and Ronald Reagan continued right up to the convention, with Ford's victory not secured until the eve of the balloting. Although the Republicans managed a convincing display of unity on the last night of their convention, with the appearance of Reagan on the podium and the selection of Robert Dole as the vice presidential nominee, it was clear that Ford began his general election effort as the heavy underdog. After the Democratic convention, Carter had an amazing 33 percent lead over Ford in the Gallup Poll,[1] and going into the traditional Labor Day kickoff of the campaign, his lead was a substantial 18 percent (see Table 7.1). The remainder of the campaign witnessed Carter trying to maintain his lead and Ford attempting to get the GOP effort rolling.

By late September and early October, Ford had dramatically closed the gap on Carter, an improvement largely attributed to Ford's performance in the first debate on September 23 and to Carter's interview with *Playboy*. In this interview, Carter talked of lust and adultery, used graphic language in discussing his own views of morality, and

---

[1] This margin was artificially inflated by the fact that the Republican nominee was not yet selected and the Carter-Mondale ticket had just gotten the traditional boost in the polls that presidential candidates get immediately after their nomination. Moreover, many Ford and Reagan supporters claimed that they would vote for Carter should their own man not win the GOP nomination, which further increased Carter's lead. Most of the Reagan supporters returned to the fold and supported Ford, although in election postmortems many Ford backers felt that Reagan himself could have worked much more strenuously for the Republican ticket.

TABLE 7.1
The Standing of Carter and Ford over the Course of the Campaign
(in percentages)

Date	Carter	Ford	Other	Undecided	Total
June 25–28	53	36	2	9	100
Democratic convention					
July 16–19, 23–26	62	29	2	7	100
August 6–9	57	32	3	8	100
Republican convention					
August 20–23	50	37	3	10	100
August 27–30	54	36	2	8	100
First debate					
September 24–27	51	40	5	4	100
September 27–October 4 . .	47	45	2	6	100
Second debate					
October 8–11	48	42	4	6	100
Mondale–Dole debate					
October 15–18	47	41	4	8	100
Third debate					
October 22–25	49	44	3	4	100
October 28–30	48	44	3	5	100
Final poll	46	47	3	4	100

Source: Extracted from *The Gallup Opinion Index*, no. 137, December 1976, p. 13.

spoke highly critically of Lyndon Johnson. The interview received substantial media coverage and served to reinforce doubts about Carter's presidential qualifications.

Throughout this period, the candidates stressed very different campaign themes. Carter ran as the anti-Washington outsider who had not been a part of the mess in Washington and talked of streamlining and reorganizing government. Ford adopted a "Rose Garden" strategy, which had him campaigning from the White House itself where he signed bills and made major announcements before the television cameras and in general acted "presidential." Carter's anti-Washington theme was a continuation of his nomination campaign when he ran against the government in Washington and the traditional power brokers in the Democratic Party.

Just as his campaign seemed to be moving into high gear, Ford committed a major gaffe in the second debate, when he claimed that Eastern Europe was not under Soviet domination. Compounding the error, Ford and his advisors failed to clarify his statement immediately so that for days after the debate the campaign was on the defensive. Eventually the Ford campaign moved back on track and narrowed the gap, but Carter held on to win 51 percent of the two-party vote on

Election Day, a far cry from his 20 to 30 percent leads in the polls in the summer. The individual state results as well as the national outcome were close; in 27 states, the losing candidate got at least 47 percent of the two-party vote. Although there was no major third party or independent candidacy on the scale of the Wallace effort in 1968, the presence of former Democratic Senator Eugene McCarthy on the ballot in 30 states may have kept Carter's margin down in some states and caused him to lose others. For example, Carter carried Ohio by only 11,000 votes as McCarthy was polling 58,000. Carter lost Oregon by only 1,700 votes with McCarthy receiving over 40,000 votes. Overall, relatively small changes in the popular vote totals could have changed the Electoral College (see Chapter 11) outcome dramatically.

THE ISSUES AND CANDIDATES

Although Carter and Ford did discuss issues, it is not unfair to assert that both candidates attempted to make their own qualities and personality the major theme of their campaigns. Carter emphasized his leadership abilities, promising to reorganize the government and make it more efficient. He also stressed his trustworthiness and his intention to restore morality to government and promised never to lie to the American people. Ford emphasized his integrity and decency and portrayed himself as having earned the trust of the American people by returning honesty to government after the Watergate scandals. When the candidates discussed issues, they often employed very subtle nuances of meaning; Carter was particularly skillful at this, which earned him the label of being fuzzy on the issues.

Both Carter and Ford received similar overall positive ratings from the electorate, but the components of their positive evaluations differed sharply. According to Miller and Miller (1977: 99), Carter was judged positively because of his personal leadership skills and his association with Democratic ideology and domestic issue positions. Ironically, Carter's lack of a national record and his status as a relative unknown made it easier for voters to view him primarily in terms of his Democratic affiliation. But for Ford, the positive evaluations were linked more to characteristics of the candidate himself; Ford was seen as more reliable, more decisive, and more competent in terms of previous public service.

Despite the emphasis on the personal qualities of the candidates, there were important issues in 1976 and these tended to work in favor of the Democrats. Table 7.2 presents the problems most frequently

TABLE 7.2
The Five Problems Most Frequently Cited as Most Important in 1976

Problem	Party Preferred on Most Important Problem					Proportion of Electorate Mentioning Problem
	Dem.	No Diff.	Rep.	Total Percent	No. of Cases	
Unemployment	49	44	7	100	668	33
Inflation	30	48	22	100	452	22
Economics (general) ..	35	47	18	100	217	11
Fuel shortage/ energy crisis	44	50	6	100	112	5
Crime/violence	18	77	4	99	93	5

Source: CPS 1976 election study. The table presents those five problems most frequently mentioned as the most important problem facing the nation. The percentages in the last column of the table are based upon all respondents who cited the problem, regardless of whether they could answer the question about the most preferred party.

cited as most important by Americans in 1976. Note that economic problems topped the list, with unemployment and inflation running first and second. Further observe that the Democrats enjoyed a slight to substantial advantage on all five of the issues. Certainly the one issue that Carter hammered home constantly was Republican mismanagement of the economy. Hence, one might wonder how the election outcome could have been so close, given the Democratic advantage on these salient issues and the overall Democratic advantage in the electorate. Figure 7.1 provides a partial answer.

Note in Figure 7.1 that four of the six attitudinal components had scarcely any impact whatsoever on the vote division. In contrast are the group-related attitudes and the opinions of Ford. The former, a traditional Democratic strong point, favored the Democrats once again in 1976; voters were more likely to see the Democrats as the party of people like themselves. And attitudes toward Ford pushed the vote split in a pro-Republican direction, much more so than attitudes toward Carter moved the vote in a Democratic direction. As Election Day approached, the economy seemed to be improving under Ford's leadership and the economic issues that were expected to benefit the Democrats lost some of their impact. Miller and Miller (1977: 109) summarized the 1976 election as "incumbent performance versus partisan ideology," with the latter narrowly emerging victorious.

According to journalist Jules Witcover (1977: 685), Ford attributed his close election loss to the "Nixon issue," particularly Ford's pardoning of Nixon. Although the pardon per se was not a continual

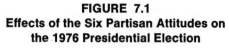

FIGURE 7.1
Effects of the Six Partisan Attitudes on the 1976 Presidential Election

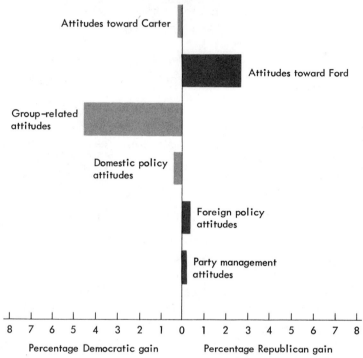

Source: Constructed from figures in a communication from Michael Kagay.

source of debate in the campaign, there is some evidence it might have tipped the vote outcome (as might have many other issues and campaign events). Miller and Miller (1977: 73–74) show that approval versus disapproval of the Nixon pardon was associated with vote choice even when the effects of party identification were considered. For example, among the 28 percent of Republican identifiers who disapproved of the pardon, 30 percent voted Democratic, compared to only 8 percent of Republicans who favored the pardon. Likewise, among the 25 percent of Democrats who supported the pardon, 44 percent voted for Ford, compared to a Ford vote of only 12 percent among Democrats who opposed the pardon. The real effect of the pardon may have occurred long before Election Day. The pardon was overwhelmingly disapproved by Americans and, after granting it, Ford's popularity plummeted. It may be that the pardon depleted much of the good will and admiration for Ford that was apparent when he assumed the Presidency, although Ford was still widely perceived in 1976 as a person of integrity and honesty despite the unpopularity of the pardon.

A comparison of the important issues in 1972 and 1976 (Tables 6.5 and 7.2) suggests one reason why the Democrats were able to oust an incumbent President. In 1972, social and lifestyle issues, such as the Vietnam War and drugs, were of great importance to the electorate. Moreover, these were issues on which Democrats were deeply divided, with large blocs favoring opposite policy alternatives. Hence a Democratic nominee risked losing substantial support from his party's adherents should he favor one side on the issue. This, of course, is what happened to McGovern in 1972; his perceived liberal stands on a number of salient social issues resulted in many Democrats voting for Nixon. The key point about 1976 is that Democrats were just as divided as ever on these issues (Miller and Miller, 1977: 38–42), but these divisions did not hurt the party at the polls. One reason for this was the lessened saliency of social issues for the voters in 1976. And this lessened saliency can be attributed to the economic problems that occupied people's attention and to the fact that the candidates avoided talking about the social issues.

Party identification made a comeback in its impact on vote choice in 1976. Overall, the proportion of defections was down substantially from 1972; almost 85 percent of citizens with a party affiliation remained loyal to their party. Yet this does not mean that citizens were automatically following an unthinking partisan loyalty. Instead, the dominant issues in 1976 coincided nicely with the traditional stances and images of the parties and thereby made partisanship a more useful cue for vote choice than it was in 1972. Although the growth of Independents seemed to level off in 1976 (see Table 2.1), there is little reason to believe that the parties were in a stronger position in 1976 than in 1972. Popular perceptions of the utility of elections and political parties remained at low levels (see Figure 1.1) and evaluations of the parties continued to decline.

THE DEBATES[2]

Like the 1960 Kennedy-Nixon debates, the Carter-Ford encounters were not debates per se but rather press conferences in which both

---

2 Parts of this discussion of the debates are based upon review essays by Sears (1977), Chaffee (1978), and Sears and Chaffee (1978). In addition, two edited books that contain many of the major studies of the 1976 debates are available; see Kraus (1979) and Bishop, Meadow, and Jackson-Beeck (1978).

candidates were present to answer reporters' questions and to comment on their opponent's replies. As such, the debates were media events, the coverage of which may have been more consequential than their actual content. There were three debates between the presidential candidates and one between the vice presidential nominees. Viewership was high, with Nielsen ratings indicating that almost 90 percent of the electorate had seen some part of the debates and that 72 percent of all households had turned on the first debate. Prior to the debates, many studies indicated that citizens looked forward to the debates to learn where the candidates stood on issues and to help them make their vote choice. Many observers expected the debates to play a critical role, particularly since more voters in 1976 than in previous elections were undecided as to their vote choice later into the campaign (see Table 11.1).

Yet it appears the debates had relatively little impact on the final outcome. According to a CBS poll (Mitofsky, 1977), 10 percent of the voters gave as a reason for candidate choice the fact that the candidate impressed them during the debates; but a survey after the third debate found that only 3 percent of the respondents claimed to have changed their vote preference as a result of the debates. Polls taken after the debates generally agreed that Ford "won" the first debate, Carter the second and third, and Mondale the vice presidential debate.

Voter reactions to the debates were highly influenced by the media coverage accorded them. Despite the fact that the debates had much issue content, the primary focus of subsequent media coverage was on who won, how the debates would affect the campaign, and related questions that reflect the horse-race mentality (discussed in Chapter 9). One study (Lang and Lang, 1978) found that citizens whose reactions to the first debate were measured four to seven days after the event were much more likely to state that Ford had won than citizens whose evaluations were obtained immediately after the debate. The authors argue that the former group was swayed by media coverage of later polls, which declared Ford the winner. The power of the media to structure people's judgments of political events was demonstrated clearly in the second debate when Ford uttered his Eastern Europe misstatement. A poll done immediately after the debate found Carter a narrow victor; but as Ford received critical media coverage over the next several days for his mistake, later polls showed that citizens viewed Carter as the overwhelming winner. Hence, "winning" a debate may be less a function of the candidate's actual performance and more a matter of media interpretation of that performance.

Generally, citizens responded to the debates in terms of their own predebate preferences and partisan predispositions. That is, people tended to claim that their preferred candidate was the winner. For example, a Roper Poll (Roper, 1977) conducted immediately after the first debate found that 70 percent of predebate Ford supporters thought Ford had won and only 8 percent Carter. Likewise, 55 percent of predebate Carter loyalists thought their candidate had won compared to only 13 percent naming Ford as the victor.

Overall, the debates seemed to have little impact on vote intention. Carter's big margin over Ford had dropped substantially prior to the first debate and it declined further after the debate; but there is little direct evidence linking the decline to the debate. There was some learning of the candidates' issue positions attributable to the debates, but even here there is little evidence that this affected the vote. One study (Abramowitz, 1978) suggested the opposite causal sequence— namely, that voters moved toward the issue positions espoused by the candidate they initially favored. That is, candidate preference influenced issue stance and not the reverse. Sears (1977) summarizes the major effect of the debates as crystalizing and reinforcing prior preferences, with little real change in vote intention due to the debates. It may be that both Ford and Carter performed sufficiently well to erase any lingering doubts that their partisans might have harbored about their competence, intelligence, and experience.

As a final point, it is questionable whether media coverage of the debates did justice to them. As mentioned before, despite the high issue content of the debates, television and newspaper coverage disproportionately focused on the question of who won. In addition, there is some evidence that post-debate media commentary critical of the debates resulted in more negative evaluations of the worth of the debates on the part of citizens. And certainly the media emphasis on who won so structured citizens viewing and discussion of the debates that they became more concerned with the horse-race aspect rather than the issue content of the debates. We will return to media coverage of the presidential selection process in Chapter 9.

THE VICE PRESIDENCY IN 1976

Normally, presidential elections can be discussed without devoting much time to the vice presidential candidates. From the perspective of the presidential nominee, a good running mate is one who at best will bring some support to the ticket and who at worst will not detract from the ticket. Despite the lip service given to the importance of a qualified Vice President capable of assuming the Presidency, vice presidential selection has generally been the afterthought of presidential politics. But in 1976 vice presidential selection achieved an unusual level of prominence at the nominating conventions and in the general election, in part because of the experiences of 1972 when McGovern's first vice presidential choice resigned from the ticket after his prior mental problems became known, and Nixon's running mate was forced to resign the Vice Presidency in disgrace in 1973.

In a bold attempt to boost his nomination chances, Reagan announced his vice presidential selection (Senator Richard Schweiker of Pennsylvania) *prior* to the convention. The Schweiker designation was an attempt to win moderate and liberal delegates away from Ford in the Northeast (and perhaps to broaden the appeal of the ticket in the general election). While the early naming of Schweiker did not secure many delegates for Reagan, it did provide him with an issue to exploit on the floor of the GOP convention—a challenge to Ford to name his running mate prior to the nomination. The reasoning behind this move was that any person named by Ford would antagonize some of his supporters, thereby enhancing Reagan's nomination prospects. The critical vote at the convention was on a proposed rules change that would have required all presidential candidates to name their running mates by the morning preceding the balloting for the presidential nomination. The Ford forces narrowly defeated the rules change and, after winning the nomination, selected a running mate in the typical fashion—an all-night session characterized by confusion, fatigue, and severe time pressures. Senator Robert Dole of Kansas was finally selected, a chief reason being that he was acceptable to the Reagan forces.

In contrast, Carter's early clinching of the Democratic nod gave him much time to choose a running mate and he orchestrated the process for maximum favorable media coverage. Three contenders— Senators Glenn, Mondale, and Muskie—went to Plains to meet with Carter, while four other prospects met with Carter in New York City, the site of the Democratic convention. The luxury of time in selecting his Vice President gave Carter the opportunity to demonstrate to the American people a decision-making style characterized by preparation, deliberation, and openness.

Although it is difficult to gauge the actual effect of the vice presidential candidates on the final outcome, it does appear that Carter was helped by Mondale's presence on the ticket more than Ford was aided by Dole. At the minimum, Mondale added an ideological and to some extent a regional balance to the Democratic ticket. His designation reassured many liberal activists of the merits of Carter's candidacy. In Dole, Ford picked someone with strengths similar to his own—a conservative, midwestern background popular with heartland Republicans—although Dole may have particularly helped in shoring up sagging GOP fortunes in the farm states. There is evidence suggesting that Mondale was viewed as a better campaigner than Dole, particularly on the vice presidential debate; Dole was often seen as a slashing, aggressive campaigner. A Gallup Poll found that 5 percent of the people who switched from Ford to Carter during the course of the campaign gave dislike of Dole as a reason, while less than 1 percent of the Carter to Ford switchers cited dislike of Mondale. And when Carter voters were asked why they supported Carter, 2 percent mentioned Mondale as a reason, compared to almost no one citing Dole as a reason for supporting Ford. Finally, a "CBS News"/*New York Times* survey done on Election Day (Mitofsky, 1977) found that 16 percent of the Carter voters mentioned Mondale as a reason for voting for Carter, compared to only 4 percent of the Ford voters mentioning Dole. It may be that the Mondale selection was critical to Carter's November success.

INTERPRETING THE 1976 ELECTION

According to the classification scheme described in Chapter 1, the 1976 election is termed a maintaining election, one in which the majority party (defined in terms of psychological attachments) was actually victorious at the polls. Not only did the Democrats win, but it appears that they enjoyed considerable success in reconstructing the New Deal coalition. However, as Miller (1978: 146–150) cautions, the support garnered by Carter differed in a number of important respects from the Roosevelt coalition. For example, while Carter and FDR both ran strongly in the South, Roosevelt's southern base consisted of solid support from white voters in the presence of a negligible black electorate. Carter's southern base, in contrast, consisted of minority support from white voters in conjunction with overwhelming support from a vastly expanded black electorate. In addition, although Carter ran well among Catholics, a traditional pillar of the New Deal coalition, religious differences in party support were actually less in

1976 than in recent elections. Between 1952 and 1972, the average Democratic vote among Protestants and Catholics was 39 and 61 percent, a difference of 22 percent. In 1976 this difference was halved as Carter won 46 percent of the Protestant vote and 57 percent of the Catholic ballots (Gallup Opinion Index, December 1976, pp. 3–4). Thus Carter's support did not have as distinctive a religious hue as that normally associated with the Roosevelt coalition.

Overall, the 1976 outcome yields little evidence of partisan realignment and instead seems more reflective of traditional voting patterns. Yet the potentiality for political change is substantial as the number of citizens with weak partisan allegiances remains high, the turnout remains low, and issues capable of tearing the parties apart (e.g., abortion and busing) remain on the political scene. Furthermore, Carter's success in regaining the South for the Democratic Party may simply be a temporary aberration in the ultimate movement of the South to the GOP. Finally, we can speculate about what will happen to the parties if the Democrats, traditionally seen as the party of economic good times, are unable to solve the economic crises of the late 1970s. Will the voters then turn to the GOP (and its negative economic images) or will they look elsewhere? Will there be any place else to look?

CONCLUSION

Throughout this and the previous two chapters an effort has been made to highlight the important features of each presidential election since 1952. Any such endeavor must of necessity oversimplify matters, omitting details that other analysts would deem important and including information that other investigators would find irrelevant. Be that as it may, the discussion should certainly indicate to the reader the variability in electoral outcomes even as the Democratic Party was commonly seen as the majority party throughout the period. Moreover, there have been substantial differences in the importance of issues, with 1956 generally viewed as a personality contest and 1972 an issue-dominated election. The types of issue concerns expressed by citizens themselves have changed dramatically in this era, from the more traditional New Deal social welfare matters in the 1950s and early 1960s to questions of race, war, and lifestyles in the late 1960s and early 1970s. Yet more traditional economic concerns have again become paramount as the economic well-being of the citizenry has been called into question. The preeminent concerns of Americans in 1979 are inflation, energy, and the state of the economy in general. Our survey of the elections has further shown that the presidential nominees themselves have differed tremendously in background and personal appeal throughout this era; the recruitment of candidates will be discussed in detail in Chapter 10. Finally, an effort was made to interpret each election outcome, particularly with respect to whether it signified a realignment. We will return to this question in the last chapter when we speculate about the future shape of presidential politics.

Part II

8

Elections: From Citizens to Candidates

INTRODUCTION

This chapter has two major aims: to summarize economically the relative importance of issues, candidates, and party identification on vote choice, and to discuss the linkages between these determinants of the vote and the conduct of campaigns. As was noted in Chapter 5, of the six partisan attitudes studied, attitudes toward the candidates were generally of greater importance than issue attitudes. And in much of the issue voting research discussed in Chapter 4 there was a concern with the relative impact of issues and candidates. For example, while Natchez and Bupp (1970) found that issue voting occurred in issue publics, they did not deny the overall importance of partisan affiliations and candidate image; in fact, they asserted that candidate image was substantially more important than issues in influencing the vote decision. The 1956 findings of *American Voter* (p. 72) support this: about 75 percent of all citizens' votes for President could be predicted accurately on the basis of their attitudes toward Eisenhower, while the addition of issue attitudes did not increase the predictive accuracy much. In an analysis of vote defections in the 1956, 1960, and 1964 presidential elections, Richard Boyd (1969) found that attitudes toward the candidates and not the issues were most useful in accounting for defection, in part because it is easier for voters to express attitudes about candidates. Overall, Boyd ranked issues behind party identification and candidate image as determinants of the vote decision. Only in the 1972 election was it claimed that issues were more important overall than candidates and party identification (Miller et al., 1976).

Thus, it would appear that party identification and candidate image generally have the greatest effect on vote choice and issues the weakest. This conclusion, however, suffers from a number of conceptual difficulties, the most crucial of which is the fact that issue and candidate attitudes are so interrelated that it may not be possible to assess their separate effects. For example, Converse and his colleagues (1970: 42, fn. 4) report that one negative comment often made about Goldwater in 1964 was that he was "implusive." Yet it was not entirely clear whether the impulsiveness resided in the candidate or in the policies he espoused. Similarly, one might argue that criticisms of McGovern in 1972 might be interpreted in both issue and personal senses. For example, did the Eagleton affair bring criticism upon McGovern because of his indecisiveness in handling the matter, a personal attribute, or because of the content of the decision eventually made, an issue concern?

The point is that evaluations of candidates often have a strong issue component, which may be indistinguishable from candidate qualities. This notion is supported by the research of Weisberg and Rusk (1970), who found that the contenders for the presidential nominations in 1968 were evaluated in both partisan and issue-related terms. Contenders such as Humphrey and Nixon who had been on the national scene for some time and who were considered national leaders within their respective parties were evaluated primarily in partisan terms; that is, Democrats tended to evaluate Humphrey positively and Nixon negatively, while the reverse held for Republican identifiers. The partisan component was weaker and the issues relatively more important for such challengers as Rockefeller, Romney, and McCarthy, who in 1968 were somewhat out of step with their respective parties, in part because of the issue positions they espoused. And with respect to a candidate such as Wallace who rejected the two major parties, issue positions were a strong determinant of evaluations. For example, the mean rating[1] of Wallace given by citizens who thought the problems of urban unrest could be resolved by solving the problems of poverty and unemployment was 18.2, while the mean rating of Wallace for citizens who preferred using all available force to stem urban unrest was 51.1. A similar situation held with respect to Vietnam issue positions. Citizens who preferred immediate withdrawal gave Wallace a mean rating of 21.8 compared to the 45.1 rating given by citizens who favored a complete military victory. Urban unrest and Vietnam positions were not nearly as related to evaluations of Humphrey and Nixon (Weisberg and Rusk, 1970: 1181–82).

Beyond our inability often to distinguish between issue and candidate attitudes, any conclusion about the weak effect of issues on election outcomes must be further hedged by the recognition that issues can have both a short-term and a long-term effect on elections. While the impact of issues in any specific election may be relatively unimportant, the long-term effect may be very consequential. As Richard Boyd argues (1969: 510):

> The impact of issues, while rarely great at any single moment, accumulates over a period of time. Overall, issues may outweigh candidates in affecting the outcome of elections, for issues have the capacity to alter the greatest single determinant of a vote, party identification.

With these cautionary statements in mind, let us turn to some research that examines the impact of issues, candidates, and partisanship over time.

THE IMPACT OF CANDIDATES, ISSUES, AND PARTY IDENTIFICATION

Research by Mark Schulman and Gerald Pomper (1975) on the 1956, 1964, and 1972 presidential elections, and updated by Mabel Hsueh for the 1976 election, provides a useful summary of the relative

---

1 The mean ratings are obtained by use of thermometer scales. Basically, respondents are asked to indicate warmth or hostility toward candidates by assigning them some number between 0 and 100. An analogy is made to a thermometer in which 0 represents a cold feeling toward the candidate and 100 a warm feeling.

impact of candidates, issues, and party identification on vote choice over time. Working from a model of voting behavior originally proposed by Arthur Goldberg (1966), Schulman and Pomper analyzed a model of the vote decision (depicted in Figure 8.1) that viewed a

FIGURE 8.1
A Causal Model of the Vote Decision

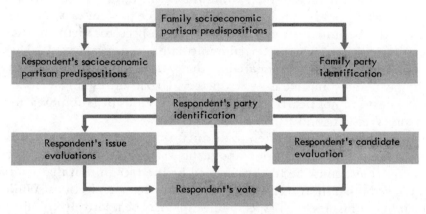

Source: Mark A. Schulman and Gerald M. Pomper, "Variability in Electoral Behavior: Longitudinal Perspectives from Causal Modeling," *American Journal of Political Science* 19 (February 1975), p. 7. Copyright 1975 by Wayne State University Press. Reprinted by permission of publisher.

person's vote as directly influenced by partisanship, issues, and candidate evaluation. The authors also posited interrelationships among these three explanatory variables; that is, party identification was seen as influencing both issue positions and candidate evaluation, while issue position was assumed to impinge upon candidate evaluations. Also included in the model were measures of the socioeconomic political predispositions of the voter and of his parents as well as the party identification of the parents. While these parental variables do not directly affect the respondent's vote decision, they do have an indirect effect via their impact on the voter's party identification.

Schulman and Pomper and Hsueh analyzed the model of Figure 8.1 for the 1956, 1964, 1972, and 1976 elections using similar measures at all four time points; this meant that observed differences could not be attributed to methodological artifacts but instead reflected genuine changes in the importance of these variables on vote choice over time. Table 8.1 summarizes the direct effects of parties, issues, and candidates on vote for the four elections; the larger the value of a coefficient,

TABLE 8.1
The Direct Effects of Party, Issues, and Candidates
on Vote Choice in 1956, 1964, 1972, and 1976*

Year	Party	Issues	Candidates
1956	.448	.060	.365
1964	.364	.224	.377
1972	.310	.233	.366
1976	.325	.086	.448

* Table entries are standardized regression coefficients. The higher the value of a coefficient, the more important was the variable in influencing vote choice.
Sources: Extracted from figs. 1, 2, and 3 in Mark A. Schulman and Gerald M. Pomper, "Variability in Electoral Behavior," *American Journal of Political Science* 19 (February 1975), pp. 7–9. Copyright 1975 by Wayne State University Press. Reprinted by permission of the publisher. And Mabel Hsueh, "Voter's Choice in the 1976 Presidential Election," unpublished paper.

the more important was that variable in influencing vote choice. The coefficients presented in the table take into account only the direct effects of the three variables on vote and do not incorporate the indirect influence of party identification on vote via its impact on both issues and candidates and the indirect influence of issues on vote via their effect on candidate evaluations.

The most important results in Table 8.1 are the increased importance of issues in 1964 and 1972, as compared to 1956 and 1976, and the decline in the impact of party identification between 1956 and 1972, with partisanship exhibiting a slight increase in importance in 1976. The strong impact of candidate evaluations across the elections is also significant, particularly given the diversity of the elections in terms of their issue content and the attractiveness of the contending candidates. Since it is the candidates who are likely to be the "new" elements in any election, it is clear that the nomination of an attractive candidate (however that be defined) is crucial for electoral sucess. That is, it is extremely difficult in any single election to upset the existing patterns of partisan allegiances or to change the generalized images of the political parties; the one element susceptible to the greatest change is the perceptions of the candidates.

Schulman and Pomper (pp. 9–10) showed that the impact of partiship on candidate evaluations declined between 1956 and 1972, while the effect of issues increased. This implied that candidates were increasingly seen in issue terms and was further evidence for the weakening of partisanship. Moreover, Schulman and Pomper showed that by 1972 most of the transmission of partisanship across generations occurred through family party identification rather than through socioeconomic and political predispositions. This meant that there was a decline in the demographic underpinnings of the New Deal partisan alignments, suggesting that the rationale underlying contemporary partisan loyalties was not as well founded as in previous decades.

However, the 1976 results indicate that party identification became more important in the evaluation of the presidential candidates and that demographic characteristics became a bit more useful in accounting for citizens' partisanship. Clearly, the 1976 political environment facilitated the reinstatement of partisanship and traditional group ties as meaningful electoral cues. Undoubtedly the economic difficulties of the mid and late 1970s helped resurrect some of the traditional New Deal cleavages. And the fact that both candidates in 1976 were relatively new to the national scene and were not associated with specific policy stances may have led voters to rely more on partisanship and candidate evaluations in making their vote choices.

Hence, the relative impact of the various determinants of the vote will depend on the current political environment. When salient issues arise that are not readily associated with the stances of the two major parties, one can expect that issues will play a greater role in vote choice and party identification a lesser one. But when issues that traditionally separate the parties dominate in an election or when there are few issues whatsoever, then one can expect party identification and candidate evaluations to be prominent. The fact that in three of the four elections in Table 8.1 candidate evaluations were the most important determinant of the vote, in conjunction with the heavy media emphasis on the candidates, suggest that the impact of candidate evaluations will remain substantial even as the role of issues and party identification fluctuates widely. Finally, the reader should keep in mind that candidates, parties, and issues are not as conceptually and operationally distinct as their different labels would suggest. When Carter is evaluated positively because he is a Democrat and when the Democratic Party is viewed positively because of its issue stances, it becomes very difficult to disentangle the separate effects of parties, issues, and candidates.

FROM CITIZENS TO CANDIDATES

In Chapters 4 through 7, and the first sections of this chapter, elections have been analyzed from the perspective of the citizen. A general approach to the study of elections has been presented as well as a discussion of the specific factors influencing presidential election outcomes between 1952 and 1976. The most important general findings have been the increased importance of issues and the diminished influence of partisanship in elections up to 1972. These findings were generally attributed to changes in the tenor of American politics in the 1960s and 1970s, particularly the rise of new and divisive issues, such as Vietnam in the 1960s and busing in the 1970s, that did not coincide with the traditional socioeconomic issues of the New Deal era. With the reemergence of traditional economic issues in 1976 and the absence of other salient issues, party identification witnessed a comeback in its effect on vote choice. The advent of new issues appears to have contributed to the decline of the political parties, in part because the parties have been unable to incorporate the new issues within their existing bases of voter support and programmatic concerns. In addition, the technological foundation of American politics has changed dramatically in the past quarter century. The electronic media permit issues to be brought directly to the public just as they enable candidates to circumvent the traditional party organizations, thereby contributing to their decline.

Thus, we observe increased issue-related voting and ideological awareness and attribute this partially to the nature of the times. But a "nature of the times" explanation is very incomplete in that issues do not arise ex nihilo, nor is their ultimate resolution a foreordained conclusion. Instead, the positions and behavior of the candidates and parties themselves are crucial determinants of the development and outcome of issue controversies. Specific candidates may emerge in times of crisis; voter perceptions of the seriousness of problems will in part be determined by the stances of the candidates. One might speculate that had Senator McCarthy not come forward as a challenger to President Johnson's renomination in 1968, the depth of anti-Johnson sentiment might never have been uncovered, perhaps resulting in a Johnson-Nixon-Wallace race in 1968. And what if George Wallace had chosen not to run in 1968? Would the internal contradictions in the Democratic Party have produced another Wallace? Would the choices offered to the electorate in 1968 have been more distinctive or less so?

The point is that the behavior of political elites does make a difference in the alternatives available to the electorate and in how the electorate responds to these alternatives. In fact, the very selection of a candidate may introduce issues and concerns into an election that otherwise would not have impinged upon the voter's consciousness.

For example, the selection of John Kennedy as the Democratic nominee in 1960 introduced the question of religion into the campaign and affected the votes of millions of citizens. Similarly, certain candidates possess characteristics that facilitate or hinder their ability to make specific kinds of appeals to the electorate. For example, it is often argued that one reason why Watergate was not more of an issue in the 1972 presidential election was that George McGovern was not the optimal candidate to exploit such an issue, in part because of a highly strident campaign style and in part because of his being tagged with a radical label. Moreover, certain candidates may be more appropriate (have a greater chance of success) under certain circumstances. One might argue that Lyndon Johnson read the mood of the post-assassination electorate accurately with his emphasis on continuity, consensus, and centrism, while Barry Goldwater misread the electorate by offering distinctive alternatives and suffered accordingly. Certainly the Watergate revelations and White House scandals in 1973 and 1974 made the country more receptive in 1976 to an inexperienced politician who emphasized his personal virtues. It is likely that the outspoken candidate will fare better in times of severe societal stress when his outspokeness reflects concerns at the forefront of citizen consciousness; certainly it is difficult to imagine the 1964 electorate being as congenial to George Wallace as the 1968 electorate. In short, voters are not responding to an inert environment that includes issues and candidates; the candidates themselves have tremendous opportunities for fashioning appeals to the electorate, which may serve to move millions of voters and to challenge the existing bases of partisan loyalties.

This is not to say that candidates have complete flexibility in formulating appeals to the electorate and in staking out issue positions. The very process of obtaining the presidential nomination imposes commitments and constraints on a candidate that may structure his campaign behavior in the general election. For example, the Humphrey presidential campaign in 1968 suffered from the close association that many voters perceived between Humphrey and the unpopular policies, particularly on the Vietnam War, of the Johnson administration. It was not until the September 30 Salt Lake City speech that Humphrey successfully moved some distance from the administration's positions. Yet Humphrey probably could not have broken from the Johnson policies much earlier even had he wanted to, since Humphrey's strategy to win the Democratic nomination bypassed the primaries and instead relied on party chieftans, labor bosses, and others to deliver blocs of delegates to him. Had Humphrey moved too fast and too far from the Johnson administration too soon, he would have lost delegate strength in states, especially southern and border states, which were more supportive of Johnson's policies and less receptive to the protest candidacies of McCarthy and Robert Kennedy.

In a similar vein, George McGovern's presidential campaign was constrained by his nomination strategy of winning delegates in both primary and nonprimary election states by reliance on an extensive organization of volunteer workers who were attracted to his candidacy largely on the basis of issue concerns. Given the coolness of many Democratic Party workers to his candidacy, McGovern could not afford to disillusion his enthusiastic supporters by waffling on certain key issues. McGovern paid dearly, however, in the general election for keeping the faith; many voters including many Democrats saw him as a radical who was out of the mainstream of politics and the Democratic Party. Carter, in contrast, forged a more diverse support coalition during the primaries that was not centered on one key issue. Hence, he had greater flexibility in shifting ground and making peace with the various segments of the Democratic Party. Of course, Carter's post-nomination task was made easier by the widespread belief that he would win in November.

McGovern's difficulties illustrate a general political rule of thumb, namely, that the primary election electorate may differ markedly from the November electorate. This means that tactics appropriate for the primaries may be inappropriate and even disastrous for the general election. Moreover, the McGovern and Carter primary and general election campaign strategies point up the crucial difference in the structure of political competition in the two elections: the primaries are often multicandidate elections in which only a plurality of the vote is needed for victory, while the presidential contest is usually a two-candidate, majority-winner race.

Another constraint that impinges upon candidates and parties is their goals, particularly with respect to the election outcome. If the major goal of a candidate or party is to win the election, then the desire for victory may limit the kinds of issue positions that a candidate or party can or should take. For example, one might argue that Senator Goldwater's disparaging comments about social security and the Tennessee Valley Authority in 1964 were electorally foolish statements given the public's attitudes on these matters, no matter what Goldwater's own principles were. For candidates or parties whose major goal is not electoral success, there is greater freedom in espousing relatively unpopular issue positions.

While the number of cases is small in which presidential candidates have not had victory as their primary goal, there have been instances in the past 35 years in which other goals became important. For example, there were four main contenders for the Presidency in 1948 and two of them—Strom Thurmond heading the Dixiecrats and Henry Wallace leading the Progressives—had no realistic chance of winning. Instead, their primary goal was to affect the policy orientation of the Democratic Party, the Dixiecrats wanting to maintain the status quo on race-related matters and the Progressives preferring a more liberal Democratic Party. The means by which the Dixiecrats and Progressives were to influence the future of the Democratic Party was the electoral process: if each group was able to siphon off sufficient votes from the party's nominee (Truman) so that he lost, then it was felt that in the future the party could not afford to ignore or offend certain blocs of voters if it hoped to win elections. It also has been argued that in 1964 some of Goldwater's chief supporters were more concerned with seizing control of the Republican Party than with winning the election.

This notion of future-oriented parties whose initial goal is not electoral success but influencing the existing party system is discussed by Anthony Downs (1957: 127), who distinguishes between two types of newly created parties—those designed to win elections and those designed "to influence already existing parties to change their policies, or not to change them." The best contemporary example of the latter kind of party is the Conservative Party in the state of New York. While the party has scored some important electoral successes, notably the election of James Buckley as United States Senator, it was originally created to influence the policy directions of the New York Republican Party, which were seen by many conservatives as too liberal. Hence, a conservative party was formed to run candidates who, it was hoped, would garner sufficient votes to insure the defeat of the Republican candidate, thereby demonstrating to the GOP leadership that it must return to conservative principles in order to win elections. What is intriguing about this situation is that conservatives were willing to let their least-preferred alternative (the Democrats) win in the short run to influence the long-term policy orientations of the parties.

The Wallace candidacy in 1968 may be interpreted to some extent along these lines, especially given Wallace's post-1968 moves back into the Democratic Party. Even when it was clear that Wallace could not win in 1968, his plea "to send a message to Washington" was an attempt to influence the policy positions of the Democratic and Republican Parties. His more recent warnings that the Democratic Party must not repeat its mistakes of 1968 and 1972 (mainly nominating candidates who were too liberal) is a not too subtle threat to the party that if it fails to move toward the center it may have a Wallace challenge on its hand, perhaps in the form of a third-party candidacy, perhaps in other forms. The point is that candidates and parties who are not first and foremost concerned with winning have greater flexibility and freedom in ranging over the political landscape.

Other constraints faced by candidates and parties are the existing distributions of citizens' opinions and preferences on political affairs. While the campaign may in part be an effort to educate and move the public in certain directions, there are issues in which the public is very unmovable and the candidate who fails to recognize this may suffer. Goldwater's comments about social security provide an example of this situation. On the other hand, the shift by liberal Democrats toward a position of opposition to busing reflects a pragmatic (some might say unprincipled) view that the busing issue is one in which the white public is not willing to listen or be educated. The busing issue illustrates a common occurrence in electoral politics, namely, the perceived need to compromise or even capitulate on certain issues in order to be around to fight the good fight on other issues. Whether such behavior represents political pragmatism at its best or political expediency at its worst is left to the judgment of the reader; clearly, the specific issues involved are likely to influence any conclusions that one reaches.

Finally, the actual means of conducting campaigns impose limitations as well as provide opportunities for candidates as they attempt to appeal to the electorate. For example, the heavy reliance today on public relations firms skilled in the use of the media, especially television, allows a prospective candidate to ignore the party organization and traditional routes of political advancement by going directly to the public, emphasizing those personal characteristics and issue stances most likely to work to the advantage of the candidate. On the other hand, the pervasiveness of the national media, again particularly television, now makes it virtually impossible for candidates to present blatantly different appeals in different regions of the country; what is said on the stump in New England is duly reported on the evening news in the South.

Thus, our attention now turns in subsequent chapters to the candidates and to the campaigns through which appeals are made to the citizenry. While citizens are limited in their electoral choices in part by the alternatives offered by the candidates, the candidates themselves are constrained by a number of factors, including the issue and partisan preferences of the citizenry. Hence our analysis of elections must include an investigation of the interactions between citizens and candidates, interactions that are largely confined to the actual political campaigns. Therefore, we will focus in Chapters 9 and 10 on the changes in the conduct of presidential campaigns that have occurred since 1952, stressing the likely consequences of these changes for election outcomes and the political system. In Chapter 11 we will consider the strategic aspects of capturing a presidential nomination and campaigning for President.

9

Changes in the Conduct of Campaigns: The Media and Presidential Politics

INTRODUCTION

Since 1952 there have been many important and interrelated changes in the conduct of presidential campaigns. One area that has witnessed dramatic change is campaign financing because the costs of waging a campaign have risen astronomically. In turn, these increased costs have spurred new attempts at campaign finance reform. Higher campaign costs are primarily due to the technological revolution that has overtaken presidential contests; today the public opinion poll, the computer, and the electronic media, especially television, have become the basic tools in the conduct of campaigns. The heavy reliance on television has had consequences for the traditional presidential nominating system, the political parties, and the types of citizens likely to be viewed as viable presidential prospects. For example, we have witnessed in recent years a proliferation of presidential primaries and a greater willingness of candidates to contest the primaries even if they do not enjoy the support of the state and local party organizations. This greater willingness to enter the political fray arises in part because television has made it more feasible for candidates to appeal directly to the voter. The proliferation of primaries has, of course, increased the amount of money spent in the electoral arena, which in turn has generated additional pressures for reform of both the nominating system and the campaign financing system. Thus, our focus in this chapter and in Chapter 10 will be on four interrelated developments: the rising costs of presidential campaigns and proposals for reform; the increased role of the media, especially television, in the conduct of campaigns; the recent patterns in the recruitment of presidential candidates; and the modes of selecting delegates to nominating conventions and proposals for reform. Our discussion of the media in this chapter is organized into two sections. The first part focuses on the role of television in presidential politics in general, summarizing many of the empirical studies on the effects of television. The second section is more speculative, analyzing how the media, particularly television and the press, intrude upon and affect the outcome of the presidential selection process.

TELEVISION AND PRESIDENTIAL POLITICS

Introduction

While presidential candidates often follow hectic campaign schedules, at times campaigning on the same day in cities separated by thousands of miles, it is clear that most voters do not experience the campaign firsthand but instead follow it through the media—television, radio, newspapers, and magazines. Television, of course, has become *the* medium through which campaigns are conducted, and in this section we will focus on two types of effects that television has had on presidential politics. These effects might be labeled "systemic" and "individual" effects, the former referring to the consequences of television for the presidential nomination and election process and the latter to the more subtle impact of television on the average citizen. Before turning to the effects of television, we will first describe the patterns of media usage in presidential elections and then present a brief history of the uses of television in contests for the Presidency.

Patterns of Media Usage over Time

The most dramatic development in media usage patterns has been the increased reliance on television as a source of information about the presidential campaign. Table 9.1 shows which media citizens have

TABLE 9.1
The Most Important Source of Campaign Information, 1952–1968*
(in percentages)

Medium	1952	1956	1960	1964	1968
Newspapers	26	27	24	26	24
Radio	32	12	6	4	4
Television	36	56	65	62	66
Magazines	6	5	5	8	6
Total	100	100	100	100	100
Number of cases	1,469	1,548	1,676	3,958	1,059

* The table entries are the percentage of respondents in each year who cited the particular medium as their most important source of campaign information.
Sources: SRC/CPS election studies.

cited as their most important source of campaign information between 1952 and 1968. The table indicates that the proportion of people naming magazines and newspapers as most important has remained relatively stable; it is with respect to radio and television that the major changes have occurred. An intriguing aspect of the figures is that the proportion of citizens claiming radio *or* television as their most important medium has been quite stable, ranging from 66 percent in 1964 to 71 percent in 1960. Without panel data, it is premature to conclude that television's gains were radio's losses, although the figures are suggestive. As of the late 1970s, television remains the dominant source of presidential campaign information, although newspapers are ranked highly for information on local political affairs.

A more complete picture of the patterns of media usage is given in Table 9.2, which indicates the percentage of Americans who have used each medium as sources of campaign information since 1952. While radio ran last in importance in 1964 and 1968, as shown in Table 9.1, magazines were consistently ranked the lowest in sheer frequency of use, as shown in Table 9.2, although the differences between magazine and radio usage were not great. With the exception of 1952, television has been the most commonly utilized medium. Unlike many innovations, the diffusion of television was rapid and

230

TABLE 9.2
The Frequency of Media Usage, 1952–1976*
(in percentages)

Medium	1952	1956	1960	1964	1968	1972	1976
Newspapers	79	68	80	78	75	57	73
Radio	70	45	42	49	41	43	45
Magazines	40	31	41	39	36	33	48
Television	51	74	87	89	89	88	89

* The table entries are the percentage of respondents in each year who report using each of the media as a source of campaign information.
Sources: SRC/CPS election studies.

widespread, occurring mainly between 1950 and 1960. The 1952 campaign is considered the first in which television played a prominent role, yet only about 40 percent of American homes had television then. By 1956 the number of television sets had doubled, and today television ownership is almost universal in the United States. The rapid growth in television ownership is reflected in the rise in television use between 1952 and 1960: a 23 percent increase in reliance on television for campaign information between 1952 and 1956 was followed by a still sizable 13 percent rise from 1956 to 1960. But since 1960 the gain has been about 2 percent, suggesting that television usage has reached a saturation point. While there are no consistent patterns with respect to the print media, one should bear in mind that the 1952–76 period witnessed the demise of many major daily newspapers and periodicals and the rapid growth of news weeklies, such as *Time, Newsweek,* and *U.S. News and World Report.* The 30–40 percent of the population who utilize magazines for campaign information becomes less impressive when one recognizes that many of these publications carry relatively little political information.

While Tables 9.1 and 9.2 chart the basic patterns of media usage, the information presented is quite crude in that one has little sense of the extent of reliance on each medium and the kind of information provided by each medium. For example, when a citizen claims television as the most important source of information, this does not tell us whether it is political advertisements or public affairs documentaries or the evening news programs that are most important for the person. One would certainly expect that the amount and quality of information conveyed by a partisan spot commercial would be appreciably lower than that provided by an hour-long documentary. Thus, to gain a more detailed perspective on citizens' media reliance, Table 9.3 shows the number of media employed by citizens as sources of campaign information. While the number of media is itself a crude indicator of the richness of the information obtained by citizens, it nevertheless yields some insight into the diversity of information available to citizens.

TABLE 9.3
The Number of Media Used by Citizens, 1952–1976*
(in percentages)

Number of Media	1952	1956	1960	1964	1968	1972	1976
None	6	8	5	3	4	5	5
One	14	19	13	12	15	21	15
Two	30	32	28	30	32	33	23
Three	35	28	35	36	34	27	34
Four	15	13	19	19	14	13	23
Total	100	100	100	100	99	99	100
Number of cases ...	1,646	1,741	1,808	1,449	1,341	1,108	2,378

* The table entries are the percentage of citizens in each year reporting they used the specified number of media.
Sources: SRC/CPS election studies.

Note in Table 9.3 there is a measurable proportion of citizens who do not follow the campaign in any of the four media. This result is a bit startling, given how readily a citizen was classified as a media user. That is, the respondent need only have claimed to have employed the medium once (e.g., watch one campaign show on television) in order to be coded as a user of that medium. The number of citizens who rely upon all four media has been above 13 percent in all elections. The most noteworthy point of Table 9.3 is that about half the citizenry relies on two or fewer media and the other half on three or four. For citizens who depend on one or two media, television and newspapers are most frequently cited.

While a detailed analysis of the characteristics of various media users is beyond the scope of this book, it is important to note that educational level is closely related to certain types of media exposure and not to others. In particular, reliance upon magazines and newspapers covaries with level of education, such that more highly educated citizens are more likely to cite the print media as a source of campaign information. Television exposure, however, has not been related to education in recent elections except that, for people with lower levels of education, television is more likely to be the only way they follow the campaign. Before television became widespread there was a moderate relationship between television reliance and education since the early owners of television sets tended to be disproportionately wealthy and highly educated.

Not only has television become the most common source of campaign information, it has also become the most trusted source. A Roper Poll in 1959 found that 32 percent of Americans said newspapers were the most believable source of news while 29 percent said television. By 1968, 44 percent of the citizens thought television was most believable and only 21 percent newspapers. Even the attacks of the Nixon administration on the television networks (and some prominent newspapers) did little to erode the credibility of television. A series of Roper Polls found that television was the major source of news about candidates for national office and that it was viewed as the source giving the clearest understanding of national issues and candidates, with newspapers running a distant second and magazines and radio a poor third and fourth. Only when it came to information about local offices did newspapers enjoy a sizable advantage over television (The Twentieth Century Fund, *Voters' Time,* Tables 1B, 1C, and 1D).

Hence, television is the preeminent source of campaign information, a situation that is upsetting to some observers because of the limited ability of television to present in-depth coverage of news stories. The half-hour national evening news programs must of necessity distill from a large number of stories those that are most newsworthy. And the stories selected for presentation must be condensed into a few minutes, thereby making it difficult to place the story in a broader context or to present the full range of relevant details. While some readers of the *New York Times* who have been overwhelmed by the amount of information presented in the paper have facetiously modified the paper's slogan from "All the News That's Fit to Print" to "All the News That Fits We Print," it is the case that major newspapers are far more able to devote substantial space to stories that give both background and analysis.[1] Television, on the contrary, is much less able to analyze and editorialize. For example, when the President

---

[1] For example, one study found that television news shows covered fewer of the key events in a major, ongoing news story than did three leading newspapers and concluded that the label of "electronic front page" often given to television news shows was quite appropriate. See Harney and Stone (1969).

makes a dramatic announcement on television, the initial coverage is most often straight reporting, with little critical evaluation. This enables the President to go directly to the people and be fairly confident that the news will be conveyed in the manner that he prefers, even if the networks do present brief instant analyses after the President's speech.

The more general point is that the only reality many events have for people is what is presented on television; the presence of both a video and a narrative component is very powerful in shaping citizens' judgments of an event. As Lang and Lang (1968: 297) point out, "the televised event, however inauthentic and unrevealing, becomes the actuality." The television camera need not tell it as it is; there is ample opportunity for staging events to achieve maximum effect, as in a televised campaign rally during which the camera pans only on the enthusiastic supporters of the candidate, thereby giving the impression of widespread warmth toward the candidate. And once an image, however inaccurate, has been transmitted, it is extremely difficult to correct that image later on.[2]

Thus, citizens rely most heavily on the medium that is least able to present detailed information about issues and candidates. This is not to say that television, particularly news reporting, is biased, only that it is incomplete. In a systematic study of network news coverage of the 1972 campaign, Hofstetter (1976) found very little evidence of any partisan bias on behalf of a party or candidate.[3] This contrasts markedly with newspaper editorial endorsement policies which have over-

---

[2] This is not to say that citizens unfailingly accept what television presents. For example, even though press and television coverage of the 1968 Democratic convention was largely sympathetic to the antiwar protestors beaten and arrested by the Chicago police, citizens tended to be far more favorable to the police and hostile to the demonstrators. See Robinson (1970).

[3] The assertion that partisan bias was absent does not mean that each candidate received the same amount and kind of coverage; in fact, Hofstetter uncovered a noticeable amount of structural and situational bias. McGovern received more coverage than Nixon, but Nixon's was more favorable. This in part reflects the deliberate strategies of the two candidates: McGovern seeking widespread coverage and being readily accessible to the media, and Nixon avoiding the media.

More generally, it has been charged (by Spiro Agnew among others) that television network news emphasizes bad news at the expense of good news. This presumably occurs for a variety of reasons, including the supposed biases of the people who select the stories to be reported and the tendency to view bad news as newsworthy and good news as routine. An actual examination of the content of the network news shows found that only about one third of the material reported could be considered bad news. While bad-news items were often reported in earlier segments of the news broadcast and received more visual emphasis, overall there was little evidence of any bias in favor of reporting bad news. See Lowry (1971).

whelmingly favored the Republican presidential candidates, with the exception of Goldwater in 1964 (Nimmo, 1970: 132). At times, the partisan biases of newspapers spill over from the editorial page to the news columns themselves. The *Manchester Union Leader*, New Hampshire's largest newspaper, is renowned as an outlet for the views of its right-wing publisher, William Loeb. The *Union Leader* is influential in New Hampshire because of the absence of statewide television stations and is important in presidential politics because of the crucial position of New Hampshire as the first state to hold a presidential primary.[4] Loeb's vendetta against Senator Muskie in 1972 (including scurrilous attacks on Muskie's wife and the publication of fabricated letters accusing Muskie of uttering ethnic slurs against Franco-Americans, an important voting bloc in New Hampshire) undoubtedly played a significant role in the unraveling of the Muskie candidacy.[5] In the 1976 Republican primary in New Hampshire, the *Union Leader* covered Ford more negatively than Reagan (Loeb's preferred candidate) in both news reports and editorials (Veblen and Craig, 1976).

The absence of widespread partisan bias in television does not alter the fact that the medium is poorly suited to provide citizens with a full, detailed, and accurate description of political events.[6] Paradoxically, this failure of television is one reason for its effectiveness since it forces citizens to fill in the partial picture presented by television according to their own predispositions. That is, television is a "cool medium": there is substantial audience involvement in completing the partial images depicted by television. The potential consequences of this situation as well as a more general analysis of television's effects

---

[4] For information about Loeb and his newspaper, see Veblen (1974).

The *Union Leader* is an atypical paper; most major newspapers do not engage in such slanted reporting of campaigns. A 1968 study by Doris Graber (1971) on the campaign coverage of 20 newspapers found that there was widespread uniformity of press coverage despite the varying editorial policies of the papers. Likewise, an analysis of television, news magazine, and major newspaper coverage of the 1972 campaign found little evidence of partisan bias. There was a slight pro-Republican bias exhibited by news magazines, but newspaper editorial policies were not reflected in their coverage of the campaign. See Evarts and Stempel (1974).

[5] For a fascinating description of the *Union Leader's* biased coverage of the New Hampshire primary, see Witcover (1972).

[6] This is not to say that newspapers perform the information dissemination function entirely satisfactorily. In her study of coverage of the 1968 election, Doris Graber found that the press tended to focus on candidate characteristics rather than issue positions. Oftentimes relevant facts were left out of campaign stories, making it more difficult for the reader to make an informed choice. See Graber (1974).

will be presented after a brief discussion of the history of television in presidential campaigns.

A Brief History of Television in Presidential Campaigns[7]

An intriguing feature in the evolution of television in presidential campaigns has been its close association with the career of Richard Nixon. One of the earliest indications of television's political power was provided by Nixon's now famous "Checkers" speech in 1952. Nixon had been accused of profiting from a political slush fund, and there were demands that he be removed as the vice presidential candidate on the Republican ticket. To counteract the criticisms, Nixon gave a speech on national television, described by Weisbord in the following manner (1966: 181–82):

> The broadcast proved Nixon a cool performer in an extremely ticklish situation. His fund, he said earnestly, was not secret; no money went for his personal use; no favors were granted in return for contributions. In a firm voice he recited his life story—the poor boy who had worked his way through college, married, gone off to war, returned to law practice, and run for Congress. He listed everything he owned—from a 1950 Oldsmobile to GI life insurance, and paid homage to his wife's "respectable Republican cloth coat."
>
> . . . Americans nodded in sympathy as Nixon bared his life, his finances, his affection for the wife and daughters flanking him on stage, and the family's affection for another gift they had received, a black and white cocker spaniel named Checkers. ". . . I just want to say this, right now, regardless of what they say about it, we are going to keep it."

Nixon's speech was television at its melodramatic best, and his closing appeal for support was answered by thousands and thousands of letters and telegrams. The impact of the speech provided an early indication of how television might effectively be utilized by candidates.

The year 1952 also witnessed the advent of the televised spot commercial in politics. The spot was a very short ad designed to convey a basic point or image without going into depth on issues or providing much informational content. One commercial showed General Eisenhower being asked, "Mr. Eisenhower, what about the high cost of

---

[7] For a more detailed discussion of the broadcast media in American politics, see Chester (1967).

living?" The General responded, "My wife, Mamie, worries about the same thing. I tell her it's our job to change that on November 4" (Rubin, 1967: 34). Note that this spot does not say anything specific about how the problem will be solved; it simply conveys the image that the candidate is sincerely concerned about the issue. The use of spot commercials has been particularly upsetting to those observers who see the function of the campaign to inform the electorate. Since that time, spot commercials have been with us, and they are often very useful vehicles for creating distorted, simplistic images of issues and candidates. In 1964 the Democrats used a very controversial spot commerical that portrayed a little girl picking daisies followed by pictures of a nuclear explosion; this was followed by the reassuring statements of Lyndon Johnson about the need for nuclear responsibility. Obvious, this spot was a blatant scare tactic designed to increase voters' fears of Senator Goldwater.

The Kennedy-Nixon television debates discussed in Chapter 5 are widely viewed as an example of the best that television has to offer politics. It was estimated that between 70 to 75 million Americans saw the first debate, with audiences of over 50 million for the other three. The Carter-Ford debates discussed in Chapter 7 enjoyed similarly large audiences, although they seem unlikely to attain the prominence of the 1960 debates.

The 1968 election witnessed a more sophisticated use of television in the Nixon campaign. In the primaries, television was successfully used to change Nixon's image from that of an untrustworthy loser to that of a confidence-inspiring winner. Commercials portrayed Nixon as a warm person with the skills to manage the nation's affairs, especially in the realm of foreign policy. And in the general election, the basic television strategy was to have Nixon appear in staged, controlled settings answering prepared questions before carefully selected audiences. The home viewer would see in these televised sessions a confident Nixon fielding questions from a highly enthusiastic audience. Nixon avoided until the very end of the campaign any appearances on spontaneous televised interview programs, such as "Face the Nation" and "Meet the Press." Long-standing concerns about the ability of the media and media experts to market candidates were reemphasized by a book entitled *The Selling of the President 1968,* which presented a behind-the-scenes description of the marketing of Richard Nixon. The following comments by Roger Ailes, the producer of the staged Nixon television shows, epitomize the marketing approach to the packaging of candidates (McGinniss, 1969: 103):

> . . . Let's face it, a lot of people think Nixon is dull. Think he's a bore, a pain in the ass. They look at him as the kind of kid who always carried a bookbag. Who was forty-two years old the day he was born. They figure other kids got footballs for Christmas, Nixon got a brief-case and he loved it. He'd always have his homework done and he'd never let you copy.
>
> Now you put him on television, you've got a problem right away. He's a funny-looking guy. He looks like somebody hung him in a closet overnight and he jumps out in the morning with his suit all bunched up and starts running around saying, "I want to be President." I mean this is how he strikes some people. That's why these shows are important. To make them forget all that.

The 1972 election was unusual in that television's major impact came in its "normal" coverage of political events rather than in any paid advertising campaigns. The immediacy with which television brought home George McGovern's inconsistencies on such matters as Eagleton and welfare reform was probably more devastating to Mc-Govern's chances than any well-orchestrated advertising campaign. Likewise, the televised coverage given to Nixon's historic trips to China and the Soviet Union served to improve his political prospects by showing him as President while the various contenders for the Democratic presidential nomination were portrayed as politicians. The power of a President to dominate the broadcast media by foreign travels, dramatic announcements, and the like means that an incumbent President seeking reelection has a tremendously important resource at his disposal. As the 1980 presidential season approaches, one can anticipate major effort by Carter to obtain favorable television coverage.

The Effects of Television

Introduction. The question of the effects of the mass media, particularly television, has given rise to numerous controversies and differences of opinion. Some observers have praised the mass media for disseminating information about public affairs widely, thereby presumably facilitating the development of the informed, independent citizenry of classical democratic theory. Other observers have asked whether television debases or perverts the political process, and have worried about the power of television and the other media to manipulate and mold the preferences and opinions of a naive public. While these latter worries have often been expressed in unnecessarily alarmist terms, they do represent genuine concerns about the consequences of television for American politics. Unfortunately, it is difficult to talk in a rigorous and systematic fashion about the effects of television in many areas because the appropriate evidence does not exist or is highly incomplete and contradictory. This situation occurs because many of the effects of the media are long term and indirect rather than short term and direct. As Joseph Klapper observes (1960: 8): "Mass communication *ordinarily* does not serve as a necessary and sufficient cause of audience effects, but rather functions among and through a nexus of mediating factors and influences." This means that an ambitious research program examining many factors over an extended time is required to determine the effects of the media. For now, we are forced in part to speculate about the effect of television, buttressing our arguments wherever possible by recourse to appropriate evidence. Two broad classes of television effects can be identified—consequences for the political system at large, such as change in the presidential nomination system, and consequences for the individual citizen, such as the acquisition of political information. While this systemic-individual distinction breaks down at times, it provides a useful organizing framework for our discussion.

Television and the Political System. Mendelsohn and Crespi (1970: 297–98) have identified four interrelated changes in American politics brought on in part by television:

1. It has altered the processes of nominating candidates at party conventions.
2. It has altered campaigning.
3. It has altered traditional party structures and functions.
4. It has helped to encourage the questioning of the traditional ways of choosing and electing candidates, and, as a consequence, will aid in ushering in the new politics of the future.

With respect to the second of the changes cited, it is now commonplace to describe presidential campaigns as being conducted primarily through the medium of television, with the planning and execution of the campaign largely in the hands of media experts and public relations and marketing specialists. This means that the party professional is no longer the central figure in the campaign nor is the party organization the major source of campaign information. And with the development of computerized, direct-mail fund-raising techniques, often aided by televised appeals, the party organization has become less important in another area traditionally within its domain.

Robert Agranoff (1972: 43) notes that the typical media campaign hurts the political party since media campaigns are designed to support a single candidate and not an entire ticket. The Nixon reelection campaign in 1972 is probably the preeminent example of this. In its concern to win an overwhelming victory, the Nixon reelection team was careful not to antagonize potential Democratic defectors to Nixon by trying to elect the entire GOP ticket. The Nixon campaign was run not through the Republican National Committee but through the President's own personal organization—the Committee to Re-elect the President (CREEP).

Agranoff has also identified some positive changes in campaigning brought about by the electronic media. Certainly it is possible for greater numbers of citizens to follow campaigns today. And it is possible for voters to get a deeper, more personal insight into both candidates since the massive flow of information in presidential campaigns make it less likely that selective processes could occur whereby one psychologically "tunes out" the opposition candidate.

Yet the prominence of television has some serious negative consequences, the most obvious one being the need to package the candidate, which results in the campaign being a merchandising enterprise rather than an effort to inform the citizenry. The 1968 Nixon campaign is the classic marketing effort. Another obvious consequence of the heavy reliance on television is the need for candidates who can at least minimally master and exploit the medium by projecting an attractive image. While this need not mean that George Washington or Abraham Lincoln would be unelectable candidates in the United States today, it does imply that the savvy candidate and his advisers will attempt to exploit the properties of television. And one such property is that television requires high involvement by the audience to complete the partial image that it conveys: this is what McCluhan (1964: 229) means when he calls television a "cool," or low-intensity, medium. This characteristic of television leads to an emphasis on audience participation and on the campaign as drama. Moreover, it suggests that candidates with very well-defined images may suffer as the opportunity for audience involvement is lessened. This has led Harold Mendelsohn to speculate (1970: 276–77):

> ... we can expect the new generation of politicians to respond to the "low intensity" demands of the TV medium in order to procure the greatest possible degree of viewer involvement well before the national conventions are convened officially ... the professionals of tomorrow must project a "cool" image.
>
> This image will be cultivated and polished over considerable periods of time—during which every opportunity for television exposure will be exploited.

The emphasis on "cool" images may result in appeals to the electorate that are based less on issue considerations and more on style, thereby making it difficult for citizens to determine the candidates' issue positions. Of course, if the circumstances are appropriate, a candidate may try to project a well-defined image based upon specific stances on key issues, but this is the exception rather than the rule.

Another effect of television on campaigning is on the day-to-day conduct of the presidential contest. Today campaigns are geared to the television coverage they will receive; rallies are scheduled early in the day so that televised news reports will be ready for the nightly news programs. Candidates' speeches are designed to provide headlines for news broadcasts, and the rallies themselves are organized to create the image of enthusiastic support for the candidate. This concern for how the campaign will come across on television leads Mendelsohn and Crespi (pp. 281–82) to talk in terms of the pseudo campaign.

There are some more subtle, more speculative systemic effects of television on American politics. If previously the political party via the machine, patronage, and constituent services served as a major link between citizens and government, today television provides that link by being the major source of information about the activities of government, particularly at the national level. The tenor of the news and information conveyed by television, however, tends to be negative, focusing on the shortcoming and failures of governmental actors. Thus, while serving as a link between citizens and government, television may serve to increase the distance between the two. The political party, on the other hand, may have served to bring government closer to the people since it was often a dispenser of direct rewards to the citizenry. Similarly, the political party often served as a unifying force, organizing a disparate variety of interests into some fairly unified whole. Television in certain ways may serve as a unifying force as it depicts the common concerns confronting citizens, but it may also exacerbate the differences that divide citizens by bringing controversies directly into the home. Thus, television's contribution to the demise of the political party may have some broader societal ramifications.

A number of observers have discussed the potential impact of television's coverage of "bad news." Michael Robinson (1972) has argued that when television news programs show two public institutions in conflict, both institutions suffer in citizens' evaluations, and citizens' feelings of political effectiveness may drop. Wamsley and Pride (1972) argue in a similar vein that television news may be creating a citizenry more cynical and negative about politics, which in the long run may set the stage for dramatic system upheavals. They write (1972: 449–450):

> It seems reasonable to assume that members of a political system are supportive of that system and see it as legitimate to the degree that it is perceived to be: effective in solving problems, efficient in doing so, morally right in its conduct, and responsive and/or solicitous of citizen welfare. *It is a possibility* that the characteristics of TV news . . . result in a sum total of effects that is denigrative of political system authority symbols rather than supportive. It should be noted this is *not* necessarily the same thing as imputing "bias" to TV news. It is rather to say that . . . TV news [may] present the authority figures of the American political system in more of a negative light than a positive one. If this possibility is affirmed by thorough research, the incredibly difficult task of analyzing effects would only have begun. But it is *possible* that the characteristics of TV news, when combined with some relatively new conceptions of impact, effects, and audience characteristics, could lead to conclusions that are quite contrary to those complacently held for so long. Certainly the need is clear to view TV news with a new, scholarly skepticism, for it may hold a far more important place in the flow of political information than social scientists have assumed up to now.

As Wamsley and Pride admit, their argument is highly tentative and in need of confirming evidence.[8]

Related to this possible effect of increasing levels of cynicism is the potentiality of television for setting the issue agenda, for determining

---

[8] It may be that cynicizing effects are not limited to television but can occur with other media. In a study analyzing newspaper content and public attitudes, Miller, Goldenberg, and Erbring (1979) found that readers of newspapers more critical of government were themselves more distrustful, although the overall press coverage of government tended to be positive or neutral. Another study (Graber, 1976), which compared campaign news on television and in the press, found that press coverage of presidential qualifications was more negative than the coverage given by television.

the kinds of issues about which citizens and candidates will be concerned. Shafer and Larson (1972) argue that television brings home to citizens information about a variety of issues, such as law and order, political protests, and deviant lifestyles, that would otherwise have not impinged upon the consciousness of citizens. In so doing, television creates issues and concerns that otherwise would not exist. For example, we often observe that residents of very safe neighborhoods express considerable fear about personal safety, undoubtedly because of television news coverage of crime in other localities.

Shafer and Larson argue that longer and more detailed news shows would help alleviate the tendency of television to oversimplify and create issues, but they further argue that the problem will not be solved until the current definition of what constitutes news is changed (1972: 16):

> The definition which almost all working journalists use—"outstanding deviations from civil norms"—exacerbates the problem of too many deviant, intrusive, incomprehensible minorities. On the other hand, if "news" were defined in a more outcome-oriented way— "events of importance to sizeable number of viewers"—actors who are merely novel or strident, but in no way influential in others' lives, would no longer fill the screen so copiously.
>
> The first to disappear would be those who are news only because the cameras record them. A news program ought to *reveal* what happened, not *create* the happening. Events which legitimately comprise news may affect more lives if the cameras arrive, but they would have impact beyond a few central actors even without publicity. With an outcome-oriented definition, events staged to manipulate the journalist's view of news as anything sufficiently outrageous would disappear.

Note that the suggestions of Shafer and Larson would result in more tranquil, more positive new programs, which perhaps would weaken the cynicism producing effects of television cited by Robinson and Wamsley and Pride. Perhaps their suggestions might also lead to unjustifiably optimistic news broadacts if decisions were made to systematically exclude bad news on the pretext that it did not fit the definition of news.

More rigorous evidence of the agenda-setting function of the media is provided by the work of McCombs and Shaw (1972) who found in Chapel Hill, North Carolina, in 1968 that the issues emphasized in the press and the evening news shows correlated strongly with the issues that citizens themselves deemed important. Likewise, Funkhouser (1973) found a relationship between media coverage of an issue and the tendency of citizens to cite the issue as an important one facing the country. However, when citizens were asked about the important problems confronting them directly, they referred to issues different than those that were the focus of media coverage. Hence Funkhouser argued that the issues which people mention in response to general questions about what issues are important are simply those they have heard about on the media and are not necessarily those that are meaningful to them, thereby weakening any claims for the agenda-setting function of the media. The work of MacKuen (1978) supports Funkhouser; the issue concerns of Americans tended to mirror media content, although in the area of economics, public concerns did not depend upon media coverage of economic matters.

While the evidence for the cynicizing effects and agenda-setting function of television is still far from conclusive, these notions nevertheless remain highly plausible, with major implications for the future shape and stability of the political system. Over the long run, it may be the media, especially television, that define the basic issues the society must confront. And given the extensive coverage of bad news, American society may be faced with a series of issues and crises, each of which contributes to a further decline in confidence in political institutions and authorities. In the more immediate future, the agenda-setting property of television may affect voting behavior by determining the issues upon which voters base their choices. Some evidence that television may indeed have created the "social issue" of the late 1960s and 1970s is provided by the finding of Robinson and Zukin (1976) that reliance on television for political information was associated with a positive evaluation of George Wallace in 1968, the candidate who most exploited the social issue.

Television and the Citizen. The evidence about the effects of television and other media on the individual citizen, particularly in the context of a voting situation, is much more thorough and convincing than the evidence dealing with the systemic effects discussed earlier. The one potential effect of television of greatest interest to students of elections is its influence on citizens' vote choices. The two classical studies of the impact of the campaign and the mass media on citizens' candidate preferences are *The People's Choice* and *Voting*. While both works predate the major introduction of television into presidential contests, the findings of both are important to discuss if for no other reason than they have become a part of our standard folklore about campaigns. The most frequently cited finding of both studies is that the mass media and the campaign act mainly to reinforce the voter's initial predispositions and attitudes rather than change attitudes. For example, Lazarsfeld and his colleagues (1968: 101–104) found that very few residents of Erie County, Ohio, changed their vote intentions between May and October of 1940. A similar result was reported in the Elmira, New York, study of the 1948 election: 96 percent of citizens who expressed a partisan preference in both August and October remained stable in their vote intention. And in the last month of the campaign, only 5 percent of the respondents changed their vote intentions (Berelson et al., 1954: 16).

Thus, it appeared from these early studies that the campaign and the mass media had little effect on citizens' preferences. And those voters who did change their preferences over the course of the campaign tended to be those less interested in the election and less exposed to campaign communications. A number of reasons were given for the primacy of the reinforcement effect. Of particular importance was selective exposure, the tendency of individuals to expose themselves primarily to communications sympathetic to their existing beliefs. Such exposure would obviously have the effect of reinforcing rather than altering predispositions. Another factor cited for the prominence of reinforcement effects was the political homogeneity of the primary and secondary groups to which the individual belonged; interacting with like-minded individuals is likely to reinforce one's own attitudes.

Thus, the classical view of the campaign and the media is that both make relatively little difference to the election outcome, that reinforcement means that the election turned out the way it would have had there been no media communications or campaign. This conclusion, however, is in need of some important caveats and modifications, particularly about the importance of the media. First of all, reinforcement is an important (though perhaps not dramatic) effect that should be credited to the media. Moreover, reinforcement implies that there exist initial predispositions to be strengthened, these initial attitudes most often being partisan loyalties. But as partisanship becomes weaker and the number of Independents grows, the opportunity for reinforcement will be less and therefore the media may have greater campaign effects. In support of the notion that the media will be more important where voters have weaker predispositions, less information, and more uncertainty, Gary Jacobson (1974) found that broadcast campaigning was more consequential in nonpresidential elections, especially primary elections where voter information was low and party identification was not available as a basis of vote decision.

Another criticism of the findings on the reinforcement effects of the campaign and the media focuses on the evidence adduced in support of the selective exposure process. Reviewing a number of studies on selective exposure, Sears and Freedman (1967) conclude that the evidence is far from convincing and that in many cases people actually expose themselves to information contrary to their existing beliefs. One might expect that the tremendous amount of information available in presidential contests would overcome any tendency toward selective exposure. Moreover, in the current era of television domination where viewers are often exposed to political communications simply because the television set is turned on to regular programming, the extent of selective exposure may be quite limited.

A final criticism of the classical research on campaigns is that it predates the era of television; findings based on the print media and radio may not be generalizable to television. While more recent evidence indicates that on the average only about a third of the electorate makes its candidate selection during the actual campaign, this does not mean that the media are ineffective in influencing vote decisions. The fact that about two thirds of citizens have made their vote decisions by the end of the nominating conventions may mean that the media play their crucial role early on. The many Democrats who decided early in 1972 that they would not support the McGovern candidacy certainly received information from the media that helped shape their decisions. Thus, while the media change relatively few preferences during the actual campaign, they still are influential in providing citizens with information and images upon which to base pre-campaign vote decisions and in structuring alternatives and depicting potential candidates throughout the inter-election period.

As we turn to the contemporary research on the media and campaigns, a few points should be kept in mind. Most of this research focuses on the general election campaign; we have relatively little solid evidence about the effects of the media during the primary season. Also, the recent work is more sophisticated in how it views the media because it not only talks about distinctive media, such as television, radio, and newspapers, but distinguishes among different types of content within a medium. For example, recent research on television has been careful not to treat the medium as a single entity; instead, it has explicitly recognized there are different types of political television, such as the nightly national news shows, public affairs documentaries, and televised political commercials. The current research is also more sophisticated in how it conceptualizes media effects in the context of a campaign. Thus, recent studies analyze not only media influences on vote choice, but also more subtle effects in such areas as information acquisition and agenda setting. Finally, the recent work takes a more realistic and complex view of how media effects occur. Rather than simply assuming that identical media content affects different people in the same way, the current research argues that, to assess media effects, one must be sensitive to the properties of the recipients of the media messages as well as to the properties of the messages themselves.

One prominent approach along these lines has been labelled the "uses and gratifications" approach; it emphasizes not what the media do to people, but how and why citizens use the media. This approach argues that the effects of campaign media on voters will depend upon the motivations that voters have for following the medium. For example, the uses and gratifications approach claims that the effect of the debates on viewers depends not only on the viewers' predispositions, such as party identification, but also on why viewers watched the debates in the first place. People who watched the debates for their entertainment value might respond to them very differently than people who watched for other reasons, such as the desire to acquire information about the candidates or the felt need to be a good citizen by watching the debates.

Like the classical studies, the contemporary research finds little effect of the media on vote preference. However, with respect to issue awareness, Patterson and McClure (1976: 49, 116) found that regular viewing of network news had no effect on the voter's issue awareness, but that viewing of political commercials was associated with higher voter awareness of candidates' issue stances. The simple explanation for this was that political advertising actually had more issue and information content to it than did the nightly network news shows. Hofstetter et al. (1976: 11) support this finding somewhat; they found that exposure to network election specials and to political advertising was more highly correlated with richness of issue perceptions than was exposure to network news programs. O'Keefe and Sheinkopf (1974) dispute the information-producing effects of political advertising. They argued that even though the political use of television in 1972 involved longer and more informative ads than the short ads used in previous elections, the television ads were not seen by viewers as important information sources. Moreover, O'Keefe and Sheinkopf concluded that no matter their length the television ads served mainly as image builders rather than information sources. The contradiction between their findings and those of Patterson and McClure can be reconciled by the notion of the inadvertent audience. While it may be true that O'Keefe's and Sheinkopf's respondents did not consciously view political commercials as important information sources, they were nevertheless acquiring information from them unknowingly. Spot commercials come on during regular programming so that many viewers who might not ordinarily tune in political programming accidently end up watching political commercials and learning from them. A study (Bowen et al., 1972) of spot commercials in the Wisconsin and Colorado gubernatorial races in 1970 supports this notion; the authors found that specific information, such as candidates' qualifications and issues stands rather than more general images, were learned from the ads.

Patterson and McClure (1976: 67–68) uncovered no effect of television news shows on the candidate images of committed voters. Among the undecided voters exposed to television, images of Nixon and McGovern changed very little until *after* the decision was made about which candidate to support. Hofstetter et al. (1976: 10) agreed with this finding in part, claiming that exposure to news programming "appeared to have increased the total amount of imagery about the candidates, but failed to influence the nature of this imagery."

Content analyses of the network evening news shows indicate that the issue stands and qualifications of the candidates receive very little attention. Instead, it is the hoopla, the rallies, the noise and excitement that are covered; network news treats the general election campaign like a horse race. For example, Patterson and McClure (1976: 31) reported that about 60 percent of the time that a presidential candidate was shown on camera in 1972, he was shown in a crowd scene. They charge (1976: 144) that the networks maintain the charade of the horse race with the active cooperation of the candidates who gear their campaigns to this kind of media coverage, a point elaborated upon in the second part of this chapter.

In contrast to television, recent studies of newspapers have identified surprisingly strong effects on information levels and vote choice.

Patterson and McClure (1976: 51) discovered that people who read the newspaper regularly became much better informed about the campaign. Three studies have indicated that newspaper endorsements have a direct effect on vote choice. Erikson (1976: 217–218) analyzed the effect of newspaper shifts in partisan endorsements between 1960 and 1964 on the Democratic presidential vote. Among other things, he found that in single major newspaper counties the 1964 vote was 5 percent more Democratic if the paper supported Johnson over Goldwater. He speculated (1976: 220) about the long-term impact of the Republican press, arguing that the cumulative effect of newspaper endorsements over time may be important. Two studies by John Robinson also demonstrate the importance of newspaper endorsements on vote choice. In one study, Robinson (1972) found that perception that a newspaper supported one candidate over the other was associated with about a 6 percent vote advantage for the preferred candidate, an effect most pronounced among respondents with weaker party loyalties. In the other study, Robinson (1974) found that there was a correlation across five presidential elections between presidential endorsements made by newspapers and the vote choice made by readers of these newspapers, controlling for relevant other variables.

If newspaper endorsements do affect vote choice as the above research suggests, then Republican presidential candidates can expect to be advantaged on Election Day. Despite Spiro Agnew's complaints about the liberal, Democratic press, the editorial policy of newspapers is heavily Republican. For example, a survey in 1976 of 661 daily newspapers showed 411 endorsing Ford, 80 Carter, and the rest uncommitted or independent. The Ford newspapers had a combined circulation of 21 million compared to 7.6 million for the Carter papers. This Republican edge is typical; only in 1964 did newspapers give more support to the Democratic candidate. In that year, Johnson was endorsed by 440 dailies and Goldwater by 359. Among the major papers in 1976, the *New York Times* and the *St. Louis Post Dispatch* endorsed Carter, while Ford was supported by the *New York Daily News,* the *Philadelphia Inquirer,* the *Miami Herald,* the *Cleveland Plain Dealer,* the *Baltimore Sun,* and many others. A number of major papers, such as the *Washington Post* and the *Los Angeles Times,* did not make endorsements. One less than enthusiastic endorsement that Ford got was from the *Manchester Union Leader;* publisher William Loeb, a Reagan enthusiast, said the election was a choice between "stupid" (Ford) and "shifty" (Carter). He wrote, "Better the fool we know than the devil we don't."

THE MEDIA AND THE PRESIDENTIAL SELECTION PROCESS[9]

Introduction

In this section of the chapter, we will focus on how the media affects the presidential selection process where that process is viewed as comprising three stages—the primary season, the national nominating conventions, and the general election campaign. The greatest attention will be given to the pre-convention period, for it is here that the media's impact is most substantial for reasons detailed shortly. I will argue that in covering the primaries the media are not neutral but actually affect the outcome of the process. This intrusiveness of the media is not due to any systematic bias or conspiracy on the part of reporters and television commentators, but instead reflects structural aspects of the news reporting enterprise as well as ambiguities and complexities inherent in the primary season.

There is a paradox as we try to analyze media effects across the three steps of presidential selection. If it is indeed the case that media impact is greatest in the primary season, it is also the case that the empirical evidence relevant to this first phase is weaker than the information on the latter stages. Hence our discussion of media effects in the primary season must of necessity take on a more speculative tone.

The Primary Season

Introduction. It seems on a priori grounds that the impact of the media should be greatest during the primary election phase of the presidential selection process. This is so because of the ambiguity and complexity inherent in the primaries, which facilitate media influences and intrusiveness. For example, primary elections are often multiple candidate contests, so that standards of victory may not be as clear as they are in the general election and the nominating conven-

---

[9] Much of this discussion is taken from Asher (1977). Because much of the following discussion emphasizes the sequential nature of the primaries, the reader may find it useful at this point to look ahead to Table 10.6 which presents, among other things, the 1976 presidential primary schedule.

tions. Unlike the general election, the structure of competition shifts over the primary season with candidates declaring themselves in and dropping out, thereby making the comparative interpretation of a series of elections more problemmatic. Furthermore, despite the apparent confusion that the Electoral College adds to the general election, the variety of primary arrangements—binding versus nonbinding, delegate versus beauty contests, winner-take-all versus proportional allocation of delegates, popular vote versus delegates won, and so on—represents a level of complexity that literally invites media interpretation and misinterpretation. Finally, the amount of information available about the candidates is low, especially early in the primary season, so that what the media chooses to emphasize can be very consequential for the candidate's fate, particularly since party identification cannot serve as a cue for candidate choice in a partisan primary.

Some theoretical perspectives on mass communications also argue for the greater impact of the media during the primaries as opposed to the later stages. There is an ongoing debate as to whether candidate images are perceiver-determined or stimulus- (e.g., television-) determined. The former view (Sigel, 1964) argues that one's candidate images are filtered by one's own predispositions, such as party identification, and that selective processes help maintain cognitive consistency. The stimulus-determined position (McGrath and McGrath, 1962; Baskin, 1976) asserts that citizens' images of candidates are more directly a function of what they actually see or read about the contenders. Although there is evidence supporting both sides, it is certainly the case that one's perceptual defenses are lower during the primaries than during the general election, and hence images of the candidates formed during the primary season, especially early on, are more likely to be stimulus-determined. In the general election as people have more information about the candidates and as the perceptual screen function of party identification comes into play, images may be less stimulus-determined. In a related vein, given the low information levels characteristic of primaries, the media, even if they do not create or alter attitudes directly, can determine the grounds (e.g., issues, personality) on which people choose between the candidates, an agenda-setting effect.

In summary, primary elections tend to be less well-defined phenomena, thereby allowing substantial leeway in media reporting and interpretation. It is difficult to demonstrate empirically that media coverage of primary election outcomes and of opinion poll presidential preferences are necessarily good or bad for the candidates or can generate bandwagons, although recent studies are suggestive. Beniger (1976) found that a candidate's standing in the preference polls had little or no effect on changes in his standing in subsequent polls, although preference poll position contributed directly to primary election success. Beniger's results also indicated that primary election success led to an improvement in a candidate's poll standing, especially for Democratic candidates in the early primaries, a finding supported by Collat et al. (1976). In a study of the 1976 nominations, Aldrich et al. (1978) argued that primary election results affected campaign momentum in the areas of poll standing, contributions, and media attention. With respect to Carter's candidacy, they found that Carter's early successes in Iowa and New Hampshire led to great increases in media coverage, popular support, and eventually financial contributions. The authors concluded that early success is vital in the presidential selection process as early setbacks result in media, contributors, and voters looking elsewhere.

A more intriguing aspect of this research is the evidence it presents that recent primary election campaigns have differed from the traditional patterns. Writing about nomination contests between 1936 and 1972, Beniger (1976) identifies only three genuine horse races—the Democratic contests in 1960 and 1972 and the Republican race in 1964. Likewise, Lucy (1973) has observed that between 1936 and 1972, only once—in 1972—in 20 cases has the presidential contender leading in the last pre-primary Gallup Poll lost primaries and permanently lost the poll lead. Although this occurred only once in 36 years, it happened again in 1976 when Jimmy Carter overcame an initial low standing in the polls to capture the Democratic nomination. The question arises as to why the traditional pattern of open and shut nomination campaigns in which the early leaders ultimately emerged victorious has been broken twice in the last four years. One answer is certainly the proliferation of primaries, which has resulted in the overwhelming majority of delegates being popularly elected. But to the proliferation of primaries must be added the manner in which the media cover the primaries, and it is to this concern that we now turn. The following discussion will show by example how the media can affect the course of the primary process. A list of examples obviously does not constitute compelling proof of the intrusiveness of the media, but the cases to be discussed are thought-provoking. The discussion will focus on three interrelated themes—the complexity of the primaries, the games that candidates play, and the emphases of the news-reporting enterprise.

The Complexity of the Primaries. The primaries are complex in many ways, one being that they are often muliple-candidate contests. At times the field of declared candidates is only a small subset of the total number of prospective nominees. The media play a very prominent role here in determining which of all the potential candidates are serious and viable. David Broder (1976: 215–17) cites one role of reporters in presidential politics as being that of the talent scout who decides which candidates merit genuine consideration as presidential aspirants. The power of this screening function is detailed very insightfully by Timothy Crouse (1973: 39, 194–99), who describes how the press gave careful scrutiny to George Romney in 1968, ultimately overplaying his "brainwashed" comment and destroying his credibility as a candidate. Whether Romney merited such treatment is not central here. What is crucial is that in the same period when Romney was undergoing intensive scrutiny, Richard Nixon was enjoying a free ride from the press because he was maintaining a low profile. After the press was through with Romney, Nixon's path to the White House was made easier. Likewise, the candidacy of Sargent Shriver in 1976 was hurt by the heavy media emphasis on his being Ted Kennedy's brother-in-law, which led observers to wonder whether Shriver was a stalking horse for Kennedy. Had Shriver's past governmental experience (e.g., Ambassador to France, Peace Corps director) been the focus of media coverage, he might then have been viewed as a more credible contender.

A more important aspect of the presence of multiple entrants in primaries is that standards of victory are less obvious. Where more than two candidates are vying, the simple majority criterion may have little utility and the media may establish their own tests of candidate performance. Passage of these tests may indicate that a candidate is running strongly, but the question arises as to why one test is chosen and not others. For example, the Florida primary in 1976 was deemed crucial to Jimmy Carter's hopes. It was argued that for Carter to establish himself as a serious contender, he had to defeat George Wallace. But why did Carter have to win, particularly since the Jackson candidacy in Florida was likely to hurt Carter more than Wallace? As an alternative test, how about simply a strong showing by Carter in Florida, especially since Wallace had swept the Florida primary in 1972?

The standards that the media establish allow for interpretation of events at some variance from what actually occurred. The classic example of this occurred in 1972 in the New Hampshire Democratic primary, in which Edmund Muskie "failed" to get the magic 50 percent of the vote needed to give his candidacy a boost, even though he defeated his chief rival George McGovern by a margin of 46 percent to 37 percent. James Perry explained how the 50 percent standard gradually emerged as the media consensus, beginning with a story by David Broder on January 9 (nearly *two* months before the primary) in which Broder wrote, "As the acknowledged front-runner and a resident of the neighboring state, Muskie will have to win the support of at least half the New Hampshire Democrats in order to claim a victory" (Perry, 1973: 85). Perry claimed that television newsmen picked up the 50 percent figure and thereby managed to infuse drama in a race whose outcome was largely a foregone conclusion. Perry (1973: 86) attributed part of Muskie's problem to a pre-primary poll showing Muskie with 65 percent of the vote. Despite the instability and unreliability of many pre-primary polls (Roper, 1975), the 65 percent and later the 50 percent mark became an albatross on the Muskie candidacy. In the first four primaries in 1972, Muskie won New Hampshire with 46 percent of the vote and Illinois with 63 percent, while Wallace carried Florida with 42 percent and McGovern Wisconsin with 30 percent. Yet it was the McGovern candidacy that was building and Muskie's that was collapsing when Wisconsin voted. Certainly media coverage of the New Hampshire primary hastened the downfall of the Muskie candidacy.

Burns Roper (1975) has called for reform of media coverage of primaries, but his message has not been heeded. And of all primary coverage, that given to New Hampshire is most in need of reform. As the first state to hold a presidential primary, New Hampshire is of course critical to the presidential selection process. Its importance is heightened, however, by the inordinate media attention given it. Michael Robinson (1978) found that of the network news stories devoted to the first eight primaries in 1976, fully 30 percent focused on New Hampshire. Moreover, media emphasis on New Hampshire increased substantially between 1972 and 1976 (Robinson, 1977: 83). Hence, the New Hampshire results, as interpreted by the media, are extremely influential in promoting or undermining a presidential candidacy. On the day before the 1976 New Hampshire primary, Walter Cronkite opined on the evening news that anything less than

55 percent of the Republican vote for Ford should be construed as a setback for the incumbent President. Luckily for Ford, this standard was not universally adopted. (In fact, other standards more favorable to Ford were adopted, a point elaborated in our later discussion of the games that candidates play.)

The point is that primary success, poll standing, and the ability to raise money and attract volunteers are all interrelated. The quest for the presidential nomination is in part a psychological battle and the media can be very influential in unwittingly creating a psychological climate beneficial to one candidate. Morris Udall complained in April of 1976 that Jimmy Carter had profited from an "orgy of publicity." Although Udall's complaint must be taken with a grain of salt, given his own aspirations, his comments (Cannon, 1976) nevertheless get to the heart of the issue:

> Never underestimate the importance of momentum in these presidential elections. We all said we weren't going to let New Hampshire do it to us again, and New Hampshirt did do it. We all said that the Iowa caucus was not that important, and the press made it that important. . . . Once that avalanche starts down the ski slope, get out of the way.
>
> . . . The people want winners and losers and if you make 27 points in a football game and I make 26, you're called a winner and I'm called a loser.

Udall's comments reflect the tendency of the media to make the primaries a sporting contest, most often a horse race, where winners and losers must be identified even if there are no clear victors. Given the emphasis on outcomes, the question still remains how to define winning and losing. If the media had decided on delegates won as the standard, instead of popular vote pluralities, then the early Democratic primaries in 1976 would not have seemed so definitive and certainly would not have given the Carter candidacy as much of an impetus. As it is, it seems that the media began to emphasize delegates won in coverage of the later primaries so that even as Carter began to lose elections to his late-entering opponents, his losses were offset by news reports emphasizing his delegate gains and his inexorable march to a delegate majority.

The notion that the media needs to identify winners and losers can be extended to say that winners and losers must be individuals and not such undefined entities as "uncommitteds," delegates pledegd to no specific candidate. In fact, throughout 1976—beginning with the precinct caucuses in Iowa in January and culminating with the New Jersey primary in June—the performance of the uncommitteds was reported in, at best, questionable ways. Even though the uncommitteds won in Iowa with 37 percent of the vote, compared to 28 percent for Carter and 13 percent for Bayh, press attention focused on Carter. Elizabeth Drew (1976a: 133) reported that as a result of his Iowa "victory," Carter was interviewed on the "CBS Morning News," while NBC's "Today Show" and ABC's "Good Morning America" also ran segments on Carter. On the "CBS Evening News," Walter Cronkite said that Iowa voters have spoken, "and for the Democrats what they said was 'Jimmy Carter'." Yet given the amount of time that Carter spent in Iowa, his performance might have been portrayed as less impressive. It may be that there was no significant political interpretation to be given by the media to the victory of the uncommitted in Iowa, beyond being a function of oddities in the delegate selection rules; but the victory of the uncommitted in New Jersey is a far different matter, a point to be developed shortly.

Given the sharp increase in the number of primaries between 1968 and 1976, an additional problem that media interpretation must address is what primaries are to be stressed. Rick Stearns, deputy campaign manager for McGovern in 1972, claimed (May and Fraser, 1973: 97) that the McGovern strategy was formulated under the assumption that primaries significant in the past would continue to be so viewed by the press in 1972. Hence, the McGovern camp stressed the Wisconsin primary and won it; but as Stearns himself said (May and Fraser, 1973: 97), there was no other reason than press inertia that "Wisconsin should have been the watershed for the McGovern campaign that it was; the Wisconsin primary fundamentally was not that important."

An additional complication associated with the increased number of primaries was that in 1976 more than one major primary occurred on the same day, whereas in previous years the major primaries unfolded in a nice temporal and geographic sequence starting in New Hampshire, moving to Wisconsin, and concluding with Oregon and California. In 1976, the media had more difficult decisions to make about which primaries to stress and it is not entirely clear they made the right choices. For example, the Wisconsin and New York primaries occurred on the same day, and it appears that the Wisconsin contest, despite allocating many fewer delegates than New York (274 versus 68), received the lion's share of media attention. This may have been due to Wisconsin's traditional importance or to the widespread feeling that Henry Jackson was expected to win in New York, which therefore made that race less exciting and less newsworthy, or due to the fact that Wisconsin was a simpler story to report since it entailed only two major candidates *and* a straightforward popular vote contest. Likewise, the Oregon primary was held on the same day as five other primaries in 1976. Oregon became the featured primary because it was deemed the most competitive race; Kentucky, Arkansas, and Tennessee were conceded to southerner Jimmy Carter; Idaho to native son Frank Church; and Nevada to neighbor Jerry Brown. But even though Oregon was the most competitive race between Carter, Church, and Brown (as a write-in), it is arguable whether this made it more newsworthy, except that it more resembled the horse race that the media seem to emphasize. The mentality underlying this view of news is illustrated by *Washington Post* columnist Ed Walsh (1976: A6) who wrote that the California primary "appeared to lose some of its luster as polls continued to show Reagan a solid favorite to take the state's 167 delegates." With this kind of reporting, a victorious candidate will gain greater mileage by defeating a rival in a hotly contested race in doubt to the end, rather than in a convincing victory evident some time prior to the actual voting.

The problem that multiple and complex primaries on the same day poses for the media is best illustrated by "Super Tuesday" of the 1976 primary season. On June 8, California, New Jersey, and Ohio all held primaries which, on the Democratic side, selected 540 delegates, more than a third of the total needed for nomination. The question was: how would these primary results be interpreted? Which state outcome would be viewed as most significant? In retrospect, it was Ohio—not California and New Jersey—that proved critical. Carter's victory in Ohio was widely seen as locking up the nomination for him. But why Ohio? Was "Super Tuesday" such an unqualified success for the former Governor of Georgia?

The *New York Times* front page story about New Jersey on the day before the primary read "Carter Victory is Forecast in Jersey Vote Tomorrow." On primary day, R. W. Apple's front page story was entitled "Carter Appears Near Goal in Last 3 Primaries Today." On Wednesday the *Times* headline was "Ford and Carter Lead in Votes in Jersey and Ohio; California Leaning to Brown and Reagan." The front page headline in the *Times* on Thursday proclaimed "Carter

Seems Due to Win on First Ballot," while on page 43 was a story entitled "Humphrey-Brown Victory in Jersey is Called Futile."

The question becomes how an anticipated Carter victory in New Jersey, which turned into an overwhelming delegate loss (83 for uncommitted, 25 for Carter), could be given so little attention. At one level, the New Jersey story did deserve less attention since the fact that Carter picked up over 200 delegates on "Super Tuesday," even while being thumped in California and New Jersey, may have been the major story of the day—it put Carter so much closer to the nomination. But in terms of the popular appeal of the candidates, the Ohio results should have been balanced by the New Jersey and California outcomes, yet they were not. The question is why.

A part of the answer is the inability or unwillingness of the media to handle complexity. An NBC television reporter argued that Ohio was the real test since there was a native son on the California ballot and in New Jersey there were uncommitted delegates, which made interpretation difficult and confused the issue. This, however, is no explanation but simply an admission that Ohio was more congenial to media coverage. One could convincingly argue that the front-runner Carter's loss in New Jersey to an uncommitted delegate slate (widely advertised as supporting Humphrey and Brown and opposing Carter) was truly the significant outcome of the day. Yet evidently this was too complicated to explain to readers and viewers. New Jersey was further complicated by a nonbinding beauty contest as well as the delegate selection vote. The fact that Carter won the former easily against token opposition and lost the latter decisively would have made the New Jersey story even more difficult to report. The lesson of all this is that the media seeks excitement and simplicity—a point developed more later.

Games Candidates Play.   While the media may inadvertently misinterpret primary results because of reasons inherent in media coverage, it is also the case that politicians try to manipulate the media to further their own ends. As Elizabeth Drew notes (1976b: 89), "A classic problem for candidates is how to inflate their prospects in order to attract allies and followers without creating a standard against which they can be measured unfavorably." This helps explain how the front-runner status hurt Muskie, but not Carter. Muskie was a strong front-runner expected to do well, but Carter was a weak one who, each time he ran well, surprised observers with his strength. By the time Carter started to lose primaries to Brown and Church, he was so far out in front that it did not matter much. As Roper (1975: 29) notes, a candidate's goal is to run better than expected and, hence, the incentive, especially for underdog candidates, is to poor-mouth their own prospects so the eventual results appear more promising.

An excellent example of successful media manipulation was Gerald Ford's quest for the Republican nomination in 1976. Despite the bungling attributed to the Ford campaign staff, one can argue that the Ford operatives were more skillful than the Reagan camp in manipulating the media to their own ends. Late in the New Hampshire primary race, the Reagan forces leaked a poll showing their candidate eight percentage points ahead. This was a tactical mistake since it created expectations of a Reagan win, against which Ford's narrow victory was seen as impressive: Ford's 51 percent of the vote was not interpreted as a weak showing for an incumbent President despite Cronkite's aforementioned judgment that an incumbent President should be able to get at least 55 percent. Clearly, the Reagan strategy should have been one of publicly hoping for 40 percent of the vote—and then New Hampshire might have served as Reagan's springboard to the nomination. Thus, Reagan's 48 percent of the New Hampshire vote in 1976 did him less good than McGovern's 37 percent in 1972.

The Ford partisans skillfully manipulated the New Hampshire results in subsequent primaries. In Florida, they were aided by Reagan's campaign manager, who had predicted a two-to-one Reagan victory. After New Hampshire, the campaign manager lowered his estimate to a 55 percent Reagan win. This allowed the Ford forces to claim a 12 percent gain and the ever-important momentum, while at the same time preserving their underdog status, a tactic that almost perfectly follows Drew's advice cited previously. Had the President lost narrowly in Florida, the Ford people might have been successful in portraying this as a moral victory even as the Reagan camp was unsuccessful in claiming New Hampshire as a moral victory. As it turned out, Ford carried Florida with about 53 percent of the vote, a victory heralded by the media as impressive, given prior expectations of a Reagan win in Florida.

After Reagan's string of primary successes in Texas, Indiana, Nebraska, and elsewhere, one can argue that the Ford campaign was very skillful in setting up the Michigan primary as one that the President might lose. It is hard to demonstrate that Ford was ever in any serious trouble in Michigan; yet the successful conveying of that impression served to inflate the significance of his Michigan win, and thereby put his campaign on the right track again. In retrospect, it is interesting to note that an incumbent President's victory in his own home state was accorded so much more importance than his challenger's victory in his own home state.

A final example of successful game playing is Mayor Daley's claim that a Carter victory in Ohio would mean that Carter "will walk in (to the nomination) under his own power." Daley had picked Ohio as decisive and it was. The question is: Which came first? Was Ohio always crucial and Daley simply recognizing a fact? Or was Ohio crucial because Daley said so? If the latter, then this helps explain why Ohio and not California and New Jersey received the most attention on Super Tuesday. The pre-primary polls in Ohio indicated that a substantial Carter victory was in the making. Thus, it appears that Daley ably manipulated the media to put himself in the position of kingmaker.

Media manipulation by candidates can affect the outcome of the primary process. Imagine if the Reagan people in New Hampshire had been more savvy and understated their expectations. Likewise, one can only speculate about what would have happened had Mayor Daley said that New Jersey and not Ohio was the ball game. Had California and New Jersey been described as major Carter setbacks instead of second-place finishes, would people have been so eager to jump on the Carter bandwagon the next day? Again, the point is that politics is in part a psychological game, and the side that can set the standard of performance adopted by the media has a tremendous advantage. To the extent that the media are successfully manipulated by the candidates, they are playing an intrusive role in presidential politics.

The News Reporting Emphasis. How the media report the primaries can be very consequential for their outcome. As mentioned earlier, the dominant perspective that news reporting takes on the primaries is the horse race, with emphasis on who's winning and losing, who's closing fast and who's fading. Perry (1973: 10) blames the "who's ahead" mentality in part on Theodore White's books on presidential elections. White, of course, had the advantage of writing after the winner's identity was already known. Newsmen following the primaries as they occur do not have this luxury, yet they may get so hooked on the importance of proclaiming "who's ahead" that they put themselves in intenable positions, such as awarding the nomination to Muskie before any of the primaries had been held in 1972. As Broder observes (1976: 217), the handicapper role of reporters may mislead readers into believing that a candidate's current standing necessarily predicts accurately his final standing.

The horse race mentality is, of course, encouraged by the need to attract readers and viewers. A horse race is by definition an exciting event—with identifiable winners and losers. And as Collat et al. (1976: 34) point out, newsmen tend to agree in their judgment of who is ahead since "they see the same polls, read the same things, and talk to the same people." This results in a certain homogeneity in news reporting about the viability of candidates and can make the media more influential in the winnowing of candidates. The focus on who is winning even shows up on election night coverage of the primaries, where the networks often seem to be in a race among themselves to be the first to call the outcome of the primary.

It has also been argued that the horse race emphasis reflects the competence of political reporters to cover politics and their inability to cover government. Charles Peters (1976: 56) described political reporters as knowing "much about the process of being elected and little about what the government does or how it could be improved." This means that coverage of what the candidates actually stand for and what they plan to do often gets overwhelmed by the concern for winning and losing, a phenomenon which also occurs in the general election campaign. The policy positions of candidates are often inadequately reported.[10] Patterson (1977) provides convincing evidence of the horse race mentality of network news. Analyzing the content of network news, he found that 60 percent of the 1976 presidential election coverage focused on the horse race, compared to only 28 percent devoted to issues, candidate qualifications, and the like. And during the height of the primary season, the proportion of time devoted to

---

[10] David Broder (1979) speculates that the horse race mentality may also be prominent on the White House staff. The ever-lengthening campaign required to seek the presidential nomination compels a candidate to surround himself with loyalists willing to make an indefinite commitment. If the candidate is successful, the faithful supporters may be rewarded with positions in the White House. Yet such staffers, usually young and relatively inexperienced in government, may be more interested and competent in winning elections than running the day-to-day affairs of government. Hence their emphasis is on the next election and not on the current happenings in government, which works to the detriment of successful public policy formulation and execution.

the horse race was even higher. In a similar vein, Graber and Kim (1977) found that the thrust of media coverage made it difficult for the voter to compare candidates' issue positions.

There are times when the political acumen of reporters may fail them and they fall back on standard operating procedures. The occurrence of major, multiple primaries on the same day in 1976 was probably a situation for which newsmen lacked clear guidelines as to which races merited major coverage; hence, reporters fell back on the criterion of competition—the horse race—to identify the critical primary.

At other times, reporters may simply not know what sort of focus should be given to a story and may therefore follow the lead of an influential journalist. The classic example of this occurred in 1972 when newsmen were perplexed about the significance of the Iowa precinct caucus results. According to Crouse (1973: 85), when R. W. Apple wrote as his lead for Iowa that McGovern had made a surprisingly strong showing, the other newsmen picked up the story and reported the same theme back to their papers. Drew (1976a: 127) reports a similar occurrence in Iowa in 1976. Apple had written a story that Carter was doing well in Iowa and this story itself became a political event "prompting other newspaper stories that Carter was doing well in Iowa, and then more newspaper, magazine, and television coverage for Carter than might otherwise have been his share."

The horse race mentality can be very intrusive. Few people would want to bet on a candidate identified in the media as a loser. The interaction between media coverage, poll results, and primary outcomes can generate interpretations and prophecies that assume a life of their own and act to promote the prospects of one candidate over another.

The Conventions

In discussing the effect of the media, especially television, on the nominating conventions, one can identify three targets of impact: the procedural and structural arrangements of the convention, the delegates to the conventions, and the home viewers of the conventions. About the first, conventions today are events staged for television. Since 1952 conventions have been streamlined to be more attractive to the television audience. For example, Judith Parris reports (1972: 150) that the 1952 Democratic convention totaled ten sessions that lasted over 47 hours, while the 1968 convention consisted of just five sessions that ran less than 29 hours. Despite McGovern giving his acceptance speech at three o'clock in the morning Eastern time, convention activities, such as the nominee's speeches, are scheduled to reach the largest possible audience.

If the effect of television on conventions was simply one of streamlining and scheduling, then it would be difficult to argue that television was intrusive in any negative or harmful sense. Unfortunately, television's effects go beyond routine shaping of the convention. For example, the Democrats in 1976 were very concerned that their convention be perceived by the American public as a harmonious and orderly affair. They believed that their raucous and conflictual conventions of 1968 and 1972 as portrayed to the American public via television were major contributing factors to Humphrey's and McGovern's defeats. Hence, the 1976 Democratic convention adopted a rule that minority reports on the platform, rules, and credentials had to have the support of 25 percent of the members of the appropriate committee in order to be brought before the full convention; only 10 percent had been required in the past. Certainly this rule change was an attempt to avoid televised divisiveness, to minimize the prominence of fringe elements, and to keep the convention on schedule.

Although making minority reports more difficult may not be the optimal way to achieve full airing of issues, one can sympathize with party professionals who are concerned with what the citizen at home sees of the conventions on television. The Republicans in 1964 and the Democrats in 1968 and 1972 left stormy conventions as seriously divided parties and all three lost in November. It is an empirical generalization that the nominee selected at the convention should gain ground in the polls right after the convention, yet McGovern actually lost ground in the post-convention polls conducted *before* the Eagleton affair. It appears that the vast majority of Americans are not enthralled by conventions characterized by conflict and rancor, nor are they sympathetic to parties and candidates whose conventions appear dominated by groups alien and threatening to the average citizen.

Paletz and Elson (1976) have presented one of the few systematic analyses of what aspects of the conventions television actually emphasizes. Their quantitative analysis of NBC's coverage of the 1972 Democratic convention demonstrated that violence and fringe elements were not given undue coverage, nor was there any bias for or against

McGovern. In their qualitative analysis of NBC coverage, however, Paletz and Elson came to a different conclusion. They argued that the predominant impression left by television of the Democratic convention was one of conflict and disorder. They attributed this not to any deliberate bias on the part of newsmen but to the norms and procedures of television news reporting. For example, they argued that the media interpret fairness to mean getting all sides. But as Paletz and Elson point out (1976: 122):

> . . . it [getting all sides] can make the "Stop McGovern Movement" seem as strong as the "Elect McGovern Movement" whether it is or not. Moreover the technique may actually create the impression of sides that do not really exist to a substantial degree among the delegates as a whole. It certainly increases the elements of conflict and drama.

Furthermore, when reporters do portray divisiveness, they do not so in ways to suggest that it represents a healthy discussion of issues, but instead that it symbolizes bitterness and hostility. Zukin (1979: 19–22) presents evidence about the effects of perceived conflict from the perspective of viewers of the 1976 conventions. He found that people had less favorable recollections of the Republican convention, with many of these negative images centering on the style of the convention and on the behavior of the delegates. He argued that the conflict associated with the hotly contested Ford-Reagan battle resulted in more negative evaluations of the Republican convention.

What Paletz and Elson are saying is that television distorts the conventions for reasons inherent in the news reporting enterprise. Warren Weaver (1976) points out that in a dull convention, television, unlike newspapers which can cut back convention column space, must fill the time and to accomplish this may seize upon an inconsequential story and blow it out of proportion. Weaver asserts that reports of anti-Carter dissension at the Democratic convention received much more attention than they deserved for just this reason.

The networks are in competition to attract viewers and this seems to be reflected in their readiness to push any story. The problem is that if substantial coverage is given to an inconsequential story, it may be elevated to a matter of genuine importance. This is reflected in the eagerness with which the network seized upon the alleged bribing of two Ford delegates from Illinois; the television coverage was replete with interviews with representatives on both sides, the reporting of heated charges and denials, and the like. On the CBS convention coverage, Cronkite himself said very dramatically that this might be the kind of issue that could shake delegates loose. It seems that the direct effect of this kind of reporting is to generate excitement, and the indirect effect is to increase the level of conflict and make party unity more difficult to achieve. The CBS pre-convention program on the GOP gathering (held in Kansas City) was entitled "Kansas City Showdown," which captures the media emphasis well. Just as the primaries are infused with drama, so are the conventions.

At times, the networks themselves are skillfully manipulated by groups seeking to use the convention and the concommitant television coverage to promote their own causes. The networks, of course, must be the final arbiters of which groups and issues merit coverage. But if the definition of news is "outstanding deviation from civil norms" rather than "events of importance to sizeable number of viewers" (Shafer and Larson, 1972: 16), then the networks may unwittingly serve to increase the appearance of discord.

Thus, the intrusiveness of television on the conventions is in large part a function of the nature and incentives of television news reporting. But sometimes television simply blows it, as evidenced by the misinterpretation of the South Carolina delegation challenge at the 1972 Democratic convention, which led some people to believe that the McGovern candidacy was in trouble when just the opposite was the case. At the 1968 Democratic convention, Sander Vanocur and John Chancellor were responsible for a Kennedy-for-President boom that electrified the convention, but was simply not accurate (Perry, 1973: 171).

One can speculate how intrusive the media might be at a deadlocked or close convention in which events are unfolding rapidly and television is the major source of information for the delegates. On the second night of the Republican convention in 1976 before the test vote on the critical rule 16–C (on vice presidential selection) had occurred, there was an uproar fanned by the television networks over alleged comments in an Alabama newspaper by Ford campaign manager Rogers Morton that the "Cotton South" would be written off by Ford. Morton claimed to have said that certain southern states would be difficult for Ford to carry because of southerner Carter heading the Democratic ticket, but denied that these states had been written off. Nevertheless, newsmen confronted the Mississippi delegation with the "fact" that Ford was writing off the South. Earlier in the day the Mississippi delegation had invoked the unit rule by a very narrow margin of 31–28 to support Ford's position on 16–C and thereby cast all 30 votes against the rule. When Morton's alleged comments became known, the Reagan forces wanted the Mississippi delegation to caucus again in the hope of changing two votes and breaking the unit rule and perhaps converting some Ford supporters. The intrusiveness of the media became absurd here. Dan Rather offered to lead Rogers Morton across the convention floor so that he might meet with the Mississippi delegation. Mike Wallace provided the Mississippi Reagan delegates with a CBS trailer in which to caucus. No votes were changed as a result of all this, but it should suggest how the media can sometimes forget that they are there to report the news and not play an active part in generating it.

The General Election

The general election campaign is a better defined situation than the primaries, with the presidential choices narrowed down to two serious candidates; hence the chances for media intrusiveness are less than during the primary season. Nevertheless, the opportunities for media manipulation and game playing by the candidates as well as misdirected coverage by the media remain substantial in the general election. Given that the empirical studies reviewed earlier generally indicated weak media effects on vote choice, one might wonder whether concern about media manipulation in the general election is warranted. One response is that successful manipulation of the media by a candidate may serve to alter the course of campaigns in ways not readily amenable to quantitative investigation. This can be illustrated by reference to Richard Nixon's reelection campaign in 1972.

The Nixon camp recognized the structural aspects of news reporting and ran a campaign designed to take advantage of these features. Nixon campaigned as President from the White House while surrogate campaigners carried the Republican message on the stump. As Jules Witcover notes (1973: 24–25), the absence of Nixon from the campaign trail resulted in intensive scrutiny of McGovern. Every little flaw in the campaign, every squabble among his advisors received substantial media attention because of the availability of the McGovern camp to the media. McGovern was covered as a candidate striving for office, while Nixon was treated as the incumbent President above the political fray. Witcover argues (1973: 26) that even had Nixon campaigned more, he would likely have kept himself insulated from press questioning, with the result that the accessible McGovern campaign would still have been subjected to intensive and critical scrutiny. Ford's Rose Garden strategy in 1976 was a variant on the 1972 Nixon effort, although Ford was more accessible than Nixon to the media.

Ben Bagdikian (1973) points out that the Nixon campaign strategy led to news coverage that effectively served as Nixon propaganda in many instances. One procedure that contributed to this was "twinning"—giving both sides of a story equal coverage even when they did not deserve such comparable treatment. McGovern himself complained about this (Ryan, 1976: 8):

> Let me register one beef from my own campaign. There were times when we would have a great rally where local leaders would tell us, "This is the biggest crowd we've ever seen at Cleveland Airport!" Or: "This is the biggest crowd we've ever had at Post Office Square in Boston!" I would turn on the television set later to see the enormous throng, and well, there *would* be a 15-second spot of me addressing this crowd. Then, under some kind of curious interpretation of the equal-time rule, since Nixon was not campaigning, they would pick up some guy along the fence who would say, "I think McGovern stinks."
>
> And this would be the way the program would end—or "Mc-Govern said this, but a disgruntled former Democrat interviewed by our roving reporter said this." And then they had some jerk get up and say that I was too radical for him or that I couldn't make up my mind on the issues. What the viewer was left with was a final negative image. It happened repeatedly during the campaign.

Bagdikian (1973: 11) did not blame Nixon for adopting the strategy that he did, arguing that this was standard behavior for a heavily favored incumbent. Instead, he criticized editors and publishers who allowed the Nixon camp to get away with such conduct. The point, however, is that a candidate could count on the networks and newspapers to try to present balanced coverage even when only one candidate was actively campaigning. Given the lesson of 1972, the media were more alert to the problem and devised some responses in 1976. For example, in response to Ford's Rose Garden strategy, television reporters in 1976 often concluded their stories with the phrase "with the Ford campaign at the White House" so that viewers would recognize Ford's actions and the media coverage of them as part of his campaign. This of course raises the question of the proper role of reporters and journalists. Is it simply to record the campaign? If so, then the media may be the vehicle of skillful candidates. Or should media personnel evaluate as well as record? This latter role is certainly controversial, opening up news organizations to charges of bias and threats of political and economic reprisals.

Candidates are also skillful in recognizing that news personnel need to file stories even when little hard news exists. Candidates can then construct media events that project desired images without much hard content. Buchanan (1976) described an excellent example of this phenomenon on how the media covered Jimmy Carter's extended stay in Plains, Georgia, after winning the Democratic nomination. Each day reporters would issue a report from Plains on who visited the candidate or how the softball game went. The television viewer was treated to pictures of Carter greeting fellow Democrats, Carter playing softball, Carter going to church, and the like. The question, of course, is whether this merits coverage. It is not the fault of the Carter camp that this occurred; its contribution was simply to recognize that the media need "news" and to provide tidbits and scenes designed to show the candidate in his best light. There is an obvious response available to the media to counter such behavior and that is simply not to report such activities. But this would require a redefinition of what constitutes news as well as a restructuring of media incentives that encourage this type of news coverage. Unfortunately, it seems that the candidates have the upper hand. It is hard to imagine the media ignoring a speech designated by the President as major which, in fact, turns out to be a rehashing of existing policy. But the media can do much more in providing context and background.

The horse race coverage characteristic of the primaries is also prominent in the general election, with events regularly interpreted in terms of how they affect the relative standing of the candidates (Swanson, 1977). Moreover, the emphasis on candidate standing and media events often results in matters of substance being given short shrift. McCartney (1977: 19) described the 1976 campaign coverage as junk news which, like junk food, "is mass-produced, has no flavor and little substance." McCartney (1977: 20) argues there were issue differences between the candidates that merited coverage but these often got overwhelmed by the media emphasis on gaffes and blunders. Such events as Ford's Eastern Europe comments or Carter's *Playboy* interview are certainly newsworthy but not at the expense of other campaign stories.

The problem again arises from the definition of news. It is not news if a candidate goes through an entire campaign day without making mistakes. But should the candidate blunder, this gets elevated to a position of prominence that outweighs the other activities and statements of the candidate. From the perspective of the reporter, it is understandable why the rare gaffe receives so much attention. Reporters traveling with the presidential candidates are likely to have heard and written about the same speech before and may therefore be looking for new leads and angles. Hence the occasional candidate mistake provides the opportunity for a new story. This is only reasonable, but when it results in a heavy emphasis on less substantive issue-related matters, one can legitimately worry whether the needs of the media are contributing to a trivializing of campaign discourse.

CONCLUSION

It is clear that the role of the media, especially television, in presidential politics has increased markedly since 1952. This increased importance is due not only to the technological advances in electronic communication but also to structural changes in the nomination process, particularly the proliferation of primaries, that provide an opportunity for media influence. With the increasing domination of television, as well as the importance of other technological developments, the financial pressures on presidential contenders became very severe and eventually resulted in the adoption of public financing of the presidential contest beginning in 1976. In turn, the developments in the areas of media, campaign financing, and delegate selection have expanded the pool from which serious presidential challengers are drawn. Thus, in Chapter 10 we will analyze changes in the conduct of campaigns in the areas of campaign financing, candidate recruitment, and delegate selection.

10

Changes in the Conduct of Campaigns:
Campaign Financing and the Recruitment
and Nomination of Presidential Candidates

CAMPAIGN FINANCING

Introduction

It was a sad commentary on the state of disrepute to which campaign financing practices had fallen when political commentators observed that one bright note in the unusual accession of Gerald Ford to the Presidency in 1974 was that the new President was not beholden to wealthy contributors and special interest groups that had helped elect him. For many citizens, the financing of election campaigns had become a national scandal that could be remedied only by major reforms. A commonly expressed belief was that no one gave sizable contributions to a candidate without an expectation of some return, and this cynical viewpoint was reinforced by reports of ambassadorships for sale, charges of increases in dairy price supports in exchange for campaign contributions, and the like. Thus, as the Watergate affair and its assorted manifestations unfolded, public attitudes moved markedly toward support of such reforms as public financing of national elections and spending ceilings. For example, Gallup found in late 1972 that 71 percent of Americans favored a law that would limit the total amount of money that could be spent for or by a candidate for office. And after much prolonged debate, Congress in late 1974 passed and the President signed a major campaign reform measure, the provisions of which governed the 1976 election.

Two basic issues involved in the question of campaign financing are the amount of money to be spent by candidates and the way in which that money is to be raised. It is commonplace to cite the tremendous increase in campaign costs in the past two decades, even allowing for the effects of inflation. For example, total costs for national level committees in the presidential campaign exceeded $17 million in 1956, rose to over $25 million in 1960, and zoomed above $59 million in 1968, an increase of 345 percent in just 12 years (Alexander, 1962: 9; Alexander, 1971: 2). And these figures understate the full costs of presidential campaigns since they exclude state and local expenditures on behalf of the national ticket. Herbert Alexander estimated that the total cost (primaries and general election) of the 1968 presidential campaign reached $100 million and rose to about $130 million in 1972. One effect of the 1974 reforms (to be discussed shortly) was to reduce the total amount of money spent on the presidential campaign between 1972 and 1976, despite the fact that inflation had made campaigning more costly and that both parties in 1976 had serious nomination contests. And these figures do not include the costs of nonpresidential elections. Alexander estimated the costs of all elections in 1968 and 1972 at $300 and $425 million respectively, a sizable jump over the $140 million spent in 1952 (Alexander, 1972a: 1; Alexander, 1973).

While costs of this magnitude may seem huge, some observers argue that the amount of money spent is less relevant than who spends it and how it is raised. Moreover, given the central role of elections in democratic politics, it is argued that election campaigns should not be unduly restricted in scope by too severe limitations on the amounts of money that can be spent. Some observers claim that the actual amount of funds spent is relatively small given, for example, the great expenditures on advertising of commercial products. Alexander notes that there are inherent features of election campaigns that inevitably raise costs. For example, he writes that "political costs tend to be high because the political season is relatively short and intensity must be high for each candidate just before an election." He further states that candidates "are not just in competition with each other, but also are in competition with commercial advertisers possessed of large budgets. . . ." (Alexander, *New York Times* off print) In short, it necessarily costs a lot to attract the voters' attention.

Thus, some critics of existing campaign practices are less concerned about the amounts spent than they are about the way the funds are collected. This position is more defensible when there are not substantial inequalities in the funds available to competing candidates. However, if one candidate has access to far greater resources, then one might argue that spending ceilings themselves are crucial if the notion of a seriously contested election is to be meaningful. And incumbent candidates are much more likely to have access to substantial campaign contributions. For example, the Citizens' Research Foundation reported that the largest defense contractors gave more than $2\frac{1}{2}$ million to the Republicans in 1972 and only slightly more than $300,000 to the Democrats (*Dollar Politics*, p. 83). Obviously, it is in the enlightened self-interest of any group to contribute to the party that it perceives to be more favorable to its aims. But incumbents, particularly an incumbent President of either party, possess tremendous potential sanctions over all sectors of the economy, thereby making contributions to incumbents an investment in the group's future. Such contributions need not involve an explicit quid pro quo, although incumbents may use heavy-handed tactics at times. The point is that not all candidates have equal access to resources. In general, incumbents have an advantage over nonincumbents, Republicans have an advantage over Democrats (although it is difficult to assign a monetary value to the substantial manpower contribution that labor unions make to the Democratic Party), and major party candidates have an advantage over minor party nominees.

Another reason for advocating campaign ceilings is that their presence reduces the temptation to collect unlimited funds, thereby perhaps lessening the likelihood of shady fund-raising practices. One explanation given for the Nixon administration's use of "dirty tricks" and the like was that there simply was too much money available; ways had to be invented to spend the money in order to justify its collection in the first place.

The concern expressed above about the need for campaign ceilings does not imply that the manner in which funds are raised is unimportant. Clearly, funds collected in large amounts from relatively few contributors raise the distinct possibility that special interest groups are buying access to political decision makers. This is not to say that all large contributions are necessarily improper; undoubtedly, in many cases such contributions are motivated simply by a desire to help elect the candidate that one thinks is best for the country. But even if there is no improper influence involved in such large gifts, they are still harmful since they serve to further weaken public confidence in government because many citizens assume the worst about such contributions.

The ways in which the 1974 election reforms address our dual concerns of spending ceilings and fund-raising practices will be discussed later in the chapter. Now we will turn directly to the costs involved in running for President, the ways in which funds are raised to meet these costs, and the purposes to which these funds are put. Then we will return to the pros and cons and political implications of alternative proposals for campaign finance reform.

The Costs of Running for President

Any attempt to chart the trends in presidential campaign costs runs into problems for a variety of reasons. First of all, monies are spent on the presidential campaign at the local, state, and national levels; and the required reporting of expenditures differs tremendously across these levels. In addition, the reporting practices themselves have changed over time, thereby leaving some doubt about the comparability of the information collected at different time points. Finally, it is often difficult to separate the pre-nomination or primary costs from the general election spending. With these caveats in mind, we can turn to Table 10.1, which indicates the trends in campaign spending by national level committees from 1952 to 1968.

Note that the table indicates a consistent increase in spending, with the GOP generally outspending the Democrats, although most of the labor-related expenditures are on behalf of the Democratic nominees. Yet these figures do not begin to indicate the amount of presidential-related expenditures. For example, Alexander's estimate of the total costs (primary and general election) of the 1964 and 1968 presidential races are $60 to $100 million respectively, far cries from the figures of

TABLE 10.1
Presidential General Election Spending at the National Level, 1952–1968
(in $ millions)

Year	Total	Democratic Committees	Republican Committees	Labor Committees	Wallace Committees	Miscellaneous Committees
1952	11.6	5.0	6.6	*	—	*
1956	14.0	5.1	7.8	.5	—	.6
1960	21.4	9.8	10.1	.8	—	.7
1964	26.6	8.8	16.0	.7	—	1.1
1968	48.1	11.6	25.4	1.9	7.2	2.0

* Missing data.
Sources: Herbert E. Alexander, *Political Financing* (Minneapolis: Burgess Publishing Co., 1972), p. 6; and Delmer D. Dunn, *Financing Presidential Campaigns* (Washington, D.C.: The Brookings Institution, 1972), p. 31. The Federal Election Campaign Act of 1971 changed the definition of a political committee from a geographical to a monetary test. Committees were to disclose their finances if they raised or spent more than $1,000 on behalf of a candidate for federal offices regardless of whether they were national, state, or local in scope or even if they operated within one state. Hence comparable figures for 1972 are not available for this table. See the chapter on spending in the 1972 election in *Financing the 1972 Election* by Herbert E. Alexander.

$26.6 and $48.1 million in Table 10.1. The discrepancy is due to the nonnational general election costs and the pre-nomination spending. To illustrate: Alexander (1971: 7) estimated the 1968 pre-nomination costs at $45 million, which leaves about $7 million spent on the general election campaign by nonnational committees.

Because of more stringent reporting requirements in recent years, the expenditures for the 1972 and 1976 elections are more readily broken down into nomination and general election costs. As Table 10.2 indicates, total spending in 1976 was lower than in 1972 mainly

TABLE 10.2
Nomination and General Election Spending
in 1972 and 1976 by Party
(in $ millions)

	1972		1976*	
	Dem.	Rep.	Dem.	Rep.
Nomination	32.6	3	38	26
General election	30	62.7	21.8	21.8

* The 1976 figures are approximations; final reports on 1976 spending may change the totals slightly. The 1976 general election figures have simply been estimated to be the amount to which the candidates were entitled and do not include any financial support from the national party organizations or contributions made independently of the candidates' knowledge.
Source: Constructed from figures presented in Alexander, *Financing Politics*, pp. 193–200, 243–49.

because of the $21.8 million in public funds to which the major party candidates were limited in the general election. The obvious reason for the disparity in the Democratic and Republican primary costs in 1972 was that the Democratic contest was fought fiercely by numerous candidates, while the challenge to Nixon's renomination (by John Ashbrook and Paul McCloskey) was much more feeble. The 1972 general election figures are surprising only to the extent that the Republicans spent as much as they did to win an election that was almost certainly theirs from the start of the campaign. As Alexander notes, the spending for Nixon and McGovern set records for each party. In 1976, both parties had substantial nomination costs, with the Democratic total being higher simply because there were more Democrats seeking the nomination.

TABLE 10.3
Radio and Television Costs for General Election and Pre-nomination Presidential Campaigns, 1952–1972, by Party
(in $ millions)

Year		General Election		Pre-nomination	
		Dem.	Rep.	Dem.	Rep.
1952	Radio and TV	1.5	2.0		
1956	Radio and TV	1.8	2.9		
1960	Radio and TV	1.1	1.9		
1964	Radio	.9	1.3		
	TV	3.8	5.1		
	Total	4.7	6.4	.2	1.3
1968	Radio	1.7	3.6		
	TV	4.4	9.0		
	Total	6.1	12.6	4.8	3.0
1972	Radio and TV	6.2	4.3	3.5	.1

Sources: Herbert E. Alexander, *Political Financing* (Minneapolis: Burgess Publishing Co., 1972), p. 10; *Congressional Quarterly Weekly Report*, May 12, 1973, pp. 1134–35; The Twentieth Century Fund, *Voters' Time*, table 3; *Dollar Politics*, vol. 2 (Washington, D.C.: Congressional Quarterly Inc., 1974), pp. 60–61.

A major reason for the rise in campaign costs has been the increased use of the broadcast media, especially television, since 1952. Table 10.3 presents the broadcast costs for general election and pre-nomination presidential campaigns from 1952 to 1972. Note that only in 1968 was there a significant disparity in the amount spent on broadcasting by the respective parties in the general election. Given the narrowness of Humphrey's defeat in 1968, it is tempting to claim that had additional money been available to the Democrats, the election outcome might have been reversed. While there is no direct evidence to support this assertion, it is the case that there were weeks early in the campaign when the Democrats spent nothing on the broadcast media, as shown in Figure 10.1. The figure indicates the common tactic of media saturation in the final stages of the campaign. The sizable broadcast expenditures for Nixon reflect his heavy reliance on the broadcast media in 1968, a topic discussed in Chapter 9.

Broadcast expenditures in the primary campaign are highly dependent on the competitiveness of the primary situation. The 1964 Demo-

FIGURE 10.1
Weekly Expenditures on Network Television by the Humphrey and Nixon Campaigns, 1968

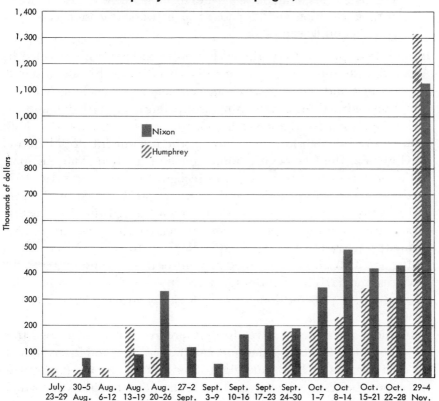

Source: *Voters' Time*, Report of the Twentieth Century Fund Commission on Campaign Costs in the Electronic Era (New York: The Twentieth Century Fund, 1969), fig. 5.

cratic and 1972 Republican primary expenditures were minmial since both parties were nominating almost unchallenged incumbent Presidents. The Republicans in 1964 and Democrats in 1972 had hotly contested primary battles, a situation reflected in the broadcast expenditures. And in 1968 when both parties had major pre-nomination struggles, the broadcast costs reached record highs.

With respect to the proportion of a campaign budget that broadcasting takes, Alexander writes (1972b: 10):

> The costs of all broadcasting today comprise about one-half of the total costs of a presidential campaign. The percentage tends to be higher when total costs are lower, indicating that broadcasting is one of the items least likely to be cut. In 1968, Nixon's $24,900,000 (general election) campaign spent 50 percent of the total, or $12,600,000, for broadcasting; Humphrey's financially starved campaign had to spend 61 percent, $6,100,000, of its $10,300,000 total for broadcasting. The Democrats would have liked to spend more. As it was, two weeks of spot television and 25 percent of network television had to be cancelled for lack of funds.

In fact, 1972 proved to be the exception to the pattern described by Alexander; despite the record overall expenditures, broadcast spending declined and more money was channeled into such activities as computerized mailings, canvassing, campaign paraphernalia, and the like. One reason for the lower broadcast costs in 1972 was that both candidates were well known, Nixon as the incumbent President and McGovern as the Democratic nominee who had risen from obscurity in the primaries to gain widespread recognition. Moreover, the 1972 candidates were campaigning under restrictions imposed by the Federal Election Campaign Act of 1971, which limited the amount that presidential nominees could spend on media (both electronic and printed) advertising to a total equivalent to 10 cents per citizen of voting age with no more than 60 percent of this amount going to the broadcast media. This statute translated into a $14.3 million limit for all media and $8.5 million for broadcast spending (*Dollar Politics*, p. 60).

In addition to media advertising, there are many other costs that must be borne by the parties and candidates. Alexander has done a detailed analysis of 1972 campaign expenditures; the GOP presidential expenditures are shown in Table 10.4. The purposes for which funds are spent are generally what one would expect in a campaign with staff, headquarters, materials, and advertising taking sizable

TABLE 10.4
Nomination and General Election Expenditures of the
Committee to Reelect the President and Related
Organizations in 1971 and 1972

Expense Category	$ Millions
Advertising (broadcast, including production costs and fees)	$ 7.0
Direct mail to voters (not including fund raising)	5.8
Mass telephoning to voters	1.3
State organizations (primary elections, personnel, storefronts, locations, travel, voter contact, etc.)	15.9
Campaign materials	2.7
Press relations, publications, and literature	2.6
Headquarters (campaign, personnel, rent, telephone, travel, legal, etc.	4.7
Travel and other expenses of President, Vice President, surrogates, and advance men	3.9
Citizen group activities	1.9
Youth activities	1.0
Polling (including White House-directed surveys)	1.6
Convention expenses	.6
Election night	.2
Fund raising (direct mail—$4 million, and major events—$1 million)	5.0
Fund raising (national administration and gifts for contributors)	1.9
Legal fees	2.1
Democratic settlement	.8
Democrats for Nixon	2.4
Total*	$61.4

* Does not include $1.4 million in miscellaneous cash, some used for "dirty tricks" or "hush" money in 1972–73, and some used for political or other purposes in 1969–70–71, not directly related to the 1972 presidential election.
Source: Herbert Alexander, *Financing Politics,* table 8–1, p. 198.

chunks of the budget. More notable is the substantial amount of money needed to raise money; for example, the Republicans in 1972 spent more than $4 million on direct-mail fund raising.

Campaign funds are collected from both small and large contributors with varying success, depending upon the specific election situation. Alexander (1972b: 24) reports that in 1968 at least 15,000 citizens gave $500 or more while 424 very large contributors (those who donated $10,000 or more) gave a total of over $12 million, an average of $27,000 per contribution. In 1972, the Nixon fund-raising effort headed by Maurice Stans was highly successful in bringing in campaign funds from major contributors prior to April 7, the date for the beginning of the strict reporting requirements provided for in the

Federal Election Campaign Act of 1971. These sizable contributions were headed by $2 million from insurance man W. Clement Stone and $1 million from Richard Scaife, heir to the Mellon oil and banking fortune (*Dollar Politics,* p. 65). Stans achieved such success in part because he promised that contributions prior to April 7 would remain anonymous; a court suit brought by Common Cause upset that promise. It was revealed that the Nixon campaign had collected almost $20 million in contributions prior to the April 7 reporting deadline with $5 million collected on April 5 and 6 alone (*Dollar Politics,* p. 66). These disclosures were a major impetus to the 1974 campaign financing reforms.

Not all campaign funds come in the form of large contributions. To the contrary, as Table 10.5 shows, the proportion of campaign contri-

TABLE 10.5
Contributions by Individuals to National Committees and Percent from Large Contributors, Democratic and Republican Parties, 1952–1968
(in $ thousands)

	Total Contributions	Large Contributions (over $500)	Percent of Monies Raised in Amounts over $500
1952			
Republicans	$ 4,329	$ 2,944	68
Democrats	3,466	2,184	63
	$ 7,795	$ 5,128	66
1956			
Republicans	$ 3,837	$ 2,839	74
Democrats	2,508	1,104	44
	$ 6,345	$ 3,943	62
1960			
Republicans	$ 6,214	$ 3,603	58
Democrats	3,376	1,992	59
	$ 9,590	$ 5,595	58
1964			
Republicans	$12,610	$ 3,475	28
Democrats	7,034	4,859	69
	$19,644	$ 8,335	42
1968			
Republicans	$22,885	$10,662	47
Democrats	11,237	8,911	79
	$34,122	$19,573	57

Source: *Voters' Time,* Report of the Twentieth Century Fund Commission on Campaign Costs in the Electronic Era (New York: The Twentieth Century Fund, 1969), table 5.

butions to national level committees collected in amounts larger than $500 has fluctuated widely since 1952. Of particular note is the small proportion (28 percent) of GOP money that came in amounts over $500 in 1964; more than 650,000 contributions under $100 were received (Alexander, 1966: 70). This Republican success in attracting small contributions was attributed to Goldwater's popularity among the conservative hardcore and to the major mailing appeals used. It is interesting to note that candidates commonly viewed as more ideological and more antiestablishment have been very successful in attracting large numbers of small contributions—Goldwater in 1964, McCarthy and Wallace in 1968, and McGovern in 1972. The entries in Table 10.5 indicate that the GOP has more than held its own in receiving its share of small contributions; the 1968 increase in the percentage of Republican funds coming from large contributors should not hide the fact that the party raised almost $12 million in small contributions. Today the professional fund raiser plays an important role in generating monies during the primary season. Particularly noteworthy in this area is Richard Viguerie, a fund raiser for conservative causes and candidates, who relies on computerized mailings to lists of likely contributors. Although his services are expensive (it may cost a dollar to raise a dollar), Viguerie's talents are very much in demand by such candidates as George Wallace in 1975 and 1976 and Philip Crane (the first announced candidate for the 1980 GOP nomination) in 1979.

Campaign Financing Reform

The problems of campaign financing confronting candidates for the Presidency are reflected in the following comments of Hubert Humphrey (*New York Times,* October 13, 1974, p. E18):

> Campaign financing is a curse. It's the most disgusting, demeaning, disenchanting, debilitating experience of a politician's life. It's stinky, it's lousy. I just can't tell you how much I hate it. I've had to break off in the middle of trying to make a decent, honorable campaign and go up to somebody's parlor or to a room and say, "Gentlemen, and ladies, I'm desperate. You've got to help me. . . .
> . . . And you see people there—a lot of them you don't want to see. And they look at you, and you sit there and you talk to them and tell them what you're for and you need help and, out of the twenty-five who have gathered, four will contribute. And most likely one of them

is in trouble and is somebody you shouldn't have had a contribution from. . . .

In response to the rising costs of politics and the abuses uncovered in the Watergate investigations, Congress passed the Campaign Reform Act of 1974, which was signed into law by President Ford with some misgivings in October 1974. Prior to the 1974 act, the most recent efforts at campaign finance reform were the Revenue Act of 1971 and the Federal Election Campaign Act of 1971. The Revenue Act was an attempt to generate public contributions to campaigns by allowing citizens to take a tax credit or deduction on their donations. The act also had a tax checkoff provision that would allow citizens to specify on their income tax return that one dollar of their tax money be used to subsidize presidential campaigns. Under the threat of a Nixon veto, this provision did not take effect until after the 1972 campaign. A similar provision was in the Presidential Campaign Fund Act of 1966, but was repealed the following year.

The tax checkoff plan in the 1971 Revenue Act is a good example of how difficult it is to institute reforms that simultaneously achieve a number of desired goals without leading to any unintended consequences. For example, one provision of the law stated that a candidate must choose between public and private financing. Yet might this not impose unconstitutional restrictions on citizens who want to give money to their preferred candidate who has already opted for public financing? One possible unintended consequence of the checkoff plan was suggested by George Thayer (1973: 291), who argued that state and local party organizations were likely to atrophy further if the responsibility of fund raising was taken from them. Furthermore, there were biases built into the checkoff plan that favored the two major parties; nominees of minor parties could receive public monies only if they received between 5 and 25 percent of the vote, and even then the amount they would get would be only a fourth of the major party amount (Dunn, 1972: 56).

As stated earlier, the major features of the 1971 Campaign Act provided for a thorough disclosure of campaign contributions received after April 7, 1972, and a limitation on the amount of money that could be spent on media advertising. The massive fund raising conducted by the Nixon campaign prior to the April 7 deadline certainly violated the spirit of the law though not the letter. The 1971 law was quickly attacked on a number of grounds, one simply being that its enforcement was not very strict. A more fundamental objection was raised to the philosophy underlying the statute: was the simple disclosure of the sources of a candidate's funds a sufficient safeguard to reduce the influence of wealth on politics or were more direct controls on spending and contributions needed?

Prior to the reform efforts of the 1960s and 1970s, the two most important statutes governing presidential campaign financing were the Federal Corrupt Practices Act of 1925 and the Hatch Act of 1940. The important features of the 1925 law relevant to presidential contests were requirements of financial reports from any committee seeking to influence the campaign in two or more states and the prohibition to corporate contributions (Alexander, 1972a: 78). This was a weak law; expenditures by committees confined to one state did not have to be reported nor did primary election gifts. Yet even this weak law helped Common Cause force disclosure of the pre-April 7 contributions to the Nixon campaign.

The Hatch Act limited individual contributions to any political committee to $5,000 and limited total spending by a committee to $3 million per year. The parties and candidates got around the law by decentralizing financing to state and local committees, particularly in states with weak to nonexistent reporting requirements, and by creating many theoretically separate national committees, each of which was allowed to spend $3 million. Thus, in 1968 there were such committees as Arts and Letters for Humphrey-Muskie, Business for Humphrey-Muskie, Citizens for Humphrey, Citizens for Humphrey-Muskie, United Chiropractors for Humphrey-Muskie, Veterans for Humphrey-Muskie, and many more. A related reason for the proliferation of committees was that donors could avoid the gift tax by giving up to $3,000 each to a large number of committees rather than a lump sum to one committee. Thus, Stewart Mott, a major McGovern financial backer, divided his contributions among a large number of committees just as Richard Mellon Scaife gave his million dollars to the Nixon campaign by giving checks of $3,000 to the requisite number of committees (*Dollar Politics,* p. 69).

The above discussion should make it abundantly clear that the campaign financing laws prior to 1974 were easily circumvented and admitted of many serious abuses. The 1974 reforms (called the Federal Election Campaign Act Amendments of 1974) addressed the problems of excessive expenditures and fund-raising practices. With respect to the former, the law set limits of $10 million per candidate for the primary elections and $21.8 million for the general election. It also limited the major parties to $2 million each for their nominating conventions and repealed the media spending limitations of the 1971 act. In addition, the law tightened the requirements for reporting contributions and required that all contributions be processed through one central campaign committee which would be responsible for reporting all contributions of $100 or more. For enforcement, Congress created an eight-member, full-time, bipartisan Federal Elections Commission, which would be able to give advisory opinions, conduct audits, subpoena witnesses, and seek civil injunctions, which would then send cases to the Justice Department for prosecution (*Congressional Quarterly Weekly Report,* October 12, 1974, p. 2867).

With respect to fund-raising activities, the law limited individual and organization contributions and provided for public financing of presidential campaigns (though not congressional campaigns). Individual contributions to a candidate were restricted to $1,000 for each primary, runoff, and general election, with an annual limit of $25,000 for all federal elections; contributions from organizations, political committees, and the like were limited to $5,000 per election. Candidates for the Presidency were entitled to public funds for their primary campaigns if they could raise on their own $100,000 in amounts of $5,000 or less from 20 or more states with contributions under $250. This provision was adopted so that frivolous candidates could not lay claim to the public treasury. If a candidate could raise the $100,000 under these conditions, then he or she would receive matching public funds for each dollar collected from contributions under $250, up to a total of $5 million (*Congressional Quarterly Weekly Report,* October 5, 1974, p. 2691). Thus, of the $10 million that candidates could spend on the primaries, half of it could come from public funds.

The parties were to choose whether they wanted public or private funding of their conventions; in either case, the $2 million spending limit held. For the general election, the incentives of the 1974 law were such that the presidential nominees in 1976 chose public funding.[1] The source of all public funds to be spent on the campaign is the Presidential Election Campaign Fund, consisting of monies designated by citizens on their income tax returns to be used for presiden-

---

[1] Future nominees can choose to reject public financing. If they do, then there is no limit on the amount they can raise and spend on their behalf. It is debatable whether a candidate who opted for private funding would be helped or hurt by the action. A candidate who spent much more than an opponent who relied on public funding might be accused of trying to buy the election. However, it is possible that the self-reliant candidate might be praised for not having tapped the public treasury.

tial elections. Minor parties were to receive money in proportion to their vote strength in the previous election, assuming they received at least 5 percent of the vote in that election.

While the 1974 reforms were intended to solve the major problems of campaign financing, they were attacked on a number of important grounds. A disparate group of citizens and organizations, including former Senator James Buckley, former Senator Eugene McCarthy, Stewart Mott, the New York Civil Liberties Union, the American Conservative Union, and others brought suit against the 1974 law on the grounds that it deprived

> . . . the plaintiffs of freedom of speech and association, of the right to petition for redress of grievances, of the right of privacy, and of due process of law and discriminates invidiously against them, all in violation of the First, Fourth, Fifth, Sixth, and Ninth Amendments to the Constitution. . . . (*Congressional Record,* January 28, 1975, p. 51106.)

The plaintiffs argued that the disclosure requirements of the law violated their right to privacy and the contribution ceilings limited their freedom of speech and association and their right to petition for redress of grievances.

The plaintiffs included a number of individuals and groups prominent in either third-party politics or antiestablishment politics within the two major parties. In fact, the 1974 law has major implications for third-party candidates as well as "maverick" challengers within the Democratic and Republican Parties. Third-party candidates can only get money if they received 5 percent of the vote in the previous election; if the party ran poorly or did not field a candidate, it obviously is penalized. The fact that John Schmitz and not George Wallace headed the American Independent Party ticket in 1972 proved costly to the AIP in 1976. Had the 1974 law been in effect in 1972, the AIP on the basis of Wallace's 1968 showing would have received millions of dollars in 1972. Likewise, the limitations on individual contributions in the 1974 law may serve to hinder third-party and maverick challenges. Oftentimes, the initial seed money that keeps an unusual candidacy alive comes from wealthy donors who believe in the causes the candidate espouses; much of the early money for the McCarthy candidacy in 1968 and the McGovern candidacy in 1972 came from wealthy contributors, such as Stewart Mott, heir to a General Motors fortune. Without these sizable contributions, now prohibited by law, these candidacies may have expired quickly.

The Supreme Court issued its decision on the constitutionality of the 1974 campaign finance law in January 1976, shortly before the start of the primary season. It upheld the contribution limits on individuals and organizations and the public financing of presidential campaigns. It struck down all expenditure limits, except for presidential candidates who accepted public funding, and invalidated the restriction on independent contributions made on behalf of a candidate so long as the donors were giving without the knowledge and encouragement of the candidate. The Court also declared the Federal Elections Commission (FEC) to be improperly constituted. As originally established, the FEC was composed of six members appointed by Congress and two by the President. The Court ruled that only the President has the power of appointment; but to avoid confusion, it let stand previous actions of the FEC and gave Congress ample time to reconstitute the commission. However, Congress delayed in reestablishing the FEC so that on March 21, at the height of the primary season, the commission was no longer able to disburse matching public funds to eligible candidates. Needless to say, this created a major hardship for the candidates, particularly for Udall and Reagan, who were unable to make strong efforts in certain states because of the lack of money. In the Federal Election Campaign Act Amendments of 1976, Congress reestablished the FEC as a six-member board appointed by the President and subject to Senate confirmation.[2]

As in the case with many reforms, the consequences of the campaign finance law were both anticipated and unanticipated. The 1976 and 1980 contestants for the nominations met the eligibility requirements for matching public funds fairly readily. Included in the 1976 group was Ellen McCormack, a single-issue (anti-abortion) candidate for the Democratic nomination. In fact, the ease with which candidates were qualifying for matching funds, and the frequency with which no longer viable candidates were able to draw public funds, led Congress in the 1976 amendments to the financing law to require that presidential candidates who withdrew from the nomination campaign had to return unspent federal funds. In addition, federal support to a candidate who won less than 10 percent of the vote in two consecutive primaries in which he or she ran was automatically cut off, although

---

[2] One result of the creation of the FEC, which oversees all federal races including the presidential campaign, is to make the accountant and lawyer an integral part of the campaign effort (Rapoport, 1979). Carter sent to the Congress a package of election reform proposals, one provision of which would grant extra money to the presidential candidates to help defray the substantial costs incurred in complying with the election laws.

provisions were made whereby a candidate could reestablish eligibility.

Although the requirements for obtaining matching public funds in the primary season were not particularly burdensome to candidates, they did serve a screening function, namely as a test which, if passed, bestowed an extra measure of legitimacy on a candidacy. Candidates attempt to establish their eligibility for matching funds quickly so as to provide evidence that theirs is a serious candidacy. George Bush was the first prospective 1980 nominee to meet the requirements, achieving this in early 1979, a full year before the first presidential primary. Hence, the campaign finance law has had the unintended effect of further lengthening the presidential season. In fact, if candidates can establish their eligibility early and begin the caucus and primary season with their matching funds in hand, then they will be able to plan and budget ahead and not have to devote extensive time and effort to fund raising. Moreover, the candidate with contributions already collected is not as much at the mercy of the early primary results. In the past, many a candidate has found himself without financial backing after an unimpressive showing in New Hampshire or some other early primary. Of course, too much can be made of advanced planning in the primaries. Given rapidly changing conditions, early commitment of funds to certain primaries or specific activities may not be all that advantageous.

The campaign finance law also has implications for incumbent Presidents seeking reelection. If an incumbent President is not challenged for renomination within his party, then the amount of money and effort required for his renomination is likely to be very low. But if the out party has a spirited contest for its nomination, then the total amount of money provided the out-party challengers during the primaries will likely far exceed that spent on the President's behalf. And this might be a disadvantage for the incumbent if these challengers are attacking his administration in well-publicized and well-financed races. In the general election, however, the effect of the spending limit ($21.8 million in 1976) may be to make it more difficult to defeat an incumbent President. The President, unlike his challenger, has many automatic advantages, such as the opportunity to travel at government expense for ostensibly nonpolitical appearances that may in fact reap great publicity for his campaign and the ability to generate newsworthy stories that will garner major media coverage.

The provisions of the campaign finance laws governing the creation and activities of political actions committees (PACs) have fostered a new development in presidential campaigning. Four 1980 Republican contenders—Ronald Reagan, Robert Dole, George Bush, and John Connally—formed political actions committees to raise and distribute funds to GOP candidates in the 1978 election, thereby hoping to gain support in their quest for the presidential nomination (Cook, 1979). Reagan's PAC, Citizens for the Republic, contributed over $500,000 to Republican U.S. House and Senate candidates in 1978. In the past, would-be presidential candidates often campaigned on behalf of fellow party members, but the direct provision of campaign funds is very new.

The actual 1976 experience with the campaign finance laws suggests some additional consequences for the general election campaign. The law certainly reduced spending in the presidential race from the bloated levels in 1972, but it also lessened the visibility of the campaign as the $21.8 million spending limit resulted in a scarcity of campaign buttons, bumper stickers, and other paraphernalia. With the limited funds available, the candidates' media campaigns received top priority and as a result the organizational effort within states suffered. For example, the Nixon reelection effort in 1972 spent about $850,000 in Ohio, while the Ford and Carter expenditures in 1976 were about $150,000 and $200,000 respectively. In 1972, there were approximately 175 Nixon storefronts and about 40 paid Nixon staff in Ohio compared to 6 Ford-only offices and 12 paid Ford operatives in 1976.

In a related vein, the limited funds available in 1976 served to alter the relationship between the national campaign organization and the state and local party organizations. In previous elections, the candidate's national organization often had sufficient money, which enabled it to contribute to the state and local organizations, thereby creating a common electoral bond by promoting the entire party ticket and providing the national ticket some leverage over the state and local efforts. There was little such money available in 1976, thereby reinforcing the trend to candidate-centered presidential contests. In many cases, the national ticket itself looked to the state and local levels for financial and other support, which often never materialized. There might have been higher levels of national, state, and local activity and coordination had the Federal Elections Commission issued a key ruling earlier in 1976. Late in the campaign, the FEC said that party committees at the city, county, congressional district, and state levels could each spend $1,000 promoting the national ticket, but many of these committees either did not have the money or had committed their funds.

The future of campaign finance reform is unpredictable; there will likely be changes in the law resulting from new congressional decisions or possible future court rulings. Certainly one area in which there is widespread agreement is the need to raise the amount of money provided in the general election beyond the inflation factor built into the law. The likely 1980 expenditure limits will be about $15 million for the primaries and $30 million for the general election. There are likely to be legal challenges against provisions of the law dealing with the treatment of third parties in such areas as eligibility and disclosure requirements. Moreover, even if the basic statutes remain unchanged, there are no guarantees that presidential candidates will opt for public funding in future contests. And the Supreme Court's ruling allowing unlimited independent expenditures on behalf of a candidate could undermine the major thrust of the finance reforms and leave political authorities once again with the problem of designing a better campaign finance system.

THE RECRUITMENT OF PRESIDENTIAL CANDIDATES

Until the capture of the Democratic nomination in 1976 by former Georgia Governor Jimmy Carter, a major development in the recruitment of presidential candidates had been the tendency for the U.S. Senate and the Vice Presidency, rather than the nation's governorships, to be the breeding ground of prospective nominees. Between 1952 and 1972, the only presidential and vice presidential nominees to have been Governors were Adlai Stevenson (of Illinois) and Spiro Agnew (of Maryland). Every other nominee, with the exceptions of General Eisenhower, William Miller (Goldwater's 1964 running mate), and Sargent Shriver (McGovern's second 1972 running mate), had served in the U.S. Senate; and Nixon, Johnson, and Humphrey followed their Senate service with a vice presidential incumbency prior to running for President. Carter's 1976 success has once again sensitized observers to the governorship as a springboard to the Presidency. As of mid-1979, one potential challenger to Carter's renomination is Governor Jerry Brown of California, while the Republican front-runner is former California Governor Ronald Reagan.

Carter's winning the nomination is important not because it represented the success of a former Governor but because it signified that an outsider with little previous political experience and scant national recognition could capture the nomination. Such an accomplishment was made possible by the expansion of the primaries as the means of selecting delegates to the national nominating conventions (see the next section of this chapter), the media coverage given to the primaries (see Chapter 9), and the campaign financing reforms discussed earlier. Hence the lesson of 1976 is that serious aspirants for the Presidency can come from diverse political backgrounds, and this is reflected in the varied field seeking the 1980 GOP nomination. In addition to former Governor Reagan are two Texans, John Connally, former Democrat who served as Secretary of the Navy, Governor of Texas, and Secretary of the Treasury, and George Bush, whose highest elective position was U.S. Representative and who also served as Republican national chairman, CIA director, and consul to the People's Republic of China. A number of U.S. Senators have declared their candidacies or expressed strong interest, including Robert Dole, Howard Baker, and Lowell Weicker, as have three U.S. Representatives—Philip Crane, John Anderson, and Jack Kemp. The size and diversity of the GOP field suggests how open and enticing the nomination process has become.

The critical issues facing the nation may help determine what kinds of experience are desired in a presidential candidate. For example, if foreign policy crises are uppermost in voters' minds, then a candidate with limited national and international experience may not be considered very favorably. It can be argued that Carter's claim in 1976 that he was an outsider without Washington connections worked to his advantage because the citizenry was upset with big government and the Watergate scandals. By mid-1979, as the energy and economic problems became acute and as Carter was continually frustrated by an independent Congress, Carter's lack of prior Washington experience was viewed by more observers as a liability rather than an asset. For the future, it seems likely that presidential aspirants will continue to come from varied backgrounds, although the visibility and significance attached to such offices as the Vice Presidency, U.S. Senator, and Governor suggest that they will be better springboards than other positions.

For the remainder of this section, we will detail how presidential recruitment shifted from the governorship to the U.S. Senate and Vice President in the 1960s and early 1970s. Louis Harris (1959: 361) put the demise of Governors as presidential prospects in historical perspective when he noted that in the first 170 years of the American Presidency, the President had formerly been a Governor in 82 of those years. But between 1945 and 1976 no former Governor occupied the White House. Robert Peabody and Eve Lubalin (1975: 27) noted that between 1960 and 1972 both parties exhibited a "deceptively simple" pattern of presidential recruitment, in which presidential nominations went to Senators or Vice Presidents who had served in the Senate before assuming the office of Vice President. To emphasize how different these recruitment patterns actually were, Peabody and Lubalin point out that the last time the Democrats gave their presidential nomination to an incumbent Senator prior to John Kennedy in 1960 was in 1860 when the nominee was Stephen Douglas. And when one examines Democratic nomination struggles since 1960, one will observe that Senators have provided the bulk of the competition. The major challengers to Kennedy in 1960 were Senators Humphrey, Johnson, and Symington, with former Governor Stevenson available should lightning strike. With the decision of Lyndon Johnson not to seek reelection in 1968, the major challengers for the Democratic nomination were Senators Humphrey, Kennedy, McCarthy, and McGovern and Governor Wallace. And in 1972 the strongest Democratic prospects were Senators McGovern, Humphrey, Muskie, and Jackson and Governor Wallace. Governors have been more prominent in challenging for the GOP nomination since 1960, although they have been no more successful than on the Democratic side.

Hence the question arises as to why the Senate and the Vice Presidency became stepping-stones to a presidential nomination as the governorships became less advantageous. This is a particularly intriguing question since the traditional political lore argued for the strength of the governorship and the weakness of the Senate and the Vice Presidency as springboards for a presidential bid. For example, Louis Harris (1959: 364–65) summarized a number of reasons why Governors were considered advantaged over Senators in quests for the presidential nomination, including the facts that Senators frequently were not real political powers in their home states while Governors were, that legislators were forced to go on record on controversial issues more so than Governors, and that Senators and Vice Presidents tended to get hidden behind the scenes while Governors often were more visible.

The traditional advantages and disadvantages of each office have been turned around by changes in the nominating process that, in turn, are related to broader changes in the American political system. Peabody and Lubalin (1975: 44–45) argue that geographical considerations in the selection of presidential nominees are no longer as important as they once were, that it is much more important today that a potential nominee have widespread national appeal rather than special appeal to one or two key states. This in turn has led to increased reliance on the mass media to develop name recognition nationwide, to widespread use of public opinion polls to measure candidate popularity, and to the contesting of many primaries to demonstrate popularity and win delegate support. And as the proportion of convention delegates chosen in primaries continues to increase along with the actual number of primaries, the need to demonstrate one's national appeal will become even more pronounced. Peabody and Lubalin (p. 45) claim that these changes have dramatically altered the nominating process:

> Pursuit of presidential nominations has become markedly more open, and lengthening preconvention campaigns have progressively focused on the cultivation of a popular national constituency as an indirect means of securing delegate support. The discretion exercised by the conventions has been reduced, and nominations have been increasingly determined before the conventions meet. Nomination is won as a result of decentralized bargaining between aspirants and delegates during which the former seek advance commitments from the latter on the basis of their poll showings.

The extended period over which presidential nomination bids are now contested helps explain some of the advantages of Senators over Governors in seeking the Presidency. The six-year term of office of Senators gives them more time to plan their presidential bids and allows them more opportunities to run in a year when their Senate seats are not up for election, thereby guaranteeing their continuation as Senators should their presidential quest fail. Governors, on the other hand, have two- or four-year terms of office, which do not provide as much electoral security for the upwardly mobile Governor. In this regard, it is noteworthy that Carter and Reagan were no longer Governor when each sought his party's nomination in 1976; hence each had the flexibility to campaign full time. In contrast, when Jerry Brown challenged Carter's renomination in 1980, he did so as the incumbent Governor, and therefore was of necessity absent from California frequently, which was a source of criticism. As of mid-1979,

Brown was already experiencing a problem in his out-of-state travels because his Lt. Governor, a Republican, was eager and able to embarrass Brown when he was not in California. Of course, incumbency gives Brown the opportunity to demonstrate problem-solving skills on contemporary problems, such as the tax revolt; despite his initial opposition to Proposition 13, Brown worked effectively in implementing it after it was approved by the voters.

The emphasis on presidential nominees with national appeal has worked to the advantage of Senators over Governors since Washington, D.C., is the hub of a national communications network, while many state capitols receive little national media coverage. Senators often can receive coverage on the nightly news shows simply by conducting hearings on some controversial public issue, while Governors are more hard-pressed to attract media attention; state problems will be less interesting to a national audience and to the national networks. Given that the public views the President as paramount in the conduct of foreign policy, would-be Presidents must establish their credentials in this area, and Senators are in a much better position to accomplish this than are Governors. An appointment to the Senate Foreign Relations Committee plus the almost obligatory fact-finding trip abroad, complete with an audience with Soviet leaders, serve to establish the Senator's expertise in the realm of foreign affairs. Despite the Senator's advantage in media coverage, the sequential nature of the primary system and the horse race emphasis given the process by the press and television allow an unknown candidate to develop a popular following.

THE NOMINATING SYSTEM

Introduction

The presidential nominating system has undergone major change, particularly since 1968, and even as this chapter was being written some nine months before the first presidential primary in 1980, significant developments were still occurring. Certainly the major change in the nomination process has been the sizable increase in the number of states employing the primary election as the means for selecting delegates to the nominating conventions. In 1972 there were 23 presidential primaries, including the District of Columbia, an increase of 6 over the 1968 figure. In 1976 there were 30 presidential primaries and the number for 1980 may go as high as 36. In 1972 about two thirds of Democratic and three fifths of Republican convention delegates were selected in primaries, while in 1976 of the Democratic and Republican delegates 76 and 71 percent respectively were chosen in primaries. The 1980 figures may well exceed 80 percent. Table 10.6 presents the tentative schedule for the 1980 primaries and the list of states which had primaries in recent years.

The number, the scheduling, and the form of the 1980 primaries were still very much up in the air as of mid-1979. Considerations of state prestige, personal and partisan advantage, and political reform resulted in substantial activity by state legislatures considering modifications of their states' primary election arrangements. For example, the New Hampshire primary is scheduled for February 26, but had the Democratic National Committee approved of Puerto Rico's February 17 primary, then the New Hampshire legislature would have advanced its primary to February 12 so that New Hampshire could maintain its strategic position as the first primary state.

An even more revealing example of how the scheduling of primaries can get caught up in a multitude of factors is provided by the case of Texas. As shown in Table 10.6, the 1980 Texas primary is scheduled for May 3, although some Texas legislators proposed separating the presidential primary from the state and local primary and moving the former up to March 11. There were many reasons for this, including helping native son John Connally; presumably an early Texas primary would enable Connally to score a victory that would help offset possible early losses in the New England primaries. And although Texas was his home state, where he would be expected to run well, nevertheless a Connally victory over Reagan in the Texas primary would be a very critical one, according to Connally supporters, since Reagan had run so well in Texas against President Ford in 1976. An early Texas primary in conjunction with primaries in other oil-producing states was advocated as a way of lessening the undue influence that New Hampshire and other New England states exercise because of their early primaries. Proponents of a South-Southwestern regional primary argued that presidential candidates tend to cater to the concerns of energy-poor New England at the expense of the energy-producing states, and that the way to redress the imbalance was for the energy states to move their primaries to an earlier date.

Local politics also helps explain the attempt to move up the Texas primary. Conservative Democratic legislators in Texas wanted separate primaries for the presidential versus state and local races because

TABLE 10.6
The Tentative 1980 Primary Schedule, the 1976 Primary Schedule, and the List of States Which Had Primaries in 1972, 1968, 1964, and 1960*

State	Tentative 1980 date	1976 date	1972	1968	1964	1960
Puerto Rico	Feb. 17–R; March 16–D	None				
New Hampshire	Feb. 26	Feb. 24	X	X	X	X
Massachusetts	March 4	March 2	X	X	X	X
Vermont	March 4	March 2				
South Carolina	March 8–R	None				
Alabama	March 11	May 4	X	X	X	X
Florida	March 11	March 9	X	X	X	X
Georgia	March 11	May 4				
Illinois	March 18	March 16	X	X	X	X
Connecticut	March 25	None				
New York	March 25	April 6	X	X	X	X
Kansas	April 1	None				
Wisconsin	April 1	April 6	X	X	X	X
Louisiana	April 5	None				
Pennsylvania	April 22	April 27	X	X	X	X
Texas	May 3–R	May 1			X	
District of Columbia	May 6	May 4	X	X	X	X
Indiana	May 6	May 4	X	X	X	X
North Carolina	May 6	March 23	X			
Tennessee	May 6	May 25	X			
Maryland	May 13	May 18	X		X	X
Nebraska	May 13	May 11	X	X	X	X
Michigan	May 20	May 18	X			
Oregon	May 27	May 25	X	X	X	X
Arkansas	May 27–D	May 25				
Idaho	May 27	May 25				
Kentucky	May 27	May 25				
Nevada	May 27	May 25				
California	June 3	June 8	X	X	X	X
Montana	June 3	June 1				
New Jersey	June 3	June 8	X	X	X	X
New Mexico	June 3	None	X			
Ohio	June 3	June 8	X	X	X	X
Rhode Island	June 3	June 1	X			
South Dakota	June 3	June 1	X	X	X	X
West Virginia	June 3	May 11	X	X	X	X
Total primaries	36	30	23	17	19	18

* As of this writing, Texas Democrats may schedule a non-binding primary on May 3. In 1964 Texas did not have a primary law, but the GOP held a non-binding presidential preference poll. For the 1960–72 period, an X indicates that the state held a presidential primary.

Sources: Constructed from information presented in *Congressional Quarterly Weekly Report,* May 19, 1979, p. 952 and November 24, 1979, p. 2661, and *Guide to 1976 Elections* (Washington, D.C.: Congressional Quarterly Inc., 1977), pp. 26–32.

they feared that if there were only one primary, many conservative Democratic voters would opt to vote in the potential Reagan-Connally Republican primary, leaving the Democratic primary with a preponderance of liberal voters who might pose a threat to the renomination of the conservative Democrats. It appears that the split-primary bill is dead, in part because of the actions of 12 liberal Democratic state legislators (labelled the "killer bees") who went into hiding so that the state senate could not achieve a quorum and pass legislation. The situation became comical as the Lt. Governor ordered the Texas Rangers to arrest the hiding legislators and bring them back to the legislature. The Texas experience demonstrates vividly how the presidential contest gets tied up in other considerations and suggests how uncertain the political environment can be for a candidate trying to plot his or her strategy early.

As of mid-1979, the states were trying to bring their delegate selection procedures into compliance with the national party rules. This was particularly a problem for the Democrats whose 1980 rules represented a change from the 1976 procedures, which in turn were different than the 1972 rules in some major ways. The Democratic Party conducted its 1976 primaries under a set of rules which, among other things, banned winner-take-all primaries and required that at least 75 percent of directly elected delegates be elected from districts no larger than congressional districts. The elimination of winner-take-all primaries was adopted to prevent a repetition of the 1972 California primary outcome in which George McGovern won a narrow popular vote victory over Hubert Humphrey, yet received California's entire bloc of 271 delegates, the largest at the convention. The intent of the 1976 Democratic rules was to guarantee that a state's delegates were allocated according to the candidates' demonstrated strength in the state. There were, however, important loopholes in the 1976 rules, the most significant one allowing winner-take-all primaries within any district (congressional or otherwise) in which delegates were directly elected. Hence a candidate could still win all or most of a state's delegates with only a small plurality of the vote, thereby undermining the move to proportional representation.

Since 1976, the Democratic Party, via the Winograd Commission, has changed the party rules once again. And since the commission was dominated by Carter supporters, many of the changes were designed to enhance Carter's renomination prospects (Crotty, 1979). For example, the Winograd Commission proposed that all primaries and caucuses take place within a three-month period, the ostensible purpose of which was to shorten the primary season and reduce the physical and financial costs incurred by candidates. However, it can be argued that the proposal favors an incumbent President, who undoubtedly begins the primary season with more resources, better organization, and higher name recognition than most prospective challengers. An exemption from this three-month rule was given to any state that in 1976 began its delegate selection before the second Tuesday in March (Crotty, 1979: 14). This in effect was an effort to insure that New Hampshire would maintain its position as the first primary. Carter backers supported this exemption because they thought their candidate would do well in New Hampshire and thus wanted the tremendous psychological boost that a New Hampshire victory brings. This move could backfire with the formal declaration of candidacy by Edward Kennedy, a native New Englander from neighboring Massachusetts. The Democrats were willing to grant New Hampshire an exemption also because they recognized that it would probably have been impossible to enforce New Hampshire compliance to any primary system in which New Hampshire was not the lead-off state.

The Winograd Commission also recommended that filing deadlines for caucuses and primaries be at least 55 to 75 days before the actual delegate selection. The aim here was to limit the field of candidates by forcing an early start on would-be challengers. As finally adopted, states were allowed to set deadlines ranging from 30 to 90 days. This move could also backfire on Carter; one can imagine circumstances in which an incumbent would have a better chance in a larger field of candidates than in a one-on-one race where all of the opponents of the incumbent coalesce around the challenger. This proposal was also designed to prevent late entries in the presidential contest, as occurred in 1976 when late starters Jerry Brown and Frank Church bested Carter in some of the later primaries.

Under the rules in effect in 1976, a candidate usually had to get at least 15 percent of the primary or caucus vote to receive his or her proportional share of delegates. The Winograd Commission initially proposed a sliding minimum of 15 percent in the first month of the primary season, 20 percent the second month, and 25 percent the third month. According to Crotty (1979: 15–16), this action favored the incumbent by discriminating against candidates with little name recognition initially and by making successful challenges to the front-runner more difficult as the primary season progressed. As finally adopted by the Democratic National Committee, the plan provided for a variable threshold, but not based on the month of the primary season. For delegates selected at state conventions and for at-large delegates in primary states, the state parties were allowed to establish a threshold of between 15 and 20 percent. For district delegates in primary states, the threshold would be determined by dividing 100 by the number of delegates elected in the district, with the proviso that the maximum threshold would be 25 percent. Hence if a district elected five delegates, the minimum percentage of the vote required to win a delegate would be 20 percent. Supporters of the plan argued that it would prevent a glut of candidates by winnowing the field and thereby facilitate the building of a consensus around the party's eventual nominee (Cook, 1978: 1571). Opponents argued that higher thresholds would make it harder for minor candidates to win delegates, thereby providing an undue advantage for the front-runner. Yet it is not entirely clear that this rule will help the front-runner. Winner-take-all is allowable within a state or district only if one candidate receives at least 90 percent of the vote. Otherwise the delegates will be allocated in proportion to the candidates' performance subject to the minimum percentage provisions. *Congressional Quarterly* (May 12, 1979, p. 909) presents the hypothetical example of a district with five delegates and three contestants. If the top candidate gets 46 percent of the vote, the runner-up 29 percent, and the third-place finisher 25 percent, then the top two would each get two delegates and the third-place candidate would get one delegate, an allocation that does not help the top candidate at all.[3]

The point of the previous discussion is that many different considerations influenced the final form of the 1980 delegate selection procedures. The reform orientation that guided the 1972 rules changes in such areas as the selection of delegates, the conduct of the convention, and the participatory opportunities within the Democratic Party has given way to a much more political and partisan and, some would say, pragmatic perspective. In conclusion, we should note that although the reform movement was most relevant to the Democratic

---

[3] For an analysis of how different minimum cutoff requirements would have affected the allocation of delegates in 1976, see Maisel and Lieberman (1977). More generally, the Maisel and Lieberman work and the Lengle and Shafer (1976) analysis of the 1972 primaries indicate how different primary rules—winner-take-all versus proportional allocation versus winner-take-all within districts would have affected the number of delegates won by candidates in 1972 and 1976.

Party, it has had consequences for the GOP. Many of the Democratic changes required state legislative enactment, which thereby affected GOP procedures. Nevertheless, Democrats and Republicans can still employ markedly different procedures within the same state. For example, the California primary for Republicans in 1976 was winner-take-all, so that Ford's 34.5 percent of the vote (versus Reagan's 65.5 percent) won him no delegates. On the Democratic side, proportional allocation of delegates was required, so that Carter's 20.4 percent of the vote (compared to Brown's 59 percent) won him 67 delegates.

Selecting the Delegates

As mentioned previously, the reliance on primary elections to select delegates to the nominating conventions has grown tremendously since 1968. Why primaries have become so popular is in part because of the rhetoric surrounding them, which asserts that primaries are the most democratic way to choose delegates. Also contributing to the prominence of primaries is the extensive coverage given them by the mass media, coverage not given to the other means of delegate selection—state party committees and state conventions. Certainly primary elections have the elements of drama, excitement, and ease of understanding that attract media attention. And many states moved to a primary between 1968 and 1976 because compliance to Democratic Party rules was easier under a primary system than under any other method of delegate selection.

Frank Sorauf (1972: 271–72) has described four types of presidential primaries: (1) those which involve the election of unpledged delegates with no presidential candidates on the ballot; (2) those which involve an expression of presidential preference only with no delegates elected; (3) those which combine the first two types of electing delegates pledged to presidential candidates; and (4) those which involve a presidential preference poll and a separate election of delegates. Beyond these four basic types, the primaries differ in several important respects. In some states a candidate must give his or her consent to be placed on the ballot, while in other states every conceivable candidate is included on the ballot. This means that some primaries give a better indication of the relative popularity of various candidates, and suggests that strategic concerns play a central role in the decision as to which primaries to contest. In some states delegates are only nominally pledged to a candidate, while in other states delegates are required by law to take a pledge of loyalty to the candidate and to continue to support the candidate through multiple ballots unless formally released from their commitment. In some states, all delegates are elected in the primary, while in other states delegates are chosen via the primary election and the state convention. And finally, in states that do employ only the primary to select delegates, the delegates may be elected from a variety of geographical units, including state legislative districts, congressional districts, and even the state at large. In short, there are many variations in primary elections that the prospective candidate must be aware of to wage an effective campaign.

While the number of delegates elected in state and district conventions has steadily decreased in the past decade, a substantial bloc of delegates are still chosen in this manner. Lacking the spectacle of the primaries, conventions were largely ignored by the mdia, although not by the savvy candidate. While Goldwater's primary election track record in 1964 was far from impressive, his nomination was assured by his success in securing delegates at state conventions (and by his California primary victory). After President Johnson's decision not to seek reelection in 1968, Hubert Humphrey announced his presidential candidacy sufficiently late that he was unable to contest most primaries, a strategically fortunate situation for him. Humphrey scored his major delegate successes in non-primary states.

In 1972 and 1976, the convention method of delegate selection received somewhat more attention, in large part because of the lessons of 1964 and 1968 and the fact that the Iowa caucus-convention system initiated the actual delegate selection process, thereby providing the first direct voter-based sounding on the relative standing of the candidates. As discussed in Chapter 9, the reporting of the Iowa caucus results became a political event in itself and the caucus results assumed a greater importance than merited. Prospective 1980 nominees are already in mid-1979 at work in Iowa. Yet with the exception of Iowa, convention states still receive relatively little coverage.

The fact that state and district conventions were so much less visible than primary elections meant that it was easier to manipulate and structure them for particular political purposes. In response to their 1968 experiences, the Democrats adopted a set of reforms designed to make the state conventions more open and representative. Delegates could not be selected until the calendar year of the nominating convention; this rule prevented the early selection of delegates at a time when most citizens were not yet attuned to presidential politics.

State parties were required to publicize the time, place, and rules of all party meetings, to hold meetings in accessible places, and to provide as much information as possible about the presidential preferences of the persons seeking to be delegates to the national convention. Formerly, party organizations often held the conventions under a veritable veil of secrecy, which resulted in very limited participation in the delegate selection process.

The Allocation of Delegates

Each party has its own formula for determining how many votes each state and territory will have at the nominating convention. These formulas take into account the population of the state and the partisan success of the party within the state at previous elections. In addition, the Republican rules provide bonus convention votes to those states with Republican presidential, congressional, and gubernatorial election victories—a procedure that has generated controversy between the party's liberal and conservative wings. The liberal Republicans, mainly from populous, urbanized states, emphasize population of the state as the major determinant of convention votes. Conservatives oppose this, arguing that the populous states are those in which the GOP fares poorest; conservatives are more supportive of rules that give a bonus to states with Republican victories. Judith Parris (1972: 27) indicates that the proportion of GOP convention votes coming from the ten most populous states has remained quite stable from 1952 to 1972, averaging about 43 percent throughout the period; the 1976 figure was 44 percent. The one area to noticeably increase its share of the convention votes has been the South; in 1972 about 22 percent of GOP convention votes were allocated to the South, an increase of about 6 percent over the 1952 figure. This increase reflects the growth and increased success of the GOP at the state and local levels in the South. In 1976, about 27 percent of the votes came from the South, but this percentage will decline to 24 in 1980 because of Carter's near sweep of the South. The 1976 GOP convention had 2,259 delegates, nearly twice as many as in previous conventions.

Unlike the Republicans, the Democrats have modified their delegate apportionment methods numerous times since 1952. Their current formula gives each state "three times its number of electoral college votes plus additional votes based on the average vote for the party's presidential ticket in the past three elections" (Parris, 1972:

30). This formula resulted in a 1976 convention with over 3,000 votes; in fact, each time the Democrats changed their rules, the number of convention votes increased. More than 53 percent of the 1972 and 1976 convention votes came from the ten most populous states, an increase of about 10 percent over the 1968 figure. This occurred because the largest states also tended to be the most loyally Democratic states throughout the 1960s. For 1980, the Winograd Commission enlarged each state's delegation by 10 percent, so that elected public and party officials would be guaranteed seats at the convention. This step reflected the belief by commission members that party service should serve as a basis for representation at the nominating convention, a position in marked contrast to the 1972 McGovern rules.

The Characteristics of Delegates

The characteristics of convention delegates have interested observers on the assumption that delegates with different backgrounds and different experiences will in fact behave differently at national conventions. With respect to voting for the presidential nominee, this seems to be a questionable assumption since many delegates are morally if not legally bound to a particular candidate. Of course, there are other activities of a convention where delegates are likely to have greater discretion, for example, on platform and credentials fights; in such areas, the delegates' background may have an independent effect on their behavior. There was considerable speculation, for example, prior to the 1972 convention that McGovern would be unable to keep his delegates united on platform and credentials disputes since many of his delegates were new to conventions, highly motivated by issue concerns, and unlikely to accept discipline. While this did not occur, it does suggest how background characteristics may plausibly be related to behavior.

Prior to 1972, the typical description of a convention delegate was that of a middle-aged white male from an upper-status background. One of the reforms adopted by the Democrats after their 1968 convention—the so-called establishment of quotas—urged that minorities, women, and young people be adequately represented on state delegations, a move that resulted in sharp increases in black, female, and youth participation at the 1972 convention (see Table 10.7). Since 1972 the Democrats have backed off from their quota requirements and, instead, have issued affirmative action guidelines that

TABLE 10.7
Some Characteristics of Delegates to
the 1968, 1972, and 1976 Conventions

Characteristic	Democratic			Republican		
	1968	1972	1976	1968	1972	1976
Race						
White	94	85	92	98	97	97
Black	6	15	8	2	3	3
Sex						
Male	87	60	67	83	65	69
Female	13	40	33	17	35	31
Age						
30 and under	4	21	14	9	7	7
over 30	96	79	86	91	93	93

Sources: John S. Jackson, III, Jesse C. Brown, and Barbara L. Brown, "Recruitment, Representation, and Political Values: The 1976 Democratic National Convention Delegates," *American Politics Quarterly* 6 (April 1978), p. 194; and Thomas H. Roback, "Recruitment and Incentive Patterns among Delegates to the 1972 and 1976 Republican National Conventions: The Individual as the Strategic Factor in the Theory of Party Organization," paper presented at the annual meeting of the American Political Science Association, Washington, D.C., September 1–4, 1977, p. 11.

state parties should follow to assure adequate representation of different groups at the national convention. The Republican Party has taken some weak and tentative steps to make the party's convention more open and diverse by calling for "positive action," but there are no serious enforcement mechanisms or sanctions for state parties that do not take positive action. As shown in Table 10.7, the group whose participation rose most substantially from 1968 to 1976 was women, yet even here female participation levels declined from 1972 to 1976. For their 1980 convention, the Democrats are considering a requirement that delegations be divided equally among men and women; the implementation and enforcement of such a provision are likely to generate some controversy.

The delegates' experience at previous national conventions has also interested political observers. It is argued that conventions dominated by newcomers are likely to be unpredictable and disorderly affairs, in contrast to conventions dominated by political veterans. Johnson and Hahn (1973: 148) report that between 1944 and 1968, the average Republican convention had 65.1 percent inexperienced delegates and the average Democratic convention 63.7 percent. Sullivan and his colleagues (1974: 24) reported that the proportion of newcomers to the 1972 Democratic convention increased to about 84 percent because of the rules changes adopted by the party and because of the attractiveness of the McGovern candidacy to citizens not normally involved in partisan and presidential politics. Demonstrating the effect of previous convention experience on convention behavior is difficult. Johnson and Hahn (1973: 161) did uncover a pattern between 1948 and 1968, which indicated that experienced delegates were more likely to support seasoned candidates and inexperienced delegates were more likely to support political newcomers to presidential politics.

A final characteristic of delegates that is receiving increased attention is whether the delegates' outlook on politics is that of an amateur (purist) or that of a professional. For the amateur, or purist, the main reason for participation in politics rests on programmatic issue concerns, with candidates judged according to their stands on issues. The professional is motivated by more traditional party concerns, such as the need to win elections; hence candidates are judged on how well they can unify the party and win the election. From this basic difference in outlook follows a number of other differences; for example, professionals are more willing to compromise on issues, since that is not their central concern, while the amateurs are more willing to contest issues to the bitter end, no matter the consequences for party unity. Obviously, a convention dominated by purists concerned only about issues and principles might not be the optimal setting for producing a winning ticket. Yet a convention dominated by party regulars may not be a productive setting for confronting controversial issues that are in need of some resolution. A convention dominated by professionals may produce a ticket and platform so bland that it will be difficult to mobilize the thousands of volunteers needed to conduct a full campaign.

Studies of the 1968 and 1972 Democratic conventions found that the amateur-professional distinction was related to the candidate preference of delegates, with amateurs favoring more issue-oriented and liberal candidates. For example, Soule and Clarke (1970: 89) report that the most typical supporter of Eugene McCarthy in 1968 was the liberal amateur, while the strongest support for Humphrey came from conservative professionals. Similarly, in an investigation of the 1972 convention, Sullivan and his associates (1974: 124) found that the centrist candidates, such as Humphrey, Muskie, and Jackson, tended to be supported by professionals, while more ideologically extreme candidates, such as Wallace and McGovern, were much more likely to be supported by purists. Overall, purists at the 1972 convention overwhelmingly favored McGovern, while professionals preferred the candidates of the center. In a similar vein, Kirkpatrick (1976) found that supporters of the centrist candidates in 1972 emphasized the role of the convention in unifying the party and putting forth a winning ticket, while the Wallace and McGovern delegates were much more likely to cite the importance of correct issue positions, party reform, and the like.

Studies of the 1976 convention delegates found distinctive orientations among supporters of Reagan versus Ford (Roback, 1977a, 1977b), but scant differences among Carter delegates versus backers of other Democratic contenders (Jackson et al., 1978). Reagan delegates were much more likely than Ford loyalists to cite support for the issue and the ideological positions of their candidate as a reason for convention participation. Compared to Ford delegates, the Reagan backers were more likely to cite purposive, programmatic matters as incentives for party activism and less likely to cite solidary and material rewards. Fortunately for Ford, many programmatically oriented Reagan supporters also highly valued party loyalty and electoral victory. At the Democratic convention, there were modest differences in the orientations of Carter delegates and supporters of the other candidates, which undoubtedly made the task of achieving party unity after the convention that much easier.

The Nominating Conventions

The nominating conventions are commonly described as having a number of functions, foremost being the nomination of the presidential and vice presidential candidates, the drafting of a platform, and the governance of the party in the inter-election period via the national committee. Certainly the nomination of the presidential candidate is the focal point of the convention, yet in recent years this decision has largely been settled prior to the start of the convention. Donald Matthews (1974: 54) points out that since 1936 the leading candidates at the beginning of the primary season have invariably won their party's nomination, the major exceptions being the failure of the early Democratic front-runner, Senator Edmund Muskie of Maine, to win the 1972 nod, and the rise of Jimmy Carter from obscurity to win the nomination in 1976. The open and shut nature of the nominating conventions is indicated in Table 10.8, which presents the number of candidates who received more than 10 percent of the convention vote and the number of ballots required to select a presidential nominee since 1952. Note that the only nomination to go beyond the first ballot was that of Stevenson in 1952.

TABLE 10.8
The Number of Ballots and the Number of Candidates Polling
10 Percent of the Votes in the Democratic and
Republican Conventions, 1952–1976

Year	Democratic Conventions		Republican Conventions	
	Candidates over 10 Percent	Number of Ballots	Candidates over 10 Percent	Number of Ballots
1952	4	3	2	1
1956	2	1	1	1
1960	2	1	1	1
1964	1	1	2	1
1968	2	1	3	1
1972	3	1	1	1
1976	3	1	2	1

Source: Frank J. Sorauf, *Party Politics in America*, 2d ed. (Boston: Little, Brown & Company, Inc., 1972), table 1, p. 293, accounts of the 1972 election; and *Guide to 1976 Elections* (Washington, D.C.: Congressional Quarterly Inc., 1977), pp. 14–15.

There was much speculation in late 1975 that the 1976 Democratic convention would break the pattern of recent conventions and require numerous ballots and extensive convention bargaining to select a nominee. This speculation was fueled by the absence of an obvious front-runner, by the presence of many candidates in the race, and by the Democratic delegate selection rules banning winner-take-all primaries. Yet not only were there no multiple ballots, the nominee was effectively decided far in advance of the convention. The question becomes how did this happen. Certainly Jimmy Carter started early, worked hard, adopted a shrewd strategy, and put together the needed resources. Yet this is only a partial explanation of how Carter emerged from the pack of candidates to secure the nomination early. One must also examine the focus of media coverage and the role the media play in winnowing candidates. As discussed in Chapter 9, the primaries and caucuses, particularly the early ones, receive extensive coverage, which serves to establish front-runners, create momentum, and eliminate candidates. Carter's early successes in Iowa and New Hampshire were certainly notable, but were not of such significance to thrust him to the head of the pack. After all, Carter came in second in the Iowa precinct caucuses with 29.1 percent of the vote, compared to 38.5 percent for uncommitted delegates. And in the highly fragmented New Hampshire primary, Carter "won" with 28.4 percent of the vote, compared to 22.7 percent for Udall, 15.2 percent for Bayh, 10.8 percent for Harris, and a scattering of votes for other candidates. How can these showings be considered so impressive that Carter was thrust to the forefront? The answer is that the media treated them as consequential—and they therefore became so. As Patterson (1977a) has demonstrated, the media's focus on winners resulted in Carter getting a disproportionate share of media coverage because of his early success, and this in turn made him better known than his opponents in subsequent primary states. Patterson labeled the phenomenon "winner-take-all" journalism, and showed that in the critical two-month period between February 23 and April 27, Carter got 43 percent of the network evening news coverage given to Democratic presidential contenders, 59 percent of the *Time* and *Newsweek* space, and 46 percent of the coverage in selected newspapers.

It is possible that convention deadlocks will occur in the future and that the convention will once again become an important bargaining site. The 1980 Democratic rules have eliminated the loophole winner-take-all primary, which should result in a broader distribution of delegates, although other rules changes will probably contribute to a winnowing, consensus-building process that works against the likelihood of a brokered convention with multiple ballots. Presently the 1980 Republican race is shaping up as a multiple-candidate contest, with Ronald Reagan the strong front-runner in mid-1979 among rank-and-file Republicans. Should Reagan fail to keep pace, the prospects of significant convention bargaining would be enhanced. The outcome of such bargaining would depend upon a variety of factors, including the number of contending candidates, their relative strengths, their acceptability to the party at large, their prospects of victory in November, and their ability to negotiate effectively with other party factions.

The fact that the nominee is most often determined prior to the convention does not mean that conventions are unexciting and lack controversy. Certainly McGovern's nomination in 1972 would have been more problematic had the challenge to his California delegates ultimately proved successful. Credentials contests, such as the California challenge and disputes over the party platform, can generate substantial excitement and conflict. Eisenhower's nomination in 1952 certainly depended on the disposition of a number of credentials fights. As mentioned in Chapter 6, moderate Republicans turned their efforts toward modifying the GOP platform in 1964 once it became clear that Goldwater had clinched the nomination. Likewise, Democratic doves in 1968 made a major effort to get a Vietnam plank to their liking while recognizing that Hubert Humphrey's nomination was virtually assured. In 1960, Nelson Rockefeller considered a challenge to the nomination of Richard Nixon and eventually focused his efforts on the party platform, which resulted in the famous "Compact of Fifth Avenue" in which Nixon pushed for platform changes desired by Rockefeller.

Some of the more consequential deliberations of the convention take place behind the scenes in the presence of a small number of party elites. The selection of the vice presidential nominee is such an activity; the selection process is best described as haphazard. The usual procedure is for the vice presidential decision to be made by the successful presidential nominee in consultation with his or her staff and a broad range of party elites. This means that the decision is often made under extreme time constraints by an exhausted candidate and the staff. This is the explanation given for the Eagleton fiasco in 1972: the McGovern staff simply did not have the opportunity to do an extensive investigation of Senator Eagleton's background. Normally the presidential nominee's choice for Vice President is routinely ratified by the convention delegates, although there was opposition to both parties' vice presidential selection in 1968 and 1972. In rare cases the determination of the vice presidential candidate is left to the convention at large; Adlai Stevenson in 1956 allowed the Democratic convention to choose his running mate. As discussed in Chapter 7, the process by which Carter selected Mondale as his running mate in 1976 was much more thorough and deliberate than is normally the case.

Reforming the Nomination System

At present there is much dissatisfaction with the shape of the nomination system and especially with the state presidential primary elections. While proponents of the primaries stress how they provide for citizen participation in the nomination process and how they increase the public's interest in politics, opponents criticize primaries on personal, political, and philosophical grounds. On personal grounds, it is argued that primaries require too much time, energy, and money, effectively ruling out candidates without access to ample financial resources and candidates unwilling to subject themselves to the indignities required to contest the primaries. Senator Walter Mondale, the first announced candidate for the 1976 Democratic nomination to drop out of the race, said, "Basically I found I did not have the overwhelming desire to be president which is essential for the kind of campaign that is required. I don't think anyone should be president who is not willing to go through fire" (*Congressional Quarterly Weekly Report*, Nov., 30, 1974, p. 3214). Evidently the rigors of the Vice Presidency are less than the demands of the primary season.

The question arises as to whether candidates should be required to endure such a trial by fire. Proponents argue that the existing primary system enables the voter to determine whether the prospective nominee has the strength and fortitude to stand up to the rigors of being President, that the grueling pace of the primaries is proper test of one's presidential capabilities. But others have argued just the opposite, asserting that the endurance contest features of the primaries have little, if anything, to say about a person's presidential fitness. Michael Robinson has extended this argument, to claim that primaries are dysfunctional for both the candidates and the country; he writes (1975: E3336):

> The primary system has made it so that the nice guys, including the competent ones, stay out of the whole ordeal. Right from the start, the primary system means that only those who possess near psychopathic ambition and temperament will get involved and stay involved.
>
> All told, the primary system is a disaster. It costs too much; it takes too long; it makes pseudo-enemies out of true political allies; and it makes pseudo-winners out of true losers. And, more importantly, the primary system has made the process of becoming President so despiriting, so distasteful, that those who would become, shouldn't.

Another set of criticisms of primaries focuses on the meaning or interpretability of the election results. It is argued that the primaries for a variety of reasons do not give an accurate indication of the voters' candidate preference. This may occur because not all candidates contest a primary or because there are multiple candidates, resulting in a plurality winner who is not preferred (and may even be opposed) by a majority of the party faithful. Certainly this was a distinct possibility in 1976 had the presence of a number of moderate and liberal Democratic candidates enabled George Wallace to score a series of plurality victories in primaries. Since only the voter's first-place choice is counted in most American elections, it is possible in a multicandidate race for a relatively unpopular candidate to emerge victorious.

Also undermining the interpretation of a primary election outcome is the representativeness, or lack thereof, of the primary electorate. In a study of 11 contested presidential primaries between 1952 and 1968, Austin Ranney (1972: 23–24) found a mean turnout rate of 39 percent, some 30 points below the general election average. The low turnout in many primaries clearly increases the probability of an unrepresentative electorate. Examining the 1968 New Hampshire and Wisconsin primaries, Ranney (1972: 36) concluded that the electorates were demographically unrepresentative and to a lesser extent atypical in their issue and candidate preferences. In a study of competitive presidential primaries in 1976, Ranney (1977: 22–26) found a mean turnout rate of only 28 percent, again raising the possibility of an unrepresentative electorate.

The New Hampshire primary is a useful target for questioning the significance given to primary results. As the first presidential primary, New Hampshire has become a crucial one, with the power to make or break candidates. Certainly Muskie's relatively unimpressive (though victorious) showing in New Hampshire signaled the beginning of his decline as a viable candidate. Yet should the voters of New Hampshire, a lightly populated, relatively unurbanized state, have so much power? In particular, should fewer than 100,000 Democratic voters in New Hampshire be in such a crucial position when these Democrats are unrepresentative of Democrats nationally? Compounding the atypicality of New Hampshire is the presence of publisher William Loeb and his influential newspaper. Loeb did his best to hurt the Muskie candidacy and apparently was successful in holding down Muskie's margin in Manchester where circulation of his paper was greatest.

A final problem with the primaries is the criteria used in interpreting the results and the effects of these interpretations on the selection process. Obviously it is highly newsworthy when the heavy underdog McGovern manages to win 37 percent of the New Hampshire vote in 1972, as against only 46 percent for the heavy favorite, Muskie. Yet the fact is that Muskie did win the primary. But being designated as the front-runner by the media entails risks, for one's performance is evaluated in terms of how strongly one wins rather than whether one wins or not. Thus, Muskie's weaker than expected showing in New Hampshire was widely interpreted and reported by the media as a major setback to his candidacy.

The general point is that primary election results are given meaning by the standards used in interpreting them; different standards may differentially affect the future course of political events. For example, one might argue that the coverage of the McGovern candidacy in 1972 served to promote his chances. That is, since McGovern was not expected to do well, his relatively strong though nonwinning performances in a number of states were widely viewed as victories. It was not until late in the primary season that the press began dissecting the McGovern campaign as closely as it had others. Likewise, Ford's winning, but weak, performance in the New Hampshire primary in 1976 was made more impressive by media interpretations grounded in expectations that Ford would actually lose. (See Chapter 9.) Hence, as one looks to 1980, expectations of weak primary showings by Carter may actually aid his prospects.

A final problem with the primaries is that the system itself is not neutral but is in fact highly manipulable, with the capacity of advantaging some candidacies and hurting others. As suggested earlier in our Texas example, the scheduling of primaries is of strategic importance; an early loss can be devastating, just as an early victory can be uplifting. One wonders what would have happened in 1976 had western states been first on the primary schedule. Would Californian Jerry Brown or Idahoan Frank Church, or both, have entered the contest earlier, and would their possible early victories have established them as the leading candidates? Finally, it is clear that victories (or losses) are not equivalent, given the serial nature of the primaries. An early loss (e.g., New Hampshire) or a late loss (e.g., California) is probably more damaging than one in the middle of the primary season. The point is that the primary system as a decision-making procedure is not neutral but instead bestows benefits on certain candidacies, thereby influencing the outcome of the process.

Numerous reforms of the primary system have been suggested that would alleviate certain shortcomings and worsen others. The most commonly mentioned alternative to the present primaries is a national primary in all 50 states. To prevent the possibility that a candidate would be victorious with only a small plurality of the vote, most proposals for a national primary include a runoff provision between the top two vote-getters should no candidate get 40 percent of the vote. A constitutional amendment establishing a national presidential primary was introduced by former Senators Mansfield and Aiken in 1972 and included the following provisions (*Congressional Quarterly Weekly Report,* July 8, 1972, p. 1651):

> The primary would be held throughout the nation on the same day, and candidates would enter by filing petitions in 17 states with signatures in each state equal to 1 percent of the vote cast in that state in the previous presidential election—10,000 signatures, for example, where one million votes were cast. Neither candidates nor voters could participate in a primary other than the one held by the party in which they were registered. The mechanics of conducting the elections would remain in the hands of the individual states. The choice of vice presidential candidates and the writing of party platforms would be left to national conventions.

The national primary certainly eliminates the possibility of any single state's primary being given undue weight. It also permits a broader, and possibly more representative, participation of citizens in the candidate selection process. And a national primary shortens the campaign period, thereby making life more civilized for the candidates. Yet the national primary has some obvious drawbacks. One is that it raises the specter of three national elections—the primary, runoff, and general—which would require substantial resources. Furthermore, it is likely that only candidates who are already well known will have a reasonable chance of victory in a national primary. By eliminating the serial nature of the present primary system, the national primary rules out the possibility of some obscure candidate (such as McGovern in 1972 or Carter in 1976) rising from obscurity to win the nomination. A national primary would prevent candidates from "testing the waters"; instead, a candidate would have to enter full force or not at all.

Proposals also have been made for regional primaries and for clusters of primaries on the same date in geographically diverse states. Each of these proposals is designed to avoid some of the pitfalls of the national primary while retaining some of the better features of existing primary system. For example, a set of grouped primaries would maintain the sequencing features of the present system and allow a candidate to enter one set of primaries before having to decide upon the remainder. None of these proposals seem likely to much reduce campaign costs.[4]

While such proposals for primary election reforms would affect both parties identically, other reform efforts have proceeded differently in each party, with the Democrats having taken the more dramatic steps. After their bitter 1968 convention, the Democrats created two reform commissions, one on party structure and delegate selection, headed by Senator McGovern, and one on rules, headed by Representative James O'Hara of Michigan. After a year of deliberations, the McGovern commission issued a list of 18 guidelines for delegate selection, many of which have been mentioned previously. The intent of the reforms was to make the convention more representative and to open up the political process to traditional nonparticipants.

The issue of representation is a tricky one, with respect to national party conventions. For example, critics in 1968 lamented that the nominees selected in the conventions (Humphrey and Nixon) were unrepresentative relics of the old politics. It was the case that nationwide polls of *all* citizens indicated Rockefeller was more popular than Nixon, and McCarthy preferred over Humphrey. But among Democrats and Republicans only, Humphrey and Nixon were the respective favorites. Thus, one can argue that the conventions in 1968 adequately reflected the desires of the partisans of each party.

The issue of representation also extends to the characteristics of the delegates making convention decisions, and here it is argued that both party's delegates were unrepresentative, mainly being white, middle-aged males. Thus, one of the McGovern commission reforms was the now infamous quotas for women, youth, and blacks; it was assumed that these groups had interests that could only be represented by members of the group. The rationale for providing quotas for these three groups and not others was in part that blacks, youth, and women were traditionally unrepresented; but this did not satisfy those groups who were without the protection of quotas.

The McGovern reforms, especially the opening of the delegation selection process in conjunction with the quotas, seemed to answer

---

4 For details of these various reform proposals, see *Congressional Quarterly Weekly Report*, July 8, 1972, pp. 1650–54. The most radical reform of the primaries suggested is their abolishment altogether; Michael Robinson urges a return to the Congressional Caucus as the mechanism for nominating presidential candidates. See Michael J. Robinson, "An Idea Whose Time Has Come—Again," *Congressional Record*, June 19, 1975, p. E3336.

the question as to whether greater loyalty was owed to one's party or to one's group in favor of the latter. Examining the 1972 Democratic delegation from California, William Cavala (1974: 40) concluded that it was very difficult to select delegates on the traditional basis of service to the party, and that the delegates finally selected had a much more distant relationship to the state and local campaign effort. Cavala (1974: 42) concluded that the new rules "hindered the efforts of the eventual winner to mount an effective electoral campaign." It seems clear that in the choice between issue purity versus electoral success, the rules resulted in an emphasis on the former.

However, since 1972 the Democratic Party, through the Mikulski and Winograd Commissions, has backed away from some of the McGovern-Fraser rules changes. As mentioned earlier, quotas have given way to affirmative action. Also, the expansion of delegation size by 10 percent for the 1980 convention—so that elected party officials would be guaranteed of attending the convention—reflects a different perspective on party service and party leadership than characterized the 1972 convention. Arterton (1978) has analyzed the consequences of party reform. He notes that the presidential selection process has become nationalized as more and more decisions are taken out of the domtain of the state political parties. Moreover, state party leaders are no longer central actors at conventions; state interests have given way to candidate-centered coalitions. Delegates themselves have less flexibility in their convention behavior as primary and caucus results bind them to supporting a particular candidate. Overall, Arterton concludes that the rules changes have made it difficult for the party establishment to control who gets the nomination; certainly McGovern and Carter were not the candidates preferred by party leaders. The ongoing controversy over Democratic Party rules reflects the inherent strain between participatory values versus party loyalty concerns. For citizens whose main priority was participation, the McGovern-Fraser reforms were probably viewed very positively as new participants became involved in the presidential selection process, even if they were more committeed to the welfare of a particular candidiate than to the political party itself. For citizens more concerned about the party per se, the modifications of the McGovern-Fraser rules since 1972 are likely seen as steps in the right direction.[5]

---

[5] For a discussion of the normative and descriptive aspects of party reform, see Ranney (1975) and Crotty (1977, 1978).

CONCLUSION

Throughout this and the previous chapter, we have focused on changes that have occurred in the strategic environment within which presidential elections are conducted. We have emphasized changes in campaign financing, media reliance, candidate recruitment, and the nomination system. While our focus was primarily descriptive, it was clear that the changes were all interrelated with major implications for the conduct and outcome of presidential elections. In Chapter 11 we will turn to the strategic aspects of seeking the Presidency, detailing the ramifications of some of the changes described in this chapter.

11

Running for President

INTRODUCTION

The presidential campaign can be analyzed and evaluated from a number of perspectives. From the perspective of the citizenry, one might view the campaign as an opportunity to inform and educate the electorate and evaluate the success of the campaign to the extent that this objective is met. Our focus in this chapter, however, is on the campaign from the candidate's vantage point. We shall assume that the candidate and his or her organization have as their primary goal electoral success and hence shall focus on the strategies employed by presidential aspirants. By strategies are meant those plans and programs adopted to promote victory. Strategies should be distinguished from tactics, which are the means by which plans and programs are executed. Our emphasis in this chapter is on strategies and not tactics, although it should be noted that the two are inexorably linked, in that certain strategies will require specific tactics to have any chance of success. For example, Nelson Rockefeller hoped to win the Republican nomination in 1968 by convincing GOP delegates of his national popularity and electability while at the same time avoiding the primaries. Rockefeller obviously had to employ such means as nationwide radio, television, and newspaper advertising campaigns; had he instead relied upon personal campaigning before small groups, his plans would have had no chance for success.

The analysis and evaluation of campaign strategies pose a number of difficulties. One is that a clear-cut statement of strategy may never be enunciated by the candidate and, even if publicly expressed, may be modified repeatedly in response to the actual course of campaign events. Related to this problem is the availability of reliable information about strategies; often one must depend upon third- and fourth-hand reports of campaign plans.

While a strategy generally deals with those features of the political environment that are manipulable by the candidate, one must recognize that many factors relevant to the election outcome—such as the existing distribution of partisan loyalties—are largely beyond the control of the candidate. Thus, evaluating a strategy makes sense only in the context of the constraints within which a candidate is operating, yet in some instances the constraints and their consequences are not immediately apparent. A sound political strategy must incorporate the realities of the situation at hand.

Finally, the evaluation of a strategy as successful or unsuccessful implies the existence of some baseline from which the campaign might be judged. The question arises as to the choice of baseline. Some might argue that victory or defeat is the appropriate standard, that the candidate who wins has employed a wise strategy and vice versa. Victory or defeat, however, seems too crude a basis for judgment; the nominee of the minority party who lost a very close election may in fact have employed the best possible strategy despite his or her loss. It has been argued that Nixon's strategy in 1968 was unsound despite his victory, since an apparent runaway election in September became a neck-and-neck race in November. Similar comments were made about Carter's 1976 performance.

Given the difficulties in discussing strategies in a detailed and thorough fashion, we will focus on the scenarios that the candidates envisaged would lead to victory. Cavala (1974: 33) describes a scenario as starting with a factual description of the candidate's present state, followed by a series of conditional statements as to what was likely to happen should certain conditions be met. We will emphasize the factors and conditions that rendered alternative plans realistic and unrealistic. We will point out how various scenarios recognized or ignored the constraints upon the candidate. And wherever possible, we will note those decisions explicitly made by presidential nominees that ultimately proved beneficial or harmful to their candidacies.

DO CAMPAIGNS MATTER?

Given the results reported in Chapter 9—that very few citizens change their mind over the course of the campaign—one might argue that studying the general election period and the strategies employed therein is an uninteresting exercise since the election outcome is largely foreordained. Apparent support for this argument is given in Table 11.1, which shows the proportion of citizens who decided on

TABLE 11.1
Time of Presidential Vote Choice, 1952–1976
(in percentages)

Decision Time	Year						
	1952	1956	1960	1964	1968	1972	1976
By the end of the conventions	68	78	62	66	59	63	54
After the conventions	21	12	25	21	19	23	22
Within two weeks of the election	9	8	10	9	15	8	17
On Election Day	2	2	3	4	7	6	7
Total	100	100	100	100	100	100	100

Source: SRC/CPS election studies.

their vote choice at various junctures in the campaign, and in Table 11.2, which shows the stability of voters' commitments to candidates. Note in Table 11.1 that about two thirds of the citizens have decided their vote choice by the end of the national nominating conventions with 1976 being the major exception to the pattern. And observe in Table 11.2 that citizens at least weakly committed to a candidate

TABLE 11.2
Stability of Voters' Commitments to Candidates over
the Course of the Campaign, 1960 and 1964
(in percentages)

	August Commitment	Election Day Vote Choice 1964	
		Johnson	Goldwater
1964			
Strongly committed to Johnson ...	34	95	5
Favor Johnson	20	84	16
Lean toward Johnson	8	59	41
Uncommitted	11	45	55
Lean toward Goldwater	4	24	76
Favor Goldwater	10	10	90
Strongly committed to Goldwater ..	3	3	97
Total	100		
Number of cases	2,271		

		1960	
		Kennedy	Nixon
1960			
Strongly committed to Kennedy ...	20	97	3
Favor Kennedy	16	94	6
Lean toward Kennedy	7	75	25
Uncommitted	13	59	41
Lean toward Nixon	5	27	73
Favor Nixon	14	12	88
Strongly committed to Nixon	25	3	97
Total	100		
Number of cases	2,672		

Source: Thomas W. Benham, "Polling for Presidential Candidates," in *The New Style in Election Campaigns,* edited by Robert Agranoff (Boston: Holbrook Press, Inc., 1972), p. 217.

prior to the traditional Labor Day start of the campaign, vote heavily for the initially favored candidate in November.

Thus, it appears from Tables 11.1 and 11.2 that the campaign is not very consequential in altering election outcomes. The tables are misleading, however, for a number of reasons. One is that a significantly large bloc of voters does make its choice during the campaign period in response to the unfolding of events; the one third of the electorate still undecided after the nominating conventions is an important battleground over which the election might be won or lost. Moreover, one must recognize that presidential contests are decided over a relatively narrow range of vote splits; seldom does the winner's share of the two-party vote much exceed 60 percent and the loser's share fall much below 40 percent, even in such landslide elections as 1964 and 1972. Thus, most election outcomes could have been reversed had only 10 percent or less of the electorate changed their vote choice in the same direction. Finally, the tables are misleading for they do not incorporate the fact that presidential races are not directly popular vote contests but electoral vote contests. And the key, large electoral vote states tend to be politically competitive, meaning that a change in the vote intentions of a small percentage of the electorate may spell the difference between victory and defeat in many crucial states. In 1976, for example, the difference between winning and losing was less than 6 percent in 27 states. Thus, candidates rightly view the campaign as an opportunity to affect their chances of victory, even if a substantial majority of voters already have made up their minds.

THE MAJOR CONSTRAINTS ON PRESIDENTIAL CANDIDATES

In Chapters 8, 9, and 10 we discussed a number of constraints and conditions that the prospective presidential candidate must consider in formulating campaign strategy. For example, we argued that the voters' positions on issues, while not immutable, are one factor that the nominee must ponder. In fact, extensive private polling is commissioned by candidates throughout the campaign to ascertain the electorate's issue preferences and candidate perceptions. We also noted that the availability of money and the services it can provide impose obvious limitations on campaign activities; the shakily financed campaign of Hubert Humphrey in 1968 is an excellent example of a situation where uncertainty about the availability of money severely hampered the conduct of the campaign. While numerous constraints impinge upon candidates, we can identify four that are crucial to the conduct of any general election campaign: (1) the need to win the nomination, (2) the presence or absence of an incumbent President seeking reelection, (3) the majority versus minority status of the candidate's party, and (4) the impact of the Electoral College on campaign strategies.

Strategic Aspects of the Nomination Process

In order to run for President in the general election, one must obviously first secure the nomination of one's party. The process by which one wins a presidential nomination imposes major constraints on the subsequent general election campaign. Donald Matthews (1974: 36) claims that the nominating process is the most critical stage of presidential selection since it is here the major screening and elimination of candidates takes place. The screening can occur at a number of points. Before the primary election season ever arrives, some candidates may have informally investigated the likely political and financial support that would be available to them should they declare a formal candidacy; if scant support for their candidacy seems likely to materialize, they may drop out of the race they never formally entered. Similarly, other potential candidates are deterred from seeking the presidency because of recognition of the rigors and sacrifices required.

The most important weeding out of candidates occurs as a result of the primary elections, and it is this aspect of the nominating process that I wish to emphasize, in part because of the recent pattern of selecting an ever-higher proportion of nominating convention delegates in primaries. Matthews claims that the presidential primary system has largely resulted in the pre-primary front-runner winning the nomination. In analyzing the record of the primaries since 1936 as they have affected the party out of power, Matthews writes (1974: 36), "when the out-party has a single leading contender before the primaries, which is most of the time, the primaries rarely change the situation. When they do alter matters, it is more often to strengthen the claim of the initial leader than substantially to weaken it." This point is elaborated in the Keech and Matthews (1977) work on nominations and convention decisions between 1936 and 1972; the authors appropriately downplay the importance of the primaries in affecting the selection of the nominee by noting that the pre-primary favorite most often emerged victorious at the convention in that era.

However, this outcome is not inevitable, as witnessed by the failure of the front-runner, Edmund Muskie, to capture the Democratic nomination in 1972 and by the success of longshot Jimmy Carter in 1976. The question is whether the Muskie and Carter examples are simply exceptions from the underlying pattern identified by Keech and Matthews, or whether the 1972 and 1976 experiences signal the arrival of an era in which the primaries assume unparalleled importance. In an epilogue to the Keech and Matthews study, Keech seems to suggest that 1976 was more of an aberration than a precursor of enduring change. But it seems that the stronger argument can be

made for the position that the primaries have indeed become critically significant for the outcome of the nomination process, not the
least because of the high proportion of the delegates elected in the
primaries. The heavy media emphasis on the primaries in conjunction with the democratic rhetoric surrounding*primaries as a selection mechanism argue for their continued importance. Also, the
horse-race emphasis of the media and the economic necessity to attract
an audience will likely result in a style of reporting detrimental to
the pre-primary favorite; after all, a horse race is less exciting to watch
if the odds-on-favorite leads the race from start to finish. Moreover,
the success of Carter and McGovern will likely result in increased
competition as many prospective candidates say, "If they can do it,
why not me?" Finally, the campaign finance and delegate selection
reforms discussed in Chapter 10 have reduced the power of the party
brokers to deliver the nomination to the pre-primary favorite. Candidates today have to compete more vigorously for delegates in the
more uncertain environment of the primaries.

The fundamental decision that a presidential aspirant must make
about the primaries is whether to enter them at all, although, as suggested earlier, it may be impossible today to skip the primaries and
hope to win unless the convention is so split that a compromise choice
becomes necessary. Adlai Stevenson in 1952, Senator Stuart Symington of Missouri in 1960, Nelson Rockefeller in 1968, and Hubert
Humphrey in 1976, among others, all hoped to be their parties'
presidential nominee without actively contesting the primaries.
Only Stevenson was successful, his candidacy representing one of the
few genuine drafts of a nominee. Symington in 1960 hoped that he
would emerge as the dark horse, compromise candidate acceptable to
all wings of the Democratic Party. He envisaged Hubert Humphrey
and John Kennedy knocking each other off in the primaries, Lyndon
Johnson being unacceptable to the liberal and labor wings of the
party, and favorite son candidates posing no serious threat. Under
these conditions, Symington hoped that the convention would turn
to him as the nominee. As mentioned earlier, Rockefeller's plan was
to demonstrate his popularity through the public opinion polls,
thereby bypassing the GOP primary electorate and appealing directly
to the convention delegates who, he hoped, would vote for the candidate mostly likely to win the general election. Humphrey's chances
in 1976 depended on a convention in which no candidate was close
to a first-ballot victory; in such a situation, it was possible that the

party would turn to its former standard bearer as a compromise, yet popular, choice.

The decision not to enter the primaries is a strategic one that recognizes the constraints confronting the candidate. For example, one might argue Symington recognized that he had neither the political nor financial resources to successfully contest the primaries; hence a passive position may have been his only plausible path to the nomination. Likewise, one might claim that Rockefeller was so unpopular with a substantial segment of the GOP rank and file and Nixon so popular that a challenge to Nixon in the primaries would have been electoral suicide. And Humphrey's formal entry in the primaries in 1976 might have reopened party wounds associated with the 1968 and 1972 conventions.

While skipping the primaries may be a reasonable response to the political environment within which the candidate is operating, it may entail certain costs. A candidate may be considered less legitimate if he or she has never demonstrated popular support in the electorate. A deadlocked convention may be wary of turning to someone who avoided the primaries, especially in an age in which the media have elevated the primaries to such an exalted status. Of course, the other side to this argument is that nonparticipation in the primaries may make one more acceptable to the warring factions battling in the primaries. Even if a candidate is successful in winning the nomination without entering the primaries, there is the potential cost that one will begin the general election campaign with a lower level of voter recognition than had one contested the primaries. One difficulty confronting Stevenson's candidacy in 1952 was that he was relatively unknown at the outset of the general election campaign, in part because of the absence of extensive primary election campaigning. This was especially harmful to him since he was facing an extremely popular and well-known war hero in the general election. The fact is, however, that candidates who wish to become President generally enter the primaries, often because they have some weakness that can be overcome only by demonstrating electoral popularity. Once the decision to enter is made, there follows the critical choice of which primaries to contest. Should one run in all primaries or in a selected few? Are certain primaries unavoidable? Should one avoid challenging a specific candidate in his or her home territory? These questions will be addressed mainly in the context of the 1972 and 1976 Democratic races.

The first point to note is that candidates must answer such questions on the basis of incomplete information. One may have to decide upon which primaries to contest before one's competition is known or before the availability of resources is assured. For example, George McGovern announced his candidacy for the 1972 Democratic nomination in January of 1971, a time when not even the number of primaries was definite yet alone the identity of the contestants. The national campaign director for McGovern, Gary Hart, stated that the basic decision to run in New Hampshire, Wisconsin, and a number of other primaries was made in July of 1970, six months before McGovern's formal announcement of candidacy (May and Fraser, 1973: 92). The McGovern camp gave serious thought to waging a strenuous campaign in the Florida primary. The decision was made not to contest Florida vigorously, which in retrospect proved to be a wise move since George Wallace surprised a number of observers by conducting his 1972 presidential bid through the Democratic Party and not his American Independent Party. Making opposition to busing his major issue, Wallace swept the Florida primary. According to Ben Wattenberg, an adviser to Senator Henry Jackson, the Jackson campaign strategy in 1972 rested on a strong showing in Florida, a state that seemed congenial to a candidate of Jackson's persuasion (May and Fraser, 1973: 39). This strategy failed because of the presence of Wallace in the Florida primary, a presence unanticipated earlier. The point is that many of the decisions that must be made about the primaries are carried out in an aura of uncertainty.

Carter announced his 1976 candidacy in December of 1974, again at a time when key pieces of information about the primaries, such as their number, scheduling, and contestants, were unknown. In fact, the basic Carter strategy was detailed in a document dated November 4, 1972, more than three years before the start of the 1976 primaries (Witcover, 1977: 119). The Carter plan was remarkably prescient, except for its assumption that Edward Kennedy would be a candidate and thereby keep the field of challengers small. Instead, Kennedy decided not to run and the number of Democratic candidates ballooned.

While an early decision to enter the primaries has its costs, it also has important advantages. If a candidate anticipates that a number of contenders will be vying for the same supporters, it may be wise to enter the race early, thereby locking up some of these supporters and freezing out other competitors. Moreover, the building of an organization and the collection of resources is a time-consuming process that must begin early. Jack Chestnut, national campaign manager for Hubert Humphrey in 1972, believed that the most damaging feature of the Humphrey primary campaign was its late start. Chestnut argued that the decision to run should have been made in July 1971, instead of the following December (May and Fraser, 1973: 74). Carter's success in 1976 and provisions of the campaign financing law have encouraged the flock of contenders for the 1980 Republican nomination to begin their campaigns early, headed by Philip Crane's August 1978 start.

The decision about which primaries to contest is critical, given the serial nature of the primaries. A strong showing early on can give a candidacy a tremendous boost, just as a poor showing can end a candidacy quickly. Yet some primaries may be considered unavoidable by the candidate, even if they do not appear to be particularly hospitable. Candidates who fail to enter the New Hampshire primary, the nation's first, may be viewed as ducking the contest because of electoral weakness. This was one reason why McGovern entered the New Hampshire primary despite the presumed invincibility of Senator Muskie, a New Englander, in that state. In reality, McGovern had little to lose in New Hampshire and much to gain. Prior to New Hampshire, his support in the public opinion polls was only a few percent and his campaign was suffering from severe financial problems. Hence a poor showing by McGovern in New Hampshire would have been interpreted as Muskie running well on his home ground, while a reputable showing would give new life to his candidacy and allow it to continue through a few more primaries. Gary Hart has explained that New Hampshire and Wisconsin were critical to McGovern's chances: the strong showing in New Hampshire helped bring in contributions and support and set the stage for the McGovern victory in Wisconsin (May and Fraser, 1973: 73).

From the start, the Carter strategy targeted New Hampshire and Florida as critical states, the goal being a respectable showing in New Hampshire and a victory in Florida; Carter achieved victories in both states. In New Hampshire, Carter profited by the lack of serious efforts on the part of Jackson and Wallace, who might have been expected to draw off some of Carter's moderate and conservative support, and by the presence of numerous liberal Democrats on the ballot, who divided up the liberal vote. Jackson himself admitted that his failure to contest New Hampshire was a serious blunder which enabled Carter to emerge as a major challenger (Witcover, 1977: 203–204). In Florida, Wallace and Jackson were on the ballot against Carter, with the liberals staying out of the contest. The contrast with Wallace established Carter as the representative of the new South and left Carter as the heir to southern support after his defeat of Wallace in Florida. Overall, the Carter strategy, as laid out in the 1972 memo, aimed to (Witcover, 1977: 123):

1. Demonstrate in the first primaries your strength as a candidate. This means a strong surprise showing in New Hampshire and a victory in Florida. [Carter won both.]
2. Establish that you are not a regional candidate by winning early primaries in medium-size states outside the south, such as Rhode Island and Wisconsin. [Carter won Wisconsin and lost Rhode Island which held a late primary.]
3. Select one of the large industrial and traditionally Democratic states which has an early primary to confront all major opponents and establish yourself as a major contender. Pennsylvania and Ohio would be possibilities. [Carter won both states, Pennsylvania in the middle of the primary season and Ohio at the very end.]
4. Demonstrate consistent strength in all primaries entered.

The McGovern and Carter strategies clearly took advantage of the sequential nature of the primaries. What is fascinating about the McGovern campaign was that it picked its spots to maximum benefit. McGovern seriously contested only two (New Hampshire and Wisconsin) of the first four primaries in 1972 and won one (Wisconsin), while Muskie challenged vigorously in all four and won two (New Hampshire and Illinois) and Wallace won the Florida primary. Yet by the time the Wisconsin results were in, the McGovern campaign was on track and the Muskie effort derailed. Since Florida and Illinois were not viewed as serious targets by McGovern, his sixth-place finish in Florida and his scant write-in votes in Illinois did not hurt him. Hence, the candidate's choice of primaries to contest and the media's designation of certain primaries as critical play an important part in determining the candidate's fate.

Thus, the present system of primary elections makes it possible for a relatively unknown and unsupported candidate to challenge successfully for the nomination by scoring early successes in carefully selected states; the institution of a national primary would eliminate this possibility. One empirical generalization about primary election results is that the winner of a primary inevitably jumps in the polls and usually receives an influx of campaign contributions. Hence it is crucial to score a victory, the sooner the better, although Rockefeller's jump in the polls after his victory in the next to last primary in Oregon in 1964 suggests that the effect may be present throughout the campaign. Table 11.3 shows how McGovern's popularity among Democrats rose after his victory in Wisconsin and how Carter's fortunes soared after successes in New Hampshire, Florida, and Pennsylvania. Traditionally, primary victories had been more important because of their impact on uncommitted delegates and less

TABLE 11.3
Choice of Democrats for the 1972 and 1976 Nominations

Survey Date	1972		
	Humphrey	McGovern	Wallace
March 3–6	31	6	15
March 7—New Hampshire primary—Muskie wins			
March 14—Florida primary—Wallace wins			
March 21—Illinois primary—Muskie wins			
March 24–27	31	5	17
April 4—Wisconsin primary—McGovern wins			
April 21–24	30	17	19
April 25—Massachusetts primary—McGovern wins			
April 25—Pennsylvania primary—Humphrey wins			
April 28–May 1	35	20	18
May 16—Maryland primary—Wallace wins			
May 23—Oregon primary—McGovern wins			
May 26–29	26	25	26

Survey Date	1976			
	Humphrey	Carter	Jackson	Wallace
January 23–26	17	4	5	18
February 24—New Hampshire primary—Carter wins				
Feb. 27–March 1	18	12	5	14
March 2—Massachusetts primary—Jackson wins				
March 9—Florida primary—Carter wins				
March 10–13	27	26	15	15
March 26–29	30	29	7	13
April 6—New York primary—Jackson wins				
April 6—Wisconsin primary—Carter wins				
April 9–12	31	28	8	13
April 23–26	33	29	7	12
April 27—Pennsylvania primary—Carter wins				
April 30–May 3	29	40	4	9

Sources: *Gallup Opinion Index*, June 1972, report no. 84, p. 10, and *Gallup Opinion Index*, August 1976, report no. 133, pp. 6–7.

so in terms of the actual number of delegates won. For example, Eisenhower in his four contested primary victories in 1952 won only 99 delegates; the real impact of his successes was on the uncommitted delegates who became convinced of his popularity (Davis, 1967: 81). The larger number of primaries today and the Democratic rules changes requiring delegates to announce their candidate preferences means there will be fewer uncommitted delegates at future conventions, so that primary victories will be important for both psychological reasons and actual delegate acquisition.

The decision whether to run in all or only some of the primaries is based upon multiple considerations. For McGovern in 1972, acute resource shortage and foresight may explain his choice. In the case of Muskie, it has been argued that as the designated front-runner he felt the need to demonstrate his popularity by sweeping the primaries. Muskie wanted to establish his reputation as a national and not simply a regional candidate, a strategy that, if successful, would have given him a running start in the general election. Muskie's strategy entailed certain risks and possessed certain advantages. Obviously, spreading oneself too thin over a number of primaries can lead to disappointing performances, which can quickly convert a front-runner to an also-ran. In many of the states he entered, Muskie had been endorsed by the party leaders and the organization, which subsequently proved unable to deliver many votes to him. The weakness of his candidacy was quickly exposed by the effectiveness of the McGovern grass-roots organization. Yet consistent success early on may lead one's opponents to drop out of the race, resulting in an easy nomination victory and a unified party in the general election.

Like Muskie, Carter ran in all the primaries (except West Virginia); but unlike Muskie, this decision worked out well for Carter for a number of reasons. First, expectations of Carter's performance were initially low, so that he risked little in running widely. After Carter merged as the front-runner and began to lose primaries to late-entrants Jerry Brown and Frank Church, there was always at least one election on each primary day that Carter managed to win, which helped maintain his progress. For example, Carter lost two of three primaries held on June 1 and two of three on June 8, but his single victories on those election days kept his campaign rolling. And even when Carter lost a primary, he still captured a respectable share of the delegates, which brought his front-running total closer to the number needed for nomination. Hence, even as Carter faltered in the latter part of the primary season, his impressive delegate totals resulted in the media emphasizing how close he was getting to the nomination rather than how poorly he was doing at the polls.

More generally, candidates decide on the number of primaries to enter on the basis of their liabilities and assets. Underfinanced candidates of necessity must opt for only a few primaries. Other candidates face other constraints. For example, John Kennedy in 1960 had to demonstrate to party leaders that his Catholicism would not drag the ticket down to defeat in November. He accomplished this by entering and winning a large number of primaries. Similarly, Estes Kefauver in 1952 sought the Democractic nomination via the primary route because his support among party leaders was so weak. And Richard Nixon in 1968 had to enter the Republican primaries to dispel his image as a loser.

The primary election system usually weeds out candidates and results in a climactic primary, the winner of which is likely to go on and secure the nomination. Gary Hart described the scenario the McGovern camp hoped for in 1972 (May and Fraser, 1973: 73):

> All the way through, our premise was that when you come to a nomination in the Democratic Party, there is, for all practical purposes, no center. Our strategy was always to co-opt the left, become the candidate of the liberal wing of the party, and then eventually get it down to a two-man race. . . . We always knew it would be a two-man race between a liberal and a conservative. There was, in fact, no center, and it was just a question of whether or not we could win on our side and who would win on the other.

While one can quarrel with Hart's liberal-conservative assessment, the race did narrow down to two men; and the California primary was climactic, just as it was for the GOP in 1964. Many observers would argue that Pennsylvania was the climactic primary in 1976; Carter's victory there ended the Jackson candidacy and thrust Carter far ahead of the field. What makes Pennsylvania unusual as a climactic primary is that it was held midway through the primary season, with more than half of the convention delegates still to be selected.

Obtaining the nomination is only the first step in the path to the Presidency, and the strategies employed to secure the nomination can promote or hinder the candidate's prospects for victory in the general election. For example, if to win the nomination the candidate must appeal to an atypical segment of the party's constituency, then it may be difficult to broaden one's base and unify the party for the general election. This description has been applied to the Goldwater and McGovern nominations. Both candidates were said to have appealed to fringes within their respective parties; both were nominated in conventions marked by sharp ideological conflict; both suffered substantial defection from their parties' loyalists; and both were overwhelmingly defeated in November. One might argue that candidates who appeal to an intense minority within their party face an almost impossible situation in trying to achieve party unity. For example, if McGovern strenuously tried to woo the labor leaders, party regulars, and others who had opposed his nomination, his supporters would have felt betrayed and McGovern himself would have been viewed as just another self-serving politician. Yet failure to win over these groups spelled electoral disaster. In 1976, the primary election process served to enhance Carter's general election prospects. As Keech (Keech and Matthews, 1977) observes, out of the diverse field that began the primaries emerged a consensus candidate around whom all factions of the party could unite.

Unlike the case for the Democrats, the 1976 primary process did not produce consensus on the Republican side but, instead, generated divisiveness as Reagan challenged the incumbent Ford for the GOP nomination. Certainly intra-party challenges to an incumbent President run the risk of tearing the party apart—so the question becomes what strategic considerations go into a decision to challenge the incumbent President. One obvious answer is that challenges to the incumbent are encouraged by political weakness and unpopularity on the part of the President; certainly Kefauver's challenge to Truman in 1952 and McCarthy's challenge to Johnson in 1968 (before both Presidents decided not to seek reelection) were fueled by widespread dissatisfaction with the incumbents' performances. And a challenge to Carter in 1980 by Kennedy, Brown, or another Democrat will be made more likely if Carter's standing in the polls remains low.

Incumbent weakness does not account very well for Reagan's decision to challenge Ford, because the polls showed Ford to be reasonably popular with Americans and to more than hold his own in trial heats with prospective Democratic candidates. Rather, Reagan's bid may have been encouraged by his having a natural and sizable base of support within the GOP; Reagan was prominent in national Republican politics long before Ford became Vice President in 1973. In general, incumbent Presidents are more vulnerable when they do not enjoy a solid base of support within their party; certainly this is one problem that may confront Carter in 1980 because many components of the Democratic coalition, such as labor, liberals, Catholics, and Jews, seem to have no special enthusiasm for Carter as they might have for Kennedy.

Taking on an incumbent is risky, of course, since Presidents have tremendous resources at their disposal. Moreover, many party professionals shudder at the prospect of an intra-party contest. And should the challenger be successful in wresting the nomination from the incumbent, it may prove to be an empty victory if the party cannot achieve unity in the general election. Yet challenges to incumbents are enticing; after all, Truman and Johnson dropped out of the race and Reagan came very close to ousting Ford. Because party professionals no longer control presidential nominations, the would-be challenger can enter the primaries knowing that his effort to defeat the incumbent will be the object of substantial media coverage.

Whether or not the primaries yield a definitive result, the formal selection of the nominee occurs at the national convention and is usually followed by an attempt to unify the party for the general election. However, the Republicans in 1964 and the Democrats in 1968 and 1972 left their conventions as seriously divided parties, and all three lost in November, while in 1976 the Democrats left their convention in uncharacteristic harmony and won on election day. Thus, we face the somewhat paradoxical situation in which the national convention may be less important in determining the identity of the nominee, but may be extremely important in starting the nominee on a successful or unsuccessful path toward the Presidency. The conventions are viewed by millions of citizens, and the images they see may be very consequential for their subsequent evaluations of the candidates and parties.

The Incumbent–Nonincumbent, Majority Party–Minority Party Status of the Candidate

Once the nomination has been secured, there are two considerations that are of immediate importance in shaping campaign strategies. The first is whether there is an incumbent President seeking reelection, and the second whether the candidate is from the majority or minority party defined in terms of the partisan allegiances of the electorate. In the situation where there is no incumbent President running, a third consideration becomes relevant: is the nominee from the party that currently controls the Presidency or not? Each of these constraints is discussed below.

An incumbent President seeking election seems to be in a formidable position. The very fact of being President, with its extensive media coverage, bestows upon the President an aura of competence, experience, and familiarity that a challenger is hard-pressed to match. If being "presidential" is an important characteristic for voter acceptance then the incumbent President possesses a tremendous advantage.

While it is true that the incumbent President will have to bear the responsibility for bad times, it is also the case there is much that Presidents can do to alleviate or submerge problems in the short term. For example, if farm income is falling, the Secretary of Agriculture can channel money to farmers through a variety of means. More generally, if the economy is sagging, the President can take a number of steps, such as releasing funds and selling materials from government stockpiles, to provide a short-term stimulus so that by Election Day the economic situation has improved at least temporarily. And from the perspective of the electorate, movement toward the solution of such economic problems as unemployment and inflation may be just as important in its vote decision as actual success in solving the problems.

While the President has some ability to alter the state of domestic affairs, in foreign affairs his advantages become overwhelming. An overseas trip to China or the Soviet Union effectively blocks out media coverage of the opposition and further serves to emphasize his presidential ability. Similarly, a vigorous defense of some American interest abroad will most often serve to rally the country behind the President. A cynic may justifiably question why two major (and premature) announcements of significant moves toward peace in Vietnam occurred shortly before the 1968 and 1972 elections.

While the President will be attacked for failing to accomplish certain goals, often he can outflank his critics by adopting some version of their proposals. The focus of media coverage is such that presidential endorsement of a program will identify it as his own in the public's mind even if the initiative for the program resided in a congressional committee or elsewhere. A message to the Congress or a speech to the public allows the President to establish his credentials on an issue.

Emphasis on the power of incumbency must be hedged by recogizing that when the country really falls apart, as in the Great Depression, the incumbent will be in severe trouble, as witnessed by President Hoover's defeat in 1932. It has been asserted that Harry Truman in

1952 and Lyndon Johnson in 1968 did not seek renomination because domestic and foreign policy crises had made their reelections doubtful. It seems clear that both could have won their party's nominations, and it certainly could be argued that Johnson would have had a better than even chance to retain the Presidency. Overall, incumbency seems to be a much more important factor than the majority-minority party status of the candidate.

The fact that Gerald Ford lost in 1976 may seem to belie the importance of incumbency. Yet only the power of incumbency can help explain how Ford was able to secure the nomination and run so strong a race in the general election, given the many strikes against him. Ford was an unelected President whose prior political base was his congressional district in Grand Rapids, Michigan. He was initially appointed Vice President by the disgraced President, whom he subsequently pardoned in a widely condemned action. During his brief Presidency, the United States experienced high rates of unemployment and inflation simultaneously, while in foreign affairs North Vietnam successfully overran South Vietnam. Not the least of Ford's election problems was his being a member of the minority party. Yet despite all these disadvantages, Ford managed to run a very close race.

At the outset, it should be noted that the majority-minority party distinction is too simple since it does not reflect whether the parties are united or not. McGovern and Humphrey were the candidates of a divided majority party and Goldwater the nominee of divided minority, and all three lost. Assuming that the parties are relatively unified, the majority-minority distinction has important implications for the kinds of strategies likely to be adopted. The majority party candidate will probably emphasize the importance of party, as did Kennedy and Carter, while the minority party nominee will stress the man and not the party, as did Nixon and Ford. Minority party candidates will want to deemphasize partisan concerns, and they can accomplish this by adopting positions close to that of the majority party or by nominating candidates with such immense popular appeal as General Eisenhower that party loyalties break down to a moderate degree.

The minority party may also attempt to win a majority of the vote by converting nonvoters to voters, recognizing that the vote difference between the candidates has been much less than the number of citizens who did not vote. This strategy has been employed by the GOP in 1952 and 1964 with markedly different results. In a campaign plan written for the Republican Party in 1952, Robert Humphreys (Lavine,

1970: 36) argued that the GOP in 1940, 1944, and 1948 adopted unsuccessful "me-too" strategies in order to win the Independent vote on the assumption that this vote was relatively liberal. Humphreys suggested that there was a fourth potential source of votes in addition to Democrats, Republicans, and Independents and these were the stay-at-homes —"those who vote only when discontent stirs them to vote against current conditions." Humphreys asserted that the stay-at-home vote heavily outnumbered the Independent, and that the best way to win this vote was to attack the incumbent party for making a mess of things. As mentioned in Chapter 5, the GOP slogan in 1952 was "Corruption, Korea, and Communism," three problems associated with the incumbent Democratic administration. Note that Humphreys' strategy assumed nothing about whether the stay-at-homes were liberal or conservative, only that they could be motivated to vote by sharp attacks on the incumbents. In fact, Humphreys was careful to advise the GOP not to try to rescind the New Deal or to take consistently conservative positions (Lavine, 1970: 36–37).

Barry Goldwater's campaign in 1964 was also premised on the notion of millions of stay-at-home voters except that these were assumed to be conservative, Republican stay-at-homes. Hence Goldwater argued that if the GOP would nominate a true conservative and offer a genuine choice rather than the "me-too" candidates of previous elections, these millions of stay-at-home conservatives voters would flock to the polls and insure a Republican victory. Goldwater's strategy was misguided since there were no millions of nonvoting conservatives; in fact, public opinion polls have consistently shown that the group with the highest turnout in presidential elections has been strong Republicans of a conservative bent.

When the majority party is split, then the minority may still try to minimize partisanship in an attempt to win over the disgruntled members of the majority; Nixon in 1972 scarcely mentioned his Republicanism, and many of his most effective television commercials were sponsored by Democrats for Nixon. At times the majority party itself will minimize partisanship, especially when victory is assured. The division in the minority GOP in 1964 guaranteed Johnson's election, so that his major concern became the magnitude of his victory. Johnson attempted to win over moderate and liberal Republicans upset by the Goldwater nomination by stressing his moderate stances and playing down his partisanship.

When there is no incumbent President running, whether the candidate is from the party presently controlling the Presidency becomes important. If so, the candidate faces a number of constraints, particularly if he is a part of the incumbent administration, such as the Vice President. For example, Richard Nixon in 1960 and Hubert Humphrey in 1968 were both caught in a dilemma. As the Vice Presidents in the outgoing administrations they were responsible for defending their parties' records. Failure to do so might have led the President to undercut their candidacies and to deny them the kind of access to decision making that would be useful in demonstrating their presidential capabilities. Yet both Nixon and Humphrey, and particularly the latter, had to establish their own identities and to explain how they would improve the condition of the nation without appearing to criticize the President. This was a difficult task and their opponents—Kennedy in 1960 and Nixon in 1968—went on the attack vigorously and successfully. Even if the candidate is not formally a part of the current administration, he or she may still be saddled with the record of that administration; Adlai Stevenson in 1952 was handicapped by criticisms of the Truman administration even though he was not a part of it.

In summary, we can array the constraints discussed in this section according to the flow diagram depicted in Figure 11.1. Note that the question of incumbency comes first; this is to suggest its paramount importance over the other factors discussed. The diagram should be read from the perspective of the candidate surveying the political environment in order to formulate a sound campaign strategy. Note that in three of four cases in which an incumbent President sought reelection, he was victorious (and by a landslide), the one exception being the unelected incumbent Ford. Also note that in the three cases (Stevenson in 1952, Nixon in 1960, and Humphrey in 1968) in which the nonincumbent candidate of the party controlling the Presidency tried to hold onto the Presidency for his party, all were unsuccessful. The number of elections covered is too small to offer any sweeping generalizations, but the results are suggestive.

The Electoral College

Technically, Americans do not vote directly for the presidential nominees but instead for a slate of electors pledged, though not formally bound, to cast their votes for the candidate receiving a plurality of the popular vote in their state; these electors are collectively referred to as the Electoral College. To become President, a candidate must receive a majority of the electoral vote, a majority that can be

334

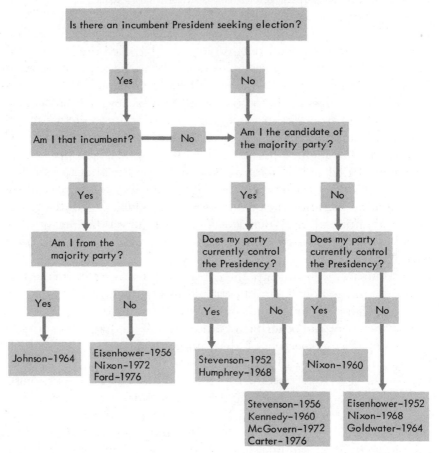

FIGURE 11.1
A Flowchart Summarizing Some Constraints
Relevant to Campaign Decision Making

achieved without a majority of the popular vote. The number of electoral votes in 1976 was 538, and to become President a candidate needed 270 votes. The number of electoral votes per state is equal to the number of U.S. Senators and Representatives from that state; in addition, the District of Columbia has three electoral votes. If no candidate receives a majority of the Electoral College vote, the U.S. House of Representatives selects the President from among the top three contenders with each state delegation in the House having one vote and a majority of 26 votes needed to elect a President. State delegations with an equal number of Democrats and Republicans will likely deadlock and be unable to vote, thereby making it difficult to attain a majority of 26 states. Wallace's goal in 1968 as a third-party candidate was to win enough electoral votes to deny either major party candidate a majority of the electoral vote, thereby establishing himself as a potential kingmaker. Finally, electoral votes are almost invariably cast as a unit; that is, the candidate carrying a state wins all of the state's electoral votes, no matter how small his plurality. This means that the candidate who carries California (with 45 electoral votes) by one vote and loses Maine (with 4 electoral votes) by 50,000 votes is far ahead in the Electoral College despite trailing in the popular vote.

The fact that the Electoral College system permits the possibility that the popular vote winner will be denied the Presidency has been the source of major criticisms of the institution. For example, Longley and Braun (1972: viii, 3) point out that a shift of less than 30,000 votes in 1948 would have made Dewey the President despite Truman's more than two-million-vote lead in the popular tally. In 1960 a shift of a total of 8,971 votes in Missouri and Illinois would have created an Electoral College deadlock because of the presence of unpledged electors, and a shift of a total of 11,424 votes in the five states of Illinois, Missouri, New Mexico, Nevada, and Hawaii would have made Nixon the President. In 1968, a shift of only 42,000 votes in three states would have sent the election to the House. And in 1976, a shift of only 5,600 votes in Ohio and 3,700 votes in Hawaii would have elected Ford despite his trailing Carter by 1.7 million votes in the popular vote figures.[1]

---

1 Many reforms of the Electoral College have been proposed, including its abolishment in favor of direct (popular vote) election of the President. Other reforms would keep the Electoral College but eliminate its winner-take-all feature by establishing a district plan, which would give electoral votes to the leading candidate in each congressional district plus two votes to the statewide winner. Other reforms would require that the electoral votes of a state be automatically cast for the candidate carrying that state, thereby eliminating the problem of the faithless elector. Finally, The Twentieth Century Fund recently developed a new proposal, labelled "the bonus plan," which would add 102 electoral votes to the current 538. These 102 electoral votes would all go to the candidate winning the national popular vote, thereby almost assuredly ending the possibility that a candidate might win the popular vote but lose the Electoral College vote and the Presidency.

Sayre and Parris favor the existing system since it makes the more populous states more influential. In order to carry these states, a candidate must run well in the metropolitan areas with their large blocs of ethnic groups, such as blacks, Jews, Poles, Italians, and others. Presidential candidates must give attention to these groups, and this provides one way in which the groups' greater needs might be met. According to Sayre and Parris, this gives a liberal bias to presidential campaigns, a bias they fear would be lost if Electoral College reforms were adopted. Longley and Braun question whether the Electoral College will continue to produce this liberal bias and argue that the Electoral College subverts the meaning of a popular election. For a discussion of the proposed alternatives to the Electoral College and their likely consequences, see Sayre and Parris (1970), Longley and Braun (1972), Yunker and Longley (1973), Yunker and Longley (1976), *Winner Take All* (1978), and *Congressional Quarterly Weekly Report*, March 10, 1979, pp. 405–410.

These examples suggest why the state and not the individual voter becomes the focus of campaign strategies, especially in close elections. When candidates map out their strategy, they talk in terms of carrying states and not the popular vote. When a candidate is far ahead in the polls that measure popular vote strength, then this advantageous position should also be reflected in an electoral vote landslide. Yet even here, candidates such as Humphrey in 1968 and McGovern in 1972 who trailed badly in the polls during the course of the campaign still talked bravely of putting together an Electoral College majority by carrying the key states. And when the election appears close, then the state results are watched very closely. Candidates commission state-wide polls to supply them the critical information about the likely Electoral College outcome.

While the Electoral College does overrepresent small states because of the constitutional provision that every state, no matter its population, is guaranteed at least three electors (two for its Senators and one for its at least one Representative), with respect to the focus of the campaign, the Electoral College and the winner-take-all rule for casting electoral votes favor the large, urbanized, industrialized states. And within these states, the Electoral College, according to Yunker and Longley (1973), tends to give greater vote power to urban ethnic groups, although suburban residents tend to be more powerful in terms of casting the decisive votes than central city dwellers. This results in the presidential constituency being more metropolitan than the nation as a whole. Black citizens are not as advantaged by the Electoral College since the black population is not concentrated only in the industrialized states but is also very prominent in the rural South and the District of Columbia.

Thus, the Electoral College system makes the large states the battle-ground of presidential elections, and this is reflected in the candidates' strategies, where they campaign, and where they spend most of their resources.[2] Even the Goldwater and Nixon strategies in 1964 and 1968, which have been labeled "southern" in orientation and which empha-

---

[2] For example, Brams and Davis (1974) report that the Democratic and Republican nominees since 1960 have spent a disproportionate amount of their campaigning time in the large states. Stanley Kelley reports (1966: 64, 75) that in 1964 Lyndon Johnson spent 30 percent of his campaign time in California, New York, and Illinois. Nixon and Kennedy in 1960 campaigned most heavily in the same six states—New York, California, Illinois, Pennsylvania, Ohio, and Michigan. Even Barry Goldwater, whose strategy was not a large state one, spent most of his scheduled campaign time in the large states, especially California, Texas, Ohio, Illinois, Pennsylvania, and New York.

sized carrying the South, the border states, the mountain states, and the western states, still required that some of the big industrialized states be won in order to secure victory. One of the best examples of the emphasis on the major states in presidential elections occurred in the 1960 Kennedy-Nixon race. Kennedy in 1960 stressed capturing the nine large states of New York, Pennsylvania, Michigan, Illinois, Ohio, New Jersey, Massachusetts, California, and Texas (Johnson's home state) which, if victorious in all, would have given him 237 of the 269 votes needed for an Electoral College majority (White, 1961: 295). The rest of the votes needed for a majority were to come from the South because of Lyndon Johnson's presence on the ticket and from a scattering of votes won in New England and the Midwest. That Kennedy's strategy worked largely as planned (California and especially Ohio were disappointments) is shown in Table 11.4; of the 269 votes needed for a majority 237 came either from the South or the large industrial states. Nixon in 1960 focused on the same large states as Kennedy did, with the exception of Massachusetts (Kennedy's home state) and New Jersey (White, 1961: 318). Unfortunately for Nixon, his pledge to campaign in all 50 states had him campaigning in Alaska, with three electoral votes, when he might better have spent the time in Illinois, which he lost very narrowly.

In 1952, 1956, 1964, and 1972 the popular vote was so one-sided that the winner was assured of an Electoral College landslide. In 1968 the state-by-state planning was very detailed. Nixon conceded Alabama, Arkansas, Mississippi, Louisiana, and Georgia to George Wallace, but challenged him in the other six states of the Confederacy and won all except Texas, thereby receiving 57 electoral votes from the South, which partially offset his losses in New York and Pennsylvania. Humphrey's strategy in 1968 was very clear: carry the major states. According to Chester, Hodgson, and Page (1969: 795–96), one campaign plan called for Humphrey to confine his activities to 27 states. Fourteen of these, such as New York, Michigan, New Jersey, Missouri, and Pennsylvania, were probable Humphrey states; nine, including Ohio and Washington, were genuine possibilities; four—California, Alaska, and the Carolinas—were outside chances; and Illinois was described as too big to ignore. Of his 14 probables, Humphrey won all but New Jersey; but he lost Ohio, Illinois, and California, all in relatively close races, and that doomed his big-state strategy. While 132 of his 191 electoral votes came from the large states (see Table 11.4), overall the best Humphrey could do was split the large states with Nixon. And given

TABLE 11.4
Large State and Southern Electoral Vote Allocation, 1952–1976

Election	Electoral Votes Needed to Win	Total Electoral Votes Won by Candidate	Southern Electoral Votes Won by Candidate	Large State Electoral Votes Won by Candidate	Large State and Southern Electoral Votes Won by Candidate
1952					
Eisenhower ...	266	442	57	247	270
Stevenson		89	71	0	71
1956					
Eisenhower ...	266	457	67	247	280
Stevenson		74	60	0	60
1960					
Kennedy	269	303	81	180	237
Nixon		219	33	67	90
1964					
Johnson	270	486	81	255	297
Goldwater		52	47	0	47
1968					
Nixon	270	301	57	123	166
Humphrey		191	25	132	132
Wallace		46	46	0	46
1972					
Nixon	270	521	130	245	332
McGovern		17	0	14	14
1976					
Carter	270	297	118	150	225
Ford		240	12	109	121

Sources: Constructed from figures presented in *Nomination and Election of the President and Vice President of the United States* (Washington, D.C.: U.S. Government Printing Office, 1972), table F, p. 7; and *Guide to 1976 Elections* (Washington, D.C.: Congressional Quarterly Inc., 1977), p. 25.

The large electoral vote states are the ten states with the largest number of electoral votes in 1976. With the exception of Florida, the same states ranked in the top ten throughout this period. Two of the ten large states are also southern (Florida and Texas), and this is adjusted for in the last column of figures presented above.

Nixon's strength in other areas, such as the border states, the plains states, the southwestern states, and the mountain states, Humphrey could not fashion an Electoral College majority.

In 1976, the Carter team developed a formula based on the size of a state, its Democratic potential, and the need to campaign in the state in order to determine how much of the campaign effort should be devoted to each state (Witcover, 1977: 551–552). According to Witcover (1977: 561–562), the Carter effort emphasized maintaining Carter's southern base, carrying traditionally Democratic states outside the South, and campaigning to some extent in Republican areas to keep the Ford effort on the defensive. The Carter team reasoned that if it could keep its southern base intact and add a few traditionally Democratic states, then only a few of the major industrial states would be required to assure victory in November. For the Ford team, unless inroads could be made in Carter's southern support, a near sweep of the large states would be required for Ford to be victorious. Hence, as

FIGURE 11.2
Candidate Stops During the 1976 Presidential Campaign

Note: States with ten or more electoral votes are indicated with number in circle.
Based on combined number of fall 1976 candidate stops by the Republican (Ford and Dole) and Democratic (Carter and Mondale) standard-bearers, as listed in the 1977 Senate Judiciary Committee report on direct vote amendment (p. 15).
Source: *Congressional Quarterly Weekly Report,* March 10, 1979, p. 406.

shown in Figure 11.2, the major industrial states, especially New York, Pennsylvania, Ohio, Illinois, and California, the South, and a few other states became the key battleground of the election.

Table 11.4 helps us illustrate some points about campaign strategy and the Electoral College. First, no candidate can afford to completely write off the major states. And in fact, most strategies, whether southern or whatever, still require carrying two or three large electoral vote states. Nevertheless, the candidate who enters the election with a bloc of votes assured is then freer to adopt any of a number of strategies to secure the remaining electoral votes needed for a majority. The distribution of the South's electoral votes since 1952 suggests how critical the region can be for Democratic and Republican prospects. If the South goes solidly for one party's candidate, then the opposition candidate is of necessity forced into a large state Electoral College strategy and the loss of only a few states will spell defeat.

Some Final Considerations on Election Strategies

It is commonplace to assert that the major strategy of any candidate in any election is to get his or her supporters to the polls and then to try to win support among uncommitted voters; efforts to convert the opposition to one's cause are usually viewed as futile. These maxims of campaigning are relevant for presidential elections: certainly nominees do not premise their campaign on the assumption that all voters are equally likely to support them. Rather, candidates recognize that certain voters are predisposed to support them and other voters to oppose.

The candidate's shorthand way of identifying likely supporters and opponents is to categorize voters into groups defined according to such demographic characteristics as race, religion, and occupation and to determine how these groups voted in previous elections. Thus, while the Electoral College makes the state the critical unit over which the election is fought, candidates do not view the state as a single entity but instead divide it into distinct areas characterized by varying patterns of party support in the past. Thus, campaign strategists often make such statements as "in order for the Democrats to carry Pennsylvania (or Illinois or New York), they must come out of Philadelphia (or Chicago or New York City) with a certain vote lead." Similarly, it is often stated that for the Republicans to carry California, they must build up a certain vote margin in Orange and San Diego counties and run strongly in Los Angeles county. These statements basically mean that a candidate must run well in his or her areas of natural support.

Statements about carrying Chicago or Orange county are further refined to identify the specific groups among which the candidate must run strongly to have a chance to carry the city or county by the necessary amount. For example, it is argued that for the Democrats to carry

Chicago by the needed margin, they will have to run well among such groups as blacks, Catholic ethnic groups, and union members—traditional sources of Democratic strength. In short, a presidential campaign tends to focus on groups that collectively add up to majority support in the electorate.

The existence of groups makes a presidential campaign possible by providing an economical way for a candidate to appeal to the citizenry at large on the basis of a limited number of concerns important to groups. Obviously, it would be impossible for a candidate to direct individual appeals to millions of citizens. And, as Froman (1966: 4) notes, the group serves as a mechanism of communication that provides its members with the standards by which political information might be evaluated.

John Kessel (1974: 116) observes that a focus on groups leads a "candidate to appeal to voters in a manner acceptable to the groups already supporting him." Kessel points out, however, that any successful campaign must do more than simply placate traditional party supporters. According to Kessel (1974: 117), one must distinguish between activists and nonactivists, the former likely being very informed about politics and highly motivated by policy concerns and the latter less so. Thus, many of the candidate's activities and speeches are geared less to rank-and-file supporters and the general public and more to the party activists. For example, Humphrey's 1968 Salt Lake City speech, in which he tried to move some distance from the Vietnam War policies of the Johnson administration, may be viewed as aimed primarily at those Democratic activists extremely upset by the war who seemed likely to withhold their critical resources and skills from the campaign unless some concessions were offered them. In retrospect, Humphrey's actual concessions in the speech seemed quite minimal, but symbolically they were significant.

Hence, the candidate enters the campaign recognizing that most groups are not politically neutral, that they in fact are predisposed to support one party over the other because of traditional ties rooted in historical events and because of more contemporary policy concerns. Benjamin Page (p. 27) found that in 1968 Humphrey and Nixon took different positions on a series of issues that reflected the differences in the issue preferences of the rank-and-file party identifiers. While the causal connection between the candidates' and the citizens' issue positions is ambiguous—candidates may be responding to citizens' wishes or citizens may be formulating issue positions according to cues provided by their preferred candidate—it seems clear that the types of issue appeals emanating from candidates are to a large degree constrained by the preferences of party activists and party loyalists.

This means efforts by a candidate to appeal to a new coalition of supporters may be highly risky in terms of losing traditional support and failing to win sufficient new adherents. One might argue that Goldwater in 1964 and McGovern in 1972 envisaged new support coalitions, which failed to materialize. Goldwater's strategy was based on the myth of the stay-at-home Republican voters and Goldwater paid heavily for succumbing to the myth. The coalition envisaged by the McGovern camp in 1972 seemed more plausible on the surface; it consisted of minorities, such as blacks and Chicanos, liberal Democrats, progressive labor union members, and young people. This latter group was particularly important since the enfranchisement of 18-year-olds plus the coming-of-voting age of the 21- to 25-year-olds too young to vote in 1968 meant that there would be 25 million new young voters in 1972. McGovern hoped for high turnout and solid support among youth and was disappointed on both counts. Young voters turned out at a rate noticeably less than the national average of 56 percent, and they divided their votes almost evenly between Nixon and McGovern. Even among college students, those young people thought to be most heavily pro-McGovern, vote preferences were almost evenly divided.

Thus, recent efforts to construct new and lasting coalitions of groups have apparently been unsuccessful. Robert Axelrod (1972: 12) has charted the loyalty rates (see Table 3.7) and the contribution that various groups have made to each party's vote support since 1952. Axelrod's analysis incorporates three elements in determining the importance of a group's contribution—the size of the group, its turnout, and its loyalty. Groups that are large in size, vote at a high rate, and overwhelmingly favor one party can make a major contribution to that party's vote support. One of Axelrod's more important findings is that the contribution of blacks to the Democratic vote total has risen dramatically: in 1952 7 percent of the Democratic vote came from blacks while in 1972 the proportion had jumped to 22 percent. Obviously black citizens comprise a significant portion of the Democratic coalition. Axelrod (1978: 622–624) also notes that the percentage of the Republican vote coming from the North has dropped from a high of 87 percent in 1952 to a low of 67 percent in 1976; this is another way of stating that the South has become an increasingly important segment of the Republican presidential coalition. Table 11.5 summarizes

TABLE 11.5
The Contribution Made to Democratic and Republican Vote
Totals by Various Groups, 1952–1976*
(in percentages)

	1952	1956	1960	1964	1968	1972	1976
Democrats							
Poor (income under $3,000)	28	19	16	15	12	10	7
Black (and other nonwhite)	7	5	7	12	19	22	16
Union member (or union member in family	38	36	31	32	28	32	33
Catholic (and other non-Protestant)	41	38	47	36	40	34	35
South (including border states)	20	23	27	21	24	25	36
Central cities (or 12 largest metropolitan areas)	21	19	19	15	14	14	11
Republicans							
Nonpoor	75	84	83	89	90	93	97
White	99	98	97	100	99	98	99
Nonunion	79	78	84	87	81	77	80
Protestant	75	75	90	80	80	74	76
Northern	87	84	75	76	80	73	67
Not in central cities	84	89	90	91	92	95	98

* The figures presented represent the percentage of the party's vote in any specific election due to the group in question.
Source: Extracted from figures presented by Robert Axelrod, "Communications," *American Political Science Review* 72 (June 1978), pp. 622–624.

the contributions made by various groups to the Republican and Democratic vote coalitions since 1952.

The 1972 Republican coalition is particularly striking since the GOP received the majority of the vote cast by poor people, union members, Catholics, and southerners (see Table 3.7). This unusual support does not stand out in Table 11.5 since the GOP increased its share of the vote among all groups in 1972. The atypical GOP coalition in 1972 illustrates a number of more general points about the voting behavior of groups. First, group voting patterns do change in response to specific campaign stimuli even as the underlying partisan attachments of the group remain fairly stable. Second, no group except blacks gives near unanimous support to one party; this means that neither party can afford to write off completely any group, with the possible exception of blacks and the GOP. And finally, the notion of a typical party coalition is a useful one so long as one does not assume that the shape of the coalition is carved in stone.

One strategic ramification that Axelrod draws from his work is that if a party wants to improve its performance among a group, it must increase the turnout or the loyalty of the group, or both. The size of the group is essentially fixed except in situations where institutional changes expand the size of the electorate, as did the Voting Rights Act of 1965. The emphasis on increasing turnout and loyalty is another variant of the fundamental strategy of appealing to one's supporters and likely supporters.

Therefore, the central task of a presidential campaign is to put together a coalition of support among groups already predisposed toward one's candidacy and to add to this coalition until victory seems assured. This emphasis on specific groups, however, may not be the strategy of the future as the proportion of citizens within groups identifying with a political party shrinks and the number of Independents increases. If this trend continues, then there will be a shrinking base of citizens who enter the campaign as likely or latent supporters of a candidate, and group appeals may be less effective in generating support. The presence of large numbers of uncommitted Independents and apoliticals raises the possibility that a candidate might use unconventional appeals to win support from such voters. The pitfalls of this strategy are threefold. First, Independents, especially in 1972 and 1976 (see Table 3.8), have not voted at as high a rate as partisans and thus seem to be a risky group upon which to base a candidacy. Second, Independents themselves are a heterogeneous group, which means it is unlikely the candidate can find one issue or one set of issues that will appeal to Independents en masse. And, finally, there are substantial numbers of voters still affiliated with the two major parties; a candidate receiving little support from partisans has major obstacles to overcome. Hence, the optimal strategy seems to be one in which a substantial share of the Independent vote is added to a core bloc of partisan support—a very traditional strategy in American presidential politics. Whether the issue preferences of citizens will permit such a traditional strategy to be successful in the future is a question considered in the last chapter.

12

Toward the Future

INTRODUCTION

Following the presidential elections of 1964, 1968, and 1972, political commentators speculated whether the election outcomes signified fundamental shifts in the strength and sources of support of the Democratic and Republican Parties. The Democratic landslide of 1964 led observers to wonder whether the GOP was dead. Gerald Pomper (1967) noted that the Democrats in 1964 ran strongest in the Northeast and weakest in the South, a reversal of traditional Democratic Party support, which led Pomper to speculate that the Democratic coalition had been permanently transformed.

The Republican victory in 1968 put to rest the question of the viability of the GOP. Political journalists began to suggest that the Republican Party was about to supplant the Democrats as the national

345

majority party. This thesis received its most prominent statement in a book by Kevin Phillips entitled *The Emerging Republican Party*. Phillips described the new Republican majority as consisting of Southern, Sun Belt, and heartland states and California. He argued that the Northeast, which formerly was the strongest Republican area, had become much less important to GOP election prospects. And even within the Northeast, Phillips (1969: 465–466) saw certain groups, such as urban Catholics, trending toward the GOP, in part because of dissatisfaction with the Democratic Party's handling of race-related matters. Phillips described the upcoming cycle in American politics as one that was likely to match a majority GOP based upon the heartland, South, and California against a minority Democratic Party based on the Northeast and Pacific Northwest and relying heavily on northern and southern black votes. Phillips (1969: 467) asserted that the GOP did not have to appeal to such groups as youth and blacks to win elections, despite what liberal Republicans said about broadening the base of the party.

The magnitude of the Republican landslide in 1972 at first glance seemed to confirm the emergence of the Republican majority. Nixon ran very strongly in the South and received a majority of the vote among such traditional Democratic supporters as union members and urban Catholics. Yet the 1972 GOP presidential victory was a very shallow one; the Democrats more than held their own in state and local races as well as in Congress. The subsequent revelations about Watergate crimes and the decline in the economy tended to dampen assertions about the inevitability of a GOP majority. And the apparent reconstruction of the New Deal coalition by Carter in 1976 (see Chapter 7) temporarily ended speculation about the imminence of the Republican majority and instead turned attention to the notion that the United States had a 1½-party system, with the GOP consigned to permanent minority status despite its strong presidential performances (Ladd, 1978c). Yet as Carter's popularity declined sharply throughout 1978 and 1979 and as conservative issue positions seemed to be gaining in popularity, political analysts once again wondered whether a brighter future awaited the GOP.

Thus, discussions about the future shape of the American party system have occupied a prominent place in contemporary political discourse. The term that is used most often in analyzing potential changes in the parties' electoral fortunes is *realignment,* which refers to a major, permanent alteration in the partisan balance in the electorate. The type of change most frequently discussed is one in which the majority party becomes the minority and vice versa, although other outcomes such as the demise of the Republican and Democratic Parties and their replacement by new parties would also be classified as realignments. Another related phenomenon is the case in which the support coalitions of the parties change dramatically even as their relative strength in the electorate remains unchanged. It was this situation that led Pomper to introduce the notion of a converting election (discussed in Chapter 1). Thus, we will focus in this chapter on the possibility of partisan realignment in the United States. First some properties of realignment, as well as some of the characteristics of the present political scene that have encouraged speculation about change, will be considered. Then some possible scenarios of realignment will be presented, followed by a summary assessment of their likelihood.

THE DEFINITION AND PROPERTIES OF REALIGNMENT

Our basic definition of realignment as a durable change in the party balance comes from work by V. O. Key, Jr. (1955). Key focused on those "critical" elections that resulted in new partisan alignments, such as the elections of 1896 and 1928. While Key viewed a single election as being critical or realigning, scholars have since argued that realignment is a process that occurs over time and have therefore shifted their attention to realigning eras rather than specific elections. For example, while we might in retrospect view the election of Roosevelt in 1932 as critical, the fact that the New Deal coalition did not achieve its peak strength until 1936 argues that important movements in the electorate were occurring throughout the period. Hence, 1932–36 might best be viewed as a realigning era.

One problem with the definition of realignment as a durable change is that one can tell only after the fact whether realignment has occurred. There are, however, certain properties of past realignments that led some contemporary observers to expect one as imminent in the United States. One characteristic of past realignments is that they have happened at regular 36–40 year intervals. Since the last realignment was in 1932–36, the cyclical nature of the phenomenon led some observers to believe that a new realignment was due in the 1972–76 era. Possible reasons for the periodicity of realignments will be presented later.

Walter Dean Burnham (1970: 6–7) states that past realigning eras have been characterized by intense political feelings that at the elite level spill over into disputes about party nominations and party platforms, as well as increased ideological polarization between the parties. At the mass level, there is increased voter involvement and issue-related voting. All of these conditions, with the exception of higher voting participation, have been present in American politics since 1964. The Republican convention of 1964 and the Democratic conventions of 1968 and 1972 were characterized by intense conflict between disparate wings of the parties. The presidential elections of 1964 and 1972 were marked by an ideological polarization uncommon in recent American politics. And, as discussed in Chapter 4, issue awareness and perceptions of party differences on the part of the citizenry increased sharply in the mid-1960s and 1970s.

There are additional changes at the mass and elite levels that have further encouraged speculation about realignment. The sizable decline in partisanship and growth in the number of Independents (see Chapter 3) suggest to many observers that a citizenry exists readily mobilizable into a new party system. The election of two nonmajor party United States Senators—Byrd of Virginia and Buckley of New York—as well as the election of an Independent Governor of Maine—Longley—were seen by some as the early indicators of the ultimate transformation of the political parties. At the elite level, the switch to the Republican Party by such former conservative Democrats as John Connally and Strom Thurmond and the switch to the Democratic party by such former GOP liberals as John Lindsay and Donald Riegle were viewed as forerunners of an eventual sorting out of elites into their ideological compatible party, which might produce substantial switches in partisanship by average citizens. However, there has been no pronounced tendency in recent years for prominent politicians to switch to the ideologically correct party; if anything, the Democrats have become more of an umbrella party encompassing liberals, moderates, and conservatives.

A final characteristic of past realignments has been the presence of serious minor party candidates in the elections preceding the realignment. The presence of George Wallace as a third-party candidate in 1968 attacking the major parties as incapable of handling the country's problems fits well with past realignment situations. Therefore, if the past is a good predictor to the future, then realignment seems likely. However, a number of key conditions must be met for a realign-

to occur, and we will discuss these after considering the causes of realignment.

THE CAUSES OF REALIGNMENT

Realignment occurs when some issue or crisis arises that cannot be handled by the political parties because the issue cuts across the existing bases of support of the parties. Not any issue can spark a realignment: rather, the issue must generate intense feelings in the electorate. Often such issues are symbolic and moral in nature rather than focusing on a specific policy area. When an issue cuts across the existing basis of a party's support, then the party is effectively immobilized from coping with the issue since any action it takes will undoubtedly antagonize some segment of the party's supporters. Race is often viewed as such an issue, particularly with respect to the Democratic Party. While the Democrats have largely come down on the pro-civil rights, pro-black side of many race-related matters, this has cost the party many of its traditional white supporters, particularly at presidential elections.

When a controversial, provocative issue arises, a number of outcomes are possible. James Sundquist (1973: 16–25) has discussed five possible outcomes, the first simply being the maintenance of the existing party system as the issue recedes in importance or is successfully finessed by the parties. More dramatic outcomes are possible, including realignment of the existing parties through shifts in allegiances by current party supporters, realignment of the existing parties through absorption of a third party, realignment through the replacement of one major party, and realignment through the replacement of both old parties.

All of these outcomes have been mentioned in current speculation about the future shape of the party system. It has been argued that the present situation, in which both parties receive support from citizens who call themselves liberals and conservatives, is an unstable one that eventually will result in massive shifts in voters' allegiances. This would lead to the continued existence of the Democratic and Republican Parties but with different sources of vote support.

The realignment of the existing parties through absorption of a third party has received much attention, given the success of the Wallace candidacy in 1968. While more of Wallace's votes came from people who called themselves Democrats, some observers believe that the American Independent Party will serve as a way station for former Democrats on their way to becoming Republicans. Under this possibility, the bulk of the Wallace support would move to the GOP, thereby creating a national Republican majority.

Realignment through replacement of one of the major parties is heard most often today in reference to the GOP. Some conservatives argue that control of the GOP is no longer their goal. Instead, many conservatives want to form a new national party because many citizens who might be attracted to the conservative cause would never be attracted to the Republican Party, either because of their existing partisanship or because of perceptions of the GOP as the party of the privileged, a point discussed later.

The occurrence of realignment through replacement of both parties has received less attention than the other possibilities. Some observers argue that the only way to get liberal and conservative citizens aligned in the proper way is to create two new parties. The attempt to make the Democrats the liberal party and the Republicans the conservative will be unsuccessful because of people's long-standing feelings about these parties. Hence, it is claimed that two new parties are required to effect a realignment.

While Sundquist has presented some thought-provoking scenarios, his discussion of the sources of realignment seems too limited. Sundquist sees alignment resulting from the switching of partisan allegiances by adherents of the existing parties. However, our discussion of party identification in Chapter 3 suggests that partisans are likely to be more immune to extraordinary political appeals than are citizens not identified with one of the two parties. Moreover, the principle that partisanship tends to become stronger the longer one has identified with a party implies that older citizens will be less promising sources of realignment than younger citizens.

In short, while Sundquist asserts that conversion—the actual switch in partisan loyalties—produces realignment, it seems more probable that realignment will be brought about by the influx of young, Independent voters and former nonvoters into the electorate, a position supported by Kristi Andersen (1976) in her analysis of the New Deal realignment. Using recall data on past partisanship from national election surveys, Andersen reconstructs the electorate of the 1920s and 1930s and finds that the Democratic majority was forged from citizens of voting age in the 1920s who had not been party adherents and from the newest voters first coming into the electorate in the 1930s. In response to the economic crisis and the appeal of Franklin

Roosevelt, both groups of citizens were mobilized into the electorate in a heavily Democratic direction; widespread conversion of Republicans into Democrats was not a significant source of the New Deal realignment.

The fact that about half of Americans under 30 in 1976 were either pure Independents or Independent leaners (see Table 3.1) means there is a sizable group of voters highly susceptible to realignment pressures. Paul Beck (1974) states that the high incidence of Independents among young people today is caused by a party system based upon New Deal cleavages that are not relevant to a younger generation that did not experience the Great Depression. Beck's argument raises some intriguing questions. If the New Deal party system is irrelevant to young people, what type of cleavage would attract young people to the political parties? Are youth so homogeneous that it is possible to appeal to them as a bloc? Might any attempt to appeal to youth run the risk of mistaking certain segments of young people as representative of all young people? Might appealing for the youth vote backfire on the political parties if youth are a negative reference point for many citizens? These questions are not easily answered, although they suggest that any youth-based realignment might be a highly unpredictable affair.

For scholars such as Burnham, the causes of realignment are reflected in their periodicity or cyclical occurrence. Burnham (1970: 9–10) views American history from a dialectical perspective, arguing that there is a fundamental contradiction between our pluralist and incrementalist political institutions and our rapidly changing socioeconomic system. Normally, the tension between the political and economic spheres can be handled within the existing party system; but in times of great social and economic stress, the slow-reacting political institutions are incapable of handling crises. In such a situation, Burnham argues, tensions build, a flashpoint is reached, realignment occurs, a new party system develops that alleviates tensions, and a period of stability ensues for a while. However, the constantly changing nature of the economic system generates new tensions and sets the realignment process in motion again, thereby making realignment a periodic occurrence. Burnham's description is fascinating, although largely unsupported by solid evidence. Burnham's explanation makes the occurrence of realignment too automatic, although he does conjecture that the realignment currently due may not happen, for reasons to be discussed shortly.

Beck (1974: 200–206) has developed a socialization theory of partisan realignment which dovetails nicely with our discusison of the learning and transmission of party identification in Chapter 3 and which provides a plausible explanation for the periodic occurrence of realignment. Beck identifies three different groups of individuals with respect to the learning of partisanship. The first group acquired their partisanship as young adults during a realignment. Partisanship learned in this period, according to Beck, will be more firmly grounded in the issues and political realities of the era and as such will have a clear-cut rationale.

The second group includes those individuals who received their preadult partisanship from parents of a realignment generation. Beck refers to these people as "children of realignment" who, while lacking direct exposure to the realignment and its causes, do learn much about the realignment from their parents. Thus, the partisanship of these individuals is grounded in meaningful cleavages and should therefore be less susceptible to change.

Finally, there are those persons who learned their partisanship at least two generations removed from a realignment and hence the rationale underlying the party system may not be clear to them. It is these citizens who will have the weakest commitments to the existing parties and who will be the most likely sources of realignment. Since the time interval between the socialization of adults during a realignment and the socialization of their grandchildren into partisanship is about 40 years, the periodicity of realignments may reflect the presence of generations far removed from the original rationale of the party system. Thus, Beck's theory suggests that the presence of a generation distant from actual experience of the earlier realignment is a necessary condition for a subsequent realignment to occur. Note that Beck is not claiming that realignment will definitely occur, only that its likelihood is increased by the existence of such a generation.

POSSIBLE ISSUE BASES OF REALIGNMENT

As discussed earlier, if a realignment is to occur, it will be precipitated by the emergence of a new issue of sufficient intensity on which the existing parties take or are perceived to take differing positions. If the parties do not take contrasting stands on the new issue and instead try to straddle it, then a new party may emerge that offers a clear-cut alternative on the issue. The question arises as to what such an issue might be.

In the late 1960s, political commentators (e.g., Scammon and Wattenberg, 1970) wrote about a new phenomenon labeled the "social issue," which was viewed as a potential source of realignment. The social issue was actually a cluster of issues dealing with such matters as race, campus unrest, law and order, and lifestyles. Presumably, working- and middle-class citizens were upset by aggressive black demands for equality, angered by the violence perpetrated by a privileged college youth, concerned by the general breakdown in law and order, and threatened by the nontraditional values espoused by the drug culture and the advocates of sexual freedom. Since many of these angry white citizens were Democrats and since the Democratic Party was presumably identified with the aspirations of blacks and college students and supportive of the new lifestyles, it was argued that the party was about to lose many of its traditional supporters. Commentators asserted that many white citizens, alternately referred to as the "center," the "silent majority," the "working man," and the "forgotten American," were ripe for appeals based on the social issue.

The Republicans and Wallace exploited the social issue with some success in 1968; and the GOP, led by the histrionics of Vice President Agnew, tried to capitalize on the issue in the 1970 congressional elections by branding the Democrats as soft on crime and violence and by associating the Democrats with elements of society feared by many white Americans. The Republican strategy failed as the Democrats refused to let themselves be portrayed as having a weaker commitment to law and order. Democratic candidates went on the attack condemning lawlessness and violence, and the social issue receded as a possible basis of realignment since there were no major differences between the parties on the issue. The association of the McGovern candidacy in 1972 with quotas for blacks and young people and with sympathy for the new lifestyles served to place the Democrats once again at a disadvantage about certain aspects of the social issue. For many citizens, however, it was McGovern himself and not the Democratic Party that was at fault. Moreover, it seems unlikely that the Democrats will allow themselves to be placed in such a position again, as evidenced by the abandonment of quotas at the 1976 convention. Overall, the social issue, although capable of generating tremendous intra- and inter-party conflict, does not seem to be a very likely basis for realignment, particularly in an era when economic matters are of paramount importance to Americans.

The economic issue has also been considered a source of realignment, but it is unclear how it might bring about a change in the partisan balance. Economic issues have traditionally favored the Democrats, although the severe economic woes in the late 1970s during a Democratic administration may erode the usual Democratic advantage in this area. The Republicans, however, have not been able to shed their negative economic image and profit at the expense of the Democrats. For example, a Gallup Poll conducted in June 1978 found that Americans cited the Democrats over the Republicans as the party best able to keep the country prosperous, by a margin of 41 to 23 percent, with the remaining 36 percent having no opinion or seeing no difference between the parties. And in a September 1978 Harris Survey, Democrats enjoyed a 42 to 26 percent margin over Republicans as the party that would do a better job in providing "some relief to taxpayers" (*Public Opinion,* September October 1978: 31). The increased public support for a balanced budget, fiscal responsibility, spending limitations, and the like, despite being traditional Republican issue stances, has not worked to the electoral advantage of the GOP because skillful Democratic politicians have managed to defuse the partisan ramifications of the issues. Hence, unless the economy takes a dramatic turn for the worse and the GOP is able to convince voters of Democratic mismanagement, economic issues do not seem to be a likely basis for realignment, although they might have such short-run political benefits as regaining control of the White House.

The one issue mentioned most frequently as a potential cause of realignment is race. Racial issues are viewed as a direct cause of the substantial Democratic decline in the South and as a likely source of continued Democratic losses among white ethnic groups in the North. Paul Abramson (1973: 7) has asserted that "the major Democratic liability is that blacks are an integral part of their coalition, and that black votes are costly." Black votes are costly, according to Abramson, in the sense that association with the aims and aspirations of black people is likely to lose a party much white support. Abramson (1973: 1–8) declares that the Democrcats are no longer the majority party (nor are the Republicans) because they cannot consistently carry the white working-class vote, which Abramson views as the heart of the New Deal coalition.

Walter Dean Burnham (1970: 142) observes that the mass migration of blacks from the South into the major cities of the North has nationalized the race issue and has led to hostile reactions by the white middle class most in competition with blacks for jobs, services, and the like. Public opinion surveys document that white attitudes toward certain aspects of the black movement for equality have become more negative in the past decade. For example, while 34 percent of the public in 1965 felt that the Johnson administration was "pushing integration too fast" and 45 percent felt that way in 1968, by 1972 70 percent agreed that "blacks and people in other minorities expect things to improve too quickly and are making unreasonable demands" (Stewart, 1974: 119–20). Thus, it appears that race has the potentiality for producing realignment.

Burnham (1970: 158) considers one possible realignment outcome —in which the Democratic Party comes increasingly to be "the party of the technologically competent and technologically superfluous strata," while the GOP becomes "the partisan vehicle for the defense of white 'middle-America.' " In this scenario, the Democratic Party would be a top-bottom coalition opposed to a middle-supported GOP. That is, the Democrats would attract the most- and least-advantaged groups in society and the Republicans the vast middle. While there is some evidence that the Democrats are running better of late among traditional Republican supporters, such as professionals, managers, and the highly educated, Burnham thinks the top-bottom coalition will not materialize.

While it sounds plausible to say that race might serve as the basis of realignment, we might ask the fundamental question as to which specific race issue would produce realignment. Is there any particular racial issue of sufficient intensity to deflect many white Democrats from their traditional party allegiances? Certainly busing is an issue that has aroused intense passions. But it seems unlikely to result in realignment for a number of reasons. First, many liberal Democratic politicians have backed away from support of busing, in response to the anger of their white constituents. Second, recent court decisions have given localities greater flexibility in handling the issue of school integration. In particular, a Supreme Court decision that ruled that busing across city lines into the suburbs was not required to solve the problem of school segregation should alleviate the fears of many suburban residents and defuse the busing issue. Moreover, it seems that second thoughts are developing among all segments of American society about the wisdom and practicality of busing, which may lead to its ultimate demise as a tool for integration. In addition, people who have no children or whose children have grown up are not likely to get aroused by busing. Thus, it appears that busing is not a likely source of realignment, although some cities still face the busing issue and it may yet intrude in presidential politics.

If busing is not the race-related catalyst to foster realignment, what other racial issue might be? On a whole host of traditional civil rights matters, such as voting rights and public accommodations, there is practically a national consensus in support of these measures, which means that they cannot serve as a basis of realignment. For example, Andrew Greeley (1974: 299–311) shows that whites overwhelmingly accept the goal of school integration today, a remarkable change in their attitudes of 15 years ago. On many other issues, including the kinds of problems about which they are most concerned, blacks and whites exhibit similar attitudes (Greeley, 1974: 339–344).

There are other race-related issues in addition to busing that have upset many whites, but these seem unlikely sources of realignment. For example, many white citizens (as well as many black citizens) are currently upset by a public welfare system which they see as unfairly advantaging blacks at the expense of the white (and black) working class. Yet this seems unlikely to generate a pro-Republican realignment, especially when it was Democratic governors in such states as California and Massachusetts who tried vigorously to bring welfare expenditures under control. Moreover, the Republicans have not offered a serious alternative to the existing welfare program (notwithstanding the tentative steps the Nixon administration made in this area), and running against "welfare cheats" does not seem to provide a sufficient basis for realignment.

In general, special treatment for blacks, be it economic or political, could serve to promote realignment. The quota system at the 1972 Democratic convention upset many long-standing white Democrats, who felt unfairly treated. Perhaps if the Democratic Party were associated with a whole series of measures that favored blacks at the expense of white, realignment might occur. Yet Democrats backed off of quotas for their 1976 convention, and it seems unlikely that they will espouse social programs that benefit blacks only. It seems more probable that future Democratic social programs will emphasize improving the quality of life of all citizens, such as national health care insurance.

If the economy, the social issue, and race are unpromising sources of realignment, then what is left? Frederick Dutton (1971: 225) has speculated that the class cleavages of an earlier era may be replaced by a cultural cleavage exemplified by the competing slogans "make the world safe for sex" versus "support your local censor." While lifestyle concerns can certainly generate intense passions, they seem an unlikely foundation for realignment since it is rare that parties will be on opposite sides on such issues, especially when the overwhelming majority of the population is on one side of the issue. Moreover, it appears that the more outrageous actions in support of and in opposition to alternative lifestyles have lessened since the early 1970s, perhaps indicating the decline in the issue's importance. Andrew Greeley (1974: 272–73) has identified a new issue, labeled "neopopulism," which he thinks might produce realignment. Basically, the issue centers around the concentration of power in American society and who is to participate in decision making. But it is difficult to specify the alternatives on the issue, where the parties stand, and the likely future shape of the issue. Greeley (1974: 274) himself argues that one of the tasks of leadership in the next decade will be to give shape and form to the issue. Along these lines, Ralph Nader has called for the creation of a new political party that would focus on what he calls the overriding issue of the times—corporate power—and would emphasize "the expansion of citizen access to all branches of government, the mass media, and corporate decision-making" (Broder, 1979: A-2). Nader envisages a new party based on consumer groups, anti-nuclear organizations, some trade unions, and local citizens' organizations. Such groups, however, are far from consensual in their issue positions, so that unless the appropriate leadership and the critical issues emerge, the prospects for realignment are negligible.

A new cluster of issues focusing on such matters as energy and nuclear power, ecology and the environment has appeared on the political agenda. These issues are still in a formative stage and may not develop to the point of generating and sustaining new political cleavages. Nevertheless, one can imagine how concerns about the environment can run headlong into concerns about jobs and economic security. The trade-off between economic expansion and job security versus environmental protection has already been a source of controversy in many localities, such as the coal mining region of Ohio where in mid-1979 the federal government relaxed pollution standards so high sulphur Ohio coal could be burned by Ohio utilities, thereby protecting the coal mining industry. It is the Democratic Party that is most threatened by the potential conflict between jobs and environmental protection. The working class and union component of the Democratic coalition is naturally more concerned about economic growth and job security, while the intellectual wing and many upper-middle-class Democrats come down on the side of the environment. These issues have not yet developed to the point where existing party allegiances are threatened and they may never reach this stage, especially as long as severe economic crises keep economic concerns paramount and make citizens more willing to compromise on environmental standards. Nevertheless, the Three Mile Island nuclear reactor incident has provided impetus to anti-nuclear power and other ecology-oriented groups. The creation of an effective mass movement seems unlikely, although in a number of European countries the environmental movement has achieved notable political clout.

Thus, it appears that realignment is unlikely, given the absence of a critical issue and the leadership required to exploit that issue. But this conclusion begs the question of whether a realignment has already occurred, perhaps in response to a plurality of issues, each of which moved a number of citizens in the same direction. Thus, we will next focus on two groups—southerners and Catholics—most often discussed in conjunction with a pro-Republican realignment and examine what evidence there is about realignment on their part. We emphasize a pro-Republican realignment because that was the outcome that received the greatest attention from political analysts until Watergate and the economy derailed the emerging Republican majority. We could also talk about pro-Democratic trends in the electorate, which have resulted in the Democrats being the dominant party within most sociodemographic groupings, as well as in most regions of the country including former GOP bailiwicks. The broad base that now characterizes the Democratic Party and its consequences for American politics will be discussed in the last section of this chapter.

SOUTHERNERS AND CATHOLICS: HAS REALIGNMENT OCCURRED?

The South

The 1976 election may seem to belie the notion of a pro-Republican realignment in the South because Carter the Democrat carried the region handily. Yet from another perspective, Carter's southern performance shows how far the GOP has come in being a major force in southern presidential politics. Despite being a native southerner of the dominant religious group, with a reputation for being a political moderate, Carter received only about 54 percent of the total southern vote and less than half of the white vote. Therefore, one might argue that the South remains very fertile ground for the GOP in presidential contests, particularly when the Democrats select a non-southern liberal as their nominee.

The traditionally Democratic South was the least Democratic section of the country in the 1964, 1968, and 1972 presidential elections. Furthermore, Democratic Party identification among southern whites has dropped from a high of 80 percent in 1952 to 47 percent in 1976, as shown in Figure 3.7. This presidential Republicanism in conjunction with the decline in Democratic loyalties would seem to indicate that massive realignment has occurred in the South. Yet other information indicates the opposite. For example, the decline in Democratic partisanship has benefited Independents and not the Republican Party. About a third of all southerners in 1976 were Independents and only one sixth Republicans. Even in 1972 when Nixon the Republican swept the South with a tremendous 70 percent of the popular vote, Democratic congressional candidates received about 60 percent of the vote, a performance surpassed slightly in 1976. In short, the evidence about southern realignment is mixed, although there has certainly been no sizable gain for the GOP in the party affiliations of southerners.

Bruce Campbell (1977) argues that a pro-Democratic realignment has occurred among black citizens in the South. Prior to the 1964 election, between 40 and 50 percent of southern blacks identified with the Democratic Party, with the second largest group of blacks classified as apoliticals and not Independents or Republicans. Since 1964, about 70 percent of southern blacks have identified with the Democratic Party and the percentage of apoliticals has dropped to about 1 percent (1977: 742). Thus, the South has witnessed a tremendous mobilization of blacks into Democratic partisanship.

Campbell (p. 744) asserts that 1964 was a critical election (as defined by V. O. Key) for southern blacks. There was a sharp and durable alteration in the existing partisan preferences of blacks, as well as intense concern about the election outcome and a high degree of electoral involvement. According to Campbell (p. 745), the issue that brought about the realignment was civil rights. The 1964 election pitted a Democratic candidate with a firm commitment to civil rights legislation against a Republican candidate who had voted against the Civil Rights Act of 1964.

Campbell (pp. 746–47) demonstrates that blacks who favored federal government intervention in civil rights affairs were the ones who shifted most toward the Democratic Party. More generally, Black and Rabinowitz (1974: 17–18) show that black images of the Democratic Party changed dramatically from the 1950s to the 1960s. In 1956 and 1960, Democratic strength among southern blacks did not rest upon civil rights issues but upon bread-and-butter domestic welfare programs. In fact, southern blacks viewed the GOP very favorably with respect to civil rights, in part because it was a Republican President who sent troops into Little Rock to enforce the Supreme Court school desegregation decision. But by the mid-1960s, black images of the parties had changed so sharply that the Democratic Party was now clearly perceived as most sympathetic to civil rights.

Among southern whites, the evidence for realignment is far more ambiguous. Borrowing a term from V. O. Key, Campbell (p. 749) argues that a *secular realignment*—"a process which involves the more or less continuous conversion of party loyalties which accumulate in trends persisting over decades"—has occurred. The secular realignment has been caused not by any one specific issue but by the continuous strain between white southern attitudes and various policies advocated by the national Democratic Party. While switches to Republican partisanship by southern whites have been infrequent, the images of the two parties have changed substantially to the disadvantage of the Democrats. For example, Black and Rabinowitz (1974: 56) report that southern whites are closer to the Republican than the Democratic Party with respect to their positions on major issues and their perceptions of which party can better handle the problems most important to them. Perhaps these changes in party imagery are forerunners to eventual growth of Republican partisanship in the South.

Paul Beck (1977) argues that the South is currently undergoing de-alignment rather than realignment. By de-alignment is meant a weakening of partisan ties in general rather than a transfer of loyalties from one party to another. Beck (1977: 485) claims that the de-alignment is due more to generational replacement rather than conversion of partisans to Independents, although both processes are important. That is, the older southern generation with strong attachments to the Democratic Party is being replaced by a younger generation predominantly Independent in its political coloration. Beck believes that southern de-alignment is probably rooted in policy dissatisfaction with both major parties, especially on the issue of race and segregation. He concludes (1977: 495) that Republican prospects in the South are even gloomier than Democratic chances on actual partisan allegiances, as evidenced by the meager increase in Republican partisanship in recent years and the lack of GOP loyalties among young southerners. Because he sees both parties being weak in the South, Beck forecasts a volatile future for southern politics.

I would modify this conclusion in three ways. While southern electoral behavior will be capable of exhibiting great volatility, this does not mean the major parties will be competing for southern votes on an equal footing. Rather, it seems the GOP will have a distinct advantage in seeking southern support in presidential elections even with racial issues on the backburner. The triumph of racial moderates and the demise of the Wallace-Maddox breed of southern politics does not mean the serious policy differences between the southern and national Democratic parties have been eliminated. If the national party and the Democratic nominee are perceived as too supportive of federal intervention, too sympathetic of minorities, and the like, then the GOP remains a more than viable alternative for white southerners.

Second, the future shape of southern politics will depend to a substantial degree on the behavior of regional elites. Speculation was rampant in the late 1960s and early 1970s about massive switches to the Republican Party on the part of elected Democratic officials. It was thought that such changes would give the GOP an instant organizational base at the state and local level and would result in many rank-and-file Democrats converting to the GOP. These massive switches by Democratic elites never came to pass, although they are still conceivable. As Donald Strong observes (1971: 255), a clash in Congress between northern and southern Democrats, in which southerners are denied chairmanships, stripped of seniority, and the like because of failure to support Democratic Party programs, could hasten realignment. Likewise, the presence of a southerner on the national ticket of one of the parties could measurably affect the election outcome in the South even if it did not result in realignment, as evidenced by Carter's candidacy in 1976.

Finally, as Beck notes, the de-alignment in the South seems to be a part of a nationwide phenomenon. For example, if one examines the partisan preferences of 18- to 25-year-olds in 1972 by region, one will observe that the relative proportions of Democrats, Republicans, and Independents in the South and non-South are almost identical. Whether this presages a nationalization of politics, in which citizens of all regions respond in similar ways to political forces and events, is unclear. It may be the case that volatility in southern electoral behavior will simply be a part of a national pattern.

Thus, while the white South may not have undergone realignment in the formal sense of massive changes in the balance of partisan allegiances, it does appear to be an increasingly hospitable area for the GOP. E. M. Schreiber (1971: 164–65) raises the possibility that the bulk of the new southern Independents may in fact be "unannounced Republicans who as yet are unwilling to identify themselves as such." If this is the case, then realignment in the South has effectively occurred. And even if the Independents are not nascent Republicans, a Republican presidential candidate can probably count on capturing the major portion of southern electoral votes unless the Democratic nominee is particularly attuned to southern preferences. Republican success in the South may force the Democrats into a large-state electoral vote strategy. Yet the GOP cannot afford to go too far in satisfying the South, particularly on racial matters, lest it guarantee Democratic victories in the large states.

Catholic Voters

Traditional Catholic allegiances to the Democratic Party rested not on religious doctrine but on historical circumstance. The waves of Catholic immigrants that settled in major American cities (with the exception of Philadelphia) encountered a Protestant-dominated Republican political establishment unsympathetic to the new arrivals. The Democratic Party, on the other hand, welcomed the Catholic ethnic groups, effectively mobilized them into politics and built urban political machines that were to last for decades. Successive waves of Catholic ethnic groups, such as the Irish and the Italians, largely gained political power through the Democratic Party.

Conjecture about a pro-Republican realignment by Catholics has been common for a number of reasons. Some scholars speculated that as Catholics moved up the economic ladded they would increasingly leave the party of their forebears and move to the party that best embodied their middle-class aspirations. More recently, it has been argued that working-class Catholic ethnic groups in major urban areas have become disenchanted with the Democratic Party because of its increasingly close association with the goals of blacks and other minorities (Phillips, 1969: 140–75). Presumably, working-class Catholic ethnics are in greatest competition with blacks for political power and economic rewards, thereby heightening tensions between the groups and facilitating Catholic movement out of the Democratic Party. Public opinion polls have indicated substantial animosity toward blacks and black aims on the part of Catholic ethnics. For example, a bare majority of all whites in the late 1960s were opposed to blacks moving into their part of town, compared to 60 percent opposition by Irish and Italian Catholics and 80 percent opposition by Polish Catholics (Dutton, 1971: 118). Finally, it has been claimed that recent Democratic Party sympathy to the liberal position on a number of lifestyle controversies, such as abortion and birth control, has been particularly offensive to Catholic citizens, thereby furthering their departure from the party.

It therefore appeared that Catholic citizens were prime targets for a Republican realignment. And in 1972 Catholics did vote heavily for Nixon, giving him 57 percent of their vote (see Table 3.7). Yet most other indicators point to continued Catholic allegiance to the Democratic Party, albeit not at levels as high as in the past. For example, according to the CPS 1972 election study, 65 percent of Catholics voted Democratic in U.S. House races, 55 percent in U.S. Senate contests, and 60 percent in gubernatorial elections. In addition, the partisan loyalties of Catholics in 1972 still showed a sizable Democratic advantage: about 51 percent were Democrats, 34 percent Independents, and less than 15 percent were Republicans. These figures represent a drop of about 10 percent from the peak Catholic Democratic loyalties in 1960, although the 1960 figure may be somewhat inflated, given the presence of a Catholic candidate at the head of the presidential ticket. In 1976, Catholic loyalties to the Democratic Party were reaffirmed with Carter receiving 57 percent of the Catholic vote, and the Democratic congressional, senatorial, and gubernatorial candidates winning 63, 67, and 50 percent of the Catholic vote.

Greeley has argued forcefully that Catholics are still an integral part of the Democratic coalition. He points out (1974: 361–67) that while Catholic ethnics are conservative on some issues they are liberal on others, including civil liberties, economic matters, and the general issue of integration. He presents evidence (1978: 285–91) which shows that Catholic Democrats are more liberal than white Protestant Democrats and black Democrats on questions of sexuality and permissiveness. With the exception of abortion, Catholics are to the left of the Democratic mean across a range of issues; only Jews are consistently more liberal. Hence, Greeley thinks it is simply incorrect and misleading to talk of Catholics leaving the Democratic coalition because of their presumed conservative social values; there are other groups within the Democratic coalition whose attitudes would make them more likely candidates for desertion from the coalition.

Thus, substantial support for the Democratic Party by Catholics in the future seems likely if the party and its candidates are perceived as sympathetic to the needs of white ethnic groups as well as blacks. It seems the Democratic Party should worry more about ethnic-racial tensions than about the possibility of upward economic mobility changing Catholics into Republicans. Fee and Greeley (1975: 31) found that as Catholics rose in socioeconomic status between 1952 and 1972, their affiliation with the Democratic Party did not lessen. Moreover, Catholics who moved to the suburbs seemed to be as strongly Democratic as their fellow Catholics in other areas.

SOME FINAL THOUGHTS ON PRESIDENTIAL ELECTIONS AND POLITICAL CHANGE

The previous discussion should make it clear that I do not expect a classical realignment to occur in the near future. An issue that would trigger the realignment and the leadership that would effectively exploit the issue do not seem readily apparent. This is not to say that important changes have not occurred or will not occur. Certainly the traditional Democratic coalition no longer exists, with the departure of the South from the fold. And among the remaining components of the New Deal Democratic coalition, there are major tensions between black and white ethnic groups which might be alleviated by traditional economic, social welfare party appeals. We should recognize that the majority party status of the Democratic Party depends in part upon its substantial advantage over the GOP in southern partisan allegiances even though the Democrats have lost the region by wide margins in recent elections, with the exception of 1976.

According to Ladd (1978c: 83–88), the Democrats have become "the everyone" party, meaning that they enjoy an advantage over the Republicans in the partisan loyalties of most sociodemographic groupings, including those which formerly favored the GOP. For example, citizens in all occupational, educational, and income categories express at least a plurality preference for the Democratic Party; this includes professionals and business executives as well as labor union members, citizens with a college degree and those with less than a high school education, and citizens at the top and bottom of the income ladder. Yet despite its broad base in the electorate, the Democratic Party has experienced difficulty in winning the Presidency in recent elections. Certainly the political party itself has become less relevant in presidential contests, as the candidates build their own personal campaign organizations and communicate directly with the voters through the mass media, rather than relying on the political party as the intermediary. Moreover, the various reforms in the areas of delegate selection and campaign financing have sharply reduced the role of the party in choosing and supporting its nominee. Yet these developments do not explain why the Democratic Party has trouble converting its majority status among voters into victory on election day.

The very encompassing nature of the Democratic Party holds the key to its problems. As discussed in Chapter 1, the political spectrum has become more complex, with the arrival of social or cultural or lifestyle issues that do not correspond to the traditional New Deal divisions. The Democratic Party includes traditional liberals concerned with New Deal issues and new liberals more concerned with lifestyle and cultural matters, and who at times may even be hostile to the philosophy of economic expansion and government activism espoused by New Deal Democrats. In addition, many of the New Deal liberals are overtly hostile to the values espoused by the party's lifestyle liberals. Hence the Democratic Party is potentially subject to severe ideological conflict; to the extent that lifestyle issues become prominent in a presidential campaign, the Democrats may be torn apart and suffer at the polls. The ideal situation for a Democratic victory is one in which traditional economic issues dominate, so that most Democrats can remain loyal to their party. If, as some believe, the traditional New Deal issues and cleavages can no longer sustain the Democratic Party in the 1980s, then the party must undergo intensive self-examination to decide what it can and does stand for.

While the Democrats have the greater schisms to confront, the future of the GOP is not entirely promising. The Republican Party of the late 1970s is the minority party, trailing far behind Democrats and Independents in citizen allegiances. And the GOP seems particularly weak among the youngest groups in the electorate, which by the simple process of population replacement will eventually comprise an ever larger segment of the voting public. Furthermore, although being a more internally homogeneous party than the Democrats, the Republican Party has its own schisms. Moderates and some moderate conservatives within the GOP have come to terms with aspects of the New Deal welfare state, while some hard-line conservatives still yearn to repeal the New Deal. Ladd argues (1978b: 20) that the economic conservatism of the GOP—along with differences in class background between working-class Democrats and Republicans —hinders the development of a new party based on Republicans and on disgruntled working-class Democrats upset with their party's support for alternative lifestyles and its de-emphasis of traditional economic issues.

Moreover, while recent polls indicate that many more Americans call themselves conservatives rather than liberals, and that opposition to a powerful federal government in the abstract is high, the GOP should not interpret these results as signifying approval of its generally conservative stance. As John Stewart (1974: 106–12) points out, there is a paradox, even a contradiction, between citizens' preferences for political labels and their opinions about specific federal government programs. That is, while more people consider themselves conservatives in response to a general question about their political ideology, they simultaneously express strong support for a whole host of domestic social programs traditionally espoused by the Democrats. This paradox leads Stewart to conclude that the Democrats should avoid general ideological positions and instead focus on specific programs. This point is further emphasized by data reported by Ladd (1978d: 33–34), which indicate that a plurality of voters who label themselves conservative identify with the Democratic Party and that self-described conservatives, by healthy pluralities, favor spending more money in such areas as national health, education, and urban problems. These figures should not be interpreted as indicating support for all federal programs and government intervention, but they do indicate the problem the Republican Party faces in coming up with a program that will advance its electoral prospects.

Finally, the GOP suffers from long-standing image problems in the electorate, as shown in Table 12.1. For example, 61 percent of the

TABLE 12.1
Images of the Parties, 1974, by Party Identification
(in percentages)

Characteristic	Total	*Which Party Characteristic Applies to*				
		Rep.	Dem.	Neither	Both	Don't Know
Too Much for Labor Unions						
All citizens	100	18	33	17	15	17
Republicans	100	10	49	10	16	14
Independents	100	16	31	18	16	19
Democrats	100	24	28	19	12	17
Too Much for Black People/ Negroes						
All citizens	100	9	24	36	16	16
Republicans	100	4	39	29	15	14
Independents	100	7	23	35	17	18
Democrats	100	12	19	38	15	14
Patriotic						
All citizens	100	12	22	11	46	10
Republicans	100	25	5	10	50	9
Independents	100	12	12	15	49	12
Democrats	100	6	38	8	41	7
Believe in the Value of Hard Work						
All citizens	100	17	30	13	31	9
Republicans	100	35	8	14	34	9
Independents	100	16	20	18	32	14
Democrats	100	10	48	8	28	6
Open to New People						
All citizens	100	7	34	10	33	16
Republicans	100	18	20	10	37	14
Independents	100	5	23	13	38	20
Democrats	100	3	49	8	26	13
Concerned for People Like You						
All citizens	100	9	48	19	17	7
Republicans	100	34	15	18	25	9
Independents	100	5	32	30	23	10
Democrats	100	1	78	10	8	3
Believe in Importance of Helping Others						
All citizens	100	6	47	13	26	8
Republicans	100	21	20	11	39	9
Independents	100	3	35	18	31	13
Democrats	100	2	70	8	16	3
Too Much for Rich People						
All citizens	100	61	8	8	15	8
Republicans	100	33	13	18	24	11
Independents	100	52	6	10	21	11
Democrats	100	81	6	3	7	4

Source: U.S. National Study for 1975 Republican Leadership Conference. Prepared by Republican National Committee, Political/Research Divisions, March 1975, table IV-6, p. 33. A national sample of 2,000 citizens was presented with a series of characteristics and asked which party was best described by each of the characteristics. The study was undertaken for the Republican National Committee by Market Opinion Research of Detroit, Mich., in November-December 1974.

American people feel that Republicans are "too much for rich people," only 7 percent say that the GOP is "open to new people," and only 9 percent believe that the Republican Party is "concerned for people like you." Highlighting the GOP's problem is that even Republican citizens ranked their party more negatively than the Democrats on a number of the items. While more citizens feel that the Democratic Party is "too much for labor unions and black people," the GOP advantage here is not very large. The Democratic Party also enjoys an advantage over the GOP as the party better able to handle such matters as keeping the country out of World War III and maintaining prosperity. And when Americans were asked in July of 1978 which party could do a better job of handling what they thought was the most important problem facing the country, 33 percent named the Democrats, 19 percent the GOP, and 48 percent either saw no difference or had no opinion (*Public Opinion*, September/October 1978, pp. 30–32).

Hence, the GOP has substantial, if not insurmountable, obstacles to overcome in order to become the majority party. Yet the presence of a large number of Independents, particularly among the youth generation, leaves open the possibility of a partisan mobilization that could change the shape of the party system. Should the proportion of Independents in the electorate remain high, then future election outcomes will likely exhibit great volatility and the notion of realignment will become less meaningful, because there will not be a stable baseline from which to evaluate partisan change. Volatility is not such an undesirable situation, from the Republican perspective; it suggests that the party stands a reasonable chance of victory even when its number of self-described loyalists is low.

Presidential elections have become less partisan affairs and seem likely to continue in this direction. In 1952, 44 percent of the vote was cast by strong party identifiers, compared to only 28 percent in 1976. Likewise, only 4 percent of the 1952 vote was cast by pure Independents, compared to 11 percent of the 1976 ballots. (See Table 3.9.) More generally, the political parties may continue to decline as meaningful political instruments. Burnham (1970: 173–74) talks of the decomposition of the party system, evidenced by the decline in party-related voting. The decline of the parties in conjunction with the rise in cynicism toward governmental institutions and authorities (discussed in Chapter 1) suggests a citizenry increasingly adrift in the political seas.

Robert Lane (1971: 293–94) talks of an era of "rootless politics" brought about by the decline in party identification, the transformation of the working class into the bourgeoisie, the enfranchisement of young voters with fewer economic and community ties and political experiences to guide them, and the relaxation of residency requirements. According to Lane (1974: 294), these developments have the effect of "reducing the weight of tradition, personal and communal, in voting, and increasing the importance of current stimuli." As party, community, and class cues become less important, the media and other sources of cues will become more important. And Lane fears that the kinds of cues provided by the media will be superficial slogans that will lower the quality of electoral decisions.

Lane's description seems unusually pessimistic, yet his notion of rootless politics is suggestive. In an era of rootless politics, how will interests be so organized that voters will be offered meaningful policy choices? In an era of rootless politics, might not a realignment occur on a scale far greater than past realignments, thereby threatening some fundamental democratic values? A massive realignment that resulted, for example, in a highly polarized party system—one in which the parties took very distinctive stands across a range of issues— might tremendously increase the stakes of politics, thereby severely weakening the traditional processes of bargaining and compromise on matters of public policy and greatly increasing societal tensions.

Another outcome is continued de-alignment such that the party in government and the party in the electorate become increasingly weak and fragmented. The present impasse in Washington is dismaying, given that Democrats control both the Presidency and the Congress. Yet it may simply reflect the state of the political parties and the consequences of an election process that puts a premium on the individual candidate rather than the political party. Carter ran as an outsider against the Washington and Democratic establishments in 1976 and may not have learned yet how to mobilize and exploit them for policy, as opposed to election, purposes. Likewise, most Democratic Congressmen ran ahead of the President in their districts in 1976 and therefore feel they owe him little, resulting in a policy individualism detrimental to any notion of political party responsibility. And the GOP minority in the Congress seems unwilling to move beyond ideological posturing, thereby calling into question its role as the opposition party and its effectiveness as a potential majority party. The 1980 election results may change the presidential and congressional incumbents, but they are not likely to reverse the decline of the party as a key actor in the organization and expression of programmatic concerns. As the political parties and party loyalties continue to weaken, what institutional arrangements will perform the functions normally associated with the parties? At present, the prospects for change in the American political system seem unusually great, yet the outcome of change need not be increased citizen satisfaction with political institutions and authorities and public policies. The end results of political change are unclear and this should lead us to view the future with both excitement and anxiety.

Appendix A

Constitutional Provisions Relevant to Presidential Selection

ARTICLE II

SECTION 1

[1] The executive power shall be vested in a President of the United States of America. He shall hold his office during the term of four years, and together with the Vice-President, chosen for the same term, be elected as follows:

[2] Each State shall appoint, in such manner as the legislature thereof may direct, a number of Electors, equal to the whole number of Senators and Representatives to which the State may be entitled in the Congress; but no Senator or Representative, or person holding an office of trust or profit under the United States, shall be appointed an Elector.

[3] The Electors shall meet in their respective States and vote by ballot for two persons, of whom one at least shall not be an inhabitant of the same

State with themselves. And they shall make a list of all the persons voted for, and of the number of votes for each; which list they shall sign and certify, and transmit sealed to the seat of government of the United States, directed to the President of the Senate. The President of the Senate shall, in the presence of the Senate and House of Representatives, open all the certificates, and the votes shall then be counted. The person having the greatest number of votes shall be the President, if such number be a majority of the whole number of Electors appointed; and if there be more than one who have such majority, and have an equal number of votes, then the House of Representatives shall immediately choose by ballot one of them for President; and if no person have a majority, then from the five highest on the list the said House shall in like manner choose the President. But in choosing the President the votes shall be taken by States, the representation from each State having one vote; a quorum for this purpose shall consist of a member or members from two-thirds of the States, and a majority of all the States shall be necessary to a choice. In every case, after the choice of the President, the person having the greatest number of votes of the Electors shall be the Vice-President. But if there should remain two or more who have equal votes, the Senate shall choose from them by ballot the Vice-President.

[4] The Congress may determine the time of choosing the Electors and the day on which they shall give their votes, which day shall be the same throughout the United States.

[5] No person except a natural-born citizen, or citizen of the United States at the time of the adoption of this Constitution, shall be eligible to the office of President; neither shall any person be eligible to that office who shall not have attained to the age of thirty-five years, and been fourteen years a resident within the United States.

[6] In case of the removal of the President from office, or of his death, resignation, or inability to discharge the powers and duties of the said office, the same shall devolve on the Vice-President, and the Congress may by law provide for the case of removal, death, resignation, or inability, both of the President and Vice-President, declaring what officer shall then act as President, and such officer shall act accordingly until the disability be removed or a President shall be elected.

[7] The President shall, at stated times, receive for his services a compensation, which shall neither be increased nor diminished during the period for which he shall have been elected, and he shall not receive within that period any other emolument from the United States or any of them.

[8] Before he enter on the execution of his office he shall take the following oath or affirmation:

"I do solemnly swear (or affirm) that I will faithfully execute the office of President of the United States, and will to the best of my ability preserve, protect, and defend the Constitution of the United States."

AMENDMENT XII
(supersedes Article II, Section 1, para. 3)

[1] The Electors shall meet in their respective States and vote by ballot for President and Vice-President, one of whom, at least, shall not be an inhabitant of the same State with themselves; they shall name in their ballots the person voted for as President, and in distinct ballots the person voted for as Vice-President, and they shall make distinct lists of all persons voted for as President and of all persons voted for as Vice-President, and of the number of votes for each; which lists they shall sign and certify, and transmit sealed to the seat of the government of the United States, directed to the President of the Senate. The President of the Senate shall in the presence of the Senate and House of Representatives, open all the certificates and the votes shall then be counted. The person having the greatest number of votes for President shall be the President, if such number be a majority of the whole number of Electors appointed; and if no person have such majority, then from the persons having the highest numbers not exceeding three on the list of those voted for as President, the House of Representatives shall choose immediately, by ballot, the President. But in choosing the President the votes shall be taken by States, the representation from each State having one vote; a quorum for this purpose shall consist of a member or members from two-thirds of the States, and a majority of all the States shall be necessary to a choice. And if the House of Representatives shall not choose a President whenever the right of choice shall devolve upon them, before the fourth day of March next following, then the Vice-President shall act as President, as in the case of the death or other constitutional disability of the President.

[2] The person having the greatest number of votes as Vice-President shall be the Vice-President, if such number be a majority of the whole number of Electors appointed; and if no person have a majority, then from the two highest numbers on the list the Senate shall choose the Vice-President; a quorum for the purpose shall consist of two-thirds of the whole number of Senators, and a majority of the whole number shall be necessary to a choice. But no person constitutionally ineligible to the office of President shall be eligible to that of Vice-President of the United States.

Passed by Congress December 9, 1803.
Ratified July 27, 1804.

AMENDMENT XX

SECTION 1

The terms of the President and Vice-President shall end at noon on the 20th day of January, and the terms of Senators and Representatives at noon on the 3d day of January, of the years in which such terms would have ended if this article had not been ratified; and the terms of their successors shall then begin.

SECTION 2

The Congress shall assemble at least once in every year, and such meetings shall begin at noon on the 3d day of January, unless they shall by law appoint a different day.

SECTION 3

If, at the time fixed for the beginning of the term of the President, the President-elect shall have died, the Vice-President-elect shall become President. If a President shall not have been chosen before the time fixed for the beginning of his term or if the President-elect shall have failed to qualify, then the Vice-President-elect shall act as President until a President shall have qualified; and the Congress may by law provide for the case wherein neither a President-elect nor a Vice-President-elect shall have qualified, declaring who shall then act as President, or the manner in which one who is to act shall be selected, and such person shall act accordingly until a President or Vice-President shall have qualified.

SECTION 4

The Congress may by law provide for the case of the death of any of the persons from whom the House of Representatives may choose a President whenever the right of choice shall have devolved upon them, and for the case of death of any of the persons from whom the Senate may choose a Vice-President whenever the right of choice shall have devolved upon them.

SECTION 5

Sections I and II shall take effect on the 15th day of October following the ratification of this article.

SECTION 6

This article shall be inoperative unless it shall have been ratified as an amendment to the Constitution by the legislatures of three-fourths of the several States within seven years from the date of its submission.

Passed by Congress March 2, 1932.
Ratified January 23, 1933.

AMENDMENT XXII

No person shall be elected to the office of President more than twice, and no person who has held the office of President, or acted as President, for more than two years of a term to which some other person was elected

President shall be elected to the office of President more than once. But this Article shall not apply to any person holding the office of President when this Article was proposed by the Congress, and shall not prevent any person who may be holding the office of President, or acting as President, during the term within which this Article becomes operative from holding the office of President or acting as President during the remainder of such term.

SECTION 2

This article shall be inoperative unless it shall have been ratified as an amendment to the Constitution by the legislatures of three-fourths of the several States within seven years from the date of its submission to the States by the Congress.

Passed by Congress March 21, 1947.
Ratified February 27, 1951.

AMENDMENT XXIII

SECTION 1

The District constituting the seat of Government of the United States shall appoint in such manner as the Congress may direct:

A number of electors of President and Vice-President equal to the whole number of Senators and Representatives in Congress to which the District would be entitled if it were a State, but in no event more than the least populous State; they shall be in addition to those appointed by the States, but they shall be considered, for the purposes of the election of President and Vice-President, to be electors appointed by a State; and they shall meet in the District and perform such duties as provided by the twelfth article of amendment.

SECTION 2

The Congress shall have power to enforce this article by appropriate legislation.

Passed by Congress June 16, 1960.
Ratified March 29, 1961.

AMENDMENT XXV
(supersedes Article II, Section 1, para. 6)

SECTION 1

In case of the removal of the President from office or of his death or resignation, the Vice-President shall become President.

SECTION 2

Whenever there is a vacancy in the office of the Vice-President, the President shall nominate a Vice-President who shall take office upon confirmation by a majority vote of both Houses of Congress.

SECTION 3

Whenever the President transmits to the President pro tempore of the Senate and the Speaker of the House of Representatives has written declaration that he is unable to discharge the powers and duties of his office, and until he transmits to them a written declaration to the contrary, such powers and duties shall be discharged by the Vice-President as Acting President.

SECTION 4

Whenever the Vice-President and a majority of either the principal officers of the executive departments or of such other body as Congress may by law provide, transmit to the President pro tempore of the Senate and the Speaker of the House of Representatives their written declaration that the President is unable to discharge the powers and duties of his office, the Vice-President shall immediately assume the powers and duties of the office as Acting President.

Thereafter, when the President transmits to the President pro tempore of the Senate and the Speaker of the House of Representatives his written declaration that no inability exists, he shall resume the powers and duties of his office unless the Vice-President and a majority of either the principal officers of the executive department or of such other body as Congress may by law provide, transmit within four days to the President pro tempore of the Senate and the Speaker of the House of Representatives their written declaration that the President is unable to discharge the powers and duties of his office. Thereupon Congress shall decide the issue, assembling within forty-eight hours for that purpose if not in session. If the Congress, within twenty-one days after receipt of the latter written declaration, or, if Congress is not in session, within twenty-one days after Congress is required to assemble, determines by two-thirds vote of both Houses that the President is unable to discharge the powers and duties of his office, the Vice-President shall continue to discharge the same as Acting President; otherwise, the President shall resume the powers and duties of his office.

Passed by Congress July 6, 1965.
Ratified February 10, 1967.

Appendix B

Presidential Election Results, 1864–1976

APPENDIX B
Presidential Election Results, 1864–1976

Year	Republican Candidate	Popular Vote	Percent Popular Vote	Electoral College Vote	Democratic Candidate	Popular Vote	Percent Popular Vote	Electoral College Vote	Major Third Party Candidate and Party	Popular Vote	Percent Popular Vote	Electoral College Vote	Other Popular Vote	Percent Popular Vote
1864	Abraham Lincoln*	2,218,388	55.0%	212	George McClellan	1,812,807	45.0%	21					692	.0%
1868	Ulysses Grant*	3,013,650	52.7	214	Horatio Seymour	2,708,744	47.3	80					46	.0
1872	Ulysses Grant*	3,598,235	55.6	286	Horace Greeley	2,834,761	43.8	63					34,683	.6
1876	Rutherford Hayes*	4,034,311	47.9	185	Samuel Tilden	4,288,546	51.0	184					90,244	1.1
1880	James Garfield*	4,446,158	48.3	214	Winfield Hancock	4,444,260	48.3	155					320,002	3.4
1884	James Blaine	4,848,936	48.2	182	Grover Cleveland*	4,874,621	48.5	219					326,197	3.3
1888	Benjamin Harrison*	5,443,892	47.8	233	Grover Cleveland	5,534,488	48.6	168					404,934	3.6
1892	Benjamin Harrison	5,179,244	43.0	145	Grover Cleveland*	5,551,883	46.0	277	James Weaver, Populist	1,024,280	8.5	22	300,690	2.5
1896	William McKinley*	7,108,480	51.0	271	William Bryan	6,511,495	46.7	176					315,763	2.3
1900	William McKinley*	7,218,039	51.7	292	William Bryan	6,358,345	45.5	155					394,086	2.8
1904	Theodore Roosevelt*	7,626,593	56.4	336	Alton Parker	5,082,898	37.6	140					809,473	6.0
1908	William Taft*	7,676,258	51.6	321	William Bryan	6,406,801	43.0	162					799,675	5.4
1912	William Taft	3,486,333	23.2	8	Woodrow Wilson*	6,293,152	41.8	435	Theodore Roosevelt, Progressive	4,119,207	27.4	88	1,142,271	7.6
1916	Charles Hughes	8,546,789	46.1	254	Woodrow Wilson*	9,126,300	49.2	277					861,933	4.7
1920	Warren Harding*	16,133,314	60.3	404	James Cox	9,140,884	34.2	127					1,479,588	5.5

Year	Candidate	Popular Vote	%	Electoral	Opponent	Popular Vote	%	Electoral	Third Party	Popular Vote	%	Electoral	Other Popular	Other %
1924	Calvin Coolidge*	15,717,553	54.1%	382	John Davis	8,386,169	28.8%	136	Robert LaFollette, Progressive	4,814,050	16.6%	13	158,187	.5%
1928	Herbert Hoover*	21,411,991	58.2	444	Alfred Smith	15,000,185	40.8	87					378,188	1.0
1932	Herbert Hoover	15,758,397	39.6	59	Franklin Roosevelt*	22,825,016	57.4	472					1,165,969	3.0
1936	Alfred Landon	16,679,543	36.5	8	Franklin Roosevelt*	27,747,636	60.8	523					1,215,124	2.7
1940	Wendell Willkie	22,336,260	44.8	82	Franklin Roosevelt*	27,263,448	54.7	449					240,735	.5
1944	Thomas Dewey	22,013,372	45.9	99	Franklin Roosevelt*	25,611,936	53.4	432					349,511	.7
1948	Thomas Dewey	21,970,017	45.1	189	Harry Truman*	24,105,587	49.5	303	Strom Thurmond, States' Rights and	1,169,134	2.4	39	290,647	.6
									Henry Wallace, Progressive	1,157,057	2.4	0		
1952	Dwight Eisenhower*	33,936,137	55.1	442	Adlai Stevenson	27,314,649	44.4	89					300,332	.5
1956	Dwight Eisenhower*	35,585,245	57.4	457	Adlai Stevenson	26,030,172	42.0	73					409,955	.6
1960	Richard Nixon	34,106,671	49.5	219	John Kennedy*	34,221,344	49.7	303					500,945	.8
1964	Barry Goldwater	27,177,838	38.5	52	Lyndon Johnson*	43,126,584	61.0	486					336,682	.5
1968	Richard Nixon*	31,785,148	43.4	301	Hubert Humphrey	31,274,503	42.7	191	George Wallace, American Independent	9,901,151	13.5	46	242,568	.4
1972	Richard Nixon*	47,170,179	60.7	520	George McGovern	29,171,791	37.5	17					1,385,620	1.8
1976	Gerald Ford	39,146,006	48.0	240	Jimmy Carter*	40,829,046	50.1	297					1,577,279	1.9

* Denotes winner.

Sources: Constructed from figures presented in *Presidential Elections since 1789* (Washington, D.C.: Congressional Quarterly Inc., 1975); and *Guide to 1976 Election* (Washington, D.C.: Congressional Quarterly Inc., 1977)

References

Abramowitz, Alan I. "The Impact of a Presidential Debate on Voter Rationality," *American Journal of Political Science* 22 (August 1978), pp. 680–90.

Abramson, Paul R. "Why the Democrats Are No Longer the Majority Party," paper presented at the annual meeting of the American Political Science Association, Jung Hotel, New Orleans, September 4–8, 1973.

———. "Generational Change and the Decline of Party Identification in America: 1952–1974," *American Political Science Review* 70 (June 1976), pp. 469–78.

———. "Developing Party Identification: A Further Examination of Life-Cycle, Generational, and Period Effects," *American Journal of Political Science* 23 (February 1979), pp. 78–96.

Agranoff, Robert. *The New Style in Election Campaigns* (Boston: Holbrook Press, Inc., 1972).

Aldrich, John H.; Gant, Michael M.; and Simon, Dennis M.   " 'To the Victor Belongs the Spoils': Momentum in the 1976 Nomination Campaigns," unpublished paper, 1978.

Alexander, Herbert E.   *Financing the 1960 Election* (Princeton, N.J.: Citizens' Research Foundation, 1962).

————.   *Financing the 1964 Election* (Princeton, N.J.: Citizens' Research Foundation, 1966).

————.   *Financing the 1968 Election* (Lexington, Mass.: D.C. Heath & Co., 1971).

————.   *Money in Politics* (Washington, D.C.: Public Affairs Press, 1972a).

————.   *Political Financing* (Minneapolis: Burgess Publishing Company, 1972b).

————.   "Campaign Spending," *Encyclopedia Year Book 1973* (New York: Grolier, Inc., 1973).

————.   *Financing Politics: Money, Elections and Political Reform* (Washington, D.C.: Congressional Quarterly, Inc., 1976).

Andersen, Kristi.   "Generation, Partisan Shift and Realignment: A Glance Back to the New Deal," chap. 5 in *The Changing American Voter* by Norman H. Nie, Sidney Verba, and John R. Petrocik (Cambridge, Mass., and London: Harvard University Press, 1976), pp. 74–95.

Arterton, F. Christopher.   "Recent Rule Changes within the National Democratic Party: Some Present and (Short Term) Future Consequences," paper presented at the annual meeting of the Social Science History Association, Columbus, Ohio, November 3–5, 1978.

Asher, Herbert B.   "The Media and the Presidential Selection Process," in *The Impact of the Electoral Process*, Sage Electoral Studies Yearbook, vol. 3, edited by Louis Maisel and Joseph Cooper (Beverly Hills and London: © Sage Publications, 1977). Adapted by permission of the Publisher, Sage Publications, Inc.

Axelrod, Robert.   "Where the Votes Come From: An Analysis of Electoral Coalitions, 1952–1968," *American Political Science Review* 66 (March 1972), pp. 11–20.

————.   "Communications," *American Political Science Review* 72 (June 1978), pp. 622–24.

Bagdikian, Ben H.   "The Fruits of Agnewism," *Columbia Journalism Review* 11 (January/February, 1973), pp. 9–21.

Barber, James David.   *The Presidential Character: Predicting Performance in the White House* (Englewood Cliffs, N.J.: Prentice-Hall, Inc., 1972).

Baskin, Otis.   "The Effects of Television Political Advertisements on Candidate Image," paper presented at the annual meeting of the International Communication Association, Portland, Oregon, April 14–17, 1976.

Beardsley, Philip L. "The Methodology of the Electoral Analysis: Models and Measurement," in David M. Kovenock, James W. Prothro et al. *Explaining the Vote, Part 1* (Chapel Hill: Institute for Research in Social Science, 1973), pp. 1–42.

Beck, Paul. "A Socialization Theory of Partisan Realignment," in *New Views of Children and Politics,* edited by Richard Niemi (San Francisco: Jossey-Bass, Inc., Publishers, 1974).

———. "Partisan Dealignment in the Postwar South," *American Political Science Review* 71 (June 1977), pp. 477–96.

———. "Youth and the Politics of Realignment," unpublished paper.

Benham, Thomas W. "Polling for Presidential Candidates," in *The New Style in Election Campaigns,* edited by Robert Agranoff (Boston: Holbrook Press, Inc., 1972), pp. 213–31.

Beniger, J. R. "Winning the Presidential Nomination: National Polls and State Primary Elections, 1936–1972," *Public Opinion Quarterly* 40 (Spring 1976), pp. 22–38.

Berelson, Bernard; Lazarsfeld, Paul; and McPhee, William *Voting* (Chicago and London: The University of Chicago Press, 1954).

Bishop, George F.; Oldendick, Robert W.; and Tuchfarber, Alfred J. 1978a "Effects of Question Wording and Format on Political Attitude Consistency," *Public Opinion Quarterly* 42 (Spring 1978), pp. 81–92.

———, and Bennett, Stephen E. 1978b "The Changing Structure of Mass Belief Systems: Fact or Artifact?" *Journal of Politics* 40 (August 1978), pp. 781–787.

Bishop, George F.; Tuchfarber, Alfred J.; and Oldendick, Robert W. 1978c "Change in the Structure of American Political Attitudes: the Nagging Question of Question Wording," *American Journal of Political Science* 22 (May 1978), pp. 250–69.

———, and Bennett, Stephen E. "Questions about Question Wording: A Rejoinder to Revisiting Mass Belief Systems Revisited," *American Journal of Political Science* 23 (February 1979), pp. 187–92.

Bishop, George F.; Meadow, Robert G.; and Jackson-Beeck, Marilyn, eds. *The Presidential Debates: Media, Electoral, and Policy Perspectives,* (New York: Praeger Publishers, 1978).

Black, Merle, and Rabinowitz, George "An Overview of American Electoral Change, 1952–1972," paper presented at the annual meeting of the Southern Political Science Association, New Orleans, November 8, 1974.

Bone, Hugh A. *American Politics and the Party System* (New York: McGraw-Hill Book Co., 1955).

Bowen, Lawrence; Atkin, Charles K.; Nayman, Oguz B.; and Sheinkopf, Kenneth G. "Quality versus Quantity in Televised Political Ads," *Public Opinion Quarterly* 37 (Summer 1972), pp. 209–24.

Boyd, Richard W. "Presidential Elections: An Explanation of Voting Defection," *American Political Science Review* 63 (June 1969), pp. 498–514.

———. "Popular Control of Public Policy: A Normal Vote Analysis of the 1968 Election," *American Political Science Review* 66 (June 1972), pp. 429–49.

———. "Structural and Attitudinal Explanations of Turnout," paper presented at the Conference on Voter Turnout, San Diego, Cal., May 16–19, 1979.

Brams, Steven J. and Davis, Morton D. "The 3/2's Rule in Presidential Campaigning," *American Political Science Review* 68 (March 1974), pp. 113–34.

Broder, David S. *The Party's Over: The Failure of Politics in America* (New York: Harper & Row, Publishers, 1971).

———. "Political Reporters in Presidential Politics," in *Inside the System*, 3d ed., edited by Charles Peters and James Fallows (New York: Praeger, 1976).

———. "Nader Says Time Nears for New Political Party," *Washington Post* (May 8, 1979), p. A–2.

———. "Carter's Staff Just 'Campaign Soldiers'," *The Columbus Dispatch*, May 27, 1979, p. B–2.

Brody, Richard A. "Stability and Change in Party Identification: Presidential to Off-Years," paper presented at the Annual Meeting of the American Political Science Association, Washington, D.C.: August 31–September 4, 1977.

——— and Page, Benjamin I. "Comment: The Assessment of Policy Voting," *American Political Science Review* 66 (June 1972), pp. 450–58.

Buchanan, Patrick "How the Networks Fall Easy Prey to Political Manipulation," *TV Guide* 24 (August 14, 1976), p. A–3.

Buchwald, Art. " 'Old' Nixon Has a Voice," *The Evening News*, September 17, 1968, p. 25.

Burnham, Walter Dean. "American Voting Behavior and the 1964 Election," *Midwest Journal of Political Science* 12 (February 1968), pp. 1–40.

———. *Critical Elections and the Mainsprings of American Politics* (New York: W. W. Norton & Co., Inc., 1970).

Campbell, Angus. "A Classification of Presidential Elections," in *Elections and the Political Order* by Angus Campbell et al. (New York: John Wiley and Sons, Inc., 1966), pp. 63–77. Material reprinted by permission of publisher.

Campbell, Angus. "Interpreting the Presidential Victory," in *The National Election of 1964,* edited by Milton C. Cummings, Jr., (Washington, D.C.: The Brookings Institution, 1966), pp. 256–81.

Campbell, Angus; Gurin, Gerald; and Miller, Warren E. *The Voter Decides* (Evanston, Ill.: Row, Peterson & Co., 1954).

———. Converse, Philip E.; Miller, Warren E.; and Stokes, Donald E., *The American Voter* (New York: John Wiley & Sons, Inc., 1960).

Campbell, Bruce A. "Patterns of Change in the Partisan Loyalties of Native Southerners: 1952–1972," *The Journal of Politics* 39 (August 1977), pp. 730–61.

Cannon, Louis. "Udall Complains 'Orgy of Publicity' Benefits Carter Drive," *The Washington Post* (April 17, 1976), p. A–4.

Cavala, William. "Changing the Rules Changes the Game: Party Reform and the 1972 California Delegation to the Democratic National Convention," *American Political Science Review* 68 (March 1974), pp. 27–42.

Chaffee, Steven H. "Are Debates Helpful to Voters?" Paper presented at the annual meeting of the International Communication Association, Chicago, April 25–29, 1978.

Chester, Edward W. *Radio, Television, and American Politics* (New York: Sheed & Ward, Inc., 1969).

Chester, Lewis; Hodgson, Godfrey; and Page, Bruce. *An American Melodrama* (New York: Dell Publishing Co., Inc., 1969).

Collat, D.; Kelley, S.; and Rogowski, R. "Presidential Bandwagons," paper presented at the annual meeting of the American Political Science Association, Chicago, September 2–5, 1976.

Converse, Philip E. "Non-voting among Young Adults in the United States," a Data Report to the American Heritage Foundation by the Political Behavior Program of the Survey Research Center, The University of Michigan, Ann Arbor, June 1963, pp. 1–36.

———. "The Concept of the Normal Vote," in Angus Campbell et al., *Elections and the Political Order* (New York: John Wiley & Sons, Inc., 1966), pp. 9–39.

———. "Religion and Politics: The 1960 Election," in Angus Campbell et al., *Elections and the Political Order* (New York: John Wiley & Sons, Inc., 1966), pp. 96–124.

———. "Of Time and Partisan Stability," *Comparative Political Studies,* 2 (July 1969), pp. 139–71.

————. "Attitudes and Non-Attitudes: Continuation of a Dialogue," in *The Quantitative Analysis of Social Problems,* edited by Edward R. Tufte (Reading, Mass.: Addison-Wesley Publishing Co., Inc., 1970), pp. 168–89.

————. "Information Flow and the Stability of Partisan Attitudes," in *Political Opinion and Behavior,* 2d ed., edited by Edward C. Dreyer and Walter A. Rosenbaum (Belmont, Cal.: Wadsworth Publishing Co., Inc., 1970), pp. 407–26.

————. "The Nature of Belief Systems in Mass Publics," in *Public Opinion and Public Policy,* rev. ed., edited by Norman R. Luttbeg (Homewood, Ill.: The Dorsey Press, © 1974), pp. 300–34.

————. *The Dynamics of Party Support: Cohort-analyzing Party Identification* (Beverly Hills, Cal.: Sage Publications, Inc., 1976).

————. "Rejoinder to Abramson," *American Journal of Political Science* 23 (February 1979), pp. 97–100.

Converse, Philip E.; Campbell, Angus; Miller, Warren E.; and Stokes, Donald E. "Stability and Change in 1960: A Reinstating Election," in Angus Campbell et al., *Elections and the Political Order* (New York: John Wiley & Sons, Inc., 1966), pp. 78–95.

Converse, Philip E.; Clausen, Aage R.; and Miller, Warren E. "Electoral Myth and Reality: The 1964 Election," *American Political Science Review* 59 (June 1965), pp. 321–36.

————. "Electoral Myth and Reality: The 1964 Election," in *Political Opinion and Behavior,* edited by Edward C. Dreyer and Walter A. Rosenbaum (Belmont, Cal.: Wadsworth Publishing Co., Inc., 1970), pp. 39–50.

Converse, Philip E., and Dupeux, Georges. "Politicization of the Electorate in France and the United States," in Angus Campbell et al., *Elections and the Political Order* (New York: John Wiley & Sons, Inc., 1966), pp. 269–91.

Converse, Philip E.; Miller, Warren E.; Rusk, Jerrold G.; and Wolfe, Arthur C. "Continuity and Change in American Politics: Parties and Issues in the 1968 Election," *American Political Science Review* 63 (December 1969), pp. 1083–105.

Cook, Rhodes. "Democrats Adopt New Rules for Picking Nominee in 1980," *Congressional Quarterly Weekly Report* 36 (June 17, 1978), p. 1571.

————. "GOP Presidential Hopefuls Gave Plenty to Party Candidates in 1978," *Congressional Quarterly Weekly Report* 37 (February 17, 1979), pp. 307–11.

Cosman, Bernard, and Huckshorn, Robert J. "The Goldwater Impact:

Cyclical Variation or Secular Decline?" *Republican Politics,* edited by Bernard Cosman and Robert J. Huckshorn (New York: Frederick A. Praeger, Inc., Publishers, 1968), pp. 234–44.

Crittenden, John. "Aging and Party Affiliation," *Public Opinion Quarterly* 26 (Winter 1962), pp. 648–57.

————. "Reply to Cutler," *Public Opinion Quarterly* 33 (Winter 1969–70), pp. 589–91.

Crotty, William. *Political Reform and the American Experiment* (New York: Thomas Y. Crowell Co., 1977).

————. *Decision for the Democrats: Reforming the Party Structure* (Baltimore: The Johns Hopkins University Press, 1978).

————. "Party Reform and Democratic Performance," paper presented at the Conference on "The Future of the American Political System: What Can be Done to Make It More Democratic and Effective?" sponsored by the Center for the Study of Democratic Politics, University of Pennsylvania, April 12–13, 1979.

Crouse, Timothy. *The Boys on the Bus: Riding with the Campaign Press Corps* (New York: Ballantine Books, 1973).

Cutler, Neal E. "Generation, Maturation, and Party Affiliation: A Cohort Analysis," *Public Opinion Quarterly* 33 (Winter 1969–70), pp. 583–88.

————. "Comment," *Public Opinion Quarterly* 33 (Winter 1969–70), p. 592.

Davis, James W. *Presidential Primaries: Road to the White House* (New York: Thomas Y. Crowell Co., 1967).

Democratic State Central Committee of Michigan. Publication no. 92767–3, 1968.

Dennis, Jack. "Support for the Institution of Elections by the Mass Public," *American Political Science Review* 64 (September 1970), pp. 819–35.

————. "Trends in Public Support for the American Political Party System," paper presented at the annual meeting of the American Political Science Association, Chicago, Ill., August 29–September 2, 1974.

Dennis, Jack, and McCrone, Donald J. "Preadult Development of Political Party Identification in Western Democracies," *Comparative Political Studies* 3 (July 1970), pp. 243–63.

DeVries, Walter, and Tarrance, V. Lance. *The Ticket-Splitter: A New Force in American Politics* (Grand Rapids, Mich.: Wm. B. Eerdmans Publishing Co., 1972).

Dobson, Douglas, and St. Angelo, Douglas. "Party Identification and the

Floating Vote: Some Dynamics," *American Political Science Review* 69 (June 1975), pp. 481–90.

Dollar Politics. Vol. 2 (Washington, D.C.: Congressional Quarterly Inc., 1974).

Downs, Anthony. *An Economic Theory of Democracy* (New York: Harper & Row, Publishers, 1957).

Drew, Elizabeth. "A Reporter in Washington, D.C.: Winter Notes—I," *The New Yorker* (May 17, 1976a), pp. 126–56.

————. "Winter Notes—II" (May 31, 1976b), pp. 54–99.

Dreyer, Edward C. "Media Use and Electoral Choices: Some Political Consequences of Information Exposure," *Public Opinion Quarterly* 35 (Winter 1971–72), pp. 544–53.

————. "Change and Stability in Party Identification," *The Journal of Politics* 35 (August 1973), pp. 712–22.

Dunn, Delmer D. *Financing Presidential Campaigns* (Washington, D.C.: The Brookings Institution, 1972).

Dutton, Frederick G. *Changing Sources of Power* (New York: McGraw-Hill Book Co., Inc., 1971).

Erikson, Robert S. "The Influence of Newspaper Endorsements in Presidential Elections: The Case of 1964," *American Journal of Political Science* 20 (May 1976), pp. 207–33.

Evans, Rowland, and Novak, Robert. "Inside Report," *Newark Sunday News,* October 27, 1968, p. C2.

Evarts, Dru, and Stempel III, Guido H. "Coverage of the 1972 Campaign by TV, News Magazines and Major Newspapers," *Journalism Quarterly* 51 (Winter 1974), pp. 645–48, 676.

Fee, Joan L., and Greeley, Andrew M. "Religion, Ethnicity and Class in American Electoral Behavior," paper presented at the annual meeting of the Midwest Political Science Association, Chicago, May 1–3, 1975.

Field, John Osgood, and Anderson, Ronald E. "Ideology in the Public's Conceptualization of the 1964 Election," in *Political Opinion and Behavior,* edited by Edward C. Dreyer and Walter A. Rosenbaum (Belmont, Cal.: Wadsworth Publishing Co., Inc., 1970), 2d ed., pp. 329–46.

Flanigan, William. *Political Behavior of the American Electorate.* Boston: Allyn & Bacon, Inc., 1972.

Froman, Lewis A., Jr. "A Realistic Approach to Campaign Strategies and Tactics," in *The Electoral Process,* edited by M. Kent Jennings and Harmon Ziegler (Englewood Cliffs, N.J.: Prentice-Hall, Inc., 1966), pp. 1–20.

Funkhouser, G. Ray. "The Issues of the Sixties: an Exploratory Study in the Dynamics of Public Opinion," *Public Opinion Quarterly* 37 (Spring 1973), pp. 62–75.

Glenn, Norval D., and Hefner, Ted. "Further Evidence on Aging and Party Identification," *Public Opinion Quarterly* 36 (Spring 1972), pp. 31–47.

Goldberg, Arthur. "Discerning a Causal Pattern among Data on Voting Behavior," *American Political Science Review* 60 (December 1966), pp. 913–22.

Graber, Doris A. "Press Coverage Patterns of Campaign News: The 1968 Presidential Race," *Journalism Quarterly* 48 (Autumn 1971), pp. 502–12.

———. "Press Coverage and Voter Reaction in the 1968 Presidential Election," *Political Scence Quarterly* 89 (March 1974), pp. 68–100.

———. "Press and TV as Opinion Resources in Presidential Campaigns," *Public Opinion Quarterly* 40 (Fall 1976), pp. 285–303.

Graber, Doris A., and Young Kun Kim. "Media Coverage and Voter Learning during the Presidential Primary Season," paper presented at the annual meeting of the Midwest Political Science Association, Chicago, April 21–23, 1977.

Greeley, Andrew M. *Building Coalitions* (New York: Franklin Watts, Inc., 1974).

———. "Catholics and Coalition: Where Should They Go?" in *Emerging Coalitions in American Politics,* edited by Seymour Martin Lipset (San Francisco: Institute for Contemporary Studies, 1978), pp. 271–95.

Greenstein, Fred I. *Children and Politics* (New Haven: Yale University Press, 1965).

Hadley, Arthur T. *The Empty Polling Booth* (Englewood Cliffs, N.J.: Prentice-Hall, Inc., 1978).

Halberstam, David. *The Best and the Brightest* (Greenwich, Conn.: Fawcett Publications, Inc., 1972).

Hargrove, Erwin C. "What Manner of Man?" in *Choosing the President,* edited by James David Barber (Englewood Cliffs, N.J.: Prentice-Hall, Inc., 1974), pp. 7–33.

Harney, Russell F., and Stone, Vernon A. "Television and Newspaper Front Page Coverage of a Major News Story," *Journal of Broadcasting* 13 (Spring 1969), pp. 181–88.

Harris, Louis. "Why the Odds Are Against a Governor's Becoming President," *Public Opinion Quarterly* (Fall 1959), pp. 361–70.

Hess, Robert D., and Torney, Judith V. *The Development of Political Attitudes in Children* (Chicago: Aldine Publishing Co., 1967).

Hofstetter, C. Richard. *Bias in the News: A Study of Network Coverage of the 1972 Election Campaign* (Columbus: Ohio State University Press, 1976).

Hofstetter, C. Richard; Zukin, Cliff.; and Buss, Terry F. "Political Imagery in an Age of Television: the 1972 Campaign," paper presented at the annual meeting of the American Political Science Association, Chicago, September 2–5, 1976.

Hsueh, Mabel. "Voter's Choice in the 1976 Presidential Election: Party Identification and Candidate Evaluations," unpublished paper, 1978.

Jackson III, John S.; Brown, Jesse C.; and Brown, Barbara L. "Recruitment, Representation, and Political Values: The 1976 Democratic National Convention Delegates," *American Politics Quarterly* 6 (April 1978), pp. 187–212.

Jacobson, Gary C. "The Impact of Broadcast Campaigning on Electoral Outcomes," paper presented at the annual meeting of the American Political Science Association, Chicago, August 29–September 2, 1974.

Jennings, M. Kent, and Langton, Kenneth P. "Mothers versus Fathers: The Formation of Political Orientations among Young Americans," *The Journal of Politics* 31 (May 1969), pp. 329–58.

Jennings, M. Kent, and Niemi, Richard G. "The Transmission of Political Values from Parent to Child," *American Political Science Review* 62 (March 1968), pp. 169–84.

―――. *The Political Character of Adolescence: The Influence of Families and Schools* (Princeton, N.J.: Princeton University Press, 1974).

―――. "Continuity and Change in Political Orientations: A Longitudinal Study of Two Generations," *American Political Science Review* 69 (December 1975), pp. 1316–35.

Johnson, Haynes. "Beyond FDR," *The Enquirer Magazine,* September 1, 1974.

Johnson, Loch K., and Hahn, Harlan. "Delegate Turnover at National Party Conventions, 1944–1968," in *Perspectives on Presidential Selection,* edited by Donald R. Matthews (Washington, D.C.: The Brookings Institution, 1973), pp. 143–71.

Kagay, Michael, and Caldeira, Greg. "Public Policy Issues and the American Voter, 1952–1972," unpublished paper.

Katz, Elihu, and Feldman, Jacob J. "The Debates in the Light of Research: A Survey of Surveys," in *The Great Debates,* edited by Sidney Kraus (Bloomington: Indiana University Press, 1962), pp. 173–223.

Keech, William R., and Matthews, Donald R. *The Party's Choice* (Washington, D.C.: The Brookings Institution, 1977).

Keith, Bruce E.; Magleby, David B.; Nelson, Candice J.; Orr, Elizabeth;

Westlye, Mark; and Wolfinger, Raymond E. "The Myth of the Independent Voter," paper presented at the 1977 annual meeting of the American Political Science Association, Washington, D.C., September 4–7, 1977.

Kelley, Stanley, Jr. *Political Campaigning* (Washington, D.C.: The Brookings Institution, 1960).

———. "The Presidential Campaign," in *The National Election of 1964,* edited by Milton C. Cummings, Jr. (Washington, D.C.: The Brookings Institution, 1966), pp. 42–81.

Kessel, John H. *The Goldwater Coalition: Republican Strategies in 1964* (Indianapolis and New York: The Bobbs-Merrill Co., Inc., 1968).

———. "Strategy for November," in *Choosing the President,* edited by James David Barber (Englewood Cliffs, N.J.: Prentice-Hall, Inc., 1974), pp. 95–119.

Key, V. O., Jr. "A Theory of Critical Elections," *The Journal of Politics* 17 (February 1955), pp. 3–18.

———. *The Responsible Electorate* (New York: Vintage Books, 1966).

Kim, Jae-On; Petrocik, John R.; and Enokson, Stephen N. "Voter Turnout among the American States: Systemic and Individual Components," *American Political Science Review* 69 (March 1975), pp. 107–23.

Kirkpatrick, Jeane J. *The New Presidential Elite: Men and Women in National Politics* (New York: Russell Sage Foundation, 1976).

Kirkpatrick, Samuel A., and Jones, Melvin E. "Issue Publics and the Electoral System: The Role of Issues in Electoral Change," in *Public Opinion and Political Attitudes,* edited by Allen R. Wilcox (New York: John Wiley & Sons, Inc., 1974), pp. 537–55.

Kirkpatrick, Samuel A.; Lyons, William; and Fitzgerald, Michael R. "Candidate and Party Images in the American Electorate: A Longitudinal Analysis," paper presented at the annual meeting of the Southwestern Political Science Association, Dallas, Tex., March 28–30, 1974.

Klapper, Joseph. *The Effects of Mass Communication* (New York: The Free Press, 1960).

Klingemann, Hans. "Dimensions of Political Belief Systems: 'Levels of Conceptualization' as a Variable. Some Results for USA and FRG 1968/69," preliminary handout prepared for the E.C.P.R. Workshop on Political Behavior, Dissatisfaction and Protest, April 12–18, 1973, Universitat Mannheim.

Kraus, Sidney, ed. *The Great Debates, 1976: Ford vs. Carter* (Bloomington: Indiana University Press, 1979).

Ladd, Everett Carll, Jr.   "The New Lines Are Drawn: Class and Ideology in America," *Public Opinion* (July/August 1978a), pp. 48–53.

———.   (September/October 1978b), pp. 14–20.

———.   "The Shifting Party Coalitions—1932–1976," in *Emerging Coalitions in American Politics,* edited by Semour Martin Lipset (San Francisco: Institute for Contemporary Studies, 1978c), pp. 81–102.

———.   *Where Have All the Voters Gone? The Fracturing of America's Political Parties* (New York: W. W. Norton & Company, Inc., 1978d).

Ladd, Everett Carll, Jr., and Hadley, Charles D.   "Party Definition and Party Differentiation," *Public Opinion Quarterly* 37 (Spring 1973–74), pp. 21–34.

Ladd, Everett Carll, Jr., with Hadley, Charles D.   *Transformations of the American Party System,* 2d ed. (New York: W. W. Norton & Company, Inc., 1978).

Lane, Robert.   *Political Life* (New York: The Free Press, 1959).

Lane, Robert E.   *Political Ideology* (New York: The Free Press, 1962).

———.   "Alienation, Protest and Rootless Politics in the Seventies," in *The Political Image Merchants,* edited by Ray Hiebert, Robert Jones, John Lorenz, and Ernest Lotito (Washington, D.C.: Acropolis Books, Ltd., 1971), pp. 273–300.

Lang, Gladys Engel, and Lang, Kurt.   "Immediate and Delayed Responses to a Carter–Ford Debate: Assessing Public Opinion," *Public Opinion Quarterly* 42 (Fall 1978), pp. 322–41.

Lang, Kurt, and Lang, Gladys Engel.   *Politics and Television* (Chicago: Quadrangle Books, 1968).

Langton, Kenneth P., and Jennings, M. Kent.   "Political Socialization and the High School Civics Curriculum in the United States," *American Political Science Review* 62 (September 1968), pp. 852–67.

Lavine, Harold.   *Smoke-Filled Rooms* (Englewood Cliffs, N.J.: Prentice-Hall, Inc., 1970).

Lazarsfeld, Paul; Berelson, Bernard, and Gaudet, Hazel.   *The People's Choice* (New York and London: Columbia University Press, 1968).

Lengle, James I., and Shafer, Byron.   "Primary Rules, Political Power, and Social Change," *American Political Science Review* 70 (March 1976), pp. 25–40.

Longley, Lawrence D., and Braun, Alan G.*The Politics of Electoral College Reform* (New Haven and London: Yale University Press, 1972).

Lowry, Dennis T.   "Gresham's Law and Network TV News Selection," *Journal of Broadcasting* 15 (Fall 1971), pp. 397–407.

Lucy, William H. "Polls, Primaries, and Presidential Nominations," *Journal of Politics* 35 (November 1973), pp. 830–48.

Macaluso, Theodore F. "The Responsiveness of Party Identification to Current Political Evaluations," mimeographed.

MacKuen, Michael. "The Press as Shepherd: A Fifteen-Year View," paper presented at the annual meeting of the Midwest Political Science Association, Chicago, April 19–21, 1979.

MacRae, Duncan, Jr., and Meldrum, James A. "Critical Elections in Illinois: 1888–1958," *American Political Science Review* 54 (September 1960), pp. 669–83.

Maggiotto, Michael A., and Piereson, James E. "Party Identification and Electoral Choice: The Hostility Hypothesis," *American Journal of Political Science,* 21 (November 1977), pp. 745–67.

Maisel, Louis, and Lieberman, Gerald J. "The Impact of Electoral Rules on Primary Elections: The Democratic Presidential Primaries of 1976," in *The Impact of the Electoral Process,* edited by Louis Maisel and Joseph Cooper (Beverly Hills and London: Sage Publications, Inc., 1977), pp. 39–80.

Margolis, Michael. "From Confusion to Confusion: Issues and the American Voter (1956–1972)," *American Political Science Review* 71 (March 1977), pp. 31–43.

Matthews, Donald R. "Presidential Nominations: Processes and Outcomes," in *Choosing the President,* edited by James David Barber (Englewood Cliffs, N.J.: Prentice-Hall, Inc., 1974), pp. 35–70.

May, Ernest R., and Fraser, Janet, eds. *Campaign '72: The Managers Speak* (Cambridge, Mass.: Harvard University Press, 1973).

Mazmanian, Daniel A. *Third Parties in Presidential Elections* (Washington, D.C.: The Brookings Institution, 1974).

McCartney, James. "The Triumph of Junk News," *Columbia Journalism Review* 15 (January/February 1977), pp. 17–21.

McCluhan, Marshall. *Understanding Media* (New York: McGraw-Hill Book Co., 1964).

McClure, Robert D., and Patterson, Thomas E. "Print vs. Network News," *Journal of Communication* 26 (Spring 1976), pp. 18–22.

McCombs, Maxwell E., and Shaw, Donald R. "The Agenda-Setting Function of the Mass Media," *Public Opinion Quarterly* 36 (Summer 1972), pp. 176–87.

McGinniss, Joe. *The Selling of the President 1968* (New York: Trident Press, 1969).

McGrath, Joseph E., and McGrath, Marion F. "Effects of Partisanship on Perceptions of Political Figures," *Public Opinion Quarterly* 26 (Summer 1962), pp. 236–48.

Mendelsohn, Harold, and Crespi, Irving. *Polls, Television, and the New Politics* (Scranton, Pa.: Chandler Publishing Co., 1970).

Michener, James A. *Report of the County Chairman* (New York: Random House, Inc., 1961).

Milbrath, Lester W. *Political Participation* (Chicago: Rand McNally & Co., 1965).

Miller, Arthur H. "Normal Vote Analysis: Sensitivity to Change over Time," *American Journal of Political Science* 23 (May 1979), pp. 406–25.

———. "Political Issues and Trust in Government: 1964–1970," *American Political Science Review* 68 (September 1974), pp. 951–72.

———. "Partisanship Reinstated? A Comparison of the 1972 and 1976 U.S. Presidential Elections," *British Journal of Political Science* 8 (April 1978), pp. 129–52.

Miller, Arthur H.; Miller, Warren E.; Raine, Alden S.; and Brown, Thad A. "A Majority Party in Disarray: Policy Polarization in the 1972 Election," paper presented at the annual meeting of the American Political Science Association, New Orleans, September 4–8, 1973.

———. "A Majority Party in Disarray: Policy Polarization in the 1972 Election," *American Political Science Review* 70 (September 1976), pp. 753–78.

Miller, Arthur H., Goldenberg, Edie N.; and Erbring, Lutz. "Type-Set Politics: Impact of Newspapers on Public Confidence," *American Political Science Review* 73 (March 1979), pp. 67–84.

Miller, Arthur H., and Miller, Warren E. "Partisanship and Performance: 'Rational' Choice in the 1976 Presidential Election," paper presented at the Annual Meeting of the American Political Science Association, Washington, D.C., September 1–4, 1977.

Mitofsky, Warren J. "1976 Presidential Debate Effects: A Hit or a Myth," paper presented at the annual meeting of the American Political Science Association, Washington, D.C., September 1–4, 1977.

Natchez, Peter B. "Issues and Voters in the 1972 Election," *University Programs Modular Studies* (Morristown, N.J.: General Learning Press, 1974).

Natchez, Peter B., and Bupp, Irvin C. "Candidates, Issues and Voters," in *Political Opinion and Behavior*, edited by Edward C. Dreyer and Walter A. Rosenbaum (Belmont, Cal.: Wadsworth Publishing Co., Inc., 1970), 2d ed., pp. 427–50.

Nie, Norman H., and Andersen, Kristi. "Mass Belief Systems Revisited: Political Change and Attitude Structure," *The Journal of Politics* 36 (August 1974), pp. 540–87.

Nie, Norman H.; Verba, Sidney; and Petrocik, John R. *The Changing American Voter* (Cambridge, Mass.: Harvard University Press, 1976).

Nie, Norman H., and Rabjohn, James N. "Revisiting Mass Belief Systems Revisited: Or, Doing Research Is Like Watching a Tennis Match," *American Journal of Political Science* 23 (February 1979), pp. 139–75.

Nimmo, Dan. *The Political Persuaders* (Englewood Cliffs, N.J.: Prentice-Hall, Inc., 1970).

O'Keefe, M. Timothy, and Sheinkopf, Kenneth G. "The Voter Decides: Candidate Image or Campaign Issue?" *Journal of Broadcasting* 18 (Fall 1974), pp. 403–11.

Page, Benjamin I. "Presidential Campaigning, Party Cleavages, and Responsible Parties," unpublished paper.

Page, Benjamin I., and Brody, Richard A. "Policy Voting and the Electoral Process: The Vietnam War Issue," *American Political Science Review* 66 (September 1972), pp. 979–95.

Paletz, David L., and Elson, Martha. "Television Coverage of Presidential Conventions: Now You See It, Now You Don't," *Political Science Quarterly* 91 (Spring 1976), pp. 109–31.

Parris, Judith H. *The Convention Problem* (Washington, D.C.: The Brookings Institution, 1972).

Patterson, Thomas E. "Press Coverage and Candidate Success in Presidential Primaries: The 1976 Democratic Race," paper presented at the 1977 annual meeting of the American Political Science Association, Washington, D.C., September 1–4, 1977a.

―――. "The 1976 Horserace," *The Wilson Quarterly* 1 (Spring 1977), pp. 73–77.

Patterson, Thomas E., and McClure, Robert D. *The Unseeing Eye: The Myth of Television Power in National Elections* (New York: G. P. Putnam's Sons, 1976).

Peabody, Robert L., and Lubalin, Eve. "The Making of Presidential Candidates," in *The Future of the American Presidency*, edited by Charles W. Dunn (Morristown, N.J.: General Learning Press, 1975), pp. 26–65.

Perry, James M. *Us and Them: How the Press Covered the 1972 Election* (New York: Clarkson N. Potter, Inc., 1973).

Peters, Charles. "The Ignorant Press," *The Washington Monthly* 8 (May 1976), pp. 55–57.

Petrocik, John. "An Analysis of Intransitivities in the Index of Party Identification," *Political Methodology* 1 (Summer 1974), pp. 31–47.

Phillips, Kevin B. *The Emerging Republican Majority* (Garden City, N.Y.: Doubleday & Co., Inc., 1969).

Pomper, Gerald M. "Classification of Presidential Elections," *The Journal of Politics* 29 (August 1967), pp. 535–66.

————. *Elections in America* (New York: Dodd, Mead & Co., Inc., 1968).

————. "From Confusion to Clarity: Issues and American Voters, 1956–1968," *American Political Science Review* 66 (June 1972), pp. 415–28.

Pool, Ithiel de Sola; Abelson, Robert P.; and Popkin, Samuel. *Candidates, Issues and Strategies* (Cambridge, Mass.: M.I.T. Press, 1965).

Porter, Kirk H., and Johnson, Donald Bruce, eds. *National Party Platforms* (Urbana: University of Illinois Press, 1970).

Ranney, Austin. "Turnout and Representation in Presidential Primary Elections," *American Political Science Review* 66 (March 1972), pp. 21–37.

————. *Curbing the Mischiefs of Faction* (Berkeley: University of California Press, 1975).

————. *Participation in American Presidential Nominations, 1976* (Washington, D.C.: American Enterprise Institute for Public Policy Research, 1977).

Rapoport, Daniel. "Campaign Politics—The Telltale Signs of a Regulated Industry," *National Journal* (January 20, 1979), pp. 92–95.

Reiter, Howard L. "The Trend toward Presidential Non-Voting," paper presented at the 1977 Annual Meeting of the American Political Science Association, Washington, D.C., September 1–4, 1977.

RePass, David E. "Issue Salience and Party Choice," *American Political Science Review* 65 (June 1971), pp. 389–400.

————. "Levels of Rationality among the American Electorate," paper presented at the annual meeting of the American Political Science Association, Chicago, August 29–September 2, 1974.

Reston, James. "Mr. Nixon and the Arts of Evasion," *New York Times*, October 2, 1968.

Roback, Thomas H. "Dimensions of Republican Amateurism: Stability and Change among National Convention Delegates: 1972–1976," paper presented at the 1977 annual meeting of the Southern Political Science Association, New Orleans, November 2–6, 1977a.

————. "Recruitment and Incentive Patterns among Delegates to the 1972 and 1976 Republican National Conventions: The Individual as the Strategic Factor in the Theory of Party Organization," paper presented at the annual meeting of the American Political Science Association, Washington, D.C., September 1–4, 1977b.

Robinson, John P. "Public Reaction to Political Protest: Chicago 1968," *Public Opinion Quarterly* 34 (Spring 1970), pp. 1–9.

———. "Perceived Media Bias and the 1968 Vote: Can the Media Affect Behavior after All?" *Journalism Quarterly* (Summer 1972), pp. 239–46.

———. "The Press as King-maker: What Surveys from the Last Five Campaigns Show," *Journalism Quarterly* (Winter 1974), pp. 587–94.

Robinson, Michael J. "Public Affairs Television and the Growth of Political Malaise: The Case of the Selling of the Pentagon," unpublished Ph.D. dissertation, The University of Michigan, 1972.

———. "An Idea Whose Time Has Come—Again," *Congressional Record,* June 19, 1975, p. E3336.

———. "The TV Primaries," *The Wilson Quarterly* 1 (Spring 1977), pp. 80–83.

———. "TV's Newest Program: The 'Presidential Nominations Game,'" *Public Opinion* 1 (May/June 1978), pp. 41–45.

Robinson, Michael J., and Zukin, Cliff. "Television and the Wallace Vote," *Journal of Communication* 26 (Spring 1976), pp. 79–83.

Roper, Burns W. "Distorting the Voice of the People," *Columbia Journalism Review* 14 (November/December 1975), pp. 28–32.

———. "The Effects of the Debates on the Carter/Ford Election," paper presented at the annual meeting of the American Political Science Association, Washington, D.C., September 1–4, 1977.

Rosenstone, Steven J., and Wolfinger, Raymond E. "The Effects of Registration Laws on Voter Turnout," *American Political Science Review* 72 (March 1978), pp. 22–45.

Rubin, Bernard. *Political Television* (Belmont, Cal.: Wadsworth Publishing Co., Inc., 1967).

Ryan, Michael. "View from the Losing Side," *TV Guide* 24 (June 12, 1976), p. 8.

Sayre, Wallace S., and Parris, Judith H. *Voting for President* (Washington, D.C.: The Brookings Institution, 1970).

Scammon, Richard M., and Wattenberg, Ben J. *The Real Majority* (New York: Coward, McCann & Geoghegan, Inc., 1970).

Schreiber, E. M. "Where the Ducks Are: Southern Strategy versus Fourth Party," *Public Opinion Quarterly* 35 (Summer 1971), pp. 155–67.

Schulman, Mark A., and Pomper, Gerald M. "Variability in Electoral Behavior: Longitudinal Perspectives from Causal Modeling," *American Journal of Political Science* 19 (February 1975), pp. 1–18.

Sears, David O. "The Debates in the Light of Research: An Overview of the Effects," paper presented at the annual meeting of the American Political Science Association, Washington, D.C., September 1–4, 1977.

Sears, David O., and Chaffee, Steven H.   "Uses and Effects of the 1976 Debates: An Overview of Empirical Studies," in *The Great Debates, 1976: Ford vs. Carter,* edited by Sidney Kraus (Bloomington: Indiana University Press, forthcoming).

Sears, David O., and Freedman, Jonathan L.   "Selective Exposure to Information: A Critical Review," *Public Opinion Quarterly* 31 (Summer 1967), pp. 194–213.

Shabad, Goldie, and Andersen, Kristi.   "Candidate Evaluations by Men and Women," *Public Opinion Quarterly* 32 (Spring 1979), pp. 18–35.

Shafer, Byron, and Larson, Richard.   "Did TV Create the 'Social Issue'?" *Columbia Journalism Review* 11 (September/October 1972), pp. 10–17.

Sheatsley, Paul B.   "White Attitudes toward the Negro," *Daedalus* 95, pp. 217–38.

Shively, W. Phillips.   "Voting Stability and the Nature of Party Attachments in the Weimar Republic," *American Political Science Review* 66 (December 1972), pp. 1203–25.

———.   "Information Costs and the Partisan Life Cycle," paper presented at the Annual Meeting of the American Political Science Association, Washington, D.C., August 31–September 4, 1977.

Sigel, Roberta A.   "Effects of Partisanship on the Perception of Political Candidates," *Public Opinion Quarterly* 28 (Fall 1964), pp. 483–96.

Sorauf, Frank J.   *Party Politics in America,* 2d ed. (Boston: Little, Brown and Co., 1972).

Soule, John W., and Clark, James W.   "Amateurs and Professionals: A Study of Delegates to the 1968 Democratic National Convention," *American Political Science Review* 64 (September 1970), pp. 888–98.

Stewart, John G.   *One Last Chance* (New York and Washington: Praeger Publishers, Inc., 1974).

Stimson, James A.   "Belief Systems: Constraint, Complexity, and the 1972 Election," *American Journal of Political Science* 19 (August 1975), pp. 393–417.

Stokes, Donald E.   "Some Dynamic Elements of Contests for the Presidency," *American Political Science Review* 60 (March 1966), pp. 19–28.

Stokes, Donald E.; Campbell, Angus; and Miller, Warren E.   "Components of Electoral Decision," *American Political Science Review* 52 (June 1958), pp. 367–87.

Strong, Donald S.   "Further Reflections on Southern Politics," *Journal of Politics* 33 (May 1971), pp. 239–56.

Sullivan, Dennis G.; Pressman, Jeffrey L.; Page, Benjamin I.; and Lyons, John J. *The Politics of Representation* (New York: St. Martin's Press, Inc., 1974).

Sullivan, John L.; Piereson, James E.; and Marcus, George E. "Ideological Constraints in the Mass Public: A Methodological Critique and Some New Findings," *American Journal of Political Science* 22 (May 1978), pp. 234–49.

———, and Feldman, Stanley. "The More Things Change, the More They Stay the Same: The Stability of Mass Belief Systems," *American Journal of Political Science* 23 (February 1979), pp. 176–86.

Sundquist, James L. *Dynamics of the Party System* (Washington, D.C.: The Brookings Institution, 1973).

Swanson, David L. "And That's the Way It Was? Television Covers the 1976 Presidential Campaign," *Quarterly Journal of Speech* 63 (October 1977), pp. 239–48.

Thayer, George. *Who Shakes the Money Tree?* (New York: Simon & Schuster, Inc., 1973).

Thompson, Hunter S. *Fear and Loathing: On the Campaign Trail '72* (New York: Popular Library, 1973).

Van Wingen, John R., and Valentine, David C. "Partisanship, Independence and the Partisan Identification Question," paper presented at the Annual Meeting of the Midwest Political Science Association, Chicago, April 20–22, 1978.

Veblen, Eric. *The Manchester Union Leader in New Hampshire Elections* (Hanover, N.H.: University Press of New England, 1974).

Veblen, Eric P., and Craig, Robert E. "William Loeb and the Manchester Union Leader: A 1976 View," paper presented at the annual meeting of the American Political Science Association, Chicago, September 2–5, 1976.

Verba, Sidney, and Nie, Norman H. *Participation in America* (New York: Harper & Row, publishers, 1972).

Voters' Time, Report of the Twentieth Century Fund Commission on Campaign Costs in the Electronic Era (New York: The Twentieth Century Fund, 1969).

Walsh, Edward. "President Hopes to Offset Likely California Loss," *Washington Post* (June 9, 1976), p. A–1.

Wamsley, Gary L., and Pride, Richard A. "Television Network News: Rethinking the Iceberg Problem," *Western Political Quarterly* 25 (September 1972), pp. 434–50.

Weaver, Warren. "Television and Politics: A Mixed Effect," *New York Times* (July 18, 1976), p. E–1.

Weisberg, Herbert F., and Rusk, Jerrold G. "Dimensions of Candidate Evaluation," *American Political Science Review* 64 (December 1970), pp. 1167–85.

Weisberg, Herbert F. "Toward a Reconceptualization of Party Identification," paper presented at the Annual Meeting of the Midwest Political Science Association, Chicago, Illinois, April 20–22, 1978.

Weisbord, Marvin R. *Campaigning for President* (New York: Washington Square Press, Inc., 1966).

White, Theodore H. *The Making of the President 1960* (New York: Pocket Books, Inc., 1961).

———. *The Making of the President 1964* (New York: Atheneum Publishers, 1965).

———. *The Making of the President 1968* (New York: Atheneum Publishers, 1969).

———. *The Making of the President 1972* (New York: Bantam Books, Inc., 1973).

Winner Take All, Report of the Twentieth Century Fund Task Force on Reform of the Presidential Election Process (New York: Holmes & Meier Publishers, Inc., 1978).

Witcover, Jules. "William Loeb and the New Hampshire Primary: A Question of Ethics," *Columbia Journalism Review* 11 (May/June 1972), pp. 14–25.

———. "The Trials of a One-Candidate Campaign," *Columbia Journalism Review* 11 (January/February 1973), pp. 24–28.

———. *Marathon: The Pursuit of the Presidency, 1972–1976* (New York: New American Library, 1977).

Wolfinger, Raymond E., and Rosenstone, Steven J. "Who Votes?", paper presented at the Annual Meeting of the American Political Science Association, Washington, D.C., September 1–4, 1977.

Yunker, John H., and Longley, Lawrence D. "The Biases of the Electoral College: Who Is Really Advantaged?" in *Perspectives on Presidential Selection* (Washington, D.C.: The Brookings Institution, 1973), pp. 172–203.

———. "The Electoral College: Its Biases Newly Measured for the 1960s and 1970s," *Sage Professional Papers in American Politics* 3, 04–031. (Beverly Hills and London: Sage Publications, 1976.)

Zukin, Cliff. "A Triumph of Form Over Content: Television and the 1976 National Nominating Convention," paper presented at the annual meeting of the Midwest Political Science Association, Chicago, April 19–21, 1979.

Bibliography

CAMPAIGN FINANCING AND COSTS

Adamany, David W., and Agree, George E. *Political Money*. Baltimore: Johns Hopkins University Press, 1975.

Alexander, Herbert E. *Financing the 1960 Election*. Princeton, N.J.: Citizens' Research Foundation, 1962.

———. *Financing the 1964 Election*. Princeton, N.J.: Citizens' Research Foundation, 1966.

———. *Financing the 1968 Election*. Lexington, Mass.: D.C. Heath & Co., 1971.

———. *Money in Politics*. Washington, D.C.: Public Affairs Press, 1972.

———. *Political Financing*. Minneapolis: Burgess Publishing Co., 1972.

———. *Financing Politics: Money, Elections and Political Reform*. Washington, D.C.: Congressional Quarterly, Inc., 1976a.

————. *Political Finance: Reform and Reality.* Philadelphia: The Annals of the American Academy of Political and Social Science, 1976b.

Dollar Politics. Vols. 1 and 2. Washington, D.C.: Congressional Quarterly, Inc., 1974.

Dunn, Delmer D. *Financing Presidential Campaigns.* Washington, D.C.: The Brookings Institution, 1972.

Heard, Alexander.*The Costs of Democracy.* Chapel Hill: University of North Carolina Press, 1960.

Nichols, David. *Financing Elections.* New York: New Viewpoints, 1974.

Thayer, George. *Who Shakes the Money Tree?* New York: Simon & Schuster, Inc., 1973.

Voters' Time. Report of the Twentieth Century Fund Commission on Campaign Costs in the Electronic Era. New York: The Twentieth Century Fund, 1969.

ELECTORAL COLLEGE

Diamond, Martin. *The Electoral College and The American Idea of Democracy.* Washington, D.C.: American Enterprise Institute for Public Policy Research, 1977.

Longley, Lawrence D., and Braun, Alan G. *The Politics of Electoral College Reform.* New Haven and London: Yale University Press, 1972.

Peirce, Neal R. *The People's President: The Electoral College in American History and the Direct-Vote Alternative.* New York: Simon & Schuster, Inc., 1968.

Sayre, Wallace S., and Parris, Judith H. *Voting for President.* Washington, D.C.: The Brookings Institution, 1970.

Winner Take All. Report of the Twentieth Century Fund Task Force on Reform of the Presidential Election Process. (New York and London: Holmes & Meier Publishers, Inc., 1978).

HISTORY OF PRESIDENTIAL ELECTIONS

Presidential Elections since 1789. Washington, D.C.: Congressional Quarterly, Inc., 1975.

Roseboom, Eugene H. *A History of Presidential Elections.* New York: The Macmillan Co., 1964.

Tugwell, Rexford G. *How They Became President: Thirty-six Ways to the White House.* New York: Simon & Schuster, Inc., 1964.

MEDIA AND CAMPAIGNING

Agranoff, Robert. *The New Style in Election Campaigns.* Boston: Holbrook Press, Inc., 1972.

Barber, James David, ed. *Race for the Presidency: The Media and the Nominating Process.* Englewood Cliffs, N.J.: Prentice-Hall, Inc., 1978.

Bishop, George; Meadow, Robert G.; and Jackson-Beeck, Marilyn, eds. *The Presidential Debates: Media, Electoral, and Policy Perspectives.* New York: Praeger Publishers, Inc., 1978.

Bloom, Melvin H. *Public Relations and Presidential Campaigns: A Crisis in Democracy.* New York: Thomas Y. Crowell Co., 1973.

Blumler, Jay G., and McQuail, Denis. *Television in Politics: Its Uses and Influence.* Chicago: University of Chicago Press, 1969.

Chaffee, Steve H. *Political Communication: Issues and Strategies for Research.* Beverly Hills and London: Sage Publications, Inc., 1975.

Chester, Edward W. *Radio, Television, and American Politics.* New York: Sheed & Ward, Inc., 1969.

Crouse, Timothy. *The Boys on the Bus.* New York: Ballantine Books, Inc., 1973.

Diamond, Edwin. *The Tin Kazoo: Television, Politics, and the News.* Cambridge, Mass.: M.I.T. Press, 1975.

Epstein, Edward Jay. *News from Nowhere: Television and the News.* New York: Random House, 1973.

Hess, Stephen.*The Presidential Campaign.* Washington, D.C.: The Brookings Institution, 1974.

Hiebert, Ray; Jones, Robert; Lorenz, John; and Lotito, Ernest, eds. *The Political Image Merchants: Strategies in the New Politics.* Washington, D.C.: Acropolis Books Ltd., 1971.

Hofstetter, C. Richard. *Bias in the News: Network Television Coverage of the 1972 Election Campaign.* Columbus: The Ohio State University Press, 1976.

Kelly, Jr., Stanley. *Political Campaigning: Problems in Creating an Informed Electorate.* Washington, D.C.: The Brookings Institution, 1960.

Klapper, Joseph. *The Effects of Mass Communication.* New York: The Free Press, 1960.

Kraus, Sidney, and Davis, Dennis. *The Effects of Mass Communication on Political Behavior.* University Park: Pennsylvania State University Press, 1976.

Kraus, Sidney, ed. *The Great Debates, 1976: Ford vs. Carter.* Bloomington: Indiana University Press, 1979.

Lang, Kurt, and Lang, Gladys Engel. *Politics and Television.* Chicago: Quadrangle Books, Inc., 1968.

MacNeil, Robert.*The People Machine: The Influence of Television on American Politics.* New York: Harper & Row, Publishers, 1968.

Mendelsohn, Harold, and Crespi, Irving. *Polls, Television, and the New Politics.* Scranton, Pa.: Chandler Publishing Co., 1970.

Nimmo, Dan. *The Political Persuaders: The Techniques of Modern Election Campaigns.* Englewood Cliffs, N.J.: Prentice-Hall, Inc., 1970.

Patterson, Thomas E., and McClure, Robert D. *The Unseeing Eye: The Myth of Television Power in National Politics.* New York: G. P. Putnam's Sons, 1976.

Perry, James M. *The New Politics: The Expanding Technology of Political Manipulation.* New York: Clarkson Potter, Inc., 1968.

Rosenbloom, David. *The Election Men: Professional Campaign Managers and American Democracy.* New York: Quadrangle Books, Inc., 1973.

Rubin, Bernard. *Political Television.* Belmont, Cal.: Wadsworth Publishing Co., Inc., 1967.

Weisbord, Marvin R. *Campaigning for President.* New York: Washington Square Press, Inc., 1966.

POLITICAL REFORM

Bickel, Alexander M. *Reform and Continuity: The Electoral College, the Convention, and the Party System.* New York: Harper & Row, Publishers, 1971.

Crotty, William J. *Political Reform and the American Experiment.* New York: Thomas Y. Crowell Co., 1977.

————. *Decision for the Democrats: Reforming the Party Structure.* Baltimore: The Johns Hopkins University Press, 1978.

Ranney, Austin. *Curing the Mischiefs of Faction: Party Reform in America.* Berkeley and London: University of California Press, 1975.

PRIMARIES, CONVENTIONS, NOMINATIONS, AND PRESIDENTIAL SELECTION IN GENERAL

Bain, Richard C., and Parris, Judith H. *Conventions, Decisions and Voting Records.* Washington, D.C.: The Brookings Institution, 1973.

Barber, James David, ed. *Choosing the President.* Englewood Cliffs, N.J.: Prentice-Hall, Inc., 1974.

Bone, Hugh A. *American Politics and the Party System.* New York: McGraw-Hill Book Co., 1971. Selected chapters.

David, Paul T.; Goldman, Ralph M.; and Bain, Richard C. *The Politics of National Party Conventions.* Washington, D.C.: The Brookings Institution, 1960.

Davis, James W. *Presidential Primaries: Road to the White House.* New York: Thomas Y. Crowell Co., 1967.

Keech, William R., and Matthews, Donald R. *The Party's Choice.* Washington, D.C.: The Brookings Institution, 1977.

Key, V. O., Jr. *Politics, Parties and Pressure Groups.* New York: Thomas Y. Crowell Co., 1964. Selected chapters.

Kirkpatrick, Jeane. *The New Presidential Elite.* New York: Russell Sage Foundation, 1976.

Matthews, Donald R., ed. *Perspectives on Presidential Selection.* Washington, D.C.: The Brookings Institution, 1973.

Nomination and Election of the President and Vice President of the United States. Washington, D.C.: U.S. Government Printing Office, 1972.

Parris, Judith H. *The Convention Problem.* Washington, D.C.: The Brookings Institution, 1972.

Polsby, Nelson W., and Wildavsky, Aaron B. *Presidential Elections.* New York: Charles Scribner's Sons, 1971.

Ranney, Austin. *Participation in American Presidential Nominations, 1967.* Washington, D.C.: American Enterprise Institute for Public Policy Research, 1977.

Sorauf, Frank J. *Party Politics in America.* 2d ed. Boston: Little, Brown and Co., 1972. Selected chapters.

Sullivan, Denis G.; Pressman, Jeffrey L.; Page, Benjamin I.; and Lyons, John J. *The Politics of Representation: The Democratic Convention 1972.* New York: St. Martin's Press, 1974.

REALIGNMENT AND POLITICAL CHANGE

Bass, Jack, and DeVries, Walter. *The Transformation of Southern Politics.* New York: Basic Books, 1976.

Broder, David. *The Party's Over: The Failure of Politics in America.* New York: Harper & Row, Publishers, 1971.

Burnham, Walter Dean. *Critical Elections and the Mainsprings of American Politics.* New York: W. W. Norton & Company, Inc., 1970.

Chambers, William Nisbet, and Burnham, Walter Dean, eds. *The American Party Systems: Stages of Political Development.* New York: Oxford University Press, 1967.

Clubb, Jerome M., and Allen, Howard W., eds. *Electoral Change and Stability in American Political History.* New York: The Free Press, 1971.

Dutton, Frederick G. *Changing Sources of Power.* New York: McGraw-Hill Book Co., Inc., 1971.

Greeley, Andrew M. *Building Coalitions.* New York: Franklin Watts, Inc., 1974.

Knoke, David. *Change and Continuity in American Politics.* Baltimore and London: The Johns Hopkins University Press, 1976.

Ladd, Everett Carll, Jr. *Where Have All the Voters Gone?* New York: W. W. Norton & Company, Inc., 1978.

Ladd, Everett Carll, Jr., and Hadley, Charles D. *Transformation of the American Party System.* 2d ed. New York: W. W. Norton & Company, Inc., 1978.

Lipset, Seymour Martin, ed. *Emerging Coalitions in American Politics.* San Francisco: Institute for Contemporary Studies, 1978.

Lubell, Samuel. *The Hidden Crisis in American Politics.* New York: W. W. Norton & Company, Inc., 1971.

Phillips, Kevin B. *The Emerging Republican Majority.* Garden City, N.Y.: Doubleday & Co., Inc., 1969.

Scammon, Richard M., and Wattenberg, Ben J. *The Real Majority.* New York: Coward, McCann & Geoghegan, Inc., 1970.

Seagull, Louis M. *Youth and Change in American Politics.* New York and London: New Viewpoints, 1977.

Stewart, John G. *One Last Chance.* New York and Washington: Praeger Publishers, Inc., 1974.

Sundquist, James L. *Dynamics of the Party System.* Washington, D.C.: The Brookings Institution, 1973.

RECENT BOOKS ON THE CONTEMPORARY PRESIDENCY

Cronin, Thomas E. *The State of the Presidency.* Boston: Little, Brown and Company, 1975.

Dunn, Charles W., ed. *The Future of the American Presidency.* Morristown, N.J.: General Learning Press, 1975.

Hargrove, Erwin C. *The Power of the Modern Presidency.* New York: Alfred A. Knopf, Inc., 1974.

Hirschfield, Robert S., ed. *The Power of the Presidency: Concepts and Controversy.* 2d ed. Chicago: Aldine Publishing Co., 1973.

Hughes, Emmet John. *The Living Presidency: The Resources and Dilemmas of the American Presidential Office.* Baltimore: Penguin Books Inc., 1973.

James, Dorothy Buckton. *The Contemporary Presidency*. 2d ed. Indianapolis and New York: The Bobbs-Merrill Co., Inc., 1974.

Kessel, John H. *The Domestic Presidency: Decision-Making in the White House*. North Scituate, Mass.: Duxbury Press, 1975.

Koenig, Louis W. *The Chief Executive*. 3d ed. New York: Harcourt Brace Jovanovich, Inc., 1975.

Neustadt, Richard E. *Presidential Power: The Politics of Leadership*. New York: John Wiley & Sons, Inc., 1960.

Reedy, George E. *The Twilight of the Presidency*. New York: World Publishing Co., 1970.

Rossiter, Clinton. *The American Presidency*. Rev. ed. New York: Harcourt, Brace & World, Inc., 1960.

Schlesinger, Arthur M., Jr. *The Imperial Presidency*. Boston: Houghton Mifflin Co., 1973.

Sundquist, James L. *Politics and Policy: The Eisenhower, Kennedy, and Johnson Years*. Washington, D.C.: The Brookings Institution, 1968.

Thomas, Norman C., ed. *The Presidency in Contemporary Context*. New York: Dodd, Mead & Co., 1975.

Tugwell, Rexford G., and Cronin, Thomas E., eds. *The Presidency Reappraised*. New York and Washington: Praeger Publishers, Inc., 1974.

Wildavsky, Aaron, ed. *Perspectives on the Presidency*. Boston: Little, Brown & Co., 1975.

SPECIFIC PRESIDENTIAL ELECTIONS

1960

Kraus, Sidney, ed. *The Great Debates*. Bloomington: Indiana University Press, 1962.

Pool, Ithiel de Sola; Abelson, Robert P.; and Popkin, Samuel. *Candidates, Issues and Strategies*. Cambridge, Mass.: M.I.T. Press, 1965.

White, Theodore H. *The Making of the President 1960*. New York: Atheneum Publishers, 1961.

1964

Cosman, Bernard, and Huckshorn, Robert J., eds. *Republican Politics: The 1964 Campaign and Its Aftermath for the Party*. New York: Frederick A. Praeger, Publishers, 1968.

Cummings, Milton C., Jr., ed. *The National Election of 1964*. Washington, D.C.: The Brookings Institution, 1966.

Kessel, John H. *The Goldwater Coalition: Republican Strategies in 1964*. Indianapolis and New York: The Bobbs-Merrill Company, Inc., 1968.

Lamb, Karl A., and Smith, Paul A. *Campaign Decision-Making: The Presidential Election of 1964*. Belmont, Cal.: Wadsworth Publishing Co., Inc., 1968.

White, Theodore H. *The Making of the President 1964*. New York: Atheneum Publishers, 1965.

1968

Chester, Lewis; Hodgson, Godfrey; and Page, Bruce. *An American Melodrama*. New York: Dell Publishing Co., Inc., 1969.

Kovenock, David M.; Prothro, James W.; and Associates. *Explaining the Vote: Presidential Choices in the Nation and the States, 1968*. Chapel Hill: Institute for Research in Social Science, 1973.

McGinniss, Joe. *The Selling of the President 1968*. New York: Trident Press, 1969.

White, Theodore H. *The Making of the President 1968*. New York: Atheneum Publishers, 1969.

1972

May, Ernest R., and Fraser, Janet, eds. *Campaign '72: The Managers Speak*. Cambridge, Mass.: Harvard University Press, 1973.

Thompson, Hunter C. *Fear and Loathing: On the Campaign Trail '72*. New York: Popular Library, 1973.

White, Theodore H. *The Making of the President 1972*. New York: Atheneum Publishers, 1973.

1976

Pomper, Gerald, ed. *The Election of 1976*. New York: David McKay Company, Inc., 1977.

Schram, Martin. *Running for President*. New York: Stein and Day, 1977.

Witcover, Jules. *Marathon: The Pursuit of the Presidency, 1972–1976*. New York: New American Library, 1977.

Wooten, James. *Dasher*. New York: Warner Books, Inc., 1979.

VOTING BEHAVIOR, POLITICAL PARTICIPATION, AND POLITICAL SOCIALIZATION

Berelson, Bernard R.; Lazarsfeld, Paul F.; and McPhee, William N. *Voting*. Chicago: University of Chicago Press, 1954.

Burdick, Eugene, and Brodbeck, Arthur J., eds. *American Voting Behavior*. New York: The Free Press, 1959.

Campbell, Angus; Converse, Philip E.; Miller, Warren E.; and Stokes, Donald E. *The American Voter*. New York: John Wiley & Sons, Inc., 1960.

————. *Elections and the Political Order*. New York: John Wiley & Sons, Inc., 1966.

Campbell, Angus; Gurin, Gerald; and Miller, Warren E. *The Voter Decides*. Evanston, Ill.: Row, Peterson and Co., 1954.

Campbell, Bruce A. *The American Electorate: Attitudes and Action*. New York: Holt, Rinehart and Winston, 1979.

Cantor, Robert D. *Voting Behavior & Presidential Elections*. Itasca, Ill.: F. E. Peacock Publishers, Inc., 1975.

Converse, Philip E. *The Dynamics of Party Support: Cohort-Analyzing Party Identification*. Beverly Hills and London: Sage Publications, Inc., 1976.

DeVries, Walter, and Tarrance, V. Lance. *The Ticket-Splitter: A New Force in American Politics*. Grand Rapids, Mich.: W. B. Eerdmans Publishing Co., 1972.

Dreyer, Edward C., and Rosenbaum, Walter A., eds. *Political Opinion and Behavior: Essays and Studies*. 2d ed. Belmont, Cal.: Wadsworth Publishing Co., Inc., 1970.

Fishel, Jeff, ed. *Parties and Elections in an Anti-Party Age*. Bloomington and London: Indiana University Press, 1978.

Flanigan, William H., and Zingale, Nancy H. *Political Behavior of the American Electorate*. 3d ed. Boston: Allyn & Bacon, Inc., 1975.

Greenstein, Fred I. *Children and Politics*. New Haven and London: Yale University Press, 1965.

Hess, Robert D., and Torney, Judith V. *The Development of Political Attitudes in Children*. Chicago: Aldine Publishing Co., 1967.

Jennings, M. Kent, and Niemi, Richard G. *The Political Character of Adolescence: The Influence of Families and Schools*. Princeton, N.J.: Princeton University Press, 1974.

Jennings, M. Kent, and Ziegler, L. Harmon, eds. *The Electoral Process*. Englewood Cliffs, N.J.: Prentice-Hall, Inc., 1966.

Key, V. O. *The Responsible Electorate*. New York: Vintage Books, 1966.

Lane, Robert. *Political Life*. New York: The Free Press, 1959.

Lazarsfeld, Paul F.; Berelson, Bernard; and Gaudet, Hazel. *The People's Choice: How the Voter Makes Up His Mind in a Presidential Campaign*. New York and London: Columbia University Press, 1968.

Maisel, Louis, and Cooper, Joseph, eds. *The Impact of the Electoral Process*. Beverly Hills and London: Sage Publications, Inc., 1977.

Milbrath, Lester W. *Political Participation*. Chicago: Rand McNally & Co., 1965.

Miller, Warren E., and Levitin, Teresa E. *Leadership and Change: Presidential Elections from 1952 to 1976*. Cambridge, Mass.: Winthrop Publishers, Inc., 1976.

Mulcahy, Kevin V., and Katz, Richard S. *American Votes: What You Should Know about Elections Today*. Englewood Cliffs, N.J.: Prentice-Hall, Inc., 1976.

Nie, Norman H.; Verba, Sidney; and Petrocik, John R. *The Changing American Voter*. Cambridge, Mass.: Harvard University Press, 1976.

Niemi, Richard G., and Weisberg, Herbert F., eds. *Controversies in American Voting Behavior*. San Francisco: W. H. Freeman and Company, 1976.

Niemi, Richard G., ed. *New Views of Children and Politics*. San Francisco: Jossey-Bass, Inc., Publishers, 1974.

Pomper, Gerald M. *Voters' Choice: Varieties of American Electoral Behavior*. New York: Dodd, Mead & Co., 1975.

Verba, Sidney, and Nie, Norman H. *Participation in America*. New York: Harper & Row, Publishers, Inc., 1972.

Name Index

Subject Index

This book has been set linotype in 11 and 10 point Baskerville, leaded 2 points. Part numbers and chapter numbers are 30 point Baskerville. Chapter titles are 18 point Baskerville. The size of the type page is 27 by 45 picas.

WHITMAN COLLEGE LIBRARY

WHITMAN COLLEGE LIBRARY

DATE DUE